Mary Lyon and Mount Holyoke

Opening the Gates

Elizabeth Alden Green

Mary Lyon and Mount Holyoke

Opening the Gates

Published by the

University Press of New England

Hanover, New Hampshire 1979

Frontispiece.
Oil painting of Mary Lyon by Joseph Goodhue Chandler.
Executed posthumously from a daguerreotype
taken between 1840 and 1845.
Mount Holyoke College Art Museum.

The University Press
of New England

Brandeis University
Clark University
Dartmouth College
University of New Hampshire
University of Rhode Island
University of Vermont

In honor of
Margaret Ball, Class of 1900
A teacher to remember

Acknowledgments

The progenitor of this volume was the late Sydney R. McLean, a true authority on Mary Lyon, who was unable to complete the biography she had planned. It was Professor McLean's informed enthusiasm and her gift to me of all her notes, full and meticulous, that set me to work.

The Mount Holyoke College community has given me generous assistance. I am most grateful for the active support of Presidents David B. Truman and Elizabeth Topham Kennan, the Faculty Grants Committee, and the Mount Holyoke Alumnae Association. The Mount Holyoke College library staff has been helpfulness itself, particularly Anne Edmonds, Nancy Devine, the entire reference department, and Elaine Trehub and Linda Wendry, whose sustained and imaginative help has made working in the archives a continuing pleasure. For timely and expert assistance with illustrations, I am indebted to Wendy Watson and to Michael Feinstein, whose contributions of time and skill were particularly generous. Cynthia Jeanne Morrell has been a dedicated typist and proof reader; one of the uncounted services of Linda Wendry was major responsibility for the index.

My special thanks go the former students who volunteered their services. Among those who preserved significant records and made them available or located documents or followed up unexplored leads or offered fruitful suggestions are Christina Huemer Bostick, Priscilla Rand Baker, Esther Goodale, Ann Louise Coffin McLaughlin, Joan Regan, Carolyn Fuller Sloat, Henrietta Howell Slote, Denise Thompson. Among the colleagues to whom I am most indebted for enlightenment and encouragement are Kathryn Kish Sklar of the University of California at Los Angeles and William McFeely of Mount Holyoke; his pragmatic enthusiasm has been particularly heartening. Among the old friends on whose combined personal and professional support I have depended are Joyce Horner, Adaline and Gordon Potter, Joseph Bottkol, Meribeth Cameron, Mary Benson.

For permission to utilize manuscript materials I am indebted to the kindness of the following sources: Amherst College Archives by permission of the Trustees of Amherst College, the Essex Institute, the Historical Society of Pennsylvania, the Houghton Library of Harvard University, Mills College Archives, Mount Holyoke College Art Museum, Mount Holyoke College Library Archives, Norwood Historical Society, Oberlin College Archives, St. Lawrence University Library, Wheaton College Archives, Wesley E. Herwig, Mrs. H. Rush Spedden.

South Hadley, Massachusetts   *E.A.G.*
February 1979

Contents

CONTENTS

Illustrations

Introduction

Among the women who affected the course of life in the United States in the nineteenth century, one of the most remarkable has been consistently overlooked in our own time. The name of Mary Lyon, founder of Mount Holyoke College, is unknown to most of the general public—yet she performed an astonishing feat. An obscure young teacher, without money, wealthy patrons, or influential friends, she managed, virtually single-handed, to create from nothing a major new educational institution and to open the way for the rapid spread of higher education for women.

The idea that women some day should be able to get a college education was by no means unheard of 150 years ago, but men who could see the desirability of such proposals were not ready to invest in them. Ministers of churches that took the lead in the multiplication of colleges for men in the first half of the nineteenth century opposed Mary Lyon's plans as impractical, unwise, even unchristian. After three years of tremendous struggle, she finally in 1837 brought into being an institution of high academic quality for mature young women of moderate means. Mount Holyoke Female Seminary was an immediate success; although it did not become a full-fledged college in her lifetime, from the start it demonstrated that young women were intellectually capable of doing college work and that such an institution, once endowed, could run without a deficit. Once Mount Holyoke was in full operation, people could see that college education for women was going to be practical after all and set about founding or supporting various types of institutions that could furnish that education.

Mount Holyoke also played a part in improving the quality of elementary and secondary education. Mary Lyon's insistence on entrance examinations that year by year became more demanding had a direct effect on teachers in both public and private schools who were preparing their most advanced and promising students for the Seminary. The strongest influence on the schools, of course, came through the Mount Holyoke graduates and non-graduates who went out in great numbers to teach. Their insistence on fundamentals and on thoroughness was proverbial, even though many of them were in the classroom only a few years before marriage. Some of Miss Lyon's brightest graduates went halfway round the world as missionaries or missionary wives and contributed to the reservoir of good will the United States once had in some of those distant places. But the great majority of her students made themselves felt in this country, whether they were founding or heading new colleges for women—Western, Lake Erie, Mills—coping with marginal one-room schools on the frontier, or devoting a lifetime to sound secondary education in the East.

Mary Lyon's achievement seems particularly remarkable in view of the fact that she was not a radical. Theologically and politically, she was conservative, like other residents of the Massachusetts hill towns, most of whom were Congregationalists and Whigs. Miss Lyon was a member of the Congregational Church and a devout Christian, but she paid little attention to denominational differences and took no part whatever in politics. She avoided the public controversy on which most reformers have battened. Even against a malicious personal attack, she declined the offer of a defense in print; to achieve her ends she relied on prayer and unremitting personal attention to even the smallest detail. Her particular form of puritanism was related not only to her religion but also to the early nineteenth-century schools she knew.

Education in the United States in 1800 was a matter of public concern, particularly in New England. Massachusetts and Connecticut had led the way with state laws which established two important principles: a modicum of schooling should be provided for everyone, and control of public schools belonged to the immediate community. Towns were required to set up and finance district schools, in whole or in part, in every neighborhood where children were living; the details of management, from choosing the teacher to setting the length of the school term, were left to local discretion.

INTRODUCTION

In New England district schools were usually built promptly, even by new and impecunious settlements. Timothy Dwight, the doughty president of Yale who spent his vacations for twenty years riding up and down New England and recording what he saw, found neat schoolhouses clear up to the Canadian border. "This attachment to education in New-England is universal," he concluded enthusiastically.*

The concept of free public schools had obviously emerged from colonial and revolutionary America and was to gather strength under the oncoming pressures of westward expansion and the population explosion. But a close look at the practice at the beginning of the nineteenth century—at what actually went on in many district schools, at the limits on further education—shows how vast was the room for improvement.

Education for women was especially deficient. True, by 1800 most communities were allowing girls to attend district school at the same time as boys. But even President Dwight found little to praise in the smattering of grammar, geography, and composition and the "accomplishments"—music, drawing, embroidery, French—which daughters of the well-to-do might acquire at female academies and boarding schools. On balance, Dwight managed to remain optimistic. He detected a "disposition to provide a superiour education for female children" and declared, "It is earnestly to be hoped, that . . . the women of this country, who, so far as they possess advantages, appear in no respect to be behind the other sex either in capacity or disposition to improve, may no longer be precluded from the best education by the negligence of men" (p. 476).

Even in his lifetime Dwight's faith in the promise of New England education seemed to be justified. The reforming zeal that swept across the country in his latter years—and for a quarter of a century after his death in 1817—not infrequently centered on education. Individually or collectively, earnest men set up or improved academies, founded colleges, sponsored kindergartens, started educational journals, organized teachers' associations. Some of

*Timothy Dwight, *Travels in New-England and New-York* (New Haven, 1822), 4:294.

these supporters of educational reform were particularly concerned about better opportunities for women. Four of the most important were women themselves, all New Englanders, by birth or residence, all personally familiar with the problems of a bright young woman determined to obtain a good education and become a first-rate teacher.

Emma Hart Willard, born in 1787 at Berlin, Connecticut, where she started teaching at the age of 17, established in 1814 the boarding school that was to become Troy Female Seminary and later Emma Willard School. Her influence spread not only through her school, which she headed until 1838, but also through her textbooks and educational articles. Catharine Beecher, whose famous father Lyman was called to the Litchfield, Connecticut, Congregational Church in 1810 when she was 10 years old, headed Hartford Female Seminary from 1823 to 1831, went west with her father to Cincinnati, where she founded another seminary (relatively short-lived), and devoted the rest of her life to promoting liberal education for women—writing books, giving lectures, collecting money, founding associations devoted to establishing colleges for women. Zilpah Grant, born in 1794 in Norfolk, Connecticut, where she began to teach at the age of 15, headed Adams Female Academy in Derry, New Hampshire, from 1824 through 1827, and Ipswich Female Seminary from 1828 to 1839. Like Mrs. Willard and Miss Beecher, Miss Grant continually increased the range and difficulty of the curriculum and exerted an expanding influence on education through her students, who went out to teach in district or "select" schools from the northern tip of New England to the valley of the Mississippi and, indeed, to mission stations in Hawaii and Burma. Miss Grant also influenced the fourth of this quartet of pioneers, Mary Lyon, who for ten years was her close friend and colleague at Adams and Ipswich.

Mary Lyon was born in 1797 in Buckland, Massachusetts, and began to teach there when she was 17. She had had to become self-supporting at the age of 13, and her rise in the educational world was relatively slow. She was over 35 when she struck out on her own to found Mount Holyoke by main force, without the help of legacy, donated building, financial backing from a church, or even one rich patron. If President Dwight on his swings through the Connecticut Valley had happened to encounter each of the four remarkable young women at a formative stage, would even his astute eye have foreseen that Mary Lyon would be the one to leave behind her a permanent institution of advanced education for women—endowed, out of debt, crowded with able students, manned by a corps of dedicated teachers, guided by an independent, disinterested board of trustees?

1
Knowledge by Handfuls

*Even a child is known by his
doings, whether his work be pure,
and whether it be right. The hearing
ear and the seeing eye, the Lord
hath made even both of them.*

PROVERBS 20:11–12

On a late October day in 1834 one of the travelers who went by stage from Ipswich, Massachusetts, to Amherst was a stocky, red-haired young woman in her middle thirties. Dressed neatly and simply, she had plain features, a fresh complexion, and a warm smile; to strangers she might have looked like a farmer's wife. Local residents would have recognized her as Miss Mary Lyon, who taught at Miss Zilpah Grant's school. But none of her fellow passengers could have guessed that this journey was her Rubicon, that she was leaving behind her in eastern Massachusetts the security of a rewarding job and a fixed residence for a most unlikely enterprise, untried and unsupported.

Mary Lyon was setting out to raise enough money to found a permanently endowed school for young women, organized and financed like the burgeoning colleges for men: buildings and equipment would be provided from gifts administered by an independent board of trustees, not by proprietors intent on making profits. The institution would offer to mature students the advanced work so hard for even wealthy young women to obtain. To keep costs well below those in the best existing seminaries, the necessary domestic work would be divided among the students.

In theory the project should have been welcomed in the enlightened 1830's when so many churchmen and public-spirited citizens agreed that more and better education for women was a crying need of the time; but when it came to specific plans and contributions, the voices of caution prevailed. Womanliness should be the first goal in all female education; the unhealthful restrictions of dormitory life and the rigors of Latin, Greek, and calculus might do irreparable damage to the future mothers of the nation. True, the best schools for young women were dependent upon the

3

solvency and physical endurance of the principals, but when these good teachers should fall by the wayside, the Lord would continue to raise up worthy successors. In any case "masculine" women who traveled alone, organized meetings, made public speeches, and canvassed for funds were entirely unsuited to be models for the flower of young womanhood.

In 1834 Mary Lyon therefore could have had few illusions about the kind of difficulties she would confront. Three years earlier she and Miss Grant together, encouraged by the spreading recognition of the excellence of Ipswich Seminary, had campaigned extensively for a somewhat similar proposal; their struggle after two years had ended in total failure. At least in her new venture she would be prepared for hostility toward "female greatness" and resigned to the sudden falling away of friends and helpers. A temporary handicap was the state of exhaustion in which she was leaving Ipswich. Although she was endowed with abounding energy, she had had an exceptionally strenuous summer. In addition to preparing for her change of base and operations, she had carried full administrative responsibility for the 130 students at Ipswich in the summer term while the principal, Miss Grant, had traveled in the West. Another time-consuming extra had been helping the Wheatons in Norton work out detailed plans for a new school for girls being set up as a memorial by the old judge.

But her physical weariness was no more of a deterrent than any of the other obstacles in her path. Miss Lyon was convinced that she was engaging in the Lord's work and that He would sustain her in all her trials. She saw herself as embarking "in a frail boat on a boisterous sea," but she knew she would be in God's care. "It is very sweet, in the midst of darkness and doubt, to commit the whole to His guidance," she had written her sister. There was, however, nothing passive about Mary Lyon's way of committing herself to divine guidance. A puritan, she believed in a God who was owed obedience and worldly goods and also the best portions of man's time and intelligence. [1]

Before she left Ipswich she had been hard at work on what she perceived as the essential preliminaries. In February 1834 she had composed and distributed a two-page circular describing her project. Throughout the spring she spent hours consulting sympathetic ministers and businessmen. By September 6 she had been able to assemble an all-day meeting of concerned gentlemen, including seven who approved her aims and were willing to serve on the sponsoring committee. Thereupon she reprinted the circular with their endorsements and started sending it out again. In the last six weeks before she left Ipswich, Mary Lyon had performed a remarkable feat: she had collected nearly $1,000 for fund-raising expenses from the ladies of Ipswich, starting with the students and teachers at the seminary and going from door to door, up and down the town, winning over not only the wives but also the husbands, who often held the family purse strings. For shelter the first winter of her campaign, she had found an admirable place, the home of her old friends, Professor and Mrs. Edward Hitchcock of Amherst College, where she could get more educational advice, fill in gaps in her own academic background and be within range of her friends in the hill towns where she had grown up and begun to teach.

When Mary Lyon left Ipswich in October 1834, it is doubtful that any of the committee members, much as they respected her, really believed that her plans could materialize, but her confidence in her great enterprise and in the coming of a new era in female education seems never to have wavered. Three heroic years later, when the five-story building stood solidly in place and four teachers and eighty young women arrived, full of anticipation, she rejoiced, but she was not surprised.

By any standards Mary Lyon was a remarkable woman. Her faith was indeed her own, but it had been shaped in part by the environment in which she grew up. Her background was New England through and through. Buckland, Massachusetts, was one of the hill towns founded in the mid-eighteenth century by settlers moving on from eastern and central Massachusetts and Connecticut. Whatever their reasons for migrating, the men who chose to farm those rocky, hilly acres and the women who churned and baked and spun and wove had to be self-sufficient and determined. Most of them were conservative in religion and politics; from the start, western Massachusetts was Congregational and Whig. Northhampton, where Jonathan Edwards had thundered doom, was less than 25 miles away; after his congregation turned him out in 1750, his words continued to reverberate. Mary Lyon's great grandfather, a resolute follower of Edwards, changed his residence for doctrinal reasons. When the Congregational Church of South Hadley rejected Edwards' stringent requirements for membership, Chileab Smith not only withdrew from the church but pulled up stakes and left town. He took his wife and eight children 30 miles northwest to what was then a clearing in the wilderness and soon became the town of Ashfield. There he and his sons organized a church of their own which was to play an important role in Mary Lyon's life.

Her ancestors, for the most part farmers and craftsmen, included ministers, deacons, selectmen. On her mother's side the line can be traced back to two unrelated men named Smith who emigrated from England about 1635 and both went with their families to Wethersfield, Connecticut. On her father's side, the family line is visible only to her grandfather, Aaron Lyon, who was born in Medway, Massachusetts, in 1729, lived in Sturbridge, and in 1764 moved to Ashfield with his growing family. The third of his eleven children, a son named Aaron, was born in Sturbridge on December 14, 1757. The four oldest Lyons, all boys, were just the right age to fight in the Revolutionary War. Aaron survived two enlistments unscathed; it was his younger brother Jonathan who lost an arm.

When Aaron junior returned, he began to farm in his own right, across the line in Buckland. He seems to have done well on the steep rocky slope where he chose to settle. Little by little he acquired additional pieces of land. At his death at the age of 45, he was employing a hired man; and his estate, including 100 acres, a yoke of oxen, two horses, a small herd of cows, and a flock of sheep, was appraised at $1800.

Aaron also accumulated family responsibilities. On September 2, 1784, he married Jemima Shepard, eldest of the six living children of Deacon Isaac Shepard, who had married Chileab Smith's daughter and was a pillar of the Baptist church that Chileab and his sons had founded just across the line in Ashfield. Aaron was 26 and Jemima 19; in the 19 years of their marriage they had eight children: two boys (one died at the age of 4) and six girls, including Mary.

1. The Lyon home in Buckland, a sketch made in 1851 by Hannah White for the Hitchcock biography, to which she also contributed substantial portions of text. Mount Holyoke College Library Archives.

The church was a central part of their lives. Jemima, who kept a journal of her religious inner life, recorded her protracted struggle until her "stubborn will bowed" and she could be baptized and join the covenant at the age of 15. Aaron, whose father and mother had left the Congregationalists to join the Baptists when he was ten years old, had no doubt for years been attending the Sunday services conducted by Ebenezer Smith without having undergone the trauma of personal conversion. But after four years Jemima's continuing prayers finally prevailed and she could write that "the Lord wrought wonders and brought him out of darkness into his marvelous light and fulfilled all my every desire." Aaron Lyon, Jr., joined the Baptist Corner Church on March 1, 1789, without getting embroiled in the doctrinal and personal quarrels to which this congregation was liable. According to report he had a remarkably equable disposition, never spoke an angry word, and was in demand to pray with the sick and dying. Mary, who was not quite six when he died, recalled 40 years later that at his funeral the neighbors had said of her father, "the peacemaker is gone."[2]

To Mary, who was born February 28, 1797, her father's death in December 1802 was surely the most significant event of her childhood, but it seems not to have left any inner scars. As was customary, all seven children, from Electa, 17, to Freelove, 16 months, watched at the death bed and received their father's dying blessing. Afterward Jemima, who seems to have subdued her grief the way she did her stubborn will, managed with major help from Electa and from young Aaron, 13, to keep the farm and the family together for a few years. Mary remembered these years as idyllic. When in 1843 she was pleading for bigger gifts to missions, she wrote down her recollections of "that wild romantic little farm" where nature and her mother had both been bountiful. Of her mother, she said:

almost always she was to be found busy, both early and late, amid her household cares, and amid the culture of the olive plants around her table. In that little domain, nothing was left to take its own way. Every thing was made to yield to her faithful and diligent hand.

The garden was a paradise:

The roses, the pinks, and the peonies, those old fashioned flowers, which keep time with Old Hundred, could no where grow so fresh, and so sweet as in that little garden. And no where else have I ever seen wild strawberries, in such profusion and richness, as were gathered into those little baskets. Never were rareripes so large and so yellow, and never were peaches so delicious and so fair, as grew on the trees of that little farm. The apples too, contrived to ripen before all others, so as to meet in sweet fellowship with peaches and plums, to entertain the aunts and the cousins.

Even the winter fare was Elysian:

The autumnal stores, so nicely sorted and arranged, always travelled hand in hand through the long winter, like the barrel of meal and the cruise of oil. The apples came out fresh in the spring, and the maple sugar, that most important grocery of that little neighborhood, was never known to fail, till the warm sun on the sparkling snow, gave delightful indications, that sugar days were near. When gathered around that simple table, no one desired a richer supply than was furnished by the hand of that dear mother.[3]

But managing such a farm without the principal farmer was a losing struggle, especially since the children were growing up and would be claiming their shares. By law, since Aaron died without a will, one third went to the widow and the other two thirds were allotted in equal portions to the seven children. In 1808 Electa, who had been teaching in district schools, married Ariel Moore and moved to New Marlborough in the southwestern part of the state. In 1810 Jonathan Taylor of Ashfield lost his second wife, Eunice, and was left with five little girls under the age of ten. When he came seeking another helpmeet, Jemima Lyon accepted. She took the youngest girls, Rosina, 11, and Freelove, 9, with her to Ashfield. The two older girls, Jemima, 23, and Lovina, 16, may already have had places as helpers in households in the area; both were to marry within a few years.

9

That left Aaron, who had turned 21, to occupy the homestead and make his own way as his father had done before him. Mary, 13, was to stay on and do for him the essential cooking, washing, preserving, weaving. This second loss was far more disturbing than the first. Henceforth she must provide for herself a living and also the means to the education for which she was so eager. Mary may not have been worried about the domestic responsibility, since she had already been putting in full days of household labor, working side by side with her mother, but she was surely distressed by the emptiness of the little house on Putnam's Hill. The departure of her mother and sisters must also have cut her off from the regular visits of neighbors and relatives, the nearby Lyons and Shepards and Smiths. Long afterward she used to say to her students, in talking of widows and the fatherless, "My father and mother forsook me, but the Lord took me up." To a young colleague she once mentioned her mother's remarriage: "I would not let it make me unhappy. I found I could love my new father; he was very kind to me. My mother was relieved of much care. I really became very happy." Thanks in part, it may be, to good health and an outgoing disposition, she does seem to have transcended this separation. Instead of being bitter, she retained warm affection for her mother and throughout her life was generously interested in her brother and sisters and the growing procession of nieces and nephews.[4]

The full responsibility of keeping house on a farm like Aaron's was certainly demanding for any young girl. There is scarcely room to mention all the domestic skills that Mary must have acquired from her mother before she was 13. She was certainly able to cook in the open fireplace and to bake good bread and pies in the adjacent brick oven, which would hold twelve pies at a time. She had no doubt helped her mother to churn, make butter and cheese, cure meat in some of the "big earthen jars of salt pork, hams, pig's knuckles, corned beef and sausage" that were "in every cellar," and boil down cider as an ingredient in apple sauce that would keep through the winter. In addition to washing and cleaning, she had to make her own soap and candles. Manufacturing the tallow candles, then the only source of artificial light, was a tricky process:

We first spin some tow with great care; it must be twisted only just enough to hold together, for if twisted too much we should get almost no light from our candles. This being rightly prepared, it was cut into proper lengths and twisted on the rods, a quantity of tallow was melted and the "dipping" began. The first dip was the most important; after this was done, every incipient candle must be made straight; this required the pressing of the thumb and finger down each, rolling it carefully all the way down, then the rest was more easily done. One rod after another was immersed in the tallow till they were as large as desired. Sometimes this required many hours, as they must be cooled before the next dip, or, if too cool, the successive layers of tallow would not unite. [5]

Spinning and weaving were the most time-consuming and difficult of all the home industries young Mary had been learning from her mother. The complexities of the successive steps and the way young girls developed the sense of craftsmanship are suggested in the detailed account which follows:

This [flax] was raised upon the farm and prepared for use by my father and elder brothers, then passed on to my mother who "hatcheled" it. The long finer part was then ready to be wound about the distaff and spun upon the little wheel which was propelled by the foot. This part of the work was done by my mother and older sisters and was for the warp of the piece. The tow, or coarser part, that which was separated from the finer portion by the hatchel, was carded by hand into what was called rolls, why so called I cannot say, for they were flat. My mother often carded a lot of them in the evening for the next day's spinning and laid a board on the pile, to keep them flat and firm; these were to be made into yarn by the younger girls. A girl of seven years was expected to spin seven knots per day; then the rest of the day might be spent in play. (A knot of yarn was forty times around the reel, each round measuring two yards.) This yarn from the tow was not so strong and was always used for filling. Our yarn next must be boiled in ashes and water to render it soft and pliable, then it must be thoroughly rinsed to remove every particle of ashes. We took ours to the brook, rinsing it in running water which saved us

11

much labor. Our yarn was now ready to be converted into cloth. Then came the spooling, warping, beaming on, the thread carefully drawn through the harness and reed, the harness hung in the pulleys, the treadles rightly adjusted, the tow yarn wound on quills and placed in the shuttle, and we are ready to weave. Recollect, all the cloth for family use is to be made, towels, table linen, bed linen, bags for grain, in short, everything.

This was scarcely finished before we must begin to prepare for winter. The sheep are sheared, wool for family use brought into the house to be cleansed, some to be dyed in the wool, and when properly prepared sent to the carding machine to be converted into rolls, which were spun into yarn. Some of this we dyed blue or any other color desired to make cloth for our winter gowns, or perchance for the fulled cloth for the clothing of the male portion of our family. . . . Some of our homespun we thought very nice, and think so still. Our best towels we were very proud of and like to show them even now. Then our blankets were fine, I have the remains of one of them yet and show it with much pride. I spun the yarn of which it was made, got in the piece, started the weaving myself, long, long ago. Could again do the same had I the strength. We also spun, colored the yarn for, and wove our stair carpet. It was a beauty . . .[6]

Mary Lyon's competence in household arts was hard-won, for although she had a strong physique, she seems never to have been deft with her hands. But it must have been worth the effort to her on many occasions, especially when she was "boarding round" to earn her keep and adding to her scanty education fund by selling the heavy blue and white coverlets she had spun, dyed, and woven. Writing after her death, one of her close friends in later life, Eunice Caldwell Cowles, observed, "With all her acknowledged inaptitude for mechanical pursuits, she could spin and weave as well as any of her kinswomen of those days. The blue fulled cloth habit, which she wore at Derry and Ipswich in 1827 and 1828, she spun and wove herself. She could make a batch of bread or a tin of biscuit without wasting a dust of flour. She could *clear-starch* as well as any laundress in the land." She could also embroider and net gloves and curtains, Mrs. Cowles noted, concluding,

"She took all the greater pleasure in doing these and the like things because they came hard to her."[7]

Some of Mary's expertise must obviously have been acquired on the job after her mother had left. Nevertheless, even in 1810 and 1811 Aaron was surely getting his money's worth when he paid his sister one dollar a week—in silver dollars, which she treasured and saved. This source of income stopped after a few years. In November 1812 Aaron married Armilla Alden, one of the 14 children of the Rev. John Alden of Ashfield. The family change was not unsettling. Armilla was only 19 and no doubt glad to have Mary stay on in the homestead, where she must have helped out in all sorts of ways even before the babies started coming. Mary, in turn, must have been happy to return to her efforts to get an education.

Very little is known about Mary's first schools and teachers. There was a school within a mile of the Lyon homestead in 1800. She attended as soon as she was able to walk that far, probably when she was 4, a customary age for starting district school. But by the time she was 7 the school had been moved another mile away, and she could seldom get there. She began very young to spend a school term—about three months—with a family living near a schoolhouse, helping in the household to pay for her board. In this fashion she attended several different schools in Buckland and Ashfield, staying mainly with relatives.

The common school in the first decade of the nineteenth century was chiefly a place of self-education. In a single room anywhere from 25 to 80 pupils might be crowded together on successive tiers of benches, the oldest boys and girls in the rear. Those not disposed toward mischief spent most of their time poring over what reading, grammar, and arithmetic books their families had been able or willing to provide or listening to what went on in the front of the room. They might have to wait hours between their brief turns at the teacher's desk to recite, individually or in small groups, giving back verbatim the definitions and paradigms from the book they had just handed over. Spelling matches and the games played at recess were apt to be the highlights of such days. It is not surprising that discipline was a major problem or that most teachers, the young women who took the summer term positions and the men who were hired for the more difficult winter term, stayed only one or two years. Indeed, under these circumstances it is remarkable that some real teachers emerged, who persisted and were admired. One such was John Porter, who saw so much in Mary Lyon as a pupil that he got her a post in the Shelburne Falls school for the summer of 1814 and started her on her career. Report has it that Mary from the first had a remarkable memory, studied hard, was equally successful at grasping principles and processes in grammar and in arithmetic, and talked so fast that she was sometimes hard to understand.[8]

Whatever her achievements in district school, a major source of intellectual development in her early years must have been the church. The Bible seems to have been the only book in the Lyon household; her mother probably knew considerable portions by heart and surely read and reread it to her growing family. Among Mary's happiest memories of childhood was the weekly trip across the Ashfield line to the church at Baptist Corner where her grandmother's brother, Elder Enos Smith, preached twice every Sunday. "But sweetest of all, through a mile or more, to that village church, was that wild winding way, traversed each Sabbath morning by that little group, while the family poney gave the mother her horseback ride. There, too, in winter, was that little sleigh, packed so snugly and gliding so gently, over that same winding way, to that same little church."[9]

Neither the Lyons nor the Shepards had had time for much formal education. There is no evidence that Mary's father, her mother, their brothers and sisters, her own brother, or her older sisters had managed more than a few years at district school. But they were considered intelligent, and it is likely that they drew intellectual as well as spiritual stimulus from the morning and afternoon services every Sunday at Baptist Corner. Elder Enos Smith, who had not trained for the ministry, favored "simple explanations of Bible truth." At least one of his sermons—on the character of God—moved Mary deeply. Years afterward she looked back to that particular Sunday in May 1816 as the time when she first experienced the personal conviction of God's presence that was essential to the true Christian. But she did not thereupon seek baptism; at 19 Mary already combined piety and independence.

When she did join six years later, it was the Congregational church into which she was baptized.[10]

In early nineteenth century New England, even remote churches in the hills spread the word of the reform movements that were stirring on both sides of the Atlantic. Revivals, though not yet at the fever pitch of the 1820's, were not infrequent; the Buckland Congregational Church recorded four between 1794 and 1823. Zeal was mounting for missionaries to save the godless frontiersmen in the West and the Indians they were driving out. The Massachusetts Baptist Missionary Society was founded in 1802 and was no doubt soon telling the churches what life was really like in the Western Reserve and the valley of the Mississippi. Most exciting of all was the great new field of foreign missions. In England, William Carey, after reading Captain Cook's journals of exploration in the Pacific, had stirred up his fellow Baptists to organize support; by 1793 he was on his way to India to save the heathen. The impulse to action in the United States started less than 30 miles from Buckland, across the hills at Williams College. In 1806 a religious gathering that had started in a meadow was driven by a sudden storm to shelter under a haystack. At this "Haystack Meeting" four intense young idealists in the freshman class were among those who dedicated their lives to foreign missions. Samuel Mills, Jr., and his classmates were so fixed in this resolve that in 1810, the year after they graduated and went to Andover Theological Seminary, they persuaded the assembled ministers of the Congregational churches of Massachusetts to set up the American Board of Commissioners for Foreign Missions. Its scope was soon nationwide, and it became a remarkably effective instrument for gathering gifts and enlisting and placing missionaries.

Both the cause and the organization excited Mary Lyon's imagination. Long afterward she told Mount Holyoke Seminary students: "Some of the brightest visions of my childhood are of Carey" and his co-workers. She had early learned the names of Mills and his associates and had been thrilled "when the subject of foreign missions first began to find its way into the family circle, and to be spoken of as one of the marvelous things of the age." She recalled getting the news when the first missionaries sailed from Salem and Philadelphia in 1812. Of the ABCFM, to

15

which she contributed generously all her life, she said, "I love the very thought that I can remember the beginnings of this great and glorious enterprise."[11]

Mary's early enthusiasms included the landscape in which she grew up. The climb to the top of the steep hill behind her house was one of her treasured memories. "I can now see that little mountain home with its sweet little rivulet, finding its way among rocks, and cliffs, and hillocks, and deep craggy dells. Then just beyond . . . was that 'top of the hill,' crowned by its high rolling rock. . . . Everyone was amply repaid, who would climb that steep hill, and ascend that high rock. There might be seen the far-off mountains in all their grandeur, and the deep valleys, and widely extended plains, and more than all, that little village below, containing only a very few white houses, but more than those young eyes had ever yet seen."[12]

Just how much time she spent on the games and gatherings of country boys and girls is an open question. She may occasionally have shared in the Arcadian festivals recalled in eloquent detail by a contemporary 60 years later:

. . . we would sit down and eat apples and snap the seeds at the girls, and the girls would snap the seeds at the boys and toss the cores over their shoulders to the next couple. Then came the pears . . . the red-cheeked old rare-ripes and white malcantoons, . . . and then we had the blue plums. Oh, those beautiful old blue plums! We eat and eat, till our teeth were set on edge. The girls tossed the stones over to the boys and the boys tossed the stones to the girls behind them. Then came the butternuts, cartloads of them on the ground. . . . So we cracked and eat and threw the shucks over our shoulders to the next pair; and with walnuts we would do the same. . . . When we were thirsty, there was the old, cold spring down in the dell below the rock. . . . By pairs we went down to the cold spring, and the boys dipped the gourd and handed it to the girl, and dipped the piggin and they drank; then the girl handed the boy the gourd and the boy handed the girl the piggin; so they both drank out of the piggin and the gourd, and handed it to the next pair waiting. O, who ever drank anything that tasted so good as that water at the old spring out of the gourd *and the piggin. . . . And then we would scatter off in groups and pairs among the wild grape-vines, and when the day was spent and we all met together again, to go home, lo! on the cheeks of the girls were many purple stains, and no wonder; for the boys had eaten so heartily of the grapes.*[13]

Whether Mary was ever one of these partners, she certainly knew country games. This same old gentleman remembered how, when he was a little boy and Mary, nine years his senior, was in her teens, "we used to jump upon that rock in playing 'gool,' go out where the water runs over the rock and spatter each other, and up the hill and crack butternuts, and go into the house and I would quill for her to weave."[14]

Mary Lyon's first teaching job was unremarkable. The ordinary one-room schoolhouse with raised seats in the rear was in the northeastern section of Buckland, which included that part of the village of Shelburne Falls lying on the western bank of the Deerfield River. At 17 she had been hired for a twenty-week summer term at the customary wage for young women—75 cents a week and board. (A young man hired for the winter term would receive $10 to $12 a month and board.) Like her predecessors, she was "boarding round," which meant that she had to work out a schedule for living an equal number of days at the home of each pupil, in this instance five apiece.

Her experience in the classroom was not unusual either—she had trouble with discipline. The summer term was ordinarily populated by the younger children, aged 4 to 10, but on a rainy day there might be an influx of big boys temporarily released from the heavy work of the fields. Even without them, keeping order was not easy. Zilpah Grant had started to teach in rural Connecticut a few years earlier; her method of getting obedience had been to put the young recalcitrants down a "dungeon hole" (a disused well?), suspending them by her garters. There is no indication that Mary Lyon tried such drastic measures, but in later life she told her students that she had "resolved many times, during that long summer, if once safely through, never to teach again."[15]

Happily, she changed her mind before the summer of 1815,

when, encouraged by John Porter, she went back again to the same school. For the rest of her life she was to spend an appreciable part of every year in the classroom, save only the three strenuous years 1835-37, when she devoted all her energies to founding Mount Holyoke. It took her some time to solve her problems of command; local opinion held that she would never equal her oldest sister Electa. No documentary evidence comes down to us concerning her early development as a teacher in the district schools of Buckland and Ashfield. Indeed, the only record of when and where she taught between 1814 and 1824 is a hasty list on the back of a letter with crossings out and corrections, made by her in 1833. What is clear about those years is that her teaching experience intensified her desire to learn.[16]

In the fall of 1817 a new educational opportunity opened in Ashfield. Sanderson Academy was founded by the bequest of a dedicated minister who had just died at the age of 36. The first teacher was a student at Williams particularly interested in mathematics and astronomy, Elijah Burritt, who took the job to be able to pay for the rest of his college course. Mary enrolled, using her accumulated savings, including the coverlets and linens she had woven, to pay for tuition for the first quarter and a place in a nearby boarding house; at 20, with four summers of district school behind her, she was fiercely eager to learn. Young Burritt, who was 23 and apparently a novice, seems nevertheless to have been effective in the classroom. Many years later she called Sanderson "one of those schools where they do nothing but *study* and *recite*. . . . You just learned what was in the book"; but on another occasion she said with equal truth, "Here I was principally educated, here my mental energies were first awakened." Certainly the experience was exhilarating to her. She is reported to have studied every waking moment, except for hurried meals, and to have slept an average of four hours a night.[17]

It was at Sanderson Academy that Mary Lyon performed the feat that became legendary in the hill towns: learning the whole of a Latin grammar text in three days. As one of the extra studies assigned partly to keep her from getting too far ahead of the rest of the class, Adams' Latin Grammar was given to her on a Friday. According to one account written long after the event, when on

Monday morning she took the recitation bench "midway of the room," general attention was soon attracted by "the promptness and rapidity of her recitation. . . . Soon all study was suspended, and with astonished interest we listened, while unconscious of her audience, she went through the Latin Grammar from beginning to end, with scarcely a correction."[18]

While she was mastering new subject matter hand over fist, she was also having other valuable experiences. At Sanderson she found another young woman just her own age with the same kinds of interests and ideals, and they formed a fast friendship on first sight. Amanda White was the oldest daughter of Thomas White, Esquire, one of the leading citizens of Ashfield. Her affection and companionship and her father's perceptive assistance made a real difference to Mary. Mr. White believed strongly in education, though he himself had dropped out of Yale, not liking the dead languages, and had learned to be a blacksmith. Settled by his father in Ashfield, he had built an impressive house, prospered, and become a public figure. He served as town selectman, state legislator, and justice of the peace, "trying most of the cases in the long kitchen of his dwelling house." He was also a trustee of Sanderson and a supporter of the recently opened subscription library. His daughter's new friend immediately caught his interest. When he found that Mary's financial resources were exhausted by a single term at the academy, he persuaded the other trustees to let her attend a second term without charge and invited her to "board" with the White family, sharing a room with Amanda.[19]

With eight children, the youngest only four, the White household must have been lively; it was certainly more sophisticated than anything Mary had previously known. She was a sturdy, well-built, energetic young woman, with a fine complexion, abundant auburn hair, bright blue eyes, and a warm smile, but she was "countrified" in her clothes, bearing, and mannerisms. The Whites were the first of a succession of friends who encouraged her to pay more attention to appearance and manner, pointing out an untidy skirt, a clumsy stride, a distracting gesture. Although she never did "excel in the graces of the drawing room," she made noticeable improvement and always accepted such corrections humbly and gratefully.[20]

Mr. White was a lifelong friend in need. He gave Mary Lyon financial advice and lent her money. As soon as she was able to pay her debts and start saving again, he acted as her banker, handling her money and investing it just as shrewdly as he did his own. When Amanda married and moved to Michigan in 1823, he and Mrs. White continued to welcome Mary to their home. They gave her practical assistance and encouragement for the next 25 years; both died less than a year before Mary herself. Two other White daughters developed personal ties: Hannah, three years younger than Mary, was to assist her in teaching and to write part of her biography, and Mary Arms, the youngest child, became a faithful pupil and follower.

Mary's studies at Sanderson merely whetted her appetite for learning. When the second term ended at the academy, for 11 days she attended a regular district school taught by Daniel Forbes, in order to practice penmanship, in which he was known to excel. She was not self-conscious about seating herself, a 21-year-old schoolmarm, on a low bench with "the common scholars"; it was the children who asked if she could have a chair at the teacher's table. (Once there she helped with the general instruction as well as working on her own p's and q's.) What she did worry about was any implication of intellectual pride. When Mr. Forbes set her a Latin sentence to copy, she asked him to write it in English lest she should be thought "wiser than she was." This intensive effort seems to have produced some immediate results. For the next decade her letters were written in a clear and regular hand; with special care she could produce a fine copper plate. In later life when her correspondence was voluminous, she wrote a hasty scrawl, difficult to decipher.[21]

A copy has survived of a letter she sent to a Sanderson school-mate just after the writing session; she was imitating the language of elegance as well as the shapes of the letters. No doubt hard at work at the Buckland homestead, where Aaron and Armilla now had three children under five, she wrote to Polly, "domestic employments engross almost my whole time . . ." and reflected "what can approach so near real society as epistolary converse?" At the end, in more familiar idiom, she twitted Polly about the visits of a Mr. B. and reported that she would be teaching that summer in the Buckland center school, starting June 1. There she put to immediate use one of the skills she had learned from Elijah Burritt; she introduced the study of geography through the making of maps.[22]

Just as soon as this session of district school was over, Mary Lyon ventured further afield. Drawing on her only remaining financial resource, she used some of her share of her father's estate (a total of about $150 when the appraisal was made in 1805) to attend the fall term at Amherst Academy. Started in 1814 under the sponsorship of Noah Webster, among others, the school was attracting students from various parts of Massachusetts and neighboring states. Girls came as well as boys. There were 76 masters and 76 misses in the catalogue dated November 1818, in which Mary Lyon's name appears; the young ladies seem to have been taught mainly by a preceptress. Mary was remembered afterward not only for her country clothes but for her kindness to fellow students in difficulty; her studies included rhetoric, logic, and chemistry. One of the friends she made was Orra White, a talented Amherst girl who became preceptress at the academy sometime in 1818 and was shortly to marry Edward Hitchcock, who would become professor and then president of Amherst College and a devoted friend of Mount Holyoke Seminary.

At the end of her term at Amherst Academy, Mary Lyon plunged into fulltime teaching. For more than a year she seems to have gone from one classroom to the next without any pause at all. District school "near Uncle Lyon's" for the winter of 1818-19 was followed in the spring by a family school in Buckland at the home of Alphaeus Brooks, the father of 16; in the summer by district school "near Mr. Alden's"; and in the fall by her first "select" or private school, also in Buckland. Immediately after that, she went back for the winter term of 1819-20 to the district school "near Mr. Alden's."

The year 1819 brought her a heavy blow. Aaron and Armilla, like many other New England farm families, decided to give up the struggle with their steep, rocky acres and move to the greener pastures of western New York. This possibility had been looming for some time. In 1817 Aaron had bought a piece of land in

Stockton, New York, where his great-uncle, Elder Ebenezer Smith, an itinerant preacher since his dismissal from the Baptist Corner Church in 1798, had finally come to rest. But when in early summer the young Lyons and their four children, the new baby in a cradle slung in ropes from the top of the covered wagon, actually set off with two other neighboring families, Mary felt desolate. She missed the whole family—she seems always to have been good with small children—and she missed her home. From this time on, until the Mount Holyoke Seminary building was ready for occupancy, she had no fixed residence or address. She would be 40 years old when she could once again claim even one room that was completely and permanently her own.[24]

There are no letters, diaries, or anecdotes about this difficult period in her life. For the next two years she went on teaching wherever she could and learning as much as she could, spending at least one term in Sanderson Academy, where she received free tuition and assisted with the younger pupils. After her death some of the friends of her youth recalled that early in life "she was easily discouraged" and "could not rise above disappointment, but would yield to great depression" and have long spells of weeping. Some of her letters written before she was 30 make reference to such states of mind. To her mother she mentioned "a kind of loneliness which is ever ready to oppress my spirits" and blamed it partly on the gloom of "the equinoctial storm"—she was writing in late September. Three months later she told Zilpah Grant, "My spirits have been unusually uniform for four weeks. I do not recollect an hour of depression." At some point she learned to control at least the outward signs of discouragement very effectively; her close friends in the latter half of her life all testified to her equanimity under stress.

In 1821, at the age of 24, Mary encountered the teaching that was to influence her strongly the rest of her life. An excellent seminary for young ladies had been opened three years earlier at Byfield, north of Boston, by the Reverend Joseph Emerson, and Squire White proposed sending Amanda. (His earlier plan to get a preceptress to hold a private school in Ashfield in the summer of 1819 had apparently fallen through for lack of support.) Mary wanted desperately to join her friend, but to finance the six-month

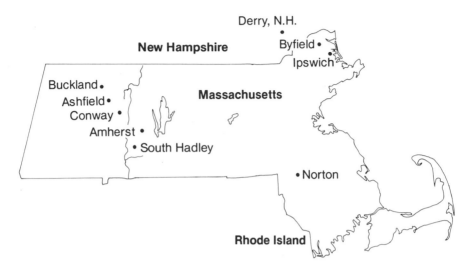

2. The map shows towns where Mary Lyon lived three months or more. After South Hadley became her home, she used to visit the Saffords in Boston and the Porters in Monson. Mount Holyoke College Library Archives.

term would take all she had—her recent earnings plus everything that was left of her inheritance from her father. Here she ran into strong opposition from friends and relatives, including her step-father, who was still exercising control over her inheritance. It took all of Mr. White's powers of persuasion to make Jonathan Taylor consent to let Mary spend her money as she wanted to. When the time came in late April for departure, Mr. White, according to a family story, had proposed to Mr. Taylor that if each of them furnished one horse, the Squire himself would provide a double carriage and drive it. Mr. Taylor did furnish the horse, but he charged Mary for it by the mile.[25]

Mary remembered the trip long afterward: they were three days on the way, they got lost in the vicinity of Boston, and she and Amanda, already homesick, cried in turn. But once there she was almost instantly absorbed and delighted. Mr. Emerson, an experienced teacher, lecturer, and preacher, communicated his continuing excitement about books and ideas as well as the range of his learning. Mary saw that the summer ought to be "peculiarly profitable." By May 13 she was writing her mother: "He renders every

23

recitation attractive. Never have I attended one, from which I might not gain valuable information, either scientific, moral, or religious." And she added, "I can complain of nothing but myself."[26]

Joseph Emerson was a puritan of unusual stamp: furiously energetic and at the same time uniformly sweet tempered, full of both conviction and intellectual curiosity, generous in his estimates of the capacity of other people, especially the young women he particularly liked to teach. He had graduated with distinction from Harvard in 1798 in the same class with William Ellery Channing and Joseph Story, the future justice. Within five years he had taken his theological training and been ordained, taught young ladies at an academy in Framingham, and persuaded one to be his wife, prepared two boys to enter Brown, and for two years as a tutor (meaning instructor) had conducted the recitations of Harvard students in mathematics, geography, and physics. For the next 13 years he was the well-loved pastor of a Congregational church in Beverly, Massachusetts.

It was poor health that made him give up the ministry and shift to teaching. He suffered from attacks of arthritis and digestive ailments of increasing severity. Although he followed strict regimens and took three long trips south for his health, his condition fluctuated; finally, after months of prostration, he died at the age of 55. Between bouts of illness, his energy seemed undiminished. He supported his growing family by conducting a seminary, giving series of public lectures, and producing textbooks and tracts. Even he was a bit surprised when he counted up what he had done in the last three months of his first southern sojourn. On June 26, 1817, he wrote from Charleston, South Carolina: "I have been in this city and in this dear family, about fourteen weeks. In that time I have formed a number of very endearing acquaintances and received favors in abundance. I have written sixteen long lectures, more than a dozen long letters, preached and lectured about forty-four times, read some, visited considerably, attended a few conferences and prayer meetings, and conversed much at home, and abroad." With this unexpected renewal of "strength and vigor," in the spring of 1818 he opened the seminary for young ladies that he would be conducting with the help of his wife and daughter in Byfield or Saugus or Wethersfield until his final illness.[27]

The subjects that Mary Lyon studied at Byfield were for the most part familiar to her, but Mr. Emerson's approach was a continuing revelation. As she wrote after his death, his estimate of the intellectual powers of women was "unusually high." Habitually "he treated ladies and gentlemen essentially in the same manner." She explained: "If a lady advanced an opinion, to which he could not assent, he did not hesitate to object . . . for he appeared to believe, that she had a mind capable of weighing an argument, and of seeing an objection." In her tribute Mary Lyon was careful to point out that this genuine respect did not keep him from approving the biblical injunction to wifely obedience. "While he considered it the universal duty of the wife to obey, restricted only by the laws of God, he did not consider it the duty of the husband, in any ordinary case, to command. . . . The obedience, which he would inculcate, would be so genuine and unaffected, as scarcely if ever to be recognized as such, by either party, the whole being clothed in the beautiful robe of mutual respect and esteem."[28]

What he expected of the earnest young women in front of him in the seminary was full understanding of what they were reading or discussing. He expected them to divide what they had been assigned into topics, to analyze, outline, and paraphrase each part, to make comparisons, to write down their questions and uncertainties, to look up every word they did not know. He probably said to them what he had written to a younger brother just about to enter Yale: "Brown's Dictionary of the Bible, Lempriere's Classical Dictionary, Jones's Biographical Dictionary, Johnson's English Dictionary, and some good Gazetteer, you ought to have constantly by you." His confidence was encouraging in the long, hard struggle for mastery. Mary wrote to her sister Rosina in Ashfield, "You know I always found difficulties, doubts, and inconsistencies in grammar; and the most I have done in that branch is to multiply these difficulties on every hand. But I must not be discouraged at this. Mr. E. remarked to us that nothing yet has been brought to perfection; and, as there are difficulties in every pursuit, if a person sees none, it argues his almost entire ignorance. Dr. Emmons observed once to Mr. E. that he often found it much harder to make a pupil discover a difficulty, than to remove it when discovered."[29]

Mr. Emerson's religious convictions were at the center of all his instruction. He believed that every act of the mind could and should contribute to the greater glory of God. Every proposition in logic, every chemistry equation, every law of physics rightly understood was a demonstration of the goodness of God and an impetus to right action. He considered the Bible "the book of books for schools, academies, colleges—the book of books, not only to direct the conduct, convert the soul, and save the world; but to discipline the faculties." He anticipated with absolute certainty the millennium, the last judgment, and an intellectually interesting eternal life in heaven for all who had been saved on earth. He was always saying, "I never expect to understand this fully before I get to heaven," or "We shall know more about this science if we ever reach heaven," or "Probably Abraham, with all his faith, had low views of this subject on earth, compared with what he has now."[30]

Mary Lyon, who had found intellectual and emotional stimulus from the church at Baptist Corner, kindled at the possibility of dedicating her life to the service of God in a way that made continuing demands on her power to learn and to reflect, as well as on her eagerness to serve. When, early in the term, Mr. Emerson asked all his students to classify themselves as Christians or unbelievers, Mary, after some hesitation, joined the group of those who "hoped they had been renewed by divine grace." She wrote her mother in great detail of the possibilities of a revival in the seminary and, as she was to do all the rest of her mother's life, asked for her prayers for a specific group. Mary knew the hazards in the process of conversion, particularly the risk of self-deception. "Four express a faint hope that they have passed from death unto life; but they hope with trembling. They feel that there is great danger of being deceived; that they shall believe stupidity to be trust in God, and thus sink down in security, and finally plunge themselves in everlasting ruin." She did not feel ready to join the church until she had returned from Byfield. When in March 1822 she did make her public profession of faith, it was not at Baptist Corner but in the Buckland Congregational Church.[31]

In the Mount Holyoke archives there are bits of the work Mary did at Byfield, which she managed to preserve through all the years of homelessness: lecture notes; comments on themes about Benevolence, the Bible, Cleopatra; and four of the themes themselves. But she needed no written reminders; Mr. Emerson's words and ways were engraved on her memory. For the rest of her life she found excitement in books he praised, made use of methods he employed, and quoted his criticism and counsel. Her enthusiasms, stirred by his, ranged almost as widely: Euclid, which had figured largely in Mr. Emerson's courtship of his first wife; Milton's *Paradise Lost*; Young's *Night Thoughts; The Improvement of the Mind* by Isaac Watts, for which Mr. Emerson was preparing a helpful text edition; the works of Jonathan Edwards. A dozen years later, when she was just beginning her heroic efforts to raise money, she solicited subscriptions for a reprint of Edwards' *History of Redemption* in the same letters in which she pled for funds to endow a seminary for young women.

The Byfield experience expanded Mary Lyon's horizons in all sorts of ways. Among the 50 pupils, no doubt a more cosmopolitan group than the one at Amherst Academy, were a number, like Mary and Amanda, in their twenties; some had already taught, and many were hoping to be teachers or missionaries. At mid-term they were joined by a minister's widow from Maine who was in her thirties. Mary particularly admired Mr. Emerson's assistant, a tall glamorous young woman from western Connecticut whose early experiences paralleled Mary's own. Zilpah Grant had a quick intelligence and a commanding presence, and her voice in the "seminary concert" or prayer meeting was eloquent. The friendship begun this summer was, during the years 1824–1834, of major importance to both young women.[32]

Mr. Emerson knew and admired notable clergymen and scholars and quoted them enthusiastically to his students. Probably Mary was most thrilled by his connection with the beginnings of foreign missions. His third wife (the first two, both intellectual and charming, had died young) was none other than Rebecca Hasseltine. Her sister, Ann Hasseltine, then living a heroic life in Burma as Mrs. Adoniram Judson, was honored in churches throughout the land as one of the first women missionaries from the United

States; she had been part of the intrepid little band that set out from Salem in 1812. It had been in part the enthusiasm of her brother-in-law which had encouraged her to accept young Judson, a close friend of Samuel Mills at Andover, and to accompany him into distant danger.

Lyman Beecher was among Mr. Emerson's acquaintances. On a trip for his health through western New England in 1816, he spent three nights in Litchfield at the Beecher home; he was particularly impressed by the eleven young ladies boarding there and, no doubt, attending Miss Pierce's school where Catharine Beecher had studied. College faculty and courses always interested him. He considered Yale "the best college in America," and especially admired President Dwight, whose judgment of his *Ecclesiastical Primer* he had gone to New Haven to obtain. He was also enthusiastic about Williams. When he had visited President Fitch just after the outbreak of the war of 1812, he had written back to his wife that the conversion within three months of 30 students and 40 townspeople was "more delightful than the alarm of war is distressing." In 1821 he was surely keeping a hopeful eye on the new college just opening its doors in Amherst. Within a few years he would be sending his oldest son there and writing to President Humphrey about ways of improving the curriculum.[33]

Though Joseph Emerson's puritanism seems remarkably outgoing and receptive, it did have limits. If as a young man he played the flute and bass viol, if he recommended to his students books by Darwin, Gibbon, and Hume, with warnings that these were the works of infidels, he nevertheless advocated total abstinence and ruled out not only novels—they were frivolous—but also practically all of classical literature, which was heathen and not useful. He was able to join the Masons and defend them under attack from the church, even though he had come to feel that the organization had serious drawbacks and would best be left to die out. He could tell a congregation, "I consider Baptists, Methodists, Congregationalists, and many other denominations, as engaged in the same great cause." But he could not tolerate either Unitarianism or Catholicism. His profound disapproval of Harvard might look to be related to his personal disappointments as an undergraduate (as a sophomore he had almost transferred to Dartmouth), but the principal cause was his dismay at the religious collapse already in process when he was a student. Fellow students who simultaneously commended the Bible and the "excellencies of christianity," praised the new liberalism in doctrine, and rejected Calvinism seemed to him set to "abandon themselves to all the horrors of atheism." A quarter of a century later his convictions were just as strong. "Next to unitarianism, I consider universalism the most dangerous of errors," he wrote his brother in July 1825.[34]

The Roman Catholic church seemed to him an equally great threat of damnation to men's immortal souls. It was on the subject of popery that in 1829 he was to preach what his brother called "the ablest sermon I ever heard from his lips." Its climax would be the denunciation of a new convent in Charlestown, the one that, five years later, was burned down by an angry mob. This violence would surely have horrified Joseph Emerson had he lived to see it. Even when he invoked a "flaming sword" against "the flag of Babylon," he was careful to explain that he meant "the sword of the spirit, the only one that ever ought to be employed against nunneries." It is not surprising that Mary Lyon took similar stands on most of these matters. The wonder is that, having come from so strict and limiting an orthodoxy, she could, at the age of 24, embrace one that was relatively open-minded.[35]

During the six months at Byfield, Amanda stepped up her campaign to get Mary to pay more attention to the way she looked: "she never went out without my inspection, to see that all was right; as she was very liable to leave off some article, or else put one on the wrong side out." If Amanda worried because Mary "did not devote sufficient time and attention" to appearances, she acknowledged her good humor at being corrected and recognized the reason for her total absorption. "Mary sends love to all," Amanda wrote home, "but time with her is too precious to spend it in writing letters. She is gaining knowledge by handfuls."[36]

Nevertheless, Mary did write letters even at Byfield; portions of two to her mother and one each to Rosina and Freelove, her younger sisters, have survived. She turned out to be a prolific correspondent, and the letters that we have are invaluable for understanding her life and the development of higher education for women. Unfortunately, the majority of these letters now exist only in the edited form in which they appear in the Hitchcock *Mary Lyon*. The four women, Hannah White, Zilpah Grant Banister, Mary Whitman, and Eunice Caldwell Cowles, who together assembled and copied the letters for the press (and, apparently, disposed of many originals), were all admirers of Mary Lyon. In particular, Mrs. Banister and Mrs. Cowles, as close personal friends, had for a number of years kept an affectionate eye on her merinos and her bonnet strings. In the same spirit they seem to have omitted words they considered repetitious or superfluous, adjusted sentence structure for a preferred emphasis, and occasionally added a sentence or phrase. More serious than these refinements are the substantive omissions, indicated by dots. These cuts—made, no doubt, in order to focus on "the power of christian benevolence"—must have eliminated fascinating instances of her observations of every day life, her immediate worries and her human warmth and liveliness.[7]

Even in the cut versions of these early letters from Byfield, there are hints of her ordinary reactions and experiences. One sentence suggests her relationship with her mother in Ashfield; she missed "the rapid conversation at the meeting hour of a mother and daughter—conversation which stops not for thoughts." She was lonesome, working by herself in the empty seminary during a two-week recess when everybody else had gone. "What think you my emotions were, when I saw my companions dispersing in all directions to embrace their parents, brothers, and sisters?" she asked Rosina. There is perhaps a touch of humor in her description to her mother of the religious state of the seminary. "Imagine to yourself a little circle of about forty females, almost excluded from the rest of the human family, all appearing solemn as eternity." To get a true picture of Mary Lyon from the letters in the Hithcock *Mary Lyon*, it is important to read closely and also to remember that Hannah White—and probably Mrs. Banister and Mrs. Cowles—considered that Mary Lyon had "a keen perception of the ludicrous, and a power of humorous description, which rendered her a very enlivening companion."[38]

Mary Lyon at 24 was in some ways still unformed. But the qualities that were to carry her through the struggles ahead were clearly visible: her unalloyed pleasure in learning, the incisiveness of her mind, her great physical energy, her warm and selfless interest in other people. It was her good fortune at this point to come under the influence of a genuine intellectual whose enthusiasm and idealism were as boundless as her own. Six weeks before his death, Joseph Emerson wrote the head of Andover Theological Seminary: "I have lately been astonished to find, that under my gray hairs, and my still more depressing infirmities, I can glow upon the most important subjects, as suddenly and as intensely as at twenty, and much more so." No wonder she treasured up even his passing remarks. In January 1822 when he dedicated the building in Saugus to which he was moving the seminary, she was back in Ashfield, but his sentiments and most of his words on that occasion had already become a part of her inner consciousness:

. . . *may we not indulge the enrapturing hope, that the period is not remote, when female institutions, very greatly superior to the present, will not only exist, but be considered as important, as are now our colleges for the education of our sons. The distinguished honor is probably reserved for our rising republic, to exhibit to the world examples of such female seminaries as the world has never witnessed. But where such an institution shall be erected, by whom it shall be founded, and by whom instructed, it is yet for the hand of Providence to develop. Possibly some of our children may enjoy its advantages.*[39]

2
A Throne of Her Own

Take fast hold of instruction:

let her not go: keep her:

for she is thy life.

PROVERBS 4:13

When Mary Lyon returned from Byfield, eager to put to use what she had been learning, she confronted the familiar question—where could she teach? There was no easy answer in the 1820's and 1830's for any young woman who had completed her apprenticeship in the district schools but had not yet built up a substantial personal following. If she could find a sponsor, classroom space, satisfactory boarding places for out-of-towners, and capital to cover advertising, fuel, and supplies, she might start a "select" school, hoping that an adequate number of bright and not wholly ignorant pupils would enroll. Or she might seek a post as second or third in command at one of the relatively established schools or academies, where the students were apt to be abler but the power of the preceptor was absolute. In any case, the chances of permanence were slight; secondary schools of all descriptions tended to be short-lived, springing up and disappearing with equal ease. Even the academies with some endowment were apt to depend heavily for survival on the reputation, physical stamina, and organizational skill of the incumbent preceptors.

Thanks to another boost from Squire White, Mary Lyon was promptly invited to return to Sanderson Academy as preceptress—heretofore she had been only a part-time assistant. The Squire had managed to persuade Abijah Cross, the young Dartmouth graduate just named principal, that she would be quite as "sufficient" as the male colleague he had thought he needed. She proved herself in short order; until the spring of 1824 when she left to work with Zilpah Grant, she held the post continuously under three successive male principals. All were Dartmouth graduates headed for the ministry.

About these two years of teaching, her last in a coeducational school, there are no records whatever. Her personal relations seem to have been cordial. On their honeymoon in 1824, Abijah Cross and his bride stopped overnight at the school in Derry, New Hampshire, where Mary was then teaching; subsequently, she spent a two-week vacation with the newlyweds at their home in Salisbury, New Hampshire. At the least, her contact with these young Sanderson principals must have enlarged her knowledge of Dartmouth courses and revivals and encouraged her interest in Dartmouth students from the hill towns.[1]

Sometime in 1822 Mary Lyon had a difficult decision to make. Her brother Aaron came from Stockton, New York, hoping to persuade her to go back with him to Chautauqua County, where good teachers were scarce. Her affection for Aaron and his family and her intense interest in all missionary enterprises, including the home missions to frontier communities, must have had a strong appeal. But in the end she chose to stay where she had already demonstrated that a young woman without funds or family influence could find unexpected opportunities for higher education and dedicated pupils to teach.

In 1823, between the spring and fall terms at Sanderson, another such opportunity arose. The Congregational minister at Conway was Edward Hitchcock, married to Orra White, whom Mary had known as a teacher at Amherst Academy. In the summer of 1823 Mary Lyon taught a select school in Conway and lived with the Hitchcocks, where she could at the same time study science with the husband and drawing and painting with the wife. Thus began one of the enduring relationships that were so important to her ultimate success. This summer gave early indication of a special talent: her ability to maintain warm personal friendships with the wives of the men who admired, advised, and supported her.

It was accepted practice then for ministers to take young men as private pupils, either those learning Greek and Latin in order to get into college or those just out of college preparing for the ministry—and less usual to take on young women, especially in chemistry. But Mr. Hitchcock was no ordinary minister. The son of a Deerfield hatter, he had, before he was 30, graduated from and become principal of Deerfield Academy, been attracted

to Unitarianism and then converted himself back to Congregational orthodoxy, because of eye trouble given up his plans to
attend Harvard, and then, without benefit of college, qualified for
the study of divinity and the ministry. He had also won attention
beyond the Connecticut Valley through articles based on his own
astronomical observations, which exposed the repeated errors in
a popular almanac.

In another two years Edward Hitchcock would be launched on
his major career as a professor at Amherst College, which had
opened in 1821 and was still scrambling to survive. He was to be
the mainstay of science teaching at Amherst for nearly 40 years,
including a decade when he served as president. He would also
become the father of the United States geological surveys, a
founder of the American Association for the Advancement of
Science, a pioneer in the investigation of the Connecticut Valley
dinosaur tracks—and an invaluable friend of Mount Holyoke
Seminary from the moment the first plans were evolved. In this
first relatively brief encounter with Mary Lyon, he must have been
impressed to discover an enthusiasm as intense as his own for both
science and salvation.[2]

As she had done at Byfield, Mary Lyon no doubt admired her
teacher's teachers. Certainly she seized the chance to learn from
one of them. Amos Eaton, the first principal of Rensselaer Poly-
technic Institute, had for a dozen years been going up and down
western New England and eastern New York, giving widely ac-
claimed lectures on science to colleges and to the general public.
His series on natural history given in the town of Amherst some
years earlier had led to personal acquaintance with Hitchcock and
had stimulated the young principal of Deerfield and his friends to
the serious study of botany and mineralogy. In the spring of 1824,
just a few months before Professor Eaton settled permanently in
Troy, New York, and began the Rensselaer courses, he was again
lecturing on chemistry and natural history to Amherst College
students and others; Mary Lyon managed to attend. What is more,
the next spring, in response to her inquiry about her difficulties
in teaching chemistry, Professor Eaton invited her to come to
Troy for help. In April 1825 she spent the two-to-three-week
interval between her winter and summer schools as the guest of the

Eatons, attending the Institute lectures on chemistry and physics and getting additional instruction from her host.

Late in 1823 an alluring teaching opportunity was extended in a letter from Zilpah Grant, Mr. Emerson's assistant and Mary Lyon's admired friend at Byfield. Zilpah had just been named principal of a new female academy which would open in April in southern New Hampshire, thanks to the $4000 bequest of a far-seeing single gentleman; would Mary like to assist her? Delighted as she was by the prospect, Mary needed time to think it over—that is, to pray for God's guidance, as she would do in making every important decision of her life. She needed to balance the attractions of the new proposal and the claims of Sanderson, to which she felt "in no small degree indebted" and in which she had begun to see future possibilities. It took several letters and a visit by Zilpah to Ashfield early in 1824 to conclude arrangements; the partnership thus begun lasted a decade and had impressive consequences.[3]

Zilpah Polly Grant, who had been born in Norfolk in the hills of western Connecticut on May 30, 1794, had grown up under circumstances startlingly reminiscent of Mary Lyon's girlhood—like Mary's shaped by frugality, self-reliance, orthodoxy. The youngest of five children, Zilpah had also lost her father in early childhood; he was killed in an accident when she was two. Her mother managed for a time to run the household and the farm, with the help of the oldest boy, then 13; ultimately she remarried. Zilpah started teaching district school just before she turned 15. At the age of 18 she joined the Congregational church; at 25, after years of successful teaching in nearby schools, she too persuaded male relatives to let her take her patrimony and savings to attend Mr. Emerson's school in Byfield.

But there were some significant differences between these two bright young women. Zilpah lacked a rugged physique and abounding energy. At the age of 21 she suffered a severe attack of pleurisy and took two years to recover; thereafter she was subject to periods of invalidism. It is hard to ascertain the seriousness of her successive physical difficulties, which occurred between periods of vigorous activity. She lived to be 80 and entertained and traveled extensively in the latter half of her life. Eunice Caldwell Cowles,

3. Zilpah Polly Grant, later Mrs. William Banister, was principal of Adams Academy and Ipswich Seminary; for ten years she was mentor and close friend to Mary Lyon. Mount Holyoke College Library Archives.

who had studied and taught under her and collaborated with her on Mary Lyon's biography, made a forthright appraisal. Zilpah, she thought, "with some exceptions, was all her life able to do anything she really wanted to do." According to Mrs. Cowles, "on no point was she [so] open to flattery as in the matter of her aches and pains; on no side so weak; only cosset her, and at the same time tell her how much she concealed, and you rode straight into her best graces."[4]

Her vulnerability in matters of health in no way diminished her personal powers. Zilpah Polly Grant was a handsome young woman, tall and dark, with expressive eyes and regal bearing. A posthumous article about her in the *North American Review* was entitled "An American Queen." According to Miss Gilchrist, "it was said after her marriage that European visitors came to this country to see Niagara and Mrs. Banister." She had charm as well as elegance. Her cousin, John Phelps Cowles, husband of Eunice, who was not given to flattery, wrote after Zilpah's death, of her "attractive power, which made it delightful to be associated with her." He recalled that "girls that wanted to grow into polished women fondly wished to be like her" and "when she spoke, you chose to listen."[5]

This magnetic quality was one factor in Zilpah's immediate success as both teacher and student. In her six-month term at Byfield in 1820 she so stood out that Joseph Emerson immediately engaged her as his assistant both in teaching and in preparing a catechism for the press. She worked with him for a year, taught a select school in Winchester, Connecticut, for a year and a half, and in response to his repeated urgings returned early in 1823, only to leave in November to head the new academy at Derry. Mr. Emerson in 1822 called her "one, who has done more than any other young lady, to raise my Seminary." He kept in touch with her all the rest of his life. In 1830 he was writing her from Wethersfield, "Do write me fifty questions upon metaphysics." In 1832 he wrote down for her the last words she had requested, as "a brother and friend" coupling concern for her own salvation—"Love yourself as your neighbor"—with a ringing exhortation to "pursue celestial truth, wherever the word and Spirit lead," that is, to "Philosophy! Metaphysics! Speculation! Human Reason! Logic! Theory! System! Disputation!"[6]

Zilpah's pupils were also warmly responsive. In February 1823 she wrote a formal letter of thanks to the young ladies of her school in Winchester for their parting gift of a book of poems; in June she wrote an even more allegorical appreciation to the young ladies in Mr. Emerson's school in Saugus for the gift of a watch.

When Mary Lyon joined Zilpah Grant in Londonderry in mid-April 1824, there was no doubt about who was commander and who lieutenant. Zilpah's age, presence, and experience singled her out: Adams Female Academy was unquestionably Miss Grant's school. Mary Lyon was listed in the printed catalogue as one of three teachers assisting the preceptress. Both Zilpah and Mary were paid $5 per week plus board for the 30-week term; Zilpah had an additional $36 for traveling expenses. Mary was full of admiration for Zilpah's skill, foresight, and inventiveness. Her letters about Derry during the four years of their tenure bear witness to how much she was learning and how hard they were both working to achieve high standards. In February 1825 Mary wrote from Buckland, where she had been holding a winter school of her own, to a fellow teacher: "I have an opportunity this winter to see the value of what I gained at Derry." Four years later, after the transfer to Ipswich, in the midst of a letter to Zilpah about many things, Mary said, "I hope you will be enabled to do as much this winter to correct the erroneous opinions of your teachers about schools, if they have any, as you have done to correct mine from year to year."[7]

What Mary particularly admired was the combination of continuity and thoroughness in Zilpah's organization. The first summer she wrote in some detail to Amanda, now married and living in Michigan, saying of Zilpah, "You know she is well fitted to guide, and I think she has improved very much since you knew her." Though Emersonian in plan, this school differed from Byfield, where

the course was too rapid for ordinary minds, and also for such as were young, or but little improved. We have more classes, our course is slower, and the increased number of teachers will enable us to execute our plans thoroughly. We have three regular classes, denominated senior, middle, and junior. . . . We have also as many preparatory classes as circumstances require. The young ladies are examined, and are placed where it is thought they will improve the most. They are classed, not at all according to the number of books they have studied, but according to the real knowledge they are found to possess. We have but very few under fifteen years of age who can enter the regular classes.[8]

To encourage thoroughness only two or three subjects were studied at one time, with repeated drills and discussions and frequent reviews. In June, Mary was spending three hours a day on grammar and three on penmanship, for which every young lady had to make her own pens. The students, Mary found, responded very well, even though, as she told Hannah White, only four of their 60 pupils could be classified as seniors and some of the young ladies had been put two classes lower than they had expected. There had not been any delinquents even at composition, "one of the most trying exercises." True, Mary had won similar cooperation on composition in her own school the preceding summer, but at Derry it was achieved "with less effort." Nevertheless, the thirty-week session, broken by a two-week recess, was strenuous. To cope with these young women, "of different ages, possessing different habits, inclinations & capacities," demanded continued exertion.[9]

Zilpah had already begun to develop at Byfield a method of discipline which Mary adopted at Adams with great enthusiasm and held to all the rest of her life. The success of this system of planned consensus and self-reporting, which survived at Mount Holyoke Seminary long after her death, stemmed in part from the popularity of revivals among all Calvinists, conservative and liberal. The nature of the approach was described in detail by Mrs. Cowles and Miss Guilford.

As she met one and another of the more docile and influential pupils, she said to her alone, "If you could avoid whispering altogether, I think it would be an advantage to you and to the school;" and when the pupil said, "I will try," Miss G. added, "Will you try for a week?" After a large number had pledged themselves to her, she discussed the subject with them all, dwelling on the evils of whispering in school, and clearly showing it to be the floodgate of idleness and disorder. When their minds were in the right state to give the right answer, she put the question, "Would you like to try and avoid whispering, and all communications equivalent to it, till this time tomorrow?" On the morrow she bestowed a look and a word of commendation on those who had kept their resolve, and by such means, in a few weeks, banished the practice from the school.

Each new rule was approved and enforced in the same way.

Having established, with argument and apt illustration, the general principle and secured such conviction as to shame dissent, she would bring forward her particular case: it might be silence in study-hour or in school, retirement at night, or rising in the morning. The pupils would see that what she had asked was wise and good. They would freely pledge themselves to observe it, and each one promise to keep a record of her success or failure.[10]

Zilpah Grant had carefully set up in advance the study of the Bible as part of the regular curriculum, although Adams was not a denominational school; she had stipulated to the trustees—as they later had reason to regret—that one seventh of the pupils' time might be put on the Bible. Mary Lyon was naturally sympathetic. "Every week of the term," she wrote, "each pupil is expected to apply her mind closely, two hours or more, to the Scripture lesson given out early in the week, and recited the next Monday morning. This study has excited more deep and universal interest than any other." In later years the exegesis of Scripture was one of Mary Lyon's acknowledged strengths.[11]

Although Zilpah had unquestioned dominance in school, the two young women seemed to have shared a genuine companionship. They may have enjoyed each other's company partly because of their unlikeness; they both welcomed the social and professional opportunities opening out before them. Zilpah was the one with the sense of style; she helped Mary decide what to wear. Mary was the one with the sense of humor; her eye for ironic detail helped keep both of them cheerful amid the contretemps of everyday life. Zilpah picked out gingham for a dress for Mary (9 yards was required), chose her bonnet trimmings, and suggested mailing to Ashfield, for a pending visit to Connecticut, the Gros-de-nap gown Mary had obviously left in Derry for the winter.[12]

In June 1825 Mary wrote to Zilpah's married sister in Connecticut, because "your sister gives herself so much to do and me so little," describing a major event—the visit of Lafayette. He arrived in the midst of a thunderstorm at the end of a long day; the young ladies, dressed in white, had been waiting for him eight hours. Both teachers and pupils were awed by this personal encounter with nobility. Mary noted that even Dr. Dana, Adams trustee and former president of Dartmouth, had a tremor in his voice when he delivered the official welcome. This same letter mentioned little Edward Parker, son of the minister with whom Zilpah and Mary were boarding. In the temporary absence of both mother and father, they had the responsibility for this "pretty looking boy," compared to whom "a mule is a pattern of docility & condescension."[13]

Another glimpse of their immediate surroundings comes from a letter written two years later, after they had shifted boarding houses. Mary described the table conversation they drew, along with better accommodations and independence. C. T. Bly Esquire, discouraged by Zilpah's "talent to evade whatever she thinks it expedient to evade," had given up trying to discuss religion. "The division of Londonderry, affairs at the city of Washington, and political subjects generally furnish us with abundance of table talk. Sometimes . . . it seems as if the last saucer of tea would be spun out to an insupportable length." When Zilpah was sick, Mary was "the chief replier," since "I suppose it very important to treat a very polite carver with all due attention." This same letter records the accident to Zilpah's ankle that turned out to be much more serious than either of them then suspected.

Last Friday we had a very amusing scene. The seats and tables were so placed as to give most of the floor to the young ladies, and as we keep the swing partitions raised to accommodate monitorial recitations, a convenient station was furnished for Miss Grant. Just imagine nearly 80 young ladies, arranged in geometrical order, all jumping at the same moment with the additional exercise of constant laughter. Miss Grant never appeared more lively and graceful. But to damp the merriment, the leader of the play received an injury to her ankle, which has confined her to the chamber ever since.[14]

The steps by which these two lively young women became acquainted with prominent clergymen and educators in the Boston area have not been recorded; but given Zilpah's glamour, the quickness and zeal of both of them, Joseph Emerson's enthusiastic endorsement, and the backing of the Adams trustees, it is not surprising that their horizons had widened even before the move to Ipswich. When Zilpah's torn tendon turned out to be a major handicap—she had to go on crutches for several years—one of her letters of sympathy came from Dr. and Mrs. Leonard Woods. Professor of theology at Andover Theological Seminary since its founding in 1808, Dr. Woods was one of the most respected voices of orthodox Congregationalism and a leader in its missionary efforts. He obviously knew both young women reasonably well and offered not only religious consolation but also practical assistance.

As soon as you are able, would it not be adviseable for you to put yourself for a little while under the care of Dr. Warren? I should be quite in favor of this. You could come here at first: then after a suitable time to rest, take our morning stage coach & go to Boston. I would write a letter to introduce you to Dr. Warren; & Dr. Farrar had better do the same, (if you think proper.) In the hospital, you would have the best attendance, & regular visits from the Physician.

Dr. John C. Warren, a professor at Harvard Medical School, was one of the most eminent physicians in Boston, and Zilpah was probably grateful for his care in spite of the slowness of her recovery. Dr. Woods sent regards to Miss Lyon, "whose duties have been very arduous, & who has, I doubt not, had grace from God according to her need." His second practical suggestion, the name of a competent young woman in Newburyport who might be a short-term substitute for Zilpah, was never taken up.[15]

Among the notable people with whom Zilpah and Mary established personal contact during their four years at Derry were the Beechers. Catharine, three years younger than Mary Lyon, began to make a name for herself and her seminary at Hartford soon after its opening in 1823. She must have learned early about the caliber of the teaching at Adams; within a few years she was mounting a campaign to get Zilpah to join her at Hartford. Two of Lyman Beecher's nieces were enrolled at Adams; in June of 1825 their mother, accompanied by Mrs. Lyman Beecher and another sister, paid an overnight visit to the school. It seems not unlikely that at the end of her winter school in March 1828 Mary did manage a projected trip to Hartford and Wethersfield, gaining what Zilpah called "just such improvement as you need" by visiting both Catharine Beecher and Joseph Emerson.[16]

In any case, Mary Lyon had been visiting schools in Boston as early as the summer of 1826; both she and Zilpah followed new developments in educational theory and practice. They both read the excellent new monthly, started in 1826, which aimed to enlarge

45

the horizons of everyone concerned with schools and colleges and recognized the urgency of improved opportunities for young women. For a decade the *American Journal of Education*, edited first by William Russell and then by William Woodbridge (he called it *American Annals of Education*), discussed Pestalozzi and others, delineated effective classroom practice, and spread the news of the rapid multiplication of colleges for men.

By 1826 the monitorial system, imported from England, was being used very successfully at Adams. Toward the end of the session Mary wrote her youngest sister Freelove a detailed account.

At present, I am deeply absorbed in grammar and arithmetic. We are conducting both the exercises on the monitorial plan. Grammar for this quarter has just commenced. Between forty and fifty now recite at the same time on this plan. We shall occupy about an hour in the recitation. I shall devote my time as I commonly do, when we have recitations in this way. We have regular monitors appointed for grammar from the senior class. These monitors study their lessons; and for the present, I shall devote about half an hour to them out of school. We have been attending to Adams's Arithmetic on the monitorial plan for a long time, with usual, or rather increasing success. We shall very soon lay it aside for the season. Between fifty and sixty have attended this exercise together, comprising all the regular classes except the senior class; and, indeed, most of this class have been engaged all the time as monitors. We have adopted the plan of having a regular monitor for every section, consisting of from five to twelve, according to the capacity of the monitors and of the students. Last spring, the school all attended to Colburn's Arithmetic. About a week since, seventy commenced a review. To this we devote an hour in school, our usual time for a recitation. As they are nearly together at present, I spend about half the time in asking questions to the whole, and then they are arranged in small monitorial classes. I pass from one class to another, assisting the monitors or listening to the recitations, as the case may require. This exercise is very pleasant. It is highly animating to observe seventy pupils, with the attention of all fixed on the same point at the same moment.[17]

There was no doubt that Adams Female Academy under Zilpah Grant was a success. Enrollment figures told the story. Mary commented repeatedly on "the happy effects of a system so long continued"; of the 90 students enrolled in the first fourteen-week term of the 1826 session, 39 had attended in a previous year. And yet, though the statistics compiled by Zilpah Grant in 1839 indicated a degree of continuity worthy of note, they also showed how far young women then were from getting the kind of sustained education that was available to their brothers. Of the 260 students enrolled at Adams from 1824 through 1827, three quarters attended for one year of twenty-eight weeks—or less; 10 percent qualified for diplomas; fewer than 5 percent attended as many as three of the four years the school was in operation.[18]

During the Derry years Mary Lyon was also developing power and prestige independently. When she returned to western Massachusetts in the late fall of 1824, Mr. Clark, the Congregational minister in Buckland, suggested that she hold a small winter school there. She agreed, accepting his invitation to board with the Clark family. This was the first of the three-month winter schools she conducted for six successive years in Buckland or Ashfield in between the seven-month summer terms she was teaching with Zilpah. Mary's standards of performance increased as rapidly as her teaching skills. She prepared for each session with intense effort and worked straight through the term without letup. A letter written toward the end of her first Buckland school suggests the nature of her concern and the extent to which it paid off. Although she concluded, "I do not think it favorable to piety to have so much anxiety as I have had this winter," she was pleased with the results.

My school here consists of twenty-five young ladies. After so large a number had been admitted, I had some anxiety respecting it. I feared that I might attempt more uniformity about books, than, considering the circumstances, would be expedient. I expected, also, a cold winter, and my design was to have the scholars study in school. And as I possess not much natural dignity, I could foresee my scholars crowding around the fire, some whispering, some idle, &c. I remembered that, several years ago, I had a school of young ladies in this town, in which there was more whispering than in all the schools in which I have been engaged for the last three or four years. The fault then was mine, and I knew not but that the effects might be felt even now.

I kept my school occupied on general subjects at first, and now I have about as much uniformity in books as we had at L. In teaching, I am constantly wishing for your or Miss G.'s advice. Indeed, I sometimes need your assistance more than words can express.

At the commencement, I thought it best to assume as much artificial dignity as possible; so, to begin, I borrowed Miss Grant's plan to prevent whispering. All, with one exception, strictly complied; and that was one of the first young ladies in age and improvement. It appeared altogether probable that the termination of this affair would be a matter of considerable importance in relation to her, her father's family, and perhaps to the school generally. But after I had passed a few almost sleepless nights about it, a kind Providence directed the result in a manner which seemed the best calculated to promote the interests of the school; for at length she came cheerfully into the arrangement.

A circumstance, in relation to the first set of compositions, was somewhat trying. One pupil refused entirely to write; but I was assisted in leading her to comply with the requirement. Some other things I could mention. Suffice it to say, that I have had just enough of such things to give me continual anxiety; but God, in his providence, has been very kind to me. Many events have terminated as I desired, when it seemed not at all in my power to control them. Perhaps I have generally been able to accomplish about what I have undertaken. My school, in many respects, is very pleasant. I have but two or three pupils under sixteen years of age. With the exception of two or three, they are very studious. On the whole, I think it the best school I ever had; the best, because the most profitable to its members; I do not mean the best in which I have been engaged. I have an opportunity this winter to see the value of what I gained at Derry.[19]

As her school became better known, the increases in enrollment brought their own problems. At the beginning of her second winter school, she explained to Zilpah that she had been prevented from writing earlier not only by unexpected duties and a bad cold but also by "much care & anxiety about making suitable preparations for a larger school than I had expected." In fact, the needs of the 45 young women enrolled were such that Mary had engaged Hannah White to help her. This same year she boarded in a family with fourteen of her students and had to preside at the table for the young ladies. To "prevent too much, if not improper, conversation at meals," she planned a suitable subject to introduce at each meal and worked out ways of getting each of the group to participate. Topics might be the operation of tract societies, United States foreign exports, the outward signs of selfishness, favorite Bible passages. Even though this took "an effort, on my part, which I had scarcely realized," she found it "pleasant indeed" and so did a number of students over the years who wrote home about it. As fast as one need was met, other possibilities presented themselves. In 1830 she had 100 pupils, two teachers, and five assistant pupils, and was writing to Zilpah, "My labors are indeed abundant, my cares almost overwhelming, and they continue to increase. I devote more attention to individuals than formerly."[20]

No amount of organization, ingenuity, or extra assistance could allay one major anxiety—a sense of personal inadequacy as a leader of revivals. Over and over she wrote about it: "You know that I frequently feel that I can do little or nothing to aid Christians in a life of holiness. In this respect, my responsibility is greater than ever before; indeed, it is so great, that I know not what to do." Her unquestioning belief in heaven and hell and her sense of the urgency of salvation for these fine young women made her recurring doubts of her own worthiness a heavy weight to bear. Even in the last months of her life, when her preeminence as a religious teacher looked unassailable, she was still asking her friends for special prayers that God would direct and inspire her religious instruction.[21]

Such anxiety would not have surprised many of Mary Lyon's fellow puritans. When in 1826 Catharine Beecher reported signs of religious stirrings in her school, Lyman Beecher wrote back immediately, cautioning her to avoid undue excitement herself during revivals. Although Catharine was practiced in religious discussion and relatively sure of herself, her father included a warning against "an overpowering weight of responsibility and care."

We can neither carry the world on our shoulders nor govern it, nor even govern the wants of a very small part of it, which are most immediately under our own eye. Settle it in your heart, therefore, that you are to exercise your best judgment, and perform in the best manner you can your duty, and leave the whole in the hands of God. You can not be accountable for consequences.[22]

Whatever Mary Lyon's inner tensions as she felt her way cautiously, week by week, for five successive years of revivals, the students responded impressively. Ultimately each year the outcome seemed to Mary herself "great and wonderful." Her approach was low keyed. She followed Joseph Emerson and Zilpah Grant in having students divide themselves into the converted and unconverted for separate instruction after hours.

The work was very still; so much so, that many in town knew scarcely any thing about it. Our school exercises were as usual. Many of our friends, who visited us, observed nothing to mark this as the place where the Spirit was operating so powerfully, except a general stillness, and here and there a deeply solemn countenance.

Her biblical instructions seemed memorable to many students; Fidelia Fiske felt that no one who had heard her could forget any detail of the mercy seat, which was pure gold, 2½ cubits long, and 1½ cubits wide, and had a cherub at each end. But it may well be that her own humility spoke louder than her words to the solemn young women before her. In any case, everyone rejoiced over the final tally. In the climactic winter of 1830, with 40 out of 99 pupils already converted at the beginning of the term, more than 30 of the others at the close "expressed some hope that they found the Savior precious to their souls."[23]

The winter schools also achieved notable material success. The enrollment started at 25, then doubled and stayed at about 50 for the two winters, 1826-27 and 1827-28, when she had Sanderson Academy in Ashfield. When she went back to a larger hall in Buckland for the last two years, the numbers rose to 74 and then 99. In the modest "catalogue" for 1830, an eight-page printed list of teachers and students, the geographical distribution showed how the word had spread. Young women came from all over western Massachusetts—Springfield, Brookfield, Amherst, Greenfield, as well as the Berkshire hill towns; two from Boston, six from Connecticut (all Zilpah's relatives), two from Vermont.

The curriculum was designed to prepare young women for elementary teaching. Mary Lyon was determined to be thorough; she and Zilpah Grant both championed systematic study for girls instead of the fashionable piling up of so-called accomplishments. As a number of her pupils discovered to their initial dismay, instead of advanced work and new subjects they began with mental and written arithmetic, reading, grammar, and geography, supplemented by practical advice about classroom management. But her insistence on mastery of the fundamentals soon won the admiration of most students—and of their parents and the general community as well.

Visitors came in numbers. In March 1829 Mary mentioned them casually to Zilpah: "More than half the days since the term commenced, I have had more or less company in school, generally from out of town." The next year, with almost 100 pupils, she restricted visits to Friday; on one Friday in January a student reported between 30 and 40 spectators. Some of the visitors were school committee members, looking for teachers for the next year; indeed, some school districts had taken to naming their committees in November instead of March in order to get a chance at Miss Lyon's most sought-after students. Among the knowledgeable visitors in the public interest was Colonel Leavitt of Heath, an enthusiastic proponent of the monitorial system, on which he was reading everything he could lay hands on. He came at the end of February 1827 to spend two or three days, observing the monitors with an eye to employment and discussing school problems with Miss Lyon, who valued his conversation. When Mary finally decided to work with Zilpah the year round, it is not surprising that the Franklin County Association of Ministers urged her to reconsider and then tried to get Miss Grant to move her school out to the western part of the state.[24]

Although the curriculum of what was in all but name a normal school centered on elementary school subject matter, Mary Lyon did manage at intervals to work in advanced subjects for her best students and regularly encouraged interest in the outer world. In 1830 "little societies" with duly elected officers met every Wednesday afternoon "to gain intelligence from newspapers" and pass it on to fellow-boarders at the next meal. Among the numerous samples of student work which Mary somehow or other preserved intact through all the long years of homelessness is a set of questions written by students in January 1830. They were an assignment in intellectual philosophy, a subject which seems to have combined psychology, logic, and ethics. Susan Smith inquired: "Does it require the greatest effort of mind, to ascertain a point in Natural Philosophy [physics], or Astronomy, or in Intellectual Philosophy? In other words, which had the greatest mind, Mr. Newton or Mr. Locke?" Lucretia Longley asked these theological daughters of Calvin and Jonathan Edwards, "How can we justify our ancestors for inflicting punishments upon other denominations of Christians, for propagating their opinion?" Sophia Lyman spoke up for Unitarian Harvard. "Why," she demanded, "is every person in the world, who enjoys any degree of civil or religious liberty, under special obligations to the early benefactors of Harvard College?"[25]

References to New England colleges abounded. Though no one was claiming equality at that point, the young ladies were able and willing to make comparisons. A cousin of Zilpah, writing to her brother who had graduated from Yale, explained that the boarding regulations were different from those he had known at college, but the rules about "study-hours, relaxation, retiring, rising, recitations etc." were very like. Like their brothers and cousins in college and their teacher, many of these young women were strongly attracted by the opportunities for service and adventure in missions, domestic as well as foreign; their carefully preserved exercises and compositions frequently referred not only to India but to the valley of the Mississippi, where some of them would be teaching within a very few years.[26]

There is no question that Mary Lyon took pleasure and satisfaction in her winter schools, no matter what they cost her in worry and exertion. Toward the end of the second winter, during which she had been struggling with the problems of doubled enrollment and worrying about her own spiritual inadequacy, she wrote to Amanda, "I enjoy so much that I sometimes almost fear lest I may have all my good things in this life." She felt the dignity and worth of her profession; to the young ladies going out to teach, she would say "Now you are to be seated on a throne of your own. You can sway a golden scepter there." Just as she would do all the rest of her life, she found each year an improvement on the last. After the close of the final term in 1830, she wrote her younger sister Rosina, "I believe that my schools have been more and more interesting every winter, and we all think this has been the most so of all."[27]

Although the exertion required for the summer and winter schedule Mary Lyon maintained between 1824 and 1830 taxed even her remarkable energy, she would probably not have given up the winter school without strong pressure from Zilpah Grant for her year-round services. Mary had never made any secret of her attachment to Zilpah, and for several years circumstances seemed to strengthen the bond. Both young women valued their family connections and sympathized with each other over the misfortunes of their relatives. When Mary first arrived at Derry in April 1824, a letter was waiting with news of the death in Ohio of Ariel Moore, husband of her oldest sister Electa. Later that summer Zilpah had a letter with grim tidings indeed; her mother, who had for some time been liable to intermittent periods of depression, had committed suicide. In May 1827 all Ashfield was shaken by the sensational tragedy of Ashfield Pond. Deacon David Lyon, Mary's uncle, and his 18-year-old son, two stepsons of his married daughter, and another young man were all drowned in the aftermath of a too convivial community sheep washing. The four young men had thought it would be fun to take two sheep out in a canoe, which overturned in deep water, and the Deacon drowned attempting rescue. Mary's most protracted and agonizing family problem, on which she consulted Zilpah at length, was the collapse of Lovina's home when the oldest of the five children was only eight. In 1828 Daniel Putnam fell seriously ill and Lovina suffered a mental breakdown that necessitated her being sent from Buckland to the Hartford Hospital for the Insane. Freelove, the youngest sister, took on the immediate daily care of the children and Mary assumed personal and financial responsibility of considerable proportions. Daniel died in December 1828; Lovina, who returned to Buckland soon afterward, never recovered. After various arrangements for care in the neighborhood, she finally had to go back to the hospital in Hartford, where she died in September 1832. In addition to time and thought, Mary spent part of her savings on Lovina; she contributed to her interim care, paid all her hospital bills, and was much involved in finding the right temporary and permanent homes for the children.

Another close tie in the early years of the friendship was created by Zilpah's physical problems. During her periods of prostration Zilpah had affectionate care, and she stored up energy; while Mary's exertions multiplied and her solicitude increased, she could not help being gratified by her power to rise to emergencies. In September 1825 when Zilpah was laid low by a "bilious fever," Mary wrote her mother, "I have been so well that I could do more, with the same effort and the same fatigue, since Miss G. has been sick, than at any other time." In August 1827 when Zilpah's tendon, torn three months earlier, had not responded to treatment, Mary wrote Freelove that she had "had more vigor of body and mind than usual" and declared, "I love Miss G's society more than ever, and I believe we may love our friends very ardently, and love them according to the principles and spirit of the gospel."[28]

During the two-week recess in July 1828 both young women visited Zilpah's relatives in Connecticut; after their return to Derry, they both came down with typhoid. Mary's surviving letters are full of Zilpah's condition: on September 3 she was delirious and Mary thought she would die; on September 26 Zilpah, still very weak, was exhausted after sitting up half an hour. By October 6 she was on the mend; Mary wrote to Boston to Deacon Melledge, father of a pupil, for ale, no doubt a prescription. In these letters Mary made no mention of her own health; she was obviously able to keep things going. That it took stoicism as well as efficiency is suggested by a casual reference to her typhoid attack in a letter to Zilpah six months later.

*You remember that, after my sickness last summer, my hair came
off by handfuls. For several weeks past, I have not lost any, so
that I hope I shall continue to have enough to support my combs.
For a while my head was very cold; but since I began to wear a
turban, it has been quite comfortable.*[29]

Though personal ties were important, what seems finally to have
brought the two friends to the point of decision about their future
together was Zilpah Grant's battle with the Adams Academy
trustees. They were well pleased with the enrollments and the
caliber of her instruction, but they had not bargained for her
persistent efforts toward a Calvinist salvation of souls. In the
summer of 1826 she was well launched on a quiet revival. She had
made her customary division of students into those who were and
those who were not professing Christians; she and her three
teachers held a daily prayer meeting; and a group of mothers was
organized to pray every Wednesday morning between eight and
nine for God's blessing on the school. By this time the trustees
were sufficiently alarmed to ask Miss Grant in July for a report
from every teacher of the exact number of hours and minutes
spent in the course of a week on religious and moral discussion.
The reports, saved for posterity no doubt by Zilpah, indicate that
the time taken from secular subjects was minimal and that all four
young women felt God was with them. Less than a week after
Mary Lyon had given her account for the trustees of the week's
religious instruction (one hour and eleven minutes of class time,
two hours in private conversation with individuals), she was
writing about the prospects of more conversions in the school.
Even though the students' "habits, education, views, feelings, and
principles are so entirely different, that it is to be expected that
there will be a great number who will feel that it is all an idle
tale . . . who will have it in their hearts to ridicule," by the end of
the term about twenty had expressed hope and there might well
be more "showers of divine grace" after the two-week recess. She
obviously expected Zilpah to continue in just the same way in
spite of the trustee warning.[30]

Although Zilpah won the skirmishes, she could see trouble ahead. In February 1827, after reproaching Mary for long silence (a letter had gone astray), Zilpah laid claim to her services in a rhetorical paragraph beginning, "Miss Lyon, you will not forget me; you will not forsake me; you will not leave me to labor alone." She concluded on a pragmatic note, "If our way should be hedged up there will be time for us to make further arrangements." After the end of the 1827 session, the trustees at their annual meeting, on November 13, were driven to action. Their ingenious plan to counteract orthodoxy without condemning religion was to vote to add music and dancing to the curriculum; they reappointed Zilpah Grant principal and nearly doubled her salary, offering her $350 plus a percentage of tuition fees. Zilpah, horrified, took an absolute stand against dancing; thereupon the trustees voted on November 23 that no teachers had been engaged. Shortly thereafter they issued a circular inviting applications for principal (women preferred) and stated the majority position.

It was the original design of the trustees to establish this seminary on liberal principles. They regret that the institution has acquired the character of being strictly Calvinistic in the religious instruction. This character has grown up in opposition to the sentiments and wishes of a majority of the trustees. It is their determination to select persons who will not attempt to instil into the minds of their pupils the peculiar tenets of any denomination of Christians, but will give that general instruction wherein all Christians agree.[31]

Partly because there was a minority among the trustees supporting Zilpah, she kept hoping for several weeks that the break could be mended without sacrificing her principles. She wrote frequently to Mary and sought counsel among her learned friends. But early in January she accepted the inevitable. She had already had an offer at Byfield but felt she could do better; as she wrote Mary, "My business, therefore, for some time will be to scratch with a goosequill and inform the public that I am disengaged." Within a month she had found just the place—a rent-free building in Ipswich, where she would have complete autonomy. Her account to Mary was business-like: the building was new and commodious, within 100 rods of it lived 25 families who would like to take boarders, there were 8 to 12 stages a day passing through the town, the town itself would supply 30 to 40 pupils, many of them in the preparatory class. She wanted Mary for the summer but at this moment thought she might best stay in Buckland in the winter.[32]

During all Zilpah's turmoil, Mary kept sending sympathy and affection. She did not proffer advice nor make any assumptions about her own future. "I do ardently desire to continue with you, if I can be useful," she wrote her "dearest earthly friend" on November 26. On December 10 she found no words adequate "to tell you how much I sympathize with you in your trials, how my heart bleeds when I think of you, and how I want to be with you, and share in your daily sorrows and joys." On December 26 she was open to all alternatives. She was eager to follow Zilpah in the summers if she left Derry and would even consider joining her in the winters, but she also saw the possibility that "Providence should so direct that you should think it not my duty to be with you" either winter or summer. On January 8 she was assuring Zilpah that her letters were not unduly worrying: "Sometimes, when I have been re-perusing your letters, sentence by sentence, to see if there was not some idea expressed or implied which I did not at first apprehend, I have thought it would be well for me to read my Bible with like care."[33]

Mary had anxieties of her own—her continuing sense of inadequacy as a spiritual leader and the question of her location in subsequent winters. The Sanderson trustees, no doubt in difficulty over meager summer enrollment, found it "undesirable to break the course of a regular school through the year, by having a school exclusively for females in the winter," which meant that Mary once again had to make arrangements elsewhere. Zilpah did not rush in to demand her services then, and Mary's letters, almost to the time in April when she left for Ipswich, suggested uncertainty. She kept talking about the importance of leaving everything in the Lord's hands and blamed herself for being "too much inclined to seek to direct my own path."[34]

In another year, however, as soon as the winter session at Ipswich was under way, Zilpah began to feel acutely that she needed Mary all year long. One fragment among her letters of appeal sent post haste to Buckland begins: "I suppose you already know, that my attachment for you has increased year by year since we were first united in business, & that I have considered your assistance & friendship among my greatest earthly blessings." Zilpah stressed the ultimate contribution to "the cause of useful education" and the importance of maintaining the reputation they had already established together. She admitted that any school Mary Lyon would teach in Buckland "wd be composed of more substantial materials, than we generally find in seaports," where some pupils had to be bribed to study, and she felt sure that Mary would base her decision not on personal inclination but on what she saw as her duty.[35]

Mary at first said "No." Her assessment of the situation was straightforward and succinct. "Had you made the proposal contained in your last two years ago, I should have had no doubt about the path of duty," she wrote. Now she was influenced not only by "the wants of this community" as compared with "the increased number of schools in the vicinity of Ipswich" but also by "your abundant ability alone to form all your plans; the ease with which you could procure experienced assistants in the winter." For nearly a year the question was argued with family and friends. Before Mary finally agreed in December 1829 to make the move the following year, an array of ministers had attempted to exert influence through letters and personal interviews, including Warren Fay of Charlestown, who was to endorse the ill-starred New England Seminary for Teachers, and Theophilus Packard of Shelburne, who would ardently support the early efforts for Mount Holyoke Seminary.[36]

Mary Lyon had had another good reason to delay her total commitment to Miss Grant's school. During much of 1829 there was some doubt as to where Zilpah Grant herself would be the next year. In May she received an invitation from Catharine Beecher to become co-head—that is, chaplain and religious director—of the Hartford Female Seminary, at a salary of a thousand dollars a year. Although Zilpah refused, Catharine was not easily discouraged and, during the summer and fall, kept renewing her proposal and expanding her arguments. At the age of 29, six years younger than

Zilpah, Catharine was a conspicuous success as a teacher and an advocate. Two years earlier she had managed to raise nearly $5,000 by stock subscriptions for a school building, and in 1829 she was confident that she could raise another $20,000 for permanent endowment. Her insistence was flattering, and so was the language of her offer. She was seeking "a woman of talent and experience and of established reputation, one who has gained that self-possession which will enable her to address the whole school in a way I have yet found no teacher prepared to attempt. . . . if I cannot obtain Miss Grant, there is no one else whom it is desirable for me to seek." The inducements included the cultural and religious advantages of Hartford and contact with the redoubtable Beechers. "You will find a personal friend in every member of my family," Catharine promised.[37]

Catharine Beecher knew perfectly well that Zilpah's acceptance would be a blow to Mary Lyon. The year before, she had offered Mary a teaching job, just on the chance that there was some truth to the rumor that Miss Lyon might leave Miss Grant, and had apparently considered making an offer to Hannah White too. In the initial letter to Zilpah, Catharine had sent her "best love" to Miss Lyon, who, she knew, "would act disinterestedly in advising," and expressed regret "that my success should in any way interfere with the comfort of so kind and generous a friend."[38]

Neither Miss Beecher nor Miss Grant seems to have felt there was anything confidential about this proposal; they both consulted friends and advisers extensively. Hannah White, who spent a part of the summer of 1829 at Ipswich as a visitor and part-time tutor, considered the arguments pro and con at some length in a letter to her mother and reported that Catharine had "enlisted on her side several gentlemen of literature & influence in Hartford Boston etc." Zilpah kept turning to such men as Leonard Woods of Andover and Joseph Emerson; when in mid-November she asked for her admired teacher's opinion a second time, she sent along her own analysis in outline form. She had six arguments for going to Hartford and eleven against, of which one was "Miss Lyon is now to me all, & probably in reality more than all I can be to Miss Beecher."[39]

Lyman Beecher himself took a hand. His letter in late November proposed a private understanding between him and Zilpah. The tacit possibility of Zilpah's coming would furnish the incentive so much needed by the gentlemen who must raise the money first. Once they succeeded and the joint enterprise was in operation, Zilpah need stay only a year or two until Catharine trained a successor from among her teachers. Whether this tipped the balance, there is no one to say, but Zilpah almost immediately gave a firm and final refusal. Shortly thereafter Mary agreed to stay the year round at Ipswich for a two-year period starting in April 1830.[40]

Having resisted the lures of the Beechers, Zilpah was proof against appeals to move her school to the western part of the state, either from the ministers of Franklin County or from a Greenfield deputation that could offer boarding as well as classroom accommodations. "Why wd the light shine further on Con. river than here?" her letter to Mary demanded. To be sure, Mary was well known in that region, but Zilpah was not, and she had no intention of being "plucked up here, & transplanted into a new soil" where she must for an interval lack some of "that reputation which I consider my most powerful talent for doing good here." Who could deny that personal reputation was a major ingredient in her success, as it was for Catharine Beecher and Emma Willard, or that Mary Lyon's name was relatively unknown? Zilpah's acts of generosity to Mary had never included equal billing. It was in the Ipswich catalogue of October 1830 that Mary was first listed as assistant principal rather than teacher.[41]

3
Trial Run

The Lord will perfect that

which concerneth me . . .

PSALM 138:8

When Mary Lyon finally opted for Ipswich throughout the year, the path of duty and common sense looked straightforward and uneventful. "The prospect of my future labors is pleasant, but excites no high anticipations," she wrote Zilpah. This letter of decision made it obvious that she was not committing herself beyond the two years of the agreement. But whatever her reservations for the long future, she could not then have possibly imagined that within four or five years she would break away altogether and embark on an unlikely enterprise that would bring her into conflict with some of the school and church leaders she particularly respected.

The four and a half years that she was settled in Ipswich full time—from April 1830 through September 1834—made extraordinary demands upon her. They demonstrated that, under pressure, she could simultaneously extend her range as a teacher, administer the finances and daily operations of a large boarding school, and learn by experience the hazards of launching a new cause.[1]

The Ipswich Female Seminary (denominated Academy in the 1828 and 1829 catalogues) raised its academic level appreciably between 1828 and 1834. Having a winter as well as a summer term increased the total possible teaching time from 28 to 40 weeks. Enrollment mounted until the first quarter of the summer term of 1831, when the catalogue listed 191 students—too many for the townspeople even of Ipswich to accommodate in suitable boarding places. This meant that thereafter the youngest and weakest applicants were refused; the catalogue beginning in the fall of 1831 announced that no one under the age of 14 would be admitted. By 1834 the catalogue specified qualifications for admission: ". . . as far as practicable young ladies before entering the Seminary, should be skilful in both mental and written Arithmetic, and thoroughly acquainted with Geography and the History of the United States." Ipswich, of course, had started on a higher level than the Adams Female Academy. More than 30 of the most enthusiastic Derry students (Zilpah Grant made the total 44 when she did a final tabulation in 1839) followed Miss Grant and Miss Lyon to Ipswich and went right on from where they had left off the year before. Similarly, when Mary Lyon gave up her winter school, about 20 of her Buckland pupils enrolled at Ipswich, including such able young women as Louisa and Jerusha Billings, Maria Cowles, Julia Brooks, and Abigail Tenney, who were almost immediately drafted as teachers or student assistants.

The curriculum of Miss Grant's school was designed to give "a thorough and extensive English education." This description explicitly excluded the Latin and Greek that still figured so largely in the standard college course for men, though the dominance of the classics was beginning to come under professorial attack. From the other 30 to 40 percent of the college curriculum that had nothing to do with the classics came the subject matter—and often the textbooks—that Miss Grant and Miss Lyon kept adding year by year. This included sciences, mathematics, theology, philosophy. In 1829 the girls at Ipswich who were sufficiently "improved" might be taking chemistry, physics, astronomy, or botany. Miss Lyon, thanks to her study under Professor Eaton in 1824 and 1825, was already conducting experiments in her chemistry classes; such demonstrations were rare enough to warrant mention in the 1829 catalogue. By 1834 three more sciences had been added—biology, geology, and physiology. The mathematical study widely approved for young women was arithmetic. Ipswich thoroughness prescribed this subject for practically all students at least once every year. In addition geometry was already in the catalogue in 1829, and algebra was added in 1832.[2]

Other texts to be found in the Ipswich catalogue by 1834 included Sullivan's *Political Class Book*, Goodrich's *Ecclesiastical History*, *Abercrombie on the Intellectual Powers*. As juniors and seniors most young men, no matter how unorthodox the college they were attending, studied defenses of Christianity against the inroads of 18th century rationalist thought and the threat of scientific inquiry. By 1834 the Ipswich young ladies were also reciting on Paley's *Natural Theology* and Butler's *Analogy of Natural and Revealed Religion*. In the winter term Miss Grant and a class of 90 took on Alexander's *Evidences of Christianity*, which directs a sustained attack against the philosophy of Hume. In the final session Miss Grant encouraged those students who felt they had barely begun to think about the questions they had been discussing and predicted that they would go on seeking answers long after the books had been laid aside. She closed the class with a prayer which one student found "very affecting."[3]

Exactly how much student time was devoted to any one of these additions to the curriculum is hard to guess. The general scheme at Ipswich and later on at Mount Holyoke Seminary was intensive study of two or three subjects for short periods, varying from two to ten weeks, followed by equally intensive study of two entirely different subjects. Fundamentals were reviewed at intervals by everyone, and some subjects continued on a regular basis throughout the term. These included the Bible, which was studied for two hours on Sunday, recited Monday morning, and reviewed later in the week; calisthenics; practice in reading aloud; the writing of compositions; and vocal music. This last was a happy addition in 1830–31, taught under the guidance of Lowell Mason, noted hymn writer and president of the Handel and Haydn Society, who was shortly to found the Boston Academy of Music and get choral singing into the curriculum of the Boston public schools.

In appraising the academic offering, it is important to recognize that Ipswich deliberately omitted the "ornamental branches" which took up part of the time of most young women in seminaries, including those studying at Troy under Emma Willard. When Zilpah exclaimed, "But *away* with French & Music & Painting from *our* school . . ." she was disapproving of the popularity of drawing room accomplishments, of a meager hold on conversational French, and of rudimentary skills in sketching and playing simple airs, in place of solid learning. The same year that she condemned "Music," she arranged for her able young cousin, Maria Cowles, to spend four weeks of her vacation in Boston, observing Lowell Mason's training of a children's choir and taking piano lessons in order to be able to accompany the singing classes she would teach at Ipswich the ensuing year. Mary Lyon, too, thought highly of this kind of music as a subject for study. She wrote Zilpah about it with considerable feeling.

Those who have been able to sing from childhood, do not know by experience the feelings which some have who cannot sing. When passing near the music-room last summer, and thinking that a large part of the choir, probably, had no more of a natural voice than myself, I found it necessary to restrain, with firm determination, a rising murmur. I have sometimes felt, that I would have given six months of my time, when I was under twenty, and defrayed my expenses, difficult as it was to find time or money, could I have enjoyed the privileges for learning vocal music that some of our pupils enjoy.[4]

By 1830 both Mary Lyon and Zilpah Grant thought of themselves as teachers of teachers. Their strong interest in the expanding efforts of the 1830's toward educational reform, along with the success of Ipswich graduates in the classroom, hastened their recognition outside their own corner of New England. They regularly attended the American Institute of Instruction, first held in Boston in August 1830 under the presidency of Francis Wayland, president of Brown. The Institute provided a week of stimulating and sophisticated lectures just before the Harvard commencement; women teachers naturally were not invited to speak or to become members, but they were allowed to attend the sessions free of charge. At such meetings Miss Grant was unquestionably the more visible, with or without crutches, but Miss Lyon too must gradually have become a recognizable figure.

The methods used at Ipswich began to attract attention, particularly in the *American Annals of Education*. The February 1833 issue carried two articles on the seminary, both covering a period when Mary Lyon was in sole charge. One was a full and complimentary report of a day's visit by a professional observer; the other was a six-page account, by "one of the teachers" (possibly Eunice Caldwell), of the process by which the students were "classed" for the following year and ultimately found eligible for a diploma. The writer supported the editorial stand of the *Annals* against marks (they stimulated undesirable rivalry) without minimizing the one exception at Ipswich. No grades were given for recitations or course work, but student performance on the individual oral examinations that determined class standing was rated 1 to 4 according to excellence. This article also suggests how deliberate and sustained the effort was to upgrade the level of instruction.

The requisites for a certificate have gradually been made more and more definite, and the standard has been constantly rising from year to year. But it is ardently hoped, that the general standard of female education, will, ere long, allow many of the branches now pursued in the Seminary as occasional and collateral studies, to be placed among those termed indispensable. The plan of individual examinations has never been fully executed exactly as described, till the last year. But in this sketch, things have been described just as they are, without the addition of a single item from the various anticipated improvements in the system of means employed in the Seminary, to rouse the mind to thought, action and industry. [5]

Mary Lyon's knowledge of textbooks, by then multiplying rapidly, was precise and discriminating. The comments scattered through her correspondence indicate the attention she paid to whatever she was preparing to teach. She noted the inexactness of a single word—Upham used "thinking" in a vague sense on page 85. She distinguished between editions of a United States history suitable for beginners—the best one had questions by Joseph Emerson. She looked for better ways of utilizing the texts she preferred. When she was teaching from Grimshaw's *Etymology*, she wished "some way could be contrived to have the English language studied with as much intensity as the Latin is." Her commendation of new texts began to be sought by their authors; Catharine Beecher wanted approval of her *Arithmetic* in 1829 and Elijah Burritt consulted Mary Lyon in 1832 before he published his very successful *Geography of the Heavens.*[6]

The nature of Mary Lyon's comments on grammars is particularly interesting. During a trip west in the summer of 1833, when she was hundreds of miles from the texts themselves, she wrote to Zilpah Grant about several possible choices. Of a volume she had tried once but would not use again, she said, "There is a lack of elevation and character about it. It is more like the work of a smart, ingenious *schoolmaster*, than of a man of fine literary taste." Of another grammar she had not yet examined closely, she observed, "a man that can write a book for children loosely can scarcely be expected to make a grammar what it ought to be." She saw the limitations even of Murray's *Grammar*, a stand-by for older students everywhere.

Besides requiring a thorough knowledge of good old Murray, embracing a clear understanding of all his notes and remarks, I have a query whether we ought not to include, as essential to completing our course, an ability to criticize in a philosophical manner his erroneous Latinisms; a knowledge of the particular resemblances and differences between Murray and our preparatory book; and an ability to arrange the differences under two heads, essential and non-essential. Finishing with a book of such an elevated style as that of Murray's Grammar, it would not be so great an evil to have the style of our preparatory book ordinary. What a pity that in our late primary school books there is not more of elevated simplicity![7]

Mary Lyon's skills in the classroom, already perceptible when she first was sought out by Zilpah Grant, were fully developed by 1830. Mrs. Cowles, who was a student in her classes in 1828 and 1829 and a fellow teacher for four years at Ipswich and one year at the still-to-be founded Mount Holyoke, could speak with authority of her procedures and her goals.

She did not think so much of a perfect lesson, nor take so much time for examination on the text-book, as many teachers do;

but she made the hour one of delightful and improving conversation, and exhilarating mental activity.

She always made that part of the lesson on which she dwelt, clear and life-like. She did not consider the learning of a few facts, less or more, as an object of supreme importance. Out of the lesson on hand, she would seize some prominent points, and exhibit them in such a light, that they could scarcely fail to find a lodgment in the understanding and memory of every one. Then she would hear the remainder of the lesson rapidly, or put it over to the review; or, what was very common with her in some branches, she would make the pupils recite to one another out of school, she arranging them in couples, and requiring them to bring in certificates, neatly written and duly signed, of the quality of those private recitations. . . .

She aimed to teach her pupils to educate themselves, to show them how to study, to help them lay the foundation of an edifice which they were themselves to finish. She was herself impressed deeply with the truth that they must soon pass from her eye and care, and could only commence their training while at school; and she conveyed this impression to them.

To go through *a book, she considered a matter of little consequence. To see it well begun, to set her pupils' minds on the right track, to open to them fields of investigation, was in her view the main business. Not but that she would generally finish a text-book; but when she did, she would always drop it when least expected, and just when the interest was highest, and when her scholars were in the precise mood to recollect the study with pleasure, and wish to pursue it farther at a more convenient season.[8]*

Classroom teaching occupied only part of Mary Lyon's time at Ipswich. When she was on the scene both summer and winter, she conducted one or two recitations every day, but according to Mrs. Cowles her major responsibilities were administrative.

The care of so mating scholars in their boarding-houses and rooms as to secure their highest good, of classing them and appropriating studies to each, and of arranging recitations, devolved at times in whole or in part upon her. She counselled the younger teachers, attended their recitations, kept order in the seminary building, and acquainted herself with the character, progress, and wants of every pupil. She gave much general instruction, had an open ear and a quick, ready sympathy for every scholar, and was regarded by all as a general friend and adviser.[9]

Scheduling course offerings for short-term intensive study must have required infinite pains and ingenuity; the whole school shifted every few weeks and the students entered with very different amounts of knowledge and habits of study. Scribbled in pencil in a teaching notebook kept by Eunice Caldwell in November 1832 are the names of eleven girls and the subjects each still had to take to qualify as a senior and earn a diploma the following April. Ten needed the history of Rome, four each the history of Greece and of England, five the history of the United States after the Revolution. Seven had still to complete Euclid, six astronomy, one chemistry.[10]

From 1830 on, the big boarding house, converted by the trustees from a tavern, offered places for Miss Grant, Miss Lyon, three or four teachers, and thirty students. All the rest of the boarders were dispersed about the town in small groups with private families. Shifts were constantly being made to have roommates congenial and landladies content, yet to achieve also a mix within each house that would favor the observance of strict rules without direct supervision. Success in enforcing these rules—for instance, three hours of silent study during which there could be no visiting from room to room—depended primarily on the system of daily public self-reporting, but no doubt frequent room reassignments helped. Two or three moves within six months were not unusual. At all these permutations and combinations, Mary Lyon was very skillful. Her organizational inventiveness seems never to have flagged. Mrs. Cowles recalls that she "often said at Ipswich, that she could suggest plans by the score, leaving Miss Grant to reject or adopt them as she chose."[11]

In October 1831 Mary became even busier than she had been for the preceding year and a half. Just before the close of the summer term Zilpah Grant left on a protracted trip to recover her health. The torn tendon had continued to hobble her. Just how long she went on crutches is never said; it must have been about four years.

Pupils of 1829 and '30 recall her as carried up the steps of the academy on a strong man's shoulders day after day, and then moving with dignity to the platform on her crutches. There the morning instructions would be given, some lesson of wisdom from Genesis, some conscience-stirring words from Paul. At another hour she would lead their minds along a fresh, inspiring track in a familiar talk, enjoying to the full their animated play of mind and feature. When it was over they were dismissed to their rooms that she might without curious observers be borne out in the same manner she had entered.

Ultimately her lameness was cured, but the treatment was drastic. "By the advice of Dr. Warren the injured limb was placed in a splint and the amount of both solid and liquid food reduced for eight months to twenty ounces a day. Emaciation was extreme, but the mind was clear." It is not surprising that she felt the need of getting clear away.[12]

No one then seems to have expected that it would be nineteen months before she returned to her place in the seminary. The catalogue for 1831, issued in October, announced that she would be absent for the winter term, which started November 30 and lasted 16 weeks. It turned out that she traveled by stages to Virginia the first winter of her absence, spent the summer of 1832 in the vicinity of Boston, and went to Georgia for the following winter. But even at such distances she did not relinquish all control. Mary sent her a long letter once a week, often partly written by a young teacher, including details of financial and disciplinary problems and summaries of her biblical lectures to the whole school.

These half-hour lectures, given two or three times a week on some scriptural text, were really short sermons and had heretofore been reserved to Zilpah Grant. Mary somehow found time for the detailed preparation she devoted to every academic exercise and, according to Mrs. Cowles, "developed her full power of interesting scholars in the discussion of religious truth." Student letters confirm the judgment that it was to many "rich entertainment" to hear Miss Lyon's exegesis, verse by verse, of the Ten Commandments, the minor prophets, or the Epistles. At the beginning of the winter term in 1832, Mary wrote enthusiastically to Zilpah Grant about the illumination cast upon the Apostle Peter, the subject of her current lecture series, by the book of Hosea. "The figurative language in the second chapter is exceedingly forcible," she observed, making applications not only to Peter's experience but also to her own. She asked Zilpah to pray "that we may all be able so to connect our temporal duties with the great business of eternity that they shall not prove a snare."[13]

What students did after they left school was a matter of active concern to both Zilpah Grant and Mary Lyon. From the first they had wanted to do for others what Joseph Emerson had done for them and had enrolled as students young women who had already been teaching district or select schools and expected to return to the classroom. As the reputation of Miss Grant's seminary grew, the placement service expanded. Before Zilpah left in October 1831, she and Mary were sending Ipswich girls out to teach in New England, the South, and the Mississippi Valley. Up to the time of Zilpah's departure to recover her health, she probably made the final choices of candidates, but Mary even then handled much of the correspondence. By the time Mary Lyon made her first move toward founding Mount Holyoke, she was in touch with principals and teachers in widely scattered parts of the country and in possession of revealing first-hand reports of the circumstances under which young teachers lived and worked.

Several letters survive involving two Ipswich graduates who were sent out to teach in a seminary in Chillicothe, Ohio, sometime in 1830. Sarah Stearns had been at Ipswich three years, two as a student and one as a teacher; Susan Smith had attended Mary Lyon's winter school at Buckland for two years and Ipswich for one year. Both young women had been student assistants as Ipswich seniors. Early in 1831 another post had to be filled at Chillicothe, to replace a third Ipswich student, Cassandra Sawyer, who had not been proposed by Miss Grant and had not been successful. In April Miss Lyon wrote a full frank answer to a letter in which Sarah and Susan had suggested that they would prefer as a replacement a classmate they knew, Eliza Capen, rather than Miss Grant's choice, Lydia Wade.

Ipswich, April 5, 1831

Misses Stearns & Smith,
  Dear Friends,
  Not long since Miss Grant received a communication from you, in which you expressed some doubt about Miss Wade's being qualified to fill the specified department in your seminary. In all the selections of teachers for the west, I believe Miss Grant's exertions have been as unwearied as if she were selecting for our own beloved seminary. (You will recollect that Miss C. S. was not of Miss Grant's selection.) I believe I may add, that after the many opportunities, Miss Grant has enjoyed during the last year of learning the character and demands of the west, she is peculiarly qualified to select teachers who bid fair for success. It is farther a settled principle with Miss Grant, in executing the many commissions she receives to send forth teachers, to send those who are the best qualified, whether every one of their acquaintances, who is disposed to look into the affair, is pleased or not.
  We have done as you requested, in endeavoring to save Miss C. Sawyer's friends from trial. They have, however, had some suspicions, because C. said nothing about removing. What they have written I know not. I thought you might need a little caution on this point, as I observed by Miss Grant's letter from you that C. S. was received as one of the judges of Miss Wade's qualifications. In selecting a teacher for ourselves or others, we always consider it important, that she should be particularly qualified for the department she is immediately to fill, whether she is preeminently qualified for other departments to which she may afterwards be called or not. We consider this principle indispensable in selecting a teacher for a primary department, of an extensive establishment. Much—very much indeed depends on the younger members being kept in order, & on their being taught accurately.
  Miss Grant knows 10 times as much of Miss W.'s character & qualifications as you or I do. She has been intimately acquainted

with her for a long time, has witnessed her improvement &
has assisted her in forming most of her plans, & has known with
what skill & success she has been able to execute them. I have
had but little personal acquaintance with her till the present
winter. Suffice it to say of my opinion, that several weeks ago in
talking about teachers for our seminary, I mentioned Miss Wade
for the younger department. Miss Grant replied, that she considered her qualified, but that her residence in town, & her
acquaintance with the misses of whom she would have the care,
would be unfavorable to success. I consider it a peculiar & excellent qualification of Miss W. that she has not studied many things
of which she knows nothing, & that she has no pretensions above
the reality.

I would not have it understood, that I have no fears about
Miss Wade's success. I can say this of no one—not even of the
ladies whom I am now addressing, successful as they have been.
And as these ladies are so well acquainted with each other, &
so well acquainted with me, there can be no harm in my speaking
freely, as it will illustrate the fact, that great confidence is consistent with much fear. I did greatly fear about Miss Smith's
limited experience, & wanted of firm health, and I feared about
as much about some things in Miss Stearns, which I have mentioned to her—such as want of simplicity & accuracy, an
inclination to too great zeal without sufficient cause, & a little
lack of nice discrimination of character. When we had decided
to send these ladies, in whom on the whole, we placed so much
confidence, & with whose success we have been so much delighted, we did not consider it expedient to trouble & discourage
by our own fears.

To take the entire charge of a primary department, to direct
their studies, form their habits and improve their manners, Miss
W. must I think excel one of these ladies in experience, & the
other in simplicity & accuracy. One more comparison, & I
have done on this point. Perhaps none would value Miss Capen's
talents, thourough education, & excellent qualifications more than
I, but I must confess that I have less fears about Miss Wade's
success in that particular department, than I should have in Miss
Capen's. I have not that evidence before me, that Miss Capen has

ever been called to labor where she had done as much, with as much success, to manage difficult dispositions as Miss Wade. Neither do I think she has so much simplicity, in communicating instruction in a manner peculiarly profitable to little misses. Though Miss Wade's knowledge is not as extensive as Miss Capen's, yet we should consider it amply sufficient to fill a similar department in our seminary.

You fully understand that on the whole, I should place Miss Capen among the first ladies with whom I am acquainted.

I do fear about Miss Wade's health, but not more than I did about Miss Smith's. Her physician says there is no danger, & her abundant & unceasing labors, prove her to be the greatest sufferer. She is retiring & modest in her manner, not inclined to bring herself forward, excellent qualifications for a teacher of little girls, who at the best have sufficient pride and forwardness. Tho she is persevering, yet she has so much sensibility & tenderness of feeling, that I could not have her placed where she would not receive the confidence of those around her, where she would meet mysterious suspicious looks.

I must acknowledge that under existing circumstances I have felt reluctant to have Miss W. go. I have greatly feared that there would be something in your manner, which you could not overcome, or that Mr. Pomroy might have received so unfavorable an impression, that he would be unprepared to estimate her worth or to repose in her that confidence so necessary to her success. But Miss Grant says as Mr. Pomroy in his last letter has finally committed the whole to her judgment, she cannot do justice to Mr. Pomroy and to her seminary by withholding Miss W. without a sufficient reason. She also says that as she has so much confidence in Mr. Pomroy's kindness & candor, & knows so much of both of you, that she thinks she shall do justice to Miss W. by sending her among you saying nothing to her of the whole affair, hoping that she will never know anything about it. She has gone, and you can believe me if I say that I never had such feelings for any of our pupils who have gone forth to labor in a far distant field. My heart yearned over her, & I longed to tell her the whole matter & to say to her that she was going away not knowing what things would befall her. But I could forbear, & I did.

And now, my dear Misses Stearns & Smith, I do not ask that you secure the friendship of Miss C. S., for perhaps that cannot be, but will you, my very dear friends, receive her [Miss W.] as a sister? Will you treat her with affection? nay more, will you treat her with confidence? Will you do all you can to lead Mr. P. to confide the responsibility of her department to herself? Will you avoid talking very much even when alone about little defects in her which can be found in abundance even in the best of us? In short, will you endeavor to place yourselves in her stead, & be all that the golden rule requires?

Your affectionate friend,
Mary Lyon.[14]

In reply Susan wrote at length; she was candid, affectionate, and informative. Miss Lyon's cautions were appreciated, although they wouldn't under any circumstances have been so unchristian as not to welcome Miss Wade warmly. Mr. Pomroy had made up his own mind about her—favorably—and she was doing well. Miss Sawyer had left for Burlington for a small school of 30 girls. Chillicothe Seminary was flourishing, although a smallpox scare had disrupted the vacation schedule. The upper school had enrolled 50 students; the lower school 30 to 40. Some of these girls would even compare favorably with their New England counterparts; one group had gone through all of *Colburn's Arithmetic* and two thirds of *Smith's Arithmetic* and might go on to geometry.[15]

The next letter from Susan, written in November, reported that she was now Mrs. Henry Little. She and her husband were living in Oxford, Ohio, a college town where he had a rapidly growing congregation (Miami University by then enrolled 180 students). Henry wrote too, expressing his gratitude for the welcome he had received at Ipswich when he had called in August 1830 and also for the kind of education that made Susan so superior a companion. In the midst of other news Susan included without comment the fact that Lydia Wade had indeed fallen ill, while off at a camp meeting with Mr. Pomroy and Sarah Stearns, and the primary school in consequence had been suspended for five weeks. Susan's letter concluded with her own gratitude for "the unwearied efforts you have both made on my behalf, particularly Miss L. during many months of youthful waywardness." The following April another expression of heartfelt thanks came from Susan's father, Obadiah Smith, back in the Connecticut Valley; he enclosed $13 which, added to the $30 dollars Susan had recently sent, should pay off what she had borrowed from Miss Lyon for her education.[16]

For several months the newly married Littles had a house guest in Oxford—no other than Eliza Capen, over whom the original question had arisen. Eliza was now Mrs. Benjamin Labaree. Her husband, a graduate of Dartmouth and Andover, was spending a few months traveling through Tennessee "on an agency"—that is, soliciting funds for the American Education Society, which gave college and theological school scholarships to poor young men wanting to become ministers.[17]

The letter to Miss Lyon from the Little ménage was written by Eliza, who had just spent a month in Cincinnati and was full of her reactions to the people and the kind of education they needed. Her findings were, not surprisingly, quite different from Mrs. Trollope's, then in press.

In most respects people here are not unlike those we find in cities at the east. They are intelligent, refined & fashionable. They possess in general more knowledge of the world, which they have gained by observation than the eastern people. In conversation their subjects are more general & less confined to persons & places, but in relation to benevolent objects, improvements of the present day & they know little or nothing, even the good people do not feel the importance of entering with all their might into a good cause . . .

Specifically, Eliza reproached them for not exerting themselves to set up sound schools—like Ipswich. There was much talk of getting Catharine Beecher to start a school, but Eliza and her acquaintances disapproved because "there would be danger of her conforming too much with public opinion, & thereby increasing the desire which is now felt for exterior accomplishments." Eliza's solution was for Mary Lyon to find two exceptionally able Ipswich graduates who together would be an acceptable substitute for Catharine Beecher. Once this pair was ready and willing, Eliza would put them in touch with potential backers in Cincinnati who could launch them before the Beechers arrived. Eliza's letter concluded with warm affectionate inquiries about Miss Lyon and the seminary and an appealing glimpse of the congenial life she was living with the Littles, reminiscent of Ipswich "system & order. We retire at ten, rise at half past six, attend family worship before breakfast, sing between that time & nine when we all commence study—have a recess once an hour for exercise, & continue study till twelve. In the afternoons we call & receive calls from the members of Mr. L's parish. Evenings attend lectures, lyceums, Temperance meetings, Bible Classes, & &."[18]

One other letter from Susan Smith Little and Henry has survived. Written in March 1833, it is a response to a special request from Mary Lyon. Two Ipswich students, stirred by the pleas for teachers for the West, had resolved to go out and offer themselves without waiting for her careful negotiations and financial agreements. Miss Lyon had obviously disapproved—and then written to ask if the Littles would look out for the pair. Both Henry and Susan were ready to welcome the young ladies and thought they might help them get a suitable school but seconded her warning about the hazards. Income was very uncertain, Susan wrote; parents out there, unlike their New England counterparts, were apt to default on subscription payments if their children were sick, away, or truant. A teacher must expect that tuition money would be paid in full for no more than two thirds of her pupils.[19]

Sarah Stearns stayed on at Chillicothe Seminary. In June 1833 her colleague was another Ipswich graduate and former teacher, Delia Allyn, but she, too, was soon to leave to be married. A letter from Delia was full of affection and personal news (although she deplored the "lack of thoroughgoing good principle" in Westerners, she was pleased that she and her husband would be living near Cincinnati) and apologetic for the trouble that she and Miss Stearns must have caused by not accepting the Ipswich candidate Mary Lyon had proposed. Miss Lyon's nomination had been slow to arrive, and in the meantime Miss Stearns had finally persuaded her brother Timothy, fresh out of Amherst, to come and teach for a year. He could teach French too and thereby eliminate an undesirable local assistant.[20]

Time was only one of the complicating factors in placement at long distance. The Rev. Charles C. Beatty was the head of a flourishing seminary in Steubenville, Ohio, who frequently sought teachers from Ipswich; indeed on a trip east he visited the seminary late in the summer of 1832. But the following winter he wrote for a teacher—not in January, as Mary Lyon urged, but at the end of March. Although Miss Lyon did manage to find one possible candidate to propose in her letter of April 8, he did not make up his mind to accept this young woman until the end of May; naturally, she was no longer available. The next winter Mr. Beatty wrote promptly and Mary Lyon was able to notify him on February 6, 1834, that she and Zilpah Grant (by then back at Ipswich) had found him a teacher. The choice fell on Louisa Packard, daughter of the minister in Shelburne who supported so many educational good causes, including Mary Lyon's schools; although she was not particularly strong in mathematics, her disposition, manners, and experience were impressive.

She is about 27 years of age, has been successfully employed in teaching most of the time for seven years, except when she has been studying. During this period, she has taught common schools, infant schools, & young ladies' schools, & has been uniformly successful. I speak with more confidence, as she has been a particular acquaintance & an intimate friend of mine for a long time. During 1830 & 1831, she was at the head of a select infant school of about 100 in the City of New York. You will of course value the experience she has had in these various departments.

Miss Packard has not studied algebra, but she will devote a few weeks to it before she leaves, & will as we hope be able hereafter to go forward with it, so as to teach it. Would you prefer to have her study Day's, Colburn's, Grund's or Bailey's? Grund's & Bailey's are recent publications.

Miss Packard is engaged only for one year, & probably will choose to stay only one year. But she can so prepare the way, that another teacher of similar qualifications would easily succeed her.

We have mentioned to Miss Packard $200, besides board, as you stated. It is the practice of many, who make application for teachers to defray their travelling expenses to the spot, leaving it to the teachers to defray their own expenses home. This is more common practice, than to leave the whole of this expense to the teacher.

What time will it be desirable, that Miss Packard should leave New England? Do you know of any desirable company that she can secure?[21]

Even such firm clear arrangements were not foolproof. As to what went wrong this time, no letters give any hint; the following September Lousia Packard was teaching not in Ohio but in Philadelphia. Like many other pupils, Louisa must have had help from Miss Lyon in getting several jobs. In the summer of 1829, she was teaching in Palmer with another of Miss Lyon's Buckland students; in 1833 she had charge of Byfield Female School, which was publicly endorsed by Miss Grant and Miss Lyon as a preparatory school for Ipswich Seminary. In Philadelphia, Louisa taught under a Miss Eaton, who was well known to Mary Lyon and had entertained her in the summer of 1833; while she was at Miss Eaton's school Miss Lyon offered her the post of superintendent of the domestic department whenever Mount Holyoke, the new seminary, should come into being. But there was obvious reluctance in Louisa's answer and Miss Lyon was soon looking elsewhere.[22]

In addition to the letters about placement, Mary Lyon had a considerable correspondence with young women who wanted advice, encouragement, and personal word of their teachers and classmates. Some were very young, like Harriet Fairchild, brand new assistant at a select school in Derry. Once she had got over the shock of finding that "my seat is before the young ladies" and curbed her impulse to laugh at their amusing blunders, she had plunged with good will into calisthenics and composition, reporting proudly all 12 subjects she had assigned so far, from the ostrich to the life of a minor Scots poet. She also included exactly the same kind of report she would have made to her section teacher at Ipswich: she had managed to be out of bed at 5 a.m.

every day for almost a week, and she had spent 18 hours reviewing the first 12 propositions of Euclid, with only one failure.[23]

No requests for specific advice were more urgent than one from Louisa Billings, who was attempting to carry on a winter school in Buckland by herself in 1830–31. Although she had been teaching with Miss Lyon for two winters and one summer, stepping into her shoes was a different matter. They were studying scriptural geography, Massachusetts geography, spelling, sentences, the Bible: was 6½ hours in school the right amount? Should the young ladies study before 6 A.M.? What did she do about homesickness? How could she head in the 16-year-old "who has been under unitarian influence, pursued higher branches, feels that these are rather small doings?" Did Miss Lyon and Miss Grant ever have to struggle over their general talks? Louisa would spend an hour preparing and then find when she got to school that she had forgotten what she was going to say. The letter was full of affection and admiration for both Miss Lyon and Miss Grant as trail-blazers. "What new plans have you adopted? new books bought?" she asked in the midst of her personal problems.[24]

On the whole Mary Lyon's young correspondents seemed to be coping effectively with the situations they confronted. Abigail Tenney, who had been a member of Miss Lyon's Buckland school in 1828–29 and then a student and teacher at Ipswich, wrote from Union Village, New York, near Troy, where she was assisting another Ipswich graduate with a select school of 28 young ladies. Although their predecessors had favored the ornamental branches, she and Miss Williams were gradually shifting to the Ipswich stress on fundamentals. Scripture, geography, and Smith's grammar had been introduced, and more than half the young ladies were taking calisthenics. Abigail included news she was sure would interest Miss Lyon: there had been revivals in Union Village and Albany. Mrs. Willard's school was flourishing, and Mrs. Willard herself was back from her trip abroad with a young French woman to teach the girls in the seminary spoken French.[25]

Young New Englanders who went out to the Mississippi Valley to teach could be severely challenged. Mary Lyon must have been proud of Eliza Adams, whom she sent out to Mount Vernon, Ohio, at the age of 20, to start a school for young ladies. Eliza managed with little difficulty to shift the curriculum from physics and rhetoric to the grammar, arithmetic, and geography her fifteen students needed acutely. But the financial arrangements were another matter. She was not surprised to have to collect her own salary, but she was shocked, when she prepared to send out bills toward the end of the first quarter, to find that she and many of the parents had been misled about the charges. The sponsoring association, with whom Miss Lyon had negotiated, had set the tuition at $4 per pupil for each quarter and indicated that they intended to bear the costs of rent and other expenses. But after Eliza arrived in Mount Vernon, the president had without her knowledge declared that the charge to each parent would be increased by his share of the rent and other costs. Eliza, who had in good faith told parents that the $4 would cover everything except board and room for out-of-towners, chose for the term just ending to absorb the extra costs out of her own pay.

Then she asked the president to hold a meeting of the entire association to work out a solution. The gentlemen who attended found one very simply. They figured the maximum possible income for the teacher, with full enrollment and no defaults, and "came to the conclusion that I could well afford to bear the whole expense." Eliza was not bitter. She could see that this was part of the prevailing climate of opinion.

The advantages of a permanent school, are not known in Mt. Vernon. Teachers have come, and begun schools for teaching the higher branches. They have sometimes continued a year, and then died away. There have been seven or eight of these little private schools at one time in Mt. Vernon. A spirit of opposition existed among them. The district schools are poorly supported. Teachers for common schools are needed very much—more than for higher schools. The people are willing to support them if they can be procured.

The rest of her letter was lively and cheerful, and she concluded in words that Mary might well have employed under such circumstances: "If the Lord is on my side, I have nothing to fear."[26]

82

The most far-reaching consequence of Mary Lyon's full time commitment to Ipswich Seminary was the decision of the two young women to make a joint bid for adequate buildings and a permanent endowment. After Mary's death, Zilpah Grant wanted it known that she had thought and talked about this idea first, but the earliest overt move was certainly taken in partnership. Between 1824 and 1829 Mary seems to have been relatively indifferent to "brick and mortar" as against "living minds to work upon." Zilpah, who had talked about the advantages of permanent endowment since she first went to Derry, seems to have lacked "time or strength . . . to labor for the object of her thoughts and hopes" until Mary was available to shoulder much of the administrative burden.[27]

The first appeal was directed in February 1831 to the Ipswich trustees in a brisk letter that referred to recent opportunities to move the seminary elsewhere and then named the two requisites to permanence: "a seminary building, free of rent, containing a hall of sufficient size to accommodate one hundred and seventy-five scholars, several recitation-rooms, a laboratory, a room for a library, and a reading-room" and "a boarding-house, completely furnished for one hundred and fifty boarders, to be situated contiguous to the seminary building, and surrounded by a few acres of play-ground." The rooms "should be pleasant and airy, so finished and furnished as to give ladies as favorable a situation, while pursuing their studies, as is afforded to young men at our colleges, or other seminaries."[28]

Although the trustees had recently had complaints from some seminary proprietors about the absence of profits, they took this request seriously and appointed a committee to investigate the possibilities. Meetings were held, prospective trustees were lined up, Zilpah herself got pledges for nearly half of what she estimated was needed. A pamphlet was circulated containing a version of the original letter to the Ipswich trustees, an explanation of the disadvantages of boarding students in private families, plans for the buildings, and an invitation to subscribe. After this apparently promising start, Zilpah Grant departed to recover her health, leaving Mary Lyon to encounter the apathy and hostility that had not been immediately visible and to confront difficult negotiations without being able to speak for Zilpah or to count on prompt replies from her by letter.

At first Mary's enthusiasm seemed to mount with the difficulties. Early in February 1832 when the seven-man board had just been completed and was about to meet, she wrote a long letter to Professor Hitchcock at Amherst, to whom she seems already to have been talking about the plans. If she could spend her days just "clearing the ground," she told him, "it would be the height of my ambition." Her series of rhetorical questions suggests how deeply concerned she had become.

What permanent female seminaries are now in existence? What one in New England, of a high character, is necessarily, from its plan, destined to outlive its present teachers? Ought this so to be? Are not a few permanent female seminaries needed?—say one or two in a state? Could there be a few of this character, designed exclusively for older young ladies preparing to teach, and soon to go forth and exert an influence in a variety of ways on the cause of education and religion,—a place of resort, where those from different parts of the country, designing to spend their lives in doing good, might come together, together receive instruction, form and mature their plans, and exert over each other's views and feelings an extensive and powerful influence,— would not great good result?[29]

She listed the trustees by name. All were substantial citizens and godly men; as resistance grew, five of them were to fall by the wayside. Two, the Rev. Joseph Felt of Hamilton and George Heard, Ipswich manufacturer and banker, turned out to be devoted supporters who gave Miss Lyon invaluable help when she finally struck out on her own.[30]

At this moment when hopes were still high, the question of site was about to be discussed, and Mary was obviously hoping that Mr. Hitchcock might be willing and able to inject himself into the scheme so that the possibility of a Connecticut Valley location might be considered.

Feeling that a genial soil would be of vast importance in this first

84

attempt, I have been exceedingly desirous that the locations on Connecticut River should receive at least a little attention, before it is finally settled in Essex county. It is not best that I should say much about it; but these trustees are capable of looking at facts as they are, if their attention should be directed to the subject. The location is to be decided before the object is presented to the public, probably at the next meeting of the trustees. My only desire is, that the state of feeling in your vicinity should be tested, and the facts laid before the trustees. I do not know that there is any way by which it could be done, but I thought it barely possible that some benevolent individuals might devise some plan.

Mary knew that she was asking a lot, but she also knew that she was addressing a fellow idealist.

I must now, my dear sir, beg that you will not look on this subject in the view of personal friendship, and feel under a kind of obligation to treat it with some little respect. Unless it commends itself to your judgment as one which has a high claim on our benevolence, I could not ask you to devote to it a single moment of your very precious time. But if it has such claims, I would most gladly raise my feeble voice, entreating all who would befriend such an object to lend a helping hand.[31]

Sometime during the summer of 1832, at the suggestion of George Heard, Mary drew up a clearly outlined prospectus entitled "New England Female Seminary for Teachers." It was endorsed by Messers Fay, Felt, and George Heard, printed under the date October 22, and circulated to friends of Ipswich Seminary. The prospectus began modestly, announcing that some "friends of education and of evangelical religion are considering the expediency of attempting to raise funds" and closed by inviting communications rather than contributions. The instituition was to be "strictly evangelical" and of high academic caliber, its plant and equipment for 100 to 200 students completely endowed, its location, as yet undetermined, central and salubrious.[32]

The dormitory plan called for a separate room for each student. This was entirely Mary Lyon's idea—Zilpah Grant never accepted it. A later draft of plans, undated but probably written in 1833, was explicit: two young ladies would share a study 16 by 14 feet and each would have a cubicle for her bed 6½ by 10 feet. Mary finally gave up on separate rooms, probably because of the expense, but her original statement gives light on one aspect of her own life that she did not discuss in letters. Until Mount Holyoke Seminary was a reality, she almost never enjoyed the privacy described in the prospectus.

The great advantages of such a privilege can scarcely be realized except by those who have often felt that they would give up almost any of their common comforts for the sake of such retirement as can be enjoyed only by assigning to each a separate apartment. But to most persons of reflection, the advantages will doubtless appear much greater than the extra expense, especially when it is considered that this institution is not designed for younger misses, but directly for the benefit of ladies of maturer age.

The aims of this 1832 proposal were unequivocal: to increase the number of well prepared teachers, to give teachers in service stimulus and means to improve their education, to open the way for more teaching jobs for women in a society that made "comparatively few demands on the time of benevolent, educated ladies," and to establish a pattern for the permanently endowed institutions of higher learning for young women needed throughout the country.[33]

By the time this appeal was in print, public indifference must have begun to seem formidable. In midsummer Mary Lyon had been writing cheerfully to Mr. Felt that Zilpah was walking easily about the house and would be entirely recovered "before our new Seminary will be ready." At the end of November, in a letter to Zilpah about acquiring buildings in Amherst, her tone had changed. "I have next to no faith that the public are now prepared to raise a sum sufficient to meet the necessities of the institution, unless it is done by stepping stones, and those must be laid by the actual progress of the institution."[34]

The inactivity of most of the trustees was a continuing disappointment. In February 1833 she conferred with an energetic young minister from Conway, the Rev. Daniel Crosby, who felt the proposal needed as supporters "those who have not every thing else in their hands, and . . . those who will not be crushed by difficulties." Although she was grateful for this new recruit, Mary was under no illusions about the difficulty of working through benevolent gentlemen. "I do not feel so much afraid as I did that they will not take the right steps, but I feel much more afraid that they will not act at all." She tried to make Zilpah understand how urgent it was that the plans "should not seem to originate with *us*, but with benevolent *gentlemen.*" How many "needless, unkind remarks" she had already suffered, she did not specify. Although there is no record of personal attacks in print at this stage, she was undoubtedly speaking out of experience when she warned that if the proposal should get popular attention, "many good men will fear the effect on society of so much female influence, and what they will call female greatness."[35]

One form of antagonism was official and public. Several proprietors—that is, stockholders—of Ipswich Seminary, already restive because Miss Grant continued to occupy the building without paying rent, decided it was time to call the whole thing quits. In December 1832 five of them called for a meeting to propose selling the building, paying the debts, and dividing the proceeds. The meeting produced only two votes in favor of liquidation; it was crowded with friends and supporters of the seminary. Even so, it must have had a chilling effect on lukewarm supporters of the new enterprise.

In view of all the difficulties, the unexpected availability of buildings occupied by a hitherto successful boys' school in Amherst at first glance had seemed providential. President Heman Humphrey of Amherst College wrote Mary Lyon in November 1832 that Mount Pleasant was up for sale. The location, on 15 acres of land, was most attractive but the purchase price turned out to be prohibitively high. However, the property could be rented for $600 a year. Mary Lyon seized on this possibility at once. If some friends of female education could scrape up that relatively modest sum for an experimental period of three to five years, wasn't there an outside chance that the success of the institution in being would generate the kind of enthusiasm required to raise $40,000? When it became apparent that the trustees were not ready for any risks whatever, Mary had urged Zilpah Grant to assume the rent charges for Mount Pleasant herself; she had even offered, in Zilpah's absence, to make the move on her own personal financial responsibility, being convinced that the rent could be "collected by dollars and cents from the farmers and mechanics all over Franklin and Hampshire counties." After three months of effort to counter mounting resistance, Mary finally abandoned all thought of moving to Amherst. But before she gave up the struggle, she had reached a significant conclusion about where the money for a permanent institution for the higher education of women would have to come from.

The funds for Amherst College have been collected, not from the rich, but from liberal Christians in common life. At the commencement of that enterprise, the prospect was held out that it would be a college of high standing, where the expenses would be low, and that it would be accessible to all. This was like a mainspring, without which it is doubtful whether it would have been possible to raise the funds. I am inclined to think that something of this kind may be indispensable to our success. The great and honorable among the good will not listen to our cause; but perhaps the more humble in life, led forward by their own ministers, may befriend this important but forsaken object. . . . If the same class of Christians who support our missionaries should contribute principally to the raising of the funds, is it not important that the style of the whole establishment should professedly be plain, though very neat?[36]

The first four months of 1833 were particularly strenuous for Mary Lyon. In addition to running Ipswich Seminary, she kept in constant touch, by note and person, with Mr. Felt and Mr. Heard, the two loyal supporters of the project on an otherwise unresponsive board; she corresponded extensively with potential backers in Amherst and the hill towns; she attended meetings in

Boston and Amherst; she wrote in detail to Zilpah Grant about each development and each roadblock. Even the final collapse of the New England Seminary for Teachers was protracted. In mid-March, a call was issued to the trustees to meet to dissolve the board, constituted just over a year earlier. Only three of the seven appeared on the specified date in early April; one of the absentees had sent a proxy and the business was accomplished. But in the meantime young Mr. Crosby of Conway had stirred up the Franklin Ministers' Association. In late February they had appointed a committee to meet with "individual friends of the Ipswich Seminary" for "inquiry and consultation." Such was the hostility by this time to the "chimerical" plan that even these cautious generalizations needed further qualification. The meeting was set for April 25 at Prof. Hitchcock's house and, Mary Lyon wrote Mr. Crosby in a much corrected and blotted note, Mr. Felt and Mr. Heard planned to come. But, to avoid embarrassment, they asked for a series of disclaimers: "that no one, who consents to attend the meeting incurs by it any responsibility . . . that the business of the meeting is not of a specific character— that it is not designed to make any direct attack of Ips. Fem. Sem."[37]

It is no wonder that before the April 25th meeting Mary wrote to Zilpah Grant: "I think there are more than nine chances out of ten that the door of Providence will be closed against all future operations towards founding a permanent institution," predicting that they themselves must expect "to give up all thought and expectation of doing anything directly for the object." Although the Amherst group set up still another committee and planned a meeting in Boston during the annual ministers' conferences at the end of May, she doubted "whether it will be of sufficient interest to advance the business a single step." She was right. The Boston meeting, very poorly attended, was adjourned; on the second try, virtually no one came and no business was transacted. After this total failure, she declared categorically, "I do not think it best to attempt to revive the subject again."[38]

But no matter how realistic her appraisal of a depressing and exhausting failure, Mary was by this time committed heart and soul to the cause of a permanently endowed institution for women, and she could not stop thinking about it for any great length of time. Her resilience was partly a function of remarkable powers of physical recuperation. A note to Mrs. Briggs, Zilpah's special friend, written three weeks after the close of the winter term and the meeting at Amherst, gives a glimpse of the process of her recovery.

A week ago yesterday I put your name on a list with nearly twenty others, to whom I wished to write forthwith. To tell the truth, I have been so immersed in cares for two or three months, and my brain has been so strained to keep in mind present duties, and not to forget any thing important, that it has often seemed as if things and circumstances which were not needed for present use would be not only forgotten at the time, but even obliterated from my memory. For a week past, in my chamber alone, in a straightforward course of business, in the midst of letters, papers, &c., I have been resting at a great rate. It does seem as if I never gained so much mental rest in a week before in my life. I have had a most curious vacation in respect to calling to mind things and circumstances which I had not thought of for weeks, and which seemed entirely forgotten. To myself I seem almost like one coming to life.[39]

By the time Zilpah finally reached Ipswich in early June, about a week after the beginning of the summer term, Mary may have appeared to be her usual vigorous self. So perhaps it is not surprising that in Zilpah's version of what happened to their joint proposal during her absence, Mary's tremendous efforts did not figure. Written some twenty years later, after Mary's death, Zilpah's account of a year and a half of struggle was indeed brief. "During my absence, Miss Lyon relinquished all hope of this being accomplished in our day, and cooperated in the dissolution of all associations under the name of trustees committees, and friends that had been formed for the promotion of the object."[40]

Whatever she ignored then or forgot later on, when Zilpah Grant returned to Ipswich in June 1833, she must have been thinking mainly of the immediate future: she and Mary Lyon were about to separate. Mary was to have the summer for rest and travel, and they would teach a last term together in the winter of 1833–34. Then Mary would take over for the summer of 1834 while Zilpah explored the West; the connection was to be finally and officially severed in September 1834.

The break was of Mary's making. Zilpah had had previous evidence of her independence; she could not have forgotten the long debate over giving up the Buckland school, and she must have known when Mary was contemplating the possibility of marriage. Although no records exist of specific young men who paid Mary Lyon attention, and the scraps of Buckland gossip are highly improbable, there is no reason to question Mrs. Cowles's statement that in the summer of 1830 Mary "gave the final negative to the question of marrying" in response to "a tempting offer which she thought held out as good a prospect of a life of love and happiness as any she could expect."[41]

After Mary agreed to teach with Zilpah winter and summer, both young women may well have seen themselves settled at Ipswich for many years to come—that is, until Zilpah's departure to recover her health. As the months of absence wore on, Mary must have felt more and more the need of daily consultation and companionship, for which the long letters south were not an adequate substitute. In the course of time she turned to a new confidante, Eunice Caldwell, later Mrs. Cowles, who was probably the ablest of all the graduates-turned-teachers on the Ipswich staff. Just when this occurred is uncertain; Mrs. Cowles was always reticent about her own role in the events she chronicled.[42]

But this shift in relationship seems to have figured only secondarily in Mary's desire for separation. What pushed her to act was her growing concern for a permanently endowed institution of higher learning for women and her growing conviction that the attempt to endow Miss Grant's seminary was doomed. She first raised the question on December 9, 1832, less than two weeks after she had urged taking a chance on the Mount Pleasant buildings in Amherst. They should both consider, she wrote, "whether my services are needed as much in our beloved seminary as in some other portion of the Lord's vineyard." Mary's main point

4. Mary Lyon in a turban. This miniature on ivory, painted by an unknown artist, was done in 1832 when Mary was Zilpah Grant's assistant and surrogate at Ipswich Seminary. Mount Holyoke College Library Archives.

was that she had found that with the help of experienced teachers "in the present improved state of the institution" the management could be handled by one person. Zilpah seems to have accepted this conclusion already, at least for the short haul; she had apparently just proposed that Mary should have the coming summer term free to travel. It was Zilpah's proposal for the summer that had persuaded Mary to raise her question by letter instead of waiting for discussion face to face; it might actually be less disturbing to the school and less strenuous for Zilpah if Mary were to leave for good at the beginning of the summer. Mary suggested that they both pray about it every morning and concluded, "You will ask about our great plan. I do not think there is one chance in twenty for it to succeed. If it should, a different course might be taken."[43]

To this bombshell Zilpah made no immediate response of any sort in any of her letters to Ipswich. Finally, at the end of February, an answer arrived. Mary sat down and wrote a long reply without a word of reproach. Her letter conveyed personal affection and concern for Miss Grant's school and showed not only that she had resigned herself to the impending demise of their joint proposal but also that she was more deeply stirred than ever by the need for endowed low-cost education for women.

Yesterday was my birthday. Thirty-six years of my life are gone, and now I am one year more than middle aged. To look back step by step, it seems a long life, and the remaining years in prospect seem few and short. But my life and strength may be prolonged for many years to come. I would that it might be so, if it is the will of the Lord. But in one thing I can rejoice,—that, as long as the Lord of the vineyard hath any need of my feeble service, he will allow me the unspeakable privilege of living and laboring; and when he sees it to be best that I should labor no longer in this dark, wicked world, which has been promised to the Savior as his inheritance, then may I be prepared to lay down this tabernacle with joy and rejoicing, and go to dwell with Christ, which is far better. Daily, my dear sister, do I endeavor to ask for you the same blessings which I ask for myself. O, this vast field, which is white already to the harvest! May laborers be raised up in great numbers, to gather in the harvest, which is continually wasting away. May those who are in the field labor while the day lasts. May you and I be so directed, that we shall spend the remainder of our days in that manner which shall be the means of the greatest possible results.

One thing I have, for several weeks, wanted to propose to you. It is this: If Providence should ever make it plainly our duty to occupy different fields of labor, and to dissolve our legal connection, I should deem it one of the greatest earthly blessings which I could possibly enjoy, to keep as many of the cords which now bind us together unbroken as could be done under existing circumstances; that we should assist each other in forming plans; that we should visit each other often; write to each other often; that we should each feel that, next to our own field of labor, that of the other is the most endearing—the field to which we have pledged our services, our influence, our hearts. A union somewhat like this would be to me an unspeakable satisfaction; it would seem to save my bleeding heart from sinking under the stroke of a separation; and my judgment says, that such a union would be suited to advance the great cause to which we have consecrated our lives.

Two days ago, I received yours, written January 10, replying to mine of December 10. After sending mine, I felt that I could leave it all with God. After that, however, there was a solemn weight resting on my soul; a feeling that one step had been taken toward accomplishing the greatest change that has ever taken place in my situation and labors, and probably the greatest that ever will take place in my life. But after receiving a few lines in Miss C.'s, acknowledging the receipt of mine of December 10, I felt that all, for the present, was done,—that God, in his own time and manner, would by his providence point out the path of duty, and I could most cheerfully and quietly wait. The peace and freedom from solicitude which I have been permitted to enjoy, with regard to the final issue, have been uncommon. When I have opened your letters, I have had no painful solicitude to find a line indicating your opinion on the question. But since the reception of yours two days ago, my mind has been most intensely occupied, and I can now give you only a few of my general, scattered thoughts.

A few words about my feelings. If it should be plain, or equally probable, that you and I could both of us accomplish as great an amount of good to spend our remaining days together as we could to occupy different fields, it would be a blessing which would be most grateful to my heart; or, if it should be equally probable that we could accomplish as much good during our lives, to continue together three years more, and then separate, I should be grateful for the privilege of being with you so much longer.

Now I will endeavor to write according to my judgment, though my opinion is not made up on any point. The reasons why it seemed to me, that were we ever to occupy different fields of labor it might be better that we should commence soon, were two,—one relating to my own usefulness, the other to yours.

If I should separate from you, I have no definite plan. But my thoughts, feelings, and judgment are turned toward the middle classes of society. For this class I want to labor, and for this class I consider myself rather peculiarly fitted to labor. To this class in society would I devote, directly, all the remainder of my strength, (God permitting,)—not to the higher classes, not to the poorer classes. This middle class contains the main springs, and main wheels, which are to move the world. Whatever field I may occupy, it must be an humble, laborious work. How I can get a footing sufficiently firm for my feet to rest upon for the remainder of my days, and where my hands can work, I know not. But by wandering around, and by resting from my labors a year or two, perhaps Providence might open the door. I should seek for nothing permanent, to continue after my death, as to the location of my labors; but I should consider it very desirable that I should occupy but one more field, that I should make but one more remove, till I remove into my grave. I shall soon be literally forty years old; and if I am ever to leave my present field of labor, and begin entirely anew, it seems desirable, for my future usefulness, that I should begin soon, before many more of my remaining days are gone, or much more of my remaining strength exhausted.

If I should journey next summer, it might be better, for you and for the school, that I should not return at all, than that I should return to spend merely a year or two. It might be less hazardous to your strength to go right forward alone, than to have these changes. You want I should write how I judge, and feel inclined to decide. I wish I could tell you more definitely than I can now. My mind seems exceedingly reluctant even to incline to one side or the other. One thing, however, is clear. Considering your views and feelings, I do not think it best that we should separate so soon as this spring, at any rate. How long it is best that we should continue together, I do not know. As your letter has been so long delayed, perhaps it will not be best to attempt to settle these questions till we meet face to face.

Your arguments against a separation now are weighty. I have considered most of them in some form, though, perhaps, not with the distinctness with which you have expressed them. My query of December 10 I designed not specifically to be, whether we ought to separate this spring, or in one, two, or three years from this time; but generally, whether it was best that we should continue together permanently, or that we should separate as soon as it could be effected to good advantage; say, at the most suitable time in the course of two or three years. I do not think I expressed this clearly. Looking at the subject in the form of this last query, I will dwell a moment on the main arguments. 1. The hope of founding a permanent seminary. This is so great an object, that it would be right to sacrifice considerable good for the sake of a small probability of success. But we must guide our steps by probabilities.

My feelings are most deeply interested in this cause, and so strong is my belief in its utility, that I do believe that such a work will be effected at some future day, perhaps some twenty or fifty years from this time. But if it must be delayed entirely for several years, I have thought that there was nothing that we could do together which we could not do separately. And as the probability in my own mind, founded, I think, on evidence, was altogether on this side, it seemed my duty to decide according to this probability, knowing, that if any indication of Providence should appear in favor of the great object, either before it should be time to act, or before I should take fast hold of any other, (which time must be considerable,) we could again unite our labors as before. My candid judgment has been, that the probability that such a seminary would be founded during our day has been constantly diminishing; but I have felt it my duty not to say much about it, but to put forth every possible effort, till we should professedly give up the subject for the present.

If, in my own mind, the chance two years ago was equal to one in five, it is now reduced to not more than one in fifty; I would say to one in one hundred, or five hundred, if we except the ray of hope which beams from the possibility that an experiment may be made at Amherst, and the possibility that something favorable may grow out of such an experiment, if it should be made. My belief has been, that unless something unexpected should be brought forward by the wheels of Providence, the time has nearly come, when it will be your duty and mine professedly to relinquish the object,—not our interest in the plan, but our attempts for its execution. This I have not expressed before, and now it pains me to acknowledge my conviction. My conviction arose from the manner in which the scheme is regarded by various individuals, who, I think, are a fair index of the public. The public, as such, know nothing of any consequence about the object, and care less than they know. The public, as such, know not, and care not, how Miss Grant and Miss Lyon are united, or when they separate, or how, if the school at Ipswich can go on well.

A few words about the importance of the prosperity of Miss Grant's school. I consider it more important that it should continue to flourish during her life, or during her ability to labor, than any other school in the land, which is the property of a private individual. But, after all, it is short-lived. I view it as just like Mr. Emerson's school. It was very important that Mr. Emerson should prosper during his days of labor, and that he should have a place where he might put forth his strength to peculiar advantage. But where is his school now? If we ask, "Where are his labors?" I would say, "All over the earth, and their record is on high."

If the plan for the permanent seminary does not succeed, I have long felt that you and I must continue to labor, and make no more attempts for any thing permanent to result, except what is planted permanently in the hearts and in the lives of those over whom God may give us a direct or indirect influence. I consider it so important that your school should continue to flourish during your remaining days of labor, that I ought to take a course which would diminish my present usefulness, and hazard my future usefulness, rather than greatly to hazard the prosperity of Miss Grant's school, and her usefulness thereby. A small hazard may be justifiable.

This letter has cost me more hours than any letter I have written you this winter, and I fear it will cost you more to read it; and how little it contains!

If the experiment is made at Amherst, the hand of Providence would, undoubtedly, make it plain duty for us to continue together.[44]

What Zilpah replied is wholly a matter of conjecture; none of her letters on this subject survive. Her tone may have varied. In May, Mary was venturing a bit of mild irony: "I am very glad, my dearest friend, that you propose to endeavor to learn that you *can* do without me. I should rejoice to have you learn this lesson fully, even if we should hereafter decide that it is our duty to continue through life to labor together." However strongly Zilpah may have disliked the idea of the break, she certainly did not hasten her return on Mary's account. Twice in May Mary Lyon wrote to Hannah White, who was teaching in Amherst. On May 10 Mary was taking the responsibility for admitting students for the summer term because Zilpah had been delayed by freshets which made the roads impassable. On May 23 Zilpah still had not arrived; her most recent letter had been mailed from Virginia on May 9 and Mary was waiting to hear whether she would be there for the opening of the summer term on May 29. She was not; she missed the opening by a week.[45]

Before Mary Lyon took off at the end of June on her trip west, she and Zilpah Grant must have worked out together the specific arrangements for their separation by stages over the next sixteen months. But when Mary finally left Ipswich late in October 1834, relations between the two were not severed. The campaign for Mount Holyoke was launched from Ipswich Female Seminary, which in all the subsequent printed appeals served as the exemplar, academically and religiously, for the new institution. Financial dealings continued as Zilpah paid back what Mary had invested in the seminary and at least once made Mary a short-term loan. In the summer of 1835 Mary took over Ipswich again for about five weeks so that Zilpah could be away. On subsequent brief visits Mary enlisted clerical assistance and further donations from Ipswich faculty and students; she even recruited Ipswich students for the upper classes at Mount Holyoke when it should open. The correspondence fell off only gradually; until after Mount Holyoke opened, it was frequent and personal enough to give important glimpses of Mary Lyon's progress and her state of mind. After Zilpah became Mrs. Banister in 1841, she visited Mount Holyoke several times and was welcomed by Mary with an intensity of feeling that the watching students remembered.

It says something about both women that this friendship could continue at all when the follower and assistant was becoming the major competitor. It certainly emphasized Mary Lyon's remarkable selflessness and warmth. She did not crave wealth or fame;

she was not envious; she harbored no resentments. She seems to have been aware of possible difficulties in their relations; in October 1833, on her way back to Ipswich from her western trip, she wrote affectionately of their coming reunion and asked Zilpah to pray with her every day "that the ensuing winter, which we anticipate spending together after so long a separation, may be for our mutual benefit, for the good of our dearly-beloved institution, and for the glory of God." Apparently Mary never forgot Zilpah's acts of generosity and never paid any attention to her displays of jealousy. After all, Zilpah had originally set the pace. As Sydney McLean observes, "Zilpah Grant may have over-estimated her influence on Mount Holyoke and its founder, who outdistanced her in intellect and drive, but she does have a part in that story." Regardless of her limitations, "she was one of the small band who, by insisting on standards, laid the foundations of future progress."[46]

To many of her friends Mary Lyon's decision to cut herself off from a regular income and a recognized base of operations to undertake an enterprise like one that had collapsed before it started must have seemed quixotic. She had saved money out of her modest pay and Mr. White had invested it for her advantageously, but she contributed generously to missions and other benevolent causes and she had taken on increasing family responsibilities. Her letters over the first year that she was managing Ipswich Seminary single-handed indicate what she was doing for her family. In late November 1831 she made a quick trip to Ashfield and borrowed cash from her sister Freelove—was it to send Lovina back to the Hartford Retreat? In late May 1832 Mary sent $52 to the hospital. After Lovina's death in September Mary paid for all the remaining hospital charges. Sometime during the year she wrote a long letter to her niece Abigail Moore in western New York, urging her to scrape up traveling expenses and come to Ipswich to prepare for teaching. Mary Lyon would pay her tuition for the year, $25, would help her "plan and economize" and would lend her additional funds if they were needed. "I should be glad to do more for you in this way, but, consistently with prior obligations, I cannot."[47]

Mary Lyon by now had another kind of capital to draw upon:

the personal authority she had been almost imperceptibly acquiring over the years. Although she was still hesitant about taking on religious functions new to her, those she did assume were handled with conspicuous success. After Zilpah's departure, saying grace before meals was at first a "trial," but gradually she grew to enjoy it very much. Another duty forced upon her by circumstances was the consolation of students who were very ill or dying; by all accounts, her presence and her prayers were comforting. Throughout her lifetime, interest in deathbeds was widespread. Friends and relatives were moved not only by solicitude and grief but also by the hope that the last words, spoken on the threshold of heaven, might give some slightest glimpse or hint of what the next world was really like. A minutely detailed account, written by a fellow student, gave in full the last words of an Ipswich student who died after a week's illness, apparently typhoid, on September 19, 1832. In her final hours she was in a state of religious excitement, praying for her family, her friends, and everybody connected with the school, including the absent Miss Grant, and even trying to convert the doctor. She seemed to find solace in having Miss Lyon by her side most of the day, praying for her and repeatedly assuring her that as a Christian she was not self-deceived. Miss Lyon was holding her hand when she died.[48]

While Miss Lyon certainly stood second to Miss Grant in the general estimation, a number of the high-minded New Englanders who were trying hard to improve public education had by 1833 come to know Mary as a remarkable teacher and propagator of the faith. Her Bible lessons and lectures on conduct impressed not only the students but also literate and sophisticated observers. The anonymous author of a six-page account in the *American Annals of Education* of a day's visit to Ipswich Seminary devoted five paragraphs to Miss Lyon's lesson from II Kings on Elisha and only regretted that he had been unable to take down every word of the recitation, which he found "a model of its kind." When Jacob Abbott was preparing to begin *The Religious Magazine*, his note to Zilpah Grant soliciting a series of contributions concluded, "Please say to Miss L. that I consider this note intended equally for herself & you."[49]

It is hard for readers today to grasp the energizing quality of

Mary Lyon's faith. Profoundly as she believed in the intervention of God in human affairs and in personal translation after death to heaven or hell, there was nothing in the least fatalistic about her kind of puritanism. As she told her students in a series of lessons on Peter the Apostle, the true worker for Christ needed to devote just as much intellect to God as to his ordinary business; all his wisdom and his invention might be needed to accomplish God's purpose. She might well have been speaking of her own still inchoate plans when she said, "I verily believe that many things God now designs to do he leaves to be thought of by his children."[50]

Mary Lyon's faith reinforced her self-reliance and intensified her energy without making her in any way forbidding. Although she was neither handsome nor elegant, she somehow seemed attractive to many of the sharp-eyed young women studying under her. They noted her sturdy frame, large head, and habit of quick movement and also her "full, smiling, happy blue eyes," "her plump rosy cheeks," and the way she seemed to radiate "intellect and intelligence." It would be a mistake to envisage her when she was about to strike out on her own as either quaint or queer. Early in January 1833 a new student arrived who must have been unusually able; she was admitted several weeks after the beginning of the winter term and the following year was named to the teaching staff. On her first day at Ipswich Seminary it was a major event to Lydia Farnham to meet "that noted and truly wonderful woman, Miss Lyon," whom she found "the perfect image of health and comfort."[51]

4
The Great Work Accomplished

But they that wait upon the Lord

shall renew their strength;

they shall mount up with

wings as eagles; they shall run,

and not be weary, and they shall walk,

and not faint.

ISAIAH 40:31

M

ary Lyon devoted the summer of 1833 to travel. Her trip was apparently proposed by Zilpah from Georgia, partly to postpone her ultimate departure from Ipswich. Although Mary never allowed herself another extended vacation, on this Grand Tour she proved an energetic and enthusiastic sightseer. In three and one-half months she covered more than 2,000 miles, by public stage, private carriage, steamship, canal boat, and even, for a few particularly uncomfortable miles, an early stretch of railroad. She visited historic landmarks, museums, factories and hospitals in New York and Philadelphia, she admired the grandeur of the Catskills and Niagara Falls, she got glimpses of the new West and the retreating frontier between Buffalo and Detroit.

How, under the pressures of the spring of 1833, she ever managed to work out a detailed itinerary, it is hard to imagine. She unquestionably left with plans not only to sightsee but also to visit notable schools and teachers and to collect precise information about the nature and function of institutional residence buildings. Her route was also obviously planned to allow her to visit her brother Aaron and sister Electa and the other relatives and friends in western New York whom she had not seen for more than ten years.

Always methodical to a point, Mary kept several records of her journey. She made day-by-day notations, from June 28 through October 10, of where she was and some of the people and things she saw. For the first six weeks she put down all her expenses, including $131.40 for scientific apparatus purchased in Philadelphia after a week of careful shopping and no doubt shipped to Ipswich. Until she reached Dunkirk, New York, she recorded all stage and boat fares; for well over 900 miles, the total cost was under $33. She listed by date 14 letters she wrote Zilpah and 12 letters Zilpah sent her; although none of this correspondence survives in the original, the Hitchcock biography contains a dozen pages of excerpts from Mary's letters. In addition, her travel notebook contains 50 pages of observations, mostly about the natural wonders that particularly impressed her. These notes seem to have been the basis of some of her subsequent letters; the crossings out and insertions show how conscious she was of the danger of "second-hand emotions" and "insipid" phrases.[1]

In some ways these records are illuminating. Bits from a letter written on July 22 in Philadelphia, where she spent three weeks, indicate the kind of attention she was paying to asylums and hospitals as well as the strenuousness of her daily program and her undiminished vigor. Obviously when this letter was written, she had recovered from the illness that had kept her house-bound the week before.

On Friday morning she went with a "Doctor B" to visit the United States Mint and a porcelain factory and, in the afternoon, with "Miss E" to a House of Refuge, where she was impressed by the "neat, whitewashed little rooms and clean beds, the orderly circle of cleanly and decently-clad girls, and the general air of neatness, order, and system . . ." She contrasted the house and its inhabitants with "the filthy children, the confusion, disorder, and misrule generally attendant on" the "dirty houses" she had often passed.

From the House of Refuge she went to the Penitentiary and the next day to the Old State House, Independence Hall, and other historic places. President Jackson was "received" in Independence Hall. One more day of sightseeing included the Navy Yard, the Marine Hospital, and the Academy of Natural Sciences. She closed the week "in fine health, except some little suffering in muscles and sinews."[2]

The Hitchcock excerpts also point up Mary Lyon's warmth and generosity toward even distant relatives. Writing of Aaron, she recalled the years when his home in Buckland had been hers and commented, "Though he is considerably altered, and appears somewhat bowed down with trials, sickness, and age, yet I find him the same kind-hearted, generous, affectionate brother. O that my visit might be profitable to his children, and to my other family friends!" It was indeed profitable. Much of the three weeks devoted to seeing family and friends went into nursing her sister Freelove, who had come out from Ashfield to visit and then fallen ill. Subsequently, she spurred on a whole succession of nieces and nephews to get an education; she found time to write them letters, and made numerous family gifts and loans.[3]

But there are some major gaps in the surviving accounts of Mary Lyon's summer of exploration. What were her reactions to the schools she visited and the teachers she consulted? She detoured to Troy to see Emma Willard. What did they talk about? She zigzagged across New York state, leaving the canal boat and going by stage in order to stop at Clinton, Auburn, Geneva, Canandaigua, to confer with men and women who must have been mainly teachers, principals, or trustees. She paid an overnight visit to the Rev. Hiram H. Kellogg, who was heading a seminary for young ladies that featured manual labor as part of the curriculum. She attended commencement at Hamilton College and Auburn Theological Seminary; she "met the teachers of Utica," apparently in a group; in a three-day stop at Rochester she "had much conversation on female education," noting specifically the name of a chambermaid with whom she had enjoyed talking.[4]

Neither the purpose nor the result of her two and one-half days in Detroit is anywhere made explicit. She arrived by steamship from Fairport, Ohio, on Wednesday morning, held several conversations with the Messers Larned, Jones, Hastings and Bates, visited Miss Tappan's school, saw a bit of the town, and Friday afternoon took a steamer back to Dunkirk. It seems likely that she had undertaken this arduous part of her trip to consider some connection with the Detroit Female Seminary; among the eleven officers elected in 1830 by the incorporators were three of the four men named in her diary. An undated paragraph, identified in Hitchcock only as written by Mary to Zilpah, might have referred to Detroit. In any case it demonstrates that

Mary could and did make incisive on-the-spot judgments.

They are talking about erecting a building for a female school in this city; but they have had no idea of doing it, except by shares, with the expectation of an income. They look at schools, generally, just as they would at mercantile business. Some persons, who knew I was coming here, hoped that I would render them some assistance about a plan; but they need something more than a plan.[5]

One unexpected aspect of Mary Lyon's exposure to new places and people was her contacts with abolitionists in the making, surprising at a time when they were so few in number and when the acquaintances she was visiting were apt to be conservative in religion and politics. Her hostess for three weeks in Philadelphia was Rebecca Eaton, a sister of Joseph Emerson's first wife, who had accompanied him to Charleston, South Carolina, on one of his trips south to regain his health and had stayed on, starting a school and making a place for herself in the community. One of her good friends was Angelina Grimké, the younger of the two sisters who were to create such a stir in the late 1830's by their articles and lectures on abolition and women's rights. First Sarah and then Angelina had left Charleston for Philadelphia and had joined the Quakers. When Rebecca Eaton came north is not apparent, but in July 1833 she was established in Philadelphia and obviously in close touch with her friends from South Carolina.

Mary Lyon was introduced to Miss Grimké on July 10, the day after her arrival in Philadelphia and, as she recorded in her diary, took tea with her on the 19th, called on her on the 24th, and saw her and Mrs. Frost, the married sister with whom Angelina was then living, at Miss Eaton's on the 25th. Angelina Grimké had one initial bond with Mary Lyon; they both knew and admired Catharine Beecher. Angelina had visited Hartford Female Seminary two summers before and arranged to return for six months to learn teaching techniques. Unhappily, the plans had fallen through; permission to return was denied the 28-year-old Angelina by the Philadelphia Friends Meeting.

There is no clue as to how Mary appraised this still unknown and not yet conspicuously radical young woman or what was discussed in those four carefully recorded meetings, but it is not improbable that the evils of slavery were considered. On Sunday, July 21, Mary attended two Presbyterian services as she did regularly throughout her trip. In the morning she heard a young missionary recently returned from Liberia, who defended the colonization scheme advocated by many conservative opponents of slavery; he believed that the weaknesses, which he did not gloss over, were inevitable but curable. She devoted seven pages of her notebook to a full account of the sermon—more space than she gave to any single experience except visiting Niagara Falls and seeing the Panorama of Mexico City, a spectacular display on exhibit in Philadelphia. This was the only sermon of all those she heard in three and one-half months that she recorded.

Lane, the new theological seminary in Cincinnati, was beyond the limits of Mary Lyon's itinerary, but she gave it close attention at least twice. She probably knew before she started that Lyman Beecher had just assumed the presidency and that the seminary was attracting idealistic students from the East, liberal Presbyterians and Congregationalists. In any case when she went to church in Catskill Village, the sermon was a plea for funds for Lane by the Rev. Franklin Vail, agent (i.e. money-raiser) and dedicated supporter of the seminary. Ten days later, during her stay in Utica, she called on her hostess's sister-in-law, the wife of the Lane student who was "monitor-general" of the farm where many Lane students were doing manual labor. Samuel Wells was a graduate of the Oneida Institute, which had pioneered in organized manual labor for all students. He was to be one of the leading dissidents in the shattering struggle a few months hence over the right of Lane students to hear abolitionist speakers. It would be rash to assume that Mary Lyon and Mrs. Samuel Wells—and the three Wells children—talked about slavery on that August afternoon. But this personal contact, like its predecessors, must have intensified Mary Lyon's interest in the issues later on when the Grimkés' lectures and Lane Seminary student protests erupted into the news.

The last entry in the journey notebook, entirely unrelated to the miscellaneous facts just recorded, reads "Messers Arthur & Lewis Tappan are strong advocates for the abolition cause. A gentleman remarked that probably Mr. A. Tappan gave $50 a week for support of publications." The Tappans, from Northampton, were dedicated and generous "new measures" Presbyterians, and the Tappan girls had attended Ipswich Seminary. Mary Lyon could hardly have helped thinking of them as potential donors for her own enterprise, though there seems to be no other reference to them by name in her letters for at least a decade.

Although she obviously did some thinking about slavery during her journey, there is no sign that anything she saw or heard modified her conservatism on this issue. Two years later in a letter to Zilpah Grant, she praised the new book, *Slavery*, by William Ellery Channing. Unitarian though he was, she felt that he had "a great soul" and found his "mildness and decision" particularly admirable in contrast with "those captious faultfindings which fill many of our newspapers." She was struck by his condemnation not only of the extremists, "the south, in their present excited and threatening attitude" and "the abolitionists, in their furious and misguided zeal" but also the compromisers, "the anti-ultras" whose "prudence and caution" were apt to lead them to concessions that would "endanger our first principles of duty." At bottom she seems to have been most distressed because clashes over slavery were keeping the church from its main business of saving souls; the evils suffered in this world by enslaved blacks probably never weighed as heavily to her as the pains of eternal damnation.[6]

After nearly two years as acting head of Ipswich Female Seminary, Mary Lyon returned in late October of 1833 to her old post as Zilpah Grant's administrative mainstay. There is no evidence of friction during their final term together, but the relationship must have been somewhat modified. In addition to organizing, supervising, and lecturing in a school of 175, Mary was actively preparing for an enterprise that was heroic if not foolhardy. To be sure, many of her fellow puritans, both men and women, were dedicated and tireless in pursuing good works, and her self-reliance would no doubt have struck Tocqueville as peculiarly American. After interviewing the president of Harvard, Tocqueville had concluded: "It is thus with everything here. Does a man conceive the idea of some social improvement, a college, a hospital, a road, it doesn't occur to him to go to the authorities. He publishes a plan, offers to execute it himself, calls the strength of other individuals to aid his own efforts, struggles hand to hand against each obstacle." Even so, it is still hard to imagine how, in pre-Victorian New England, a single woman without money or influence, largely self-educated, relatively unknown, could set out on her own to establish an advanced educational institution for women, without exact precedents.[7]

Most of the printed appeals for support of the new seminary were to be the work of Mary Lyon, in spite of the fact that she found such composition difficult and had to revise extensively. Of eight detailed descriptions designed for publication between 1834 and 1837 to solicit funds and recruit students, seven were from her hand. In March 1836 when she was at work on "Address to the Public," the fourth statement of purpose and method she had composed within two years, she wrote to Eunice Caldwell, "I consider the first draught about a fourth part of the work." The end product of these protracted struggles with words was not always the kind of public attention she had been aiming at. No religious or educational magazine accepted any of her offerings and some of them were the focus for hostile attacks. But, read in succession, the pamphlets and unpublished manuscripts show what careful thought Mary Lyon had given to every aspect of her plan.[8]

One early effort, much revised but apparently never published or distributed, analyzed the situation of the young woman on her own who was considering borrowing money to improve her education. Without a single personal allusion or a word of complaint, it says volumes about the way society hedged up the independent woman who wanted to be a first-rate teacher.

Motives which may induce young ladies to hire money & make extraordinary efforts to improve their education.
1. The prospect of doing more good through life may be a most

powerful motive. This if sufficiently strong, clear & well defined in the mind, may of itself justify the greatest efforts, & even those, which under other circumstances would merit the imputation of imprudence. When the desire to do the greatest possible good becomes firm & unshaken, I know not what may not be attempted. But this desire must be firmly fixed, or the career of doing good, will end in selfishness under the cloak of benevolence. But I do believe there is such a thing as knowing our own hearts, & becoming unalterably fixed in our purpose, & in the strength of Christ, going forward till the day of our death unchangeable in our pursuits. To such I would say, Go forward, attempt great things, accomplish great things.

2. The anticipated pleasure of an elevated education, for an elevated object may form another motive. There are peculiar sweets derived from gaining knowledge, from possessing a mind more elevated, & soul more enlarged, & from having a greater & nobler object of pursuit. These are delights known only to those who have tasted them, they are not coveted by others. Those who have tasted may thirst for an abundant supply at the fountain. This motive is lawful & may be allowed a place in the argument urging forward to the accomplishing of the desire of the heart.

3. The hope of future, & final pecuniary advantage may be another motive operating on the heart. This is a very strong, & very common motive to action in the various pursuits of life. It is so tangible, & so material in its character, that the soul need not be raised above the very dust to be under its most powerful control. But this is a motive, which ought not to be allowed at all to bear on the question under consideration. Suppose a young lady, who is without property, & without parents to aid her, & who already [has] a respectable education is considering the expediency of attempting by extraordinary efforts to avail herself of additional means, to prepare herself for future usefulness, with a hope that she shall be thus enabled to do more good all the remainder of her life. In weighing the arguments & considering the motives let not a hope of pecuniary advantage have any place in her heart. Let her not go forward with such an undertaking, encouraged by the hope, that in consequence, she may be able to lay up a little more annual income for a time of sickness—or be able to support herself more handsomely—or that she shall be less liable to embarrassment & difficulty in providing for her own support. . . . She ought firmly to resolve to be always in future satisfied, provided that, after her extra efforts to prepare herself for future usefulness, her pecuniary prospects should be as favorable as they were before she commenced. . . .

She made a quick survey of elementary and secondary schools in various parts of the country to show how few schools anywhere could be expected to offer young women salaries commensurate with superior education and teaching skill, and also observed that the pupils in the expensive institutions that paid well were often spoiled and not very rewarding to teach. She concluded by accepting it as a fact of life that a self-supporting woman was not apt to earn enough to provide for illness or other emergency.

The query very naturally arises, If teachers of such qualifications devote themselves to such schools for a very small compensation, & that frequently only a part of the year, what will they do, if they should be sick? I would say, let them do just what they would have done, if they had not received a superior education, let them do just what other unmarried females, in good standing in society, but without property do, in case of sickness. Most of these, in time of health just live along, coming out even at the end of the year, & no more. And they may be very happy in living on mutual acts of kindness, & perhaps those who by their good deeds, lay up a large store in the hearts of others, are made as comfortable in time of sickness, & feel as little solicitude as any other females who are dependent on their own exertions. It is often remarked that Providences are fitted to each other. That same hand of Providence, which has closed almost every door to wealth & independence against the personal efforts of females, does provide for them in cases of sickness & dependence much more comfortably & respectably than for the other sex in similar cases of sickness & dependence.[9]

In February 1834 when Mary Lyon issued her first printed

appeal for funds, the important features of her proposed seminary were already firmly fixed. The institution was to be permanently endowed through gifts of public-spirited donors sufficient to cover all the costs of plant and equipment. Its affairs were not to be controlled in any of the usual ways: not by local merchants and ministers concerned about income as well as the educational needs of the immediate vicinity, nor by members of some sect or faction, nor by the school head for his sustenance and profit. Instead, management was to rest in the hands of a disinterested board of trustees. Costs were to be kept very low—perhaps as low as half the charges at Ipswich—by several measures. Teachers, who would dedicate themselves to the cause, like missionaries, would accept low salaries, students would perform the necessary domestic work, any operating profits would be turned back to further reduce charges. Addressed specifically "To the Friends and Patrons of Ipswich Female Seminary," the first appeal took for granted that the recipients approved religious instruction and a rigorous academic program.

This single sheet must have figured centrally in Mary Lyon's correspondence in 1834, especially during the Ipswich summer term when she was in complete charge, Zilpah Grant having taken the opportunity for a five-month trip to the West. After the first meeting of potential sponsors for the new seminary in September, the reverse side of the sheet was filled with the names and votes of the newly formed committee and other endorsements; thus embellished, Mary Lyon's first printed statement was the one piece for fund-raising literature in circulation for another nine months.

"School for Adult Females," a much corrected draft of what may have been designed as a magazine article, seems to have been written late in 1834. It dwelt on the advantages of the domestic arrangements for the mature young women being sought as students. Neither little girls nor young misses, they would be adults who, by living in a dormitory, would profit from one another's company, instead of being parceled out by threes and fours to board with private families in the neighborhood. The domestic work would not only help to cut costs but also give students healthful exercise and practice in making personal efforts for the good of society. Mary Lyon was at considerable pains to reject the notion that hers would be a "manual labor school," a misconception that persisted during her lifetime. Her original reasoning about including the domestic work "as a mere appendage" is spelled out in a letter to Hannah White written some five months earlier.

And if any institution should ask for public support, would it not be desirable that, in some particulars, it should present certain marked features which would be approved by common Christians? On this account, I have thought that, in the proposed seminary, it would be well to have the domestic work done by the members of the school, not as an essential feature of the institution, but as a mere appendage. But this mere appendage ought, by no means, to give the name of manual labor *to the scheme. I have not the least faith in any of the proposed kinds of manual labor, by which it is supposed that females can support themselves at school, such as raising silk, attending to grape-vines, spinning, sewing, etc. I should expect that any attempt of the kind would become a bill of expense, rather than an income, to any female seminary. After the acquaintance I have had with many cultivated and interesting families, where the daughters, in a systematic manner, performed all the labor, I have the greatest confidence that a system might be formed, by which all the domestic work of a family of one hundred could be performed by the young ladies themselves, and in the most perfect order, without any sacrifice of improvement in knowledge or of refinement. Might not this simple feature do away much of the prejudice against female education among the common people? If this prejudice could by any means be removed, how much would it do for the cause? Some of the specific features of the great object in which I am engaged will seem to some of our friends like new views, different from my former ones. Not so new as might seem; they are of no very recent date. The only difference is, that I did not consider it expedient, while I was connected with Miss Grant and this institution, to say much about these views.*[10]

The next mailing piece, the "Address to the Christian Public," dated June 15, 1835, was written not by Mary Lyon but by three committee members, all ministers, who stressed the Christian bias of the new institution as well as its permanence and low cost. In addition they celebrated the scenic beauty and accessibility of South Hadley, made specific the analogy to public support of colleges for men, and emphasized the shortage of teachers, which "the spirit of enterprise" would prevent young men from supplying, when relatively idle young women would gladly teach if they were qualified. The signatories also deplored the misunderstanding and misrepresentation that the project had suffered, and praised the purity of motive of "those who have been praying this Seminary into existence."[11]

The academic quality of the new institution was hard to describe because, in Mary Lyon's words, "There is no acknowledged standard of female education by which an institution can be measured." She tackled the subject in 1835, in a twelve-page description of methods and course of study, directed to the young women whom she wanted to apply. Her appeal was primarily to idealists, those eager "to use all their talents in the great work of serving their generation." To them she promised an academic program equivalent to that available at Catharine Beecher's Hartford Seminary or at Emma Willard's Troy Seminary; it was to be closely modeled on the Ipswich program with "the same slow, thorough, and patient manner of study; the same systematic and extensive course of solid branches." Two pages were devoted to reproducing the Ipswich course of study from the latest catalogue, and there was an inconspicuous reminder that just as Ipswich had been raising its standard year by year, "there will be room for a continued advancement" at Mount Holyoke. The last five pages gave detailed advice about studying for entrance examinations and admission with advanced standing and concluded by speaking again to the idealists who wanted to help raise for women "a higher standard of science and literature—of economy and refinement—of benevolence and religion."[12]

An article written in the early spring of 1836 and published in three installments in the *Boston Recorder* in May made a vigorous bid for support from the church which had for so long supported colleges for men. In the rhetorical questions she was fond of employing, Mary Lyon reiterated her point:

Who can survey the ground for the last 20 years, and count up the thousands, and tens of thousands of dollars, which have been generously raised in behalf of these institutions, and not be filled with gratitude to Him, who has opened the hearts of the benevolent in behalf of this cause. But while we thus rejoice in what had been done, we cannot but inquire with painful emotions, why has not the hand of public beneficence been equally extended towards the higher institutions for the other sex? . . . Is this the result of mature deliberation; of sound wisdom and discretion? or is it not rather the result of the remaining principles and customs of heathenism, still lingering upon our shores?

She had clear convictions about the future preeminence and academic influence of the institution not yet in being. "The design of this enterprise, is to give our country an institution for females, founded on as benevolent and liberal a plan, and as permanent in its existence and character, as those for the other sex; an institution directly suited to exert a salutary influence on our higher female seminaries, and on all our systems of female education, and as directly suited to aid in promoting the great work of renovating the world, as are our higher institutions for young men." Hitherto, appeals for Mount Holyoke had been modest and low key but "the time has now come, when we may venture to speak more freely of our great, but original designs." The declaration that this was "the first great, public, persevering effort of the kind in the United States" was qualified by an editorial footnote referring to other unnamed attempts that were abortive or started after Mount Holyoke was. But the editor raised no question about Mary Lyon's basic assumption that young women were intellectually equal to young men and just as capable of higher education. She seems not to have engaged in public discussion about the capacity of young women to learn and to think; it was too fundamental a tenet of her belief for her to waste time in arguing.[13]

Late in 1836, probably in November, she once again took pen in hand for a specialized money-raising project. She was attempting to enlist, town by town, enough benevolent—and efficient—ladies to organize local groups, each of which would accumulate a collective contribution of $50 to $60 to furnish one student room. (The results turned out to be disappointing but she could not have guessed that the country's financial difficulties, which had already dealt such blows to every kind of fund-raising effort, would intensify in 1837.) This three-page printed letter, with a blank page for personal messages, focused on the desperate need for well trained women teachers. With enough "female teachers of enlarged views, of active benevolence, and self-denying zeal," New England would experience a vast improvement "in all our domestic and social relations . . . in our political men, who are wielding the destinies of the nation . . . in the health, habits, and disinterested zeal of many of the ministers of the gospel." In the rest of the country the need was even greater. Especially in the West, money for the education of girls in convent schools was pouring in from Catholics in Europe, constituting what Mary Lyon, along with many other United States protestants, saw as a threat to "the safety of the country." After reiterating her belief in the numbers of young women anxious for a chance to equip themselves to serve their nation and their religion and lamenting the indifference of the church to its waiting daughters, she reached a rhetorical climax: "Had I a thousand lives, I could sacrifice them all in suffering and hardship for its [the new seminary's] sake. Did I possess the greatest fortune, I could easily relinquish it all, and become poor, and more than poor, if its prosperity should demand it." Finally, after the customary list of the characteristics distinguishing the Mount Holyoke Seminary, she urged the importance of its success. Once it was effectively in operation, widespread responsibility for contributing to the higher education of women would be established for all time. "It is like signing the Declaration of Independence; the battles were still to be fought, but the question of independence was then settled. . . . Let this enterprise be carried through, and sustained by the prompt liberality of the Christian community, and it will no longer be doubted, whether the great work of supplying our country with well qualified female teachers, shall be allowed a standing among the great benevolent operations of the day."[14]

By the beginning of 1837 it had become evident that even more heroic efforts to get money must be made if the Seminary was to open in the fall. In February, Mary Lyon produced still another full-dress appeal, a pamphlet entitled "General View of the Principles and Design of the Mount Holyoke Female Seminary." In twenty pages she rehearsed the salient features of her plan, the progress to date and the urgent need for teachers able to educate in the largest sense of the word. As usual, there was nothing radical or militant in the way she presented the claims of young women. She made it clear that she was only asking to prepare them for jobs that young men would not accept and that she considered it "Providence" that had shut off women from business careers which were "lucrative and at the same time honorable." It was not even her intention to train young women who would devote their entire lives to the profession; what she wanted was to enable them to make real contributions to society in the years intervening between education and marriage.

In this version she wound up with rhetorical pleas for further contributions from seven different groups of prospective donors: men of moderate means, the wealthy, old men, young men, ministers, women, and "the intelligent of all classes." Her appeal to the ministers was characteristic. After reminding them that they had enjoyed large-scale public benefactions for their own education, she praised their generosity to colleges and scholarships for men and then expressed special gratitude to those who had also concerned themselves about young women. "They have given of their time, and of their influence, and they have contributed of their substance, notwithstanding the pecuniary trials of the last year." Among all groups of people it was the men and women of vision, concerned with the future, of whom she was asking help:

The object of this institution penetrates too far into futurity, and takes in too broad a view, to discover its claims to the passing multitude. We appeal in its behalf to wise men, who can judge what we say. We appeal to those who can venture as pioneers in

*the great work of renovating a world. Others may stand waiting
for the great multitude to go forward, but then is the time when
these men feel themselves called upon to make their greatest
efforts, and to do their noblest deeds of benevolence. Thus we
hope it will be in behalf of this institution.*[15]

A "Prospectus" or catalogue for students hoping to attend the
first year was dated South Hadley, May 1. Issued at a very difficult time, it bore marks of haste. The date of opening, when it
was finally fixed, was to be supplied by "public notice." (It was
August before ads could be placed in the *New York Observer*,
Boston Recorder, and *Hampshire Gazette* to announce that the
opening date was November 8.) The three-year course of study
was simply a reprint of the curriculum in the most recent Ipswich
catalogue; the possibility was mentioned of extra branches, specifically Latin. To be admitted to the junior, i.e. beginning, class,
students would have to pass examinations after arrival in grammar,
geography, United States history, Watts on the Mind, Colburn's
mental arithmetic, Adams's written arithmetic. For the first time
Mary Lyon specified the minimum entrance age, 16. Previously she
had spoken only of "mature" or "adult" young ladies; had she
been perturbed by the trustee appeal in 1835 which said "open
to all whose age exceeds 14 or 15"? With this, as with other
requirements, a few exceptions might be made. But, without
exception, everyone should come for the opening day and bring
with her a Bible, a dictionary and an atlas.

There had been nothing hasty about setting the fees; students
were expected to pay only the actual operating costs. Since
precise amounts could be ascertained only through experience, the
rate specified, $64 a year ($52 for board and $12 for tuition),
was to be considered tentative. After the first quarter, which
would cost $16, charges might go up or down slightly. It turned
out that Mary Lyon's calculations had been phenomenally close;
in 1838-39 the fees were lowered to $60 a year and stayed there
for fifteen years.

No matter how laborious the process of composition, finding
the best words to convey the essence of her proposal was not
nearly as difficult as finding the right men to lead the fight for

public acceptance and financial support. The unsuccessful struggle for the New England Seminary for Teachers had convinced Mary Lyon, as she had written Zilpah Grant, that "the whole business must, in name, devolve on benevolent gentlemen, and not on yourself or on myself." She had already encountered plenty of the fear of "female greatness." At the same time, she also knew by experience that benevolent gentlemen who would enlist in a controversial cause were not necessarily ready to sustain extraordinary efforts in its behalf when the odds against it became too great.[16]

Nevertheless, men of remarkable energy and dedication did rally to her support, and when one dropped out, vexed or exhausted, another turned up to take his place. On September 6, 1834, seven of the dozen "gentlemen of known benevolence and candor" gathered in an Ipswich Seminary parlor were constituted a committee "to devise ways and means for founding a permanent female seminary." Three years later Mount Holyoke opened under the guidance of ten trustees; only two had been present at the original meeting. Of the 18 men who served on the committee or the board during some part of the three years of intense struggle, ten were ministers; the laymen included a lawyer, a teacher, a merchant, a manufacturer, a farmer. What they had in common seemed to be a penchant for good works and genuine admiration for Mary Lyon. In any age the public-spirited citizen who gets things done is apt to have convictions about which are the best policies and procedures; these nineteenth-century New England puritans were strong individualists.[17]

Four of the original committee of seven had been loyal supporters of the ill-starred effort to achieve permanence for Ipswich Seminary. George Heard, Ipswich mill owner, distiller, and banker, was a Harvard graduate who was actively concerned about education and must have had a remarkably equable disposition. He had been a leader in planning for an academy in Ipswich and erecting the building in 1826, and was a trustee for the first two years of Zilpah Grant's principalship. He served as treasurer of the Mount Holyoke committee from its inception until February 1836, when the new institution received its state charter and the corporate responsibility was officially assumed by five trustees. At what must have been a stormy three-day meeting the preceding October, Mr. Heard had helped to smooth the shift from committee to board of trustees and the consequent withdrawal of three of the "eastern" members; earlier he had involved himself disinterestedly in the struggle over choosing a location. Probably his major contribution was his unflagging interest in Mary Lyon's plans in the months before the committee was formed. "With Mr. Heard she had held more conference than with any other man," according to Mrs. Cowles. "Evening after evening, while she was connected with the Ipswich school, she had spent at his house, conversing with him on her favorite subject." After his official withdrawal, Mary Lyon still depended upon him for help in fund-raising; she always spoke of him with special affection and gratitude. It was a measure of Mr. Heard's quality that he managed to remain a strong supporter of both Zilpah Grant and Mary Lyon; he acted as treasurer for the revolving loan fund for intending teachers that Miss Grant solicited for her students in 1835.[18]

The dynamo of the original committee was a 65-year-old minister who had been pastor of the Shelburne Congregational Church for thirty-five years. The Rev. Theophilus Packard already had to his credit a major role in the founding of Amherst College in 1821. At his home six years earlier, in 1815, Franklin County ministers had proclaimed the need for a college in the area and declared the town of Amherst the best location. Dr. Packard, a Dartmouth graduate, was a trustee of Williams from 1810 to 1825—and subsequently an overseer or trustee of Amherst from 1821 to 1854. As a Williams trustee, he was a strong supporter of President Moore, who resigned at Williams in order to head the new institution and took with him fifteen students, who constituted one third of the enrollment at Amherst during its first year. Dr. Packard had no qualms about his stand; indeed, he urged the rest of the Williams faculty and students to follow suit because he was convinced that no college could survive in such an inaccessible spot as Williamstown.[19]

He was an old friend and admirer of Mary Lyon. At least four of his daughters had attended her Buckland schools and he had been in the forefront of those who had tried to persuade her not to leave for year-round service at Ipswich Seminary, and then attempted to get Zilpah Grant to move her whole operation to the Connecticut Valley. At the time Mary made her decision to leave, Dr. Packard advised her to make no promises about returning but to fix upon "one to two confidential friends" who, if she did want to return, might expedite arrangements. Naturally she sent a copy of her first printed appeal promptly to Dr. Packard, with a request for comments. Writing back toward the end of March 1834, he approved cautiously; "the wings of your imagination," he thought, might need just a bit of clipping. But within a few weeks he had flung himself into the enterprise with prodigious energy.[20]

By mid-May he had won the endorsement of the Franklin and Hampshire County Association of Ministers, consulted with some friends in Amherst and Conway, and written to others. In early July he was reporting a setback or two: two centers of Congregational power in Massachusetts, the Pastoral Association and the General Association, by parliamentary maneuvers had defeated his attempt to gain their public approval. He had thereupon canvassed all the regional associations separately, though he knew their endorsements would be slow to come in. He had already visited eight communities in the Connecticut River area, consulting and passing out circulars; in Belchertown an unfinished school building might be available. But nowhere had he found a disposition to give enough money to support the new seminary or "the *very right* sort of persons for trustees." He urged Mary Lyon to "relax from school" and come up to consult with him on the next steps. Whether she got to Shelburne is unknown, but unmistakably Dr. Packard got to Ipswich on Wednesday evening for the first committee meeting scheduled for Saturday, September 6, and the two of them spent the intervening days talking over problems and prospects. It was Dr. Packard who was chosen moderator. In two days at Andover he solicited many of the 15 individual endorsements which reinforced the committee names and resolutions on the original 1834 circular; he also solicited funds.[21]

Still another of his major services in the fall of 1834 was enlisting the interest of the Rev. Roswell Hawks, minister in

Cummington. After considerable talk with Mary Lyon, Mr. Hawks obtained a leave of absence from his church and undertook what he supposed to be a temporary job as solicitor of funds for the proposed seminary. It turned out to be his life-long occupation. He continued as full-time fund-raiser not only in the painfully difficult period before the seminary opened but also for the next twenty years.[22]

Even Mary Lyon was awed by Dr. Packard's zeal and activity. She wrote Zilpah Grant in December 1834, "Dr. Packard's whole soul is enlisted. It is his first and great object, occupying his time by day, and many of his thoughts by night. I sometimes think that in interest he will even go beyond myself." But major collisions were just ahead. He had been won over to the proprietary scholarship scheme which persuaded so many colleges for men to mortgage the future for immediate gain. Contributors of sufficient sums were entitled thereafter to name students to be admitted at reduced tuition or none at all. Dr. Packard's version was cautious: $250 scholarships owned in full, half or quarter shares, would entitle owners to send pupils at $15 per year less than the set fees. Both Mary Lyon and Mr. Hawks were strongly opposed, and at the three-day meeting of the committee in Ipswich, December 3 to 5, the proposal was voted down. This vote did not convince Dr. Packard; on December 25 he wrote down his scheme in detail and sent it, with an urgent request for immediate written comment, to some of the best known members of the American Board of Commissioners of Foreign Missions. They may have had reservations; no further references to the plan have come to light.[23]

Another disagreement erupted at the December meeting in Ipswich over the choice of a location. Could the pledges from South Deerfield, the only place recommended by Dr. Packard's "western subcommittee," be counted on? And was it the best possible site? Mary Lyon, for one, thought not—and, even though she was never physically present at any trustee meeting, her ideas seemed to figure in the discussion. In this instance she doubted the validity of a local contribution list padded with the names of groups and individuals from other towns. Where there was no immediate commercial advantage, she felt that donors would

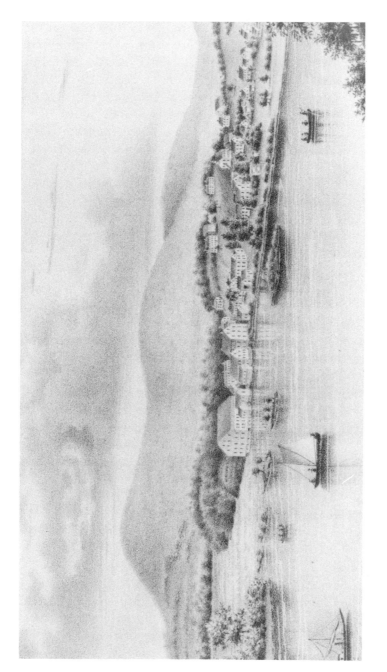

5. South Hadley Falls, the business center served by the canal, was three and a half miles from the site of Mount Holyoke Seminary. The drawing was made by Orra White Hitchcock, wife of Professor Hitchcock. Amherst College Library; by permission of the Trustees of Amherst College.

contribute—or fail to complete their pledges—no matter what site was chosen. After a day's debate the committee was on the verge of voting for South Deerfield, but the next morning they "received, read and discussed communications from the Town of Sunderland, from Miss Mary Lyon and from Professor Hitchcock" and promptly voted to reconsider. At a follow-up meeting on January 8, 1835, in Worcester, representatives from South Deerfield, Sunderland, and South Hadley were heard. South Hadley was chosen on condition that the amount pledged to the seminary should be raised from $5,000 to $8,000 within 15 days; Dr. Packard and Mr. Hawks were delegated to report the decision to South Hadley and help to raise subscriptions. After an unpromising start, pressure was applied by Mr. Hawks, the $8,000 total was reached, and the question settled for good before the end of January.[24]

These two struggles obviously dampened Dr. Packard's enthusiasm. He remained a member of the committee until it was officially superseded by the naming of five trustees in the charter application. He withdrew—along with General Asa Howland of Conway, whom he had probably recruited—along with all the "eastern" members except David Choate; their places were filled by supporters living nearer the seminary site: Rev. William Tyler and William Bowdoin of South Hadley Canal; Rev. John Todd and Rev. Joseph Penney of Northampton; and Rev. Joseph Condit, newly installed pastor of the South Hadley church. Dr. Packard faithfully attended and presided at committee meetings through 1835; what else he was doing is nowhere hinted at except for one cryptic remark in an urgent plea by Mr. Todd for a special meeting in April: "I will just whisper to you, that this meeting will shew us what course Dr. P. and Gen. H. have determined to take." The only illumination from the minutes discreetly kept by the Rev. Joseph Felt is that the "western subcommittee" at their own request were released from all executive responsibility and a new executive committee named on April 15. It can have been no surprise to Mary Lyon when he bowed out completely in October; she no doubt took his leaving with good grace. As Mrs. Cowles observed, "there were many persons, first and last, who came into her plans for a time, but, unable to see things just as she did, silently withdrew. She saw the hand of the Lord as clearly in their withdrawal as in their enlistment."[25]

Some of the early trustees dropped out because they were leaving the area for new posts; it was a period of great mobility among ministers. The Rev. Joseph Penney, a graduate of Trinity College, Dublin, had made a name for himself among New York State Congregationalists before he took over Jonathan Edwards's church in Northampton in 1832. He was named to the Mount Holyoke committee on April 15, 1835, and assigned to a subcommittee, along with Mr. Todd and Mr. Hawks, to compose and sign a new appeal for funds, the "Address to the Christian Public," issued June 15. In late September he spent a day and a half going over immediate problems and prospects with Mr. Tyler and Miss Lyon, encouraging her at a particularly discouraging time. But he did not attend the crucial meeting of the committee on October 7, 8, 9 in South Hadley, and by mid-November Mary Lyon knew that he was leaving Northampton for good, having accepted the presidency of Hamilton College.[26]

The Rev. John Todd, pastor of a new Congregational church in Northampton had impeccable orthodox credentials; he had graduated from Yale and Andover Theological Seminary and had a record of early success as a preacher and writer. He had been one of very few to attend the meeting at Professor Hitchcock's house in April 1833, called in the hope of a last-minute rescue of the New England Seminary for Teachers. He assumed considerable responsibility for the new project as soon as he was named to the committee on January 8, 1835. In April he was put on the executive committee as well as the subcommittee to prepare an appeal for funds; in October he was one of the five to be named trustees on the charter application; in March 1836 he was elected president of the board. His resignation on July 21, 1836, because he had been called to the First Congregational Church in Philadelphia must have been a blow to his fellow board members; it seemed appropriate to have him return to deliver the address at the laying of the cornerstone in October. It was Mr. Todd who suggested naming the new school Mount Holyoke after the mountain of that name in South Hadley. Professor Hitchcock had been promulgating his choice of name, "Pangynaskean,"

6. The Reverend John Todd was named to the sponsoring committee in 1835 and, when the charter was granted in 1836, was elected first president of the board of trustees. Silhouette by Augustin Edouart. Mount Holyoke College Library Archives.

compounded from Greek as the equivalent for "whole-woman-making"; his articles had occasioned some ridicule both of the name and the project. The committee vote on April 15, 1835, must have been nearly unanimous to call the new institution Mount Holyoke Female Seminary.[27]

Early in 1836 Mary Lyon made the acquaintance of three men who would provide major support in the struggles immediately ahead and also help with the day-to-day operations of the Seminary throughout her lifetime and afterward. Joseph Avery was an able, modest, and generous Conway farmer. He "probably, during the past twenty years, has given more to benevolent objects, in proportion to his property and family, than any other man in New England," Mary Lyon wrote exuberantly to Eunice Caldwell after calling upon his family in January. On April 13 he was named a trustee. Andrew Porter, one of the proprietors of a flourishing cotton mill in Monson, was suggested as a likely prospect for special responsibility by Mr. Tyler, who had the previous year enlisted the considerable services of William Bowdoin, lawyer and leading citizen of South Hadley Falls. The story was often told to Seminary students of how Miss Lyon, Mr. Tyler, and Mr. Hawks arrived at the Porter home in Monson during an April snowstorm only to find that Mr. Porter would not be back from Boston until late that evening, which was a Saturday. Mr. Tyler and Mr. Hawks had to leave for Sabbath duties, but Mary Lyon, cordially welcomed by Mrs. Porter once she had introduced herself and explained her errand, stayed with the Porters through Monday. Although in her room she prayed earnestly that Deacon Porter would accept, Miss Lyon did not all day Sunday once mention to him the business that had brought about this unexpected visit; she did not want to break the Sabbath or, probably, to usurp the prerogatives of the gentlemen who would be returning the next day to present the proposal officially. The outcome was altogether satisfactory. Deacon Porter was elected a trustee at once, at an adjourned meeting April 19. As Mary Lyon wrote immediately afterward, "He has had more experience in superintending workmen and in putting up buildings than any one on our board. Benevolent, disinterested, and of sound judgment, he is also one of the first of accountants." Within a few months—after some initial hesitation, partly because of his health, about taking on so much responsibility—he did commit himself to almost full-time supervision of building operations. According to Mrs. Stow, "Through that season he spent several days each week at South Hadley. The next year, from March to November, nearly every Monday he drove there, twenty-one miles, returning home Saturday. During all this time he left his own extensive business in other hands, provided his own conveyance, entertained himself and horse, and made no charge whatever."[28]

Daniel Safford was a Boston blacksmith, well known for the quality of his craftsmanship; his shop produced the iron fence around the Boston Common and the first furnace installed in the Capitol building in Washington. He also had a name for his acts of benevolence. When in April 1836 Mary Lyon wrote asking if she could call, both he and his wife, who had read Professor Hitchcock's Pangynaskean articles, were already interested in advancing education for women and had heard good things of Miss Lyon. From the moment she crossed their threshold, she and the Saffords were in rapport. He contributed $500 right away and the following March organized the Boston fund-raising meeting that she and Mr. Hawks had not dared attempt; at his death in 1856 Deacon Safford was the largest donor of money to the Seminary and had rendered a whole range of other services like purchasing and shipping supplies. He was elected a trustee in April 1837.

These three men, who gave substantive help when it was desperately needed, differed from one another, but they had certain experiences in common. All of them were, like Mary Lyon, self-educated and self-made. They had succeeded against odds by tremendous personal efforts begun early in life, and all of them could call upon a variety of practical skills. All laymen, they were devout churchgoers; as deacons they carried parish responsibilities as well as pursuing charitable projects of their own. Apparently they all liked Mary Lyon on sight; they admired her directness and enthusiasm, respected her aims, and could sympathize with methods that were often unorthodox. Not least important, they all had wives who became advocates of the Mount Holyoke enterprise and from the first were warmly disposed toward its progenitor. After her first call, Mary Lyon always stayed with the Saffords whenever she went to Boston, and the Porter house in Monson became her refuge whenever she needed to get away from the Seminary for a few days of rest.

It would be misleading to imply that the good deacons understood Mary Lyon better or counted for more in her own litany of patron saints than any of her earlier supporters. First among equals on the trustee roll of honor might rather be Professor Edward Hitchcock of Amherst College. Since the summer of 1823 when she had boarded and studied with the Hitchcocks and conducted a school in Conway, he had known her as a good teacher and an exceptionally bright and responsive pupil. In the struggle over the New England Seminary for Teachers, he had been her chief backer in the Connecticut Valley. It was not surprising that he should be on the original committee of seven to gather at Ipswich on September 6, 1834, or that Mary Lyon should have already asked Mrs. Hitchcock if she could again find in their house a temporary home. In a letter written early in July, Mary explained at length why she was leaving Ipswich and then made her request directly.

7a. Deacon and Mrs. Safford. Trustee from 1837 until his death in 1856, Mr. Safford, a manufacturer of ironware, was the largest donor to the Seminary in Miss Lyon's lifetime. Mrs. Safford encouraged her husband's benevolence and welcomed Miss Lyon on her business trips to Boston. Mount Holyoke College Art Museum.

7b. Deacon and Mrs. Porter. Another dedicated lifetime trustee, Mr. Porter absented himself for several months from his textile mill in order to superintend the construction of the Seminary building. The Porter home in Monson was a vacation refuge for Mary Lyon and also for a number of the young teachers. Mount Holyoke College Library Archives.

What I shall do in future I know not. It is safe & delightful to commit everything to God. The first six months after closing my labors here, I wish to spend as a boarder in the family of some friend, where I can quietly & without interruption spend my time in reading, studying & accomplishing various kinds of business, which I have on hand. Should no field be open for my direct labors for two or three years, I should have an abundance of business but I make no definite calculation for more than six months. In looking over my circle of friends, my mind for a few weeks has often dwelt on you & your family; & I have come to the conclusion to ask you two questions, begging of you frankly to answer in the negative, if you cannot reply in the affirmative. Have you a chamber in your house that you could spare for my use next winter? If so, would it be convenient for you to add myself to your family? If so, it will give me great pleasure to spend the next winter with you.

After tearing my heart away from this dear & delightful sphere of labors, which for so many years has been my home—the home where all my desires have centered, and all my greatest efforts have found an adequate object, it would be a great gratification, & a soothing comfort to find a quiet & sweet abode with those whom I have long regarded as dear friends. As I shall be so much of a wanderer, for sometime to come, access to a good library, wherever I may be, will be an important consideration. I should be glad too to spend the winter in a place, which is somewhat accessible, as I shall be more in the way occasionally of meeting one, may [sic] give advice with regard to the object in which I am so much interested. These & other reasons you will at once see, renders your house a very desirable home for me next winter, but I would by no means have you incommode yourself & yours to accommodate me.[29]

The Hitchcock hospitality was comprehensive. Mary Lyon occupied a room for much of the next two winters. In 1834-35 she brought with her a roommate, Eunice Caldwell, who had succeeded Zilpah Grant as Mary's confidante and companion. Eunice, then 23, was preparing to take charge of Wheaton Seminary when the building was ready in the spring and then, when

8. Professor Edward Hitchcock, a longtime friend of Mary Lyon, supported her plans from the first. He was a trustee from 1836 until his death in 1864. Amherst College Library; by permission of the Trustees of Amherst College.

Mary's plans came to fruition, to become her associate principal. At meals the young women enjoyed the company of the Hitchcocks and their four children and also of their fellow-boarders, the Amherst College tutors, i.e. instructors, three or four able young graduates with lively minds. Professor Hitchcock enabled Mary Lyon to tap other Amherst resources. Both winters she attended college lectures, notably his on geology. Later, after the Seminary was open, he encouraged academic and social interchange between Amherst and Mount Holyoke. In the fall of 1836, when financial problems were mounting everywhere, the Rev. Melancthon Wheeler, minister in Conway, raised $1200 for the Seminary in his own territory. He was released from his parish duties for a few weeks of intensive fund-raising in eastern Massachusetts because the Amherst faculty offered to fill his pulpit, 20 miles up in the hills, while he was gone.[30]

Of all the early trustees, Professor Hitchcock was the most ready to take up his pen in support of the enterprise and the most able to command public attention. In February and March

1835 the *Boston Recorder* carried a three-part article of nearly 5,000 words, detailing the history, principles, prospects, and need for contributions of the Pangynaskean Seminary. These three installments, unsigned, and a letter of reply in the April 1835 issue of *The Religious Magazine*, also using the name Pangynaskean, seem to have received more notice than any other early efforts at publicity. The vigor with which he defended Mary Lyon and her principles is particularly striking in some unpublished letters, notably a rejection of the 1837 attack of *The Religious Magazine* and a challenge to trustee policies two years after Mary Lyon's death. Of course his role in preparing her biography while documentary material abounded was invaluable.[31]

Collectively, the first trustees made a major contribution to the founding of Mount Holyoke; it is impossible to imagine how Mary Lyon could have succeeded without them. But no matter how much time, skill, and money they gave, they themselves felt that Mount Holyoke Female Seminary was essentially the creation of one woman. David Choate of Essex, who was not only one of the original committee of seven but also one of the five incorporators and a board member until 1843, sent to the twenty-fifth anniversary celebration his recollection of how it really began.

I shall never forget . . . how gently we tried to rock its cradle, or how carefully we endeavored, at Miss Lyon's bidding, to carry it in our arms! You, who know the history from the beginning hardly need to be reminded that it was Packard and Hawks and Howland, from the Connecticut Valley, and Dana and Felt and Heard and my humble self, from the neighborhood of the salt sea, that, in the early autumn of 1834, I should say, met at a private parlor in Ipswich and inspected a few small seeds which Miss Lyon was wishing to put into the ground somewhere, at some time, allowing us to have something to say as to the place and time and so forth, yet, not wholly surrendering anything entirely up to any; and still allowing us the innocent fancy of thinking ourselves, for the time being, co-workers with her.[32]

There is no doubt that Mary Lyon concerned herself with trustee undertakings. Although she seems never to have attended a formal trustee meeting, she customarily stationed herself in the house where one was being held, to be available for instant consultation. Increasingly she felt free to offer suggestions when she thought they were needed; sometimes she provided secretarial assistance, which must have been welcome to men who wrote all their own letters and made their own travel arrangements. Before the Worcester meeting on January 8, 1835—called because of the disagreement over the location—she wrote a rather hesitant letter to the secretary, Mr. Felt, suggesting that the Temperance House might be a more agreeable meeting place than the stage house, that a conference room might need to be engaged in advance, that he might want to take into account the time the morning stages arrived from Amherst and Boston when he set the meeting hour. In any case, she wanted to know the hour, on the chance that she might go too (she did) and she would be glad to pass along the information to the western contingent in his name, if he would write her by the first mail.[33]

There was nothing diffident in her letter to Mr. Tyler, written just before the next meeting, held at Amherst April 15, 1835. This meeting had been called at the urging of Mr. Todd and others, understandably alarmed by committee disaffection, lack of public response, and generally bleak prospects. "We have worked hard in this town [Northampton] for the past week," Mr. Todd wrote Mr. Felt, "but language is a poor medium thro' which to shew you its unpopularity. One thing is certain, that the whole plan of having the pupils labor must be given up, (& this cannot & ought not to be thought of) or else we must relinquish every idea that the rich will aid it in the least by sending their children; i.e. It must be an Institution for "commonfolks" or for the rich." Mary Lyon felt anxious not so much about these immediate setbacks as about the committee's failure to forge ahead with plans for building or even to prepare an agenda in advance. She enclosed two pages of questions, which she obviously wanted every member to have thought through before the meeting began.

Amherst April 12, 1835

Rev. Mr. Tyler,

I have had many thoughts lately, & many queries about our

new enterprize. I send you a few of these queries on the preceding page. Though I am very fearful of a long delay about commencing the buildings, I have not the ability of judging about the expediency of commencing them this season, so that I dare form an opinion. If the gentlemen of the Committee take time to consider the subject carefully, I shall be perfectly satisfied with their decision, whatever it may be. My only anxiety is, that this great question may receive so much time & thought, as to be carefully examined, & deliberately decided. Relative to the two last meetings, the fact seems to be, that the gentlemen were so oppressed, & troubled with the one question of location, that they had no time nor energies left to reach out & bring up for consideration other great questions relating to the enterprize.

If the business of raising funds has been somewhat retarded, or any other business, in consequence of the peculiar situation of the committee, there has been no fault anywhere. But the next meeting will be different and the work is now to be begun as it were. While I have the utmost confidence in the ability, & candid decisions of the committee, I must confess that I feel a degree of painful solicitude lest the gentlemen will some of them come together with so little reflection on the business which should be accomplished, & in so much haste to get through & return home to other important concerns, that some urgent business will be left unexamined, or that some important questions will be hastily decided.

Respectfully yours,
Mary Lyon

I shall also take the liberty to write Mr. Todd a few lines on this subject.[34]

A second agent to augment Mr. Hawks's efforts at money-raising was engaged after the October 1835 committee meeting—namely, the Rev. Barbour of Philadelphia. He arrived in mid-November with his family; in addition to his salary of $600 for the year, he had been given $100 for moving expenses. Not finding accommodations to his liking in South Hadley, he rented a house in Northampton. Mr. Hawks, strongly dismayed, drove over at once to Amherst to see Miss Lyon; she, too, thought this action "very undesirable." At dawn the next day Mr. Hawks returned to South

Hadley; Miss Lyon followed by stage after attending Professor Hitchcock's geology lecture, and stayed for five days, until after a hastily called meeting of the executive committee. Whether the persuasion came from this meeting or from the "considerable conversation" beforehand, in which she participated, Mr. Barbour finally gave in. He "engaged part of a house in South Hadley" for the winter, and Mary Lyon, "greatly rejoiced," returned to Amherst.[35]

The choice of a building site in the summer of 1836 occasioned another sustained difference of opinion. Mary Lyon's primary concern about this "dark cloud" was not over the site finally picked, at the May 19th trustee meeting, although she was not particularly enthusiastic about it. What she dreaded was still more delay and the possibility of further erosion of trustee support. After much discussion with Mr. Tyler and Mr. Bowdoin, both members of the building committee and both opposed to the majority choice, one day in early July she went out with the gentlemen to measure the land and take the elevation all over again. The discussion went on "abundantly" until late in the month, when a second meeting of the full board confirmed the original choice. The proponents of a higher elevation and a better view silently swallowed their disappointment, and ground was finally broken in August. "After the erection of the edifice," according to Mrs. Cowles, "Miss Lyon was accustomed to preclude all criticisms on the selection, by taking her visitors to the upper story, and directing their attention to the magnificent views from the southern and western windows."[36]

Mary Lyon's conception of her responsibility for backstopping trustee efforts extended to finding ready money. If, out of her teacher's salary, which was always used partly for gifts to family and church, she had saved—and Squire White had managed to invest profitably—just enough to sustain herself for three years without any regular source of income, her achievement would have been commendable. How she accumulated an additional $1200 to $1400, which she contributed to the Seminary between 1834 and 1838, it seems impossible to imagine. The surviving fragments of correspondence with Mr. White, mainly through Hannah, who must also have spent considerable time on Mary's affairs, suggest that he had made for her a number of short-term loans to farmers and small businessmen. The Whites seem to have had unending patience as well as financial acumen, and Mary apparently had command of the intricacies of her account and was ready both to lend and to borrow. Even so, how did she build up so large a sum? And what instinct told her to hold on to a considerable part until 1836 and 1837, when the financial difficulties of the whole country multiplied those of the struggling Seminary?[37]

The deft and inconspicuous way in which Mary Lyon supplied funds is suggested in a letter to Zilpah Grant written in November 1836 when she was still collecting what Zilpah owed her.

Granby, November 16, 1836

My dear Miss Grant,

I should be exceedingly glad of that $80, which is my due, if you can conveniently let me have it. I will just tell you the case. The building committee had a meeting a few days since to look over their funds, which are immediately available. They have a large amount of money to make out this month, & it is besides of the utmost importance that they purchase the lumber immediately. I urged this very much. They are to have a meeting again a week from Monday. The truth is it is very slow getting the money here which is now due, & I have some fear, that Dea. Porter, who says he can generally find money to hire but that he cannot now, & who by the way is the only man who can bear any part of this burden in this part of the business, that will lift a little finger, I fear that when Dea. Porter finds how things stand & how many of the subscriptions have not come in, that he will be discouraged, & feel that his associates put all on him. Mr. Hawks would be glad to borrow some to advance in behalf of the subscribers on money now due. I am going to undertake to raise some & lend to him. This is the use I want to make of the $80. Mr. Hawks & myself will be in quite another direction before the time of the meeting. I have therefore committed the acct to Mr. Tyler, who is a very safe confidential man. If you can conveniently send it, you may just send a check to Rev. William Tyler, South Hadley Canal, & just state that it is sent by my request & he will understand.

I want to give you a history of what I am trying to do. I am here & under the wing of a very efficient lady am looking up & collecting some subscriptions which have been due here so long, that they are almost considered as outlawed. I shall write again soon & tell you of some of the ludicrous things which I am trying to do. You may write, & direct to Northampton till you hear from me again.

Affectionately yours,
Mary Lyon

Your letter will of course, as trust reach Mr. next week so that he will have it before the meeting. You must send it from Ipswich as early as Thurs. It would be better to have it sent earlier so that Mr. Tyler would have time to send it & get the money.

Can you say to Miss Clarissa Eastman that I am staying with her aunt Harvey Eastman a few days, & that she sends her love. That young lady has been at Westfield, but was not satisfied with the school & left for Ipswich. Many things were said to her in Westfield to discourage her going. I hope & trust that she will now be satisfied.[38]

Mary Lyon's intervention in trustee affairs came to be sought rather than resisted. Mrs. Porter, who handled much of her husband's correspondence about the Seminary, wrote in mid-May 1837 of the discouragement of the building committee, who feared that they could not possibly raise the necessary $10,000 before October first. She urged Mary to keep to her intention of being in South Hadley the next week: "Now if you can come, it may raise their drooping spirits."[39]

Deacon Porter was probably also pleased by her active presence at the construction site whenever she was in South Hadley. The Rev. Theron Baldwin, one of the dedicated "Illinois Band" from Yale who spent most of his life spreading higher education westward, was the first principal of Monticello Seminary in Illinois, which opened its doors to young women in the spring of 1838. Before making his final plans in the summer of 1837 he toured eastern colleges and seminaries. In early September he made a three-day stop at South Hadley, where he was happy to find himself in substantial accord with Miss Lyon. Afterward he recalled how he had "spent an entire day on a pile of bricks with

Miss Lyon discussing the whole subject of education of girls, while she kept count of the cartloads of brick that were delivered."[40]

The relation between Mary Lyon and the trustees was succinctly characterized by Mrs. Cowles, who had a very close view of the events of 1834 through 1837. Mary was,

as she very well knew, set in her opinions; but she was set only when sure she was right. She understood the subject better than any gentleman, because she had studied it a hundred times as much. When she differed from any of her coadjutors, the result generally proved that she was in the right. The trustees came, as one of them said, to be afraid to oppose her plans, because they had so much proof that the Lord was with her, and that what she proposed to do he had purposed to prosper.[41]

But there was a striking exception. On one issue of major importance, Mary Lyon did give in. Even though the general financial situation worsened in 1836 and 1837, the critical year for the survival of her undertaking seems to have been 1835. Her heartening success in raising $1,000 in contingent funds from women in the fall of 1834 was followed by a satisfactory conclusion to the struggle over location when the citizens of South Hadley in January 1835 raised their pledges to $8,000. But after that the bottom dropped out of everything. The committee staged a good-sized rally in Northampton on February 18 with vigorous speeches and resolutions, but getting subscriptions, let alone cash, was another matter. It was going to take, as Mr. Todd said, "an immense amount of hand lifting & heartsinking." That the committee was fighting not just apathy but opposition became increasingly apparent as the weeks and months went by. Effort to get approval from the state association of ministers at their annual meeting in June 1835 was carefully planned. But the best that skillful maneuvering could achieve was three watered-down resolutions. One acknowledged that women should have a good Christian education, a second admitted that insufficient efforts had been made thus far, and a third approved Mount Holyoke Female Seminary—"and any other institution which designs to effect a similar object."[42]

When Mary wrote to her mother and sister late in July, she made mention—very unusual for her—of "trial and discouragement," though only as the prelude to blessing at the hand of the Lord. In a letter to Zilpah, written at the same time, her phrasing was less optimistic: "We have every reason to believe, that the more we seek to draw the public to aid us in doing good, the more perplexing will be our cares and labors." The following week she left the Connecticut Valley to take over Ipswich Seminary for the last six weeks of the summer term, so that Zilpah could take another trip. By her absence she missed the chance to encounter Harriet Martineau, whose visit to Northampton and environs included a journey to the top of Mount Holyoke and also attendance at Professor Hitchcock's geology lecture August 8. It seems unlikely, however, that Mary Lyon would have been invited to social gatherings arranged for this urbane and well-connected traveler or that she would on her own have sought out so staunch a Unitarian, even to talk about education for women.[43]

What happened—or failed to happen—to members of the committee during the summer and early fall is totally unrecorded. Somehow or other before October 1 several of them must have agreed that Mary Lyon's name alone was not sufficient to launch the new Seminary. Their solution was to invite Zilpah Grant to be co-head. Did they feel that, admirable as Mary was, she could never transcend her background—that this unpretentious but persistent countrywoman could not persuade the people with money to support so ambitious and unconventional a project? Zilpah, whose striking presence and personal charm were well known to most of the committee, disapproved of some of Mary's proposals, particularly the one requiring domestic work of every student; if Zilpah shared in the planning and direction, committee members could well have felt that the whole enterprise would inevitably be more acceptable to the solid citizens of New England.

What Mary Lyon felt has to be inferred from ambiguous evidence. Mrs. Cowles, who was scrupulously truthful but reticent about friction, recorded this development in two sentences. "The general committee, at their meeting, October 7, invited Miss

Grant to unite with Miss Lyon in taking charge of the contemplated seminary. Miss Lyon cordially seconded this invitation." Three letters of Mary Lyon which touch on the invitation have survived. On October 1 Mary was for the second time urgently requesting Zilpah to come to South Hadley the next week at the time of the meeting; she was expected at Mr. Condit's. On October 17, ten days after the committee action, while Zilpah was apparently still in the Connecticut Valley, Mary wrote a very urgent note to Mr. Tyler as a member of the executive committee, begging him to exert all his influence to get Miss Grant's assent. The body of the note follows.

You have doubtless received a letter from Mr. Todd, requesting yourself & Mr. Bowdoin to meet a few gentlemen here on Monday morning at 9 oclock. I hope you will both come, & use all your influence to effect the object under consideration. It does appear to me to be an object of immense importance not only to our seminary, but to the great cause of education. If we should now, while Miss Grant is here fail, of making our impression sufficiently strong to incline her to the plan, we can never do anything hereafter. One or two steps farther in the progress of affairs at Ipswich would place her labors entirely beyond our reach. These steps must be taken immediately unless Miss Grant decides to engage in this enterprize. I hope you will come early on Monday.
Excuse my extreme haste.[44]

In another ten days Mary wrote to Zilpah from Norton, where she was staying at Wheaton with Eunice Caldwell. Zilpah, back in Ipswich, obviously had not committed herself either way. Mary's letter conveyed deep anxiety for the right decision in the sight of God, and deep uncertainty as to what that was. "I dare not pray for anything in particular," she wrote. But her concluding paragraph suggests that the reasoning that had made her accept and support the attempt to include Miss Grant was no longer so persuasive. "My first desires for the proposed change, were too much for the sake of receiving for us, the approbation of the wise & good on earth," she said flatly.

Norton, Tues. A.M. Oct. 27, [1835]

My dear Miss Grant,

It has occurred to me, that you might have young ladies come to Ipswich without application whom you cannot receive, & whom you would be glad to send directly here, provided you knew that there were any vacancies here. Miss Caldwell has had several failures within the last week, so that there are now three vacancies in the boarding houses, that it is desirable to fill. Besides she may yet have other failures as several have not yet arrived whom she expects.

Miss Reed & Miss Hunt arrived last evening. I think it will be a very good place for Miss Hunt here this winter. The scholars are older than they were in the summer.

I design to go to Ipswich on Thurs. or Friday unless I receive a letter from you leading me to alter my decision. I have thought of you very much since we separated. I greatly fear that all the trying questions which are now taxing your mental energies, besides the care of the school just now at the commencement, will be more than you can sustain. May the Lord give you strength equal to your wants, & may he give you wisdom from on high to guide your thoughts, your views of things, & your present important decisions.

When all human help & human wisdom fail, & all knowledge of future events, as connected with present causes, & present actions, seems entirely cut off, how sweet it is to go to One, who knows all from the beginning to the end—to One who can direct our very thoughts, & who can take us individually by the hand, & lead us in a plain path. Everything appears to me as dark as Egyptian darkness, only as I turn my thoughts to Him, who is the fountain of light. I dare not pray for anything in particular, only that the will of the Lord may be done—that all interested in this new institution may be so humble, & so submissive, that his will towards this enterprize may be done, as it is done towards those on whom he smiles, & not as it is done towards those whom he chastens & afflicts. My daily feeling is "Lord thou knowest—not my will O God but thine be done."

How often have I endeavored to consecrate all the part, all the interests, which God has given me in this contemplated institution, most sacredly & solemnly to his service, & how often have

I endeavored to pray, that every one, who had any thing to do in building up this institution, may never call aught his own. O that every one, who puts a finger to the work, by giving the smallest contribution of time—of money— or of influence, might feel that this is a work of solemn consecration—a work to be reviewed by the light of eternity. May the Lord so direct all, who shall bear a part in forming the character of this institution, that no considerations, shall have any influence except those, which will bear the scrutiny of eternity.

For a few weeks past, I have thought a little too much about gaining the approbation of the wise & good towards the cause pursued in the institution, compared with my desires that everything connected with the institution may receive the approbation of GOD. My first desires for the proposed change, were too much for the sake of receiving for us, the approbation of the wise & good on earth. I have feared that this might receive the chastening hand of God towards the institution, & that the means of promoting a desirable object might become the means of exactly the reverse effect. I do hope that my views are more single. Let the will of the Lord be done. And the approbation of Heaven gained, whatever we receive from the hand of man.

Truly yours,
Mary Lyon[45]

There is no surviving word from Zilpah about this episode, but it is obvious that she did not respond immediately to Mary's intensity. Mary did go to Ipswich the following Monday and spent the better part of a week there, but it was not until after the middle of November, when she was back in Amherst, that that Mr. Todd received Miss Grant's refusal. Mr. Todd, it was reported, thought the decision "doubtless for the best" and was more decided than ever to go forward. Some of the supporters of Miss Grant might have been given pause by the six weeks of suspended motion, when the situation was so precarious, while she made up her mind about an enterprise on which she had from the first been so fully informed and so often consulted.[46]

It was a trustee who ultimately provided the most convincing evidence of Mary's reservations even during the period when she had been persuaded that Zilpah's participation was the only way to keep the whole project from immediate extinction. The Rev. Joseph Felt as secretary of the committee was so discreet that in the official record there is no mention of Miss Grant or of any proposal for changes in policy or administration. Whatever happened on October 7, the minutes say only: "Discussed various questions relative to the concerns of the Seminary." But Mr. Felt kept a diary. When the biography of Mary Lyon appeared in 1851, he wrote Professor Hitchcock his general approval and, in case a second edition was planned, suggested some minor corrections. One concerned Mrs. Cowles's statement that "Miss Lyon cordially seconded this invitation." He quoted directly from his diary:

after the question about this matter came before them, at the Oct. session of 1835, I waited on Miss L. and asked how such an arrangement met her views. She opened not her mouth. Her whole appearance indicated a disinclination for such a connection. My record says substantially, "It is very evident, that Miss L. does not wish for Miss G. to be associated with her." I was aware, that there were reasons sufficient to justify her in the wish to be the principal, perfectly consistent with her long and strong friendship for Miss G. and equally consistent with their mutual esteem and affection.[47]

The committee members who had proposed making Miss Grant co-head must have questioned Mary's power to attract large contributions, but they could not have doubted her ability to collect small amounts from unexpected sources. Everybody who had any connection with the project knew how she had collected the first $1,000 from ladies, in a whirlwind of activity over less than two months. This sum, designed for the expenses of fund-raising, came first from students and teachers of Ipswich Seminary—$269 from 130 girls and 7 teachers in the summer term, and second from the women living in the town—$475 from passing acquaintances as well as those who were related to or boarded students. The rest was made up quickly from former students and other friends. Mrs. Cowles, who probably accompanied her on many of her visits, described just how Mary went from house to house, soliciting subscriptions.

The Ipswich ladies have a vivid recollection of her farewell visits that autumn. She represented her object as calling the most loudly for aid, because, though very deserving, it was the most unknown, unnoticed, and unappreciated by the benevolent community. She talked, now with the lady of the house, now with the husband. She told the husbands, in a very good-natured but earnest way, that she had come to get them to cut off one little corner of their estates, and give it to their wives to invest in the form of a seminary for young ladies. She held before them the object dear to her heart—the bringing of a liberal education within the means of the daughters of the common people, till it loomed up to them, for the time, as it did ever before her eyes. She put it to the lady whether, if she wanted a new shawl, a card-table, a new carpet, or some other article of elegance in her furniture or wardrobe, she could not contrive means to procure it. She spread out the whole subject, talking so fast that her hearers could hardly put in a word, anticipating every objection before it was uttered, and finally appealing to their individual humanity and benevolence. She uttered no falsehood; she poured out truth; she offered arguments to make out her case; and, last and best of all, she carried the will of nearly every person with whom she labored. Ladies that, in ordinary subscriptions to benevolent objects, did well to put down their fifty cents, gave her five or ten dollars of hard-earned money, collected by the slow gains of patient industry, and gave it of their own free will, yea, gave it as a privilege from which they would not have been willing to be debarred.[48]

In June 1835 when the best efforts of the gentlemen seemed to be producing nothing at all, the committee voted to invite the ladies of the Connecticut Valley to contribute another thousand. No further reference seems to have been made to this proposal of last resort, either by the committee or by Mary Lyon, who knew the kind of personal relationship on which she had based her remarkable feat at Ipswich and may even then have had in mind the more difficult effort in 1837 to have the room furnishings given by ladies. In the meantime, it turned out that she was needed for getting the big gifts too. Mr. Hawks as agent crisscrossed southern New England, interviewing prospective donors; increasingly Miss Lyon went too. Her correspondence in 1836 and 1837 indicates that, week after week at short notice, she went on successive nights to different towns, wherever a possible interest was reported; often she joined forces with Mr. Hawks. Sometimes she teamed up with other trustees and sometimes she made important calls on her own. A letter to Zilpah suggests how painful such efforts could be.

I cannot tell you how much I dreaded it. I sent a line to him, asking his advice in such a manner that I knew he would not give it, unless he would also give his aid. I mentioned that I should call directly after dinner, and that I was to leave the city at four. I called. His look, and his manner of shaking hands, left no doubt what would be the issue. I spent a little while conversing on the subject, when he told me that he could not give me advice, as he could not go forward in this object. He said he felt himself pledged to aid the Ipswich school, and that he did not consider it his duty to engage in our enterprise. I do not know whether he designed to be understood that he would not contribute to it, or only that he would not take any responsibility about it. I asked him whether there was any objection to my saying, that the reason he could not engage in this was, that he was pledged to Ipswich. He replied that it was the truth, and that he felt no objection to its being stated. I came away with mingled emotions. I felt as if I had undergone a severe operation. On the whole, gratitude seemed to be the preponderating emotion—gratitude that I had gone through this trying effort, and that the question was finally settled; and especially that so good a reason could be assigned for its being settled in the negative.[49]

Certainly it was Mary Lyon in person who enlisted the support of Deacon and Mrs. Safford. Deacon Safford was the major contributor to the Seminary for the first twenty years of its history and also stimulated other givers. On March 9, 1837, he held in his home the Boston fund drive meeting that had for the last two years seemed so essential—and so impossible. The half dozen ministers and 15 to 20 laymen present agreed with Deacon Safford that "there would be no impropriety in their admitting three ladies to hear what was said on the subject—Mrs. Safford, Miss Caldwell & myself," as Mary wrote to Zilpah. Among other speakers was the Rev. Rufus Anderson of the American Board of Commissioners of Foreign Missions, who read part of a letter from Miss Grant, urging support of what she acknowledged might be considered a less than perfect plan, because of the overwhelming need for educated women and the simple justice of giving the same kind of help to institutions for young women that had repeatedly been given to colleges for young men. Deacon Safford led off with a $1,000 pledge, followed by two promises of $500 and four of $250; the total came to more than $3,000 that evening and reached $4,365 within ten days. These subscriptions, to be paid over five years in annual installments, were affected by the financial disasters of 1837; both the men who pledged $500 and one of those who pledged $250 were bankrupt within a few months. It was fortunate that Deacon Safford was able to keep up his payments and supplement them generously. For the calendar year 1837 he gave to the Seminary almost $1,200 in cash.[50]

Perhaps the most heroic fund-raising effort of all was Mary's plan to furnish the rooms by gifts from women in the towns and villages of New England. In November 1836 she produced the three-page printed appeal with a fourth page blank for a personal message. In the next four or five months she sent out more than a hundred of these letters, each asking "one efficient lady" to organize a drive in her community to collect $50 or $60—in cash and kind—to supply the furniture and bedding for one dormitory room. (That she could muster the names of former students, friends, and friends of friends in so many different towns and villages says something about the extent to which she was known in rural New England, even though her undertaking was for the most part ignored by the educational and religious press in Boston and New York.) The responses came back with devastating similarity from Chicopee, Shelburne, Gill, Waldoboro,

Maine; no money could be had or only a very little, perhaps a few articles of bedding, "The times are so hard." Some of these replies were full of affection and concern for the enterprise and offered suggestions. Betsy Chickering, a former Ipswich student, asked if two towns together might furnish one room. She explained that "nearly all the ladies of Phillipston are chiefly dependent on their palm leaf hats to procure contributions for charitable objects" but they might be able to get hold of feathers as well as other items for making bedding. Her final suggestion was echoed by others and ultimately adopted: a visit from Miss Lyon would be apt to "make the ladies feel willing to make effort and sacrifice adequate to raising 50 or 60 dollars."[51]

Evidence piled up that Miss Lyon's presence did have a powerful effect on both ladies and gentlemen in modest circumstances, even when money was so scarce. The students and teachers at Wheaton, under the double suasion of Miss Lyon's repeated visits and Eunice Caldwell's devotion to her and to the idea of Mount Holyoke, raised $100 in the fall of 1836 toward furnishing a parlor. The following spring they managed to collect an additional $135 to complete the amount needed—a most unlikely achievement for a new school of 40 to 50 pupils. One of the students at Ipswich, where Miss Lyon's visits were fewer and shorter by the end of 1836, wrote at least twice trying to persuade her sister in Newbury, Vermont, to organize a local drive to furnish a room.

Miss Lyon has been here to give us a little about her favorite enterprise. The cornerstone has been laid, every thing is made fast & sure & they are in want of nothing but funds to carry it on. She seemed so much interested & so energetic, I wish she could go about as her own agent—no Christian or any one who loves the best interests of his country could resist her warm hearted appeals. They are going to make an effort to have one town furnish a room—reckoning $50 for one. Can you not get $50 by making vigorous untiring efforts. Try.[52]

The effect of Mary Lyon's visit to the hill town of Heath in

January 1837 was reported in detail by a young woman who, until that time, had aspired to attend Ipswich.

We have been favored with a visit from Miss Lyon, she interested us much in behalf of her Sem. I believe with you that no one can hear her speak upon the subject without having their feelings enlisted in favor of the cause. Will you believe me when I tell you the people in Heath gave $1200.00 for the Sem. She presented the subject in such a manner that no one could fail grasping it at once, she removed all objections so that many who decided not to give before seeing her, cheerfully subscribed $50.00. I do believe it will do this people good, it will enlarge their hearts, & at least make them more interested in the school, if it does not enable them to give more for other benevolent objects. The ladies here will probably furnish a room. I never was personally acquainted with Miss Lyon before, my expectations were more than realized. What a fund of information she possesses. Some of the people here impeach her motives, by saying "self" is at the foundation, she wants to get herself a "name". Is not that impeachment without any cause? I do not think her perfect, but believe the cause she is engaged in is of God, & will be blessed by Him, & that He will enable the church to sustain it. Miss L. is desirous that Sister H. & myself should enter her school at the commencement, & we have engaged to go. I do not believe another individual in the country could procure as much here as Miss L. did.[53]

The need for stirring this kind of enthusiasm became more and more obvious as months passed without nearly enough furniture in view. At the end of June Mary Lyon wrote her niece Abigail the chilling facts: the trustees had had to borrow so much to finish the construction that she could not hope to draw on general seminary funds and "the trying times" had made her furniture project "exceedingly difficult. I suppose we have not yet pledged from ladies so much as one third the necessary amount." She seems to have engaged in intensive trouble shooting for the next few weeks. On July 29 Mrs. Porter wrote urgently to Eunice Caldwell at Norton. She and her husband had been expecting

Miss Lyon for the past three or four weeks; they had thirty-one letters for her, and the carpenters were about to make the basement divisions which she wanted to oversee. Would Miss Caldwell please try to get word to her? But no matter how difficult the unscheduled trips were for Mary Lyon and her collaborators, the results seem to have justified the frantic activity. As she wrote to Mr. Choate in late September:

I have felt very anxious to raise the means for furniture independent of the funds. I have been trying to do what I could among my circle of friends, & could I have 6 months more to visit many of my friends I think we should have done much towards completing it, or had it been a usual time, we could have done it by correspondence. After I gave up the hope of doing any thing by letters, having written almost a hundred, & mostly in vain, & when I began as far as my efforts were concerned to depend on my visits, I met with some success. Considering the short time, which I devoted, & the peculiar times, our success has been good. But a few weeks since, I saw plainly that I must relinquish any further efforts on this subject except what I could do by letters, or I should sink under the weight of cares, & many other things must be left undone.

She was right about the need of additional time. Even without further visits the ladies kept sending in contributions for several months after the Seminary opened. A list of cash receipts for furniture shows a total of $1,150 received by November; when the list stopped in July 1838, the total had risen to $1,900.[54]

It is impossible to follow Mary Lyon's activities from 1834 through 1837 without feeling that she was remarkably well endowed to withstand adversity. Her unusual physical energy had been conspicuous even in girlhood; she worked hard all the days of her life and still was able to muster extra strength under extreme pressure. As her responsibilities increased, she developed a technique for recouping physically after periods of severe strain. Mrs. Cowles described her practice.

When, from long and close application, Miss Lyon became brain-

weary, it was her practice, at this period of her life, to sink voluntarily into a state of partial stupor for one, two, or three days, as the case might require, keeping her bed most of the time, and taking very little food. From such seasons of rest she would come forth rejunevated, and ready for a campaign that would exhaust any body else.

One such period of heavy strain came when the enterprise was being launched in September and October 1834. She was simultaneously engineering the organization of the sponsoring committee, collecting the first $1,000 in small gifts and, in Zilpah Grant's absence, closing the summer term and preparing for the fall opening of Ipswich Seminary. But soon after Mary reached Amherst in late October, her extreme fatigue had abated and her usual vigor returned. Similar renewals must have occurred repeatedly in the next three years.[55]

Mary Lyon was a remarkable organizer, resourceful and, once she had reached a decision, quick to act. She had repeatedly demonstrated in the Derry, Buckland, and Ipswich schools that when one scheme fell through, she could devise another almost right away. Her own readiness engendered a confidence that was invaluable to her fellow workers when, after the long delays in getting funds, a series of misfortunes occurred during construction. When the foundation was finally excavated in August 1836, some defect was found—perhaps quicksand—which required moving the site twenty-five feet further back from the road. Then a question as to the quality of the bricks required another pause until an expert declared them sound. The following April, when construction was going forward on the third story, the flooring and part of the walls collapsed. Encountered at the site, Mary, instead of being downcast, was rejoicing that no one was seriously hurt. The following week the trustees announced in the papers that the damage would be repaired within two weeks.[56]

The extent to which her resilience depended upon her habit of planning ahead, it is hard to estimate, but she was certainly looking toward the long future. She repeatedly talked about the rising structure as the first building, and she started recruiting members of the faculty before the original committee had been formed. There is no record of when Eunice Caldwell agreed to become associate principal of the still nonexistent institution projected by her best friend; she had surely committed herself before July 1834, when she first debated the possibility of taking charge of Wheaton Seminary in the meantime. Before the end of 1835 there were two well qualified candidates for the difficult post of superintendent of the domestic department: Mary's niece Abigail Moore, who had attended Ipswich and was teaching in Charlottesville, Virginia, and Miss Peters, a student and then a teacher under Joseph Emerson. Recruiting of students also began early, particularly potential members of the senior class, whose ability and attainments Mary Lyon considered of major importance in establishing a high academic standard. In June 1835 she wrote to Eunice Caldwell:

Give a large share of love to Miss A. from me. I want to see her, to talk with her about the good which she can do, by being a member of the school the first year. Ought we not to ascertain what young ladies of our acquaintance, who are advanced in their education, intend at some time to become members of the institution, and lay before them the good that they would do by joining the school, the very first year?[57]

Hopeful as she was most of the time, Mary nevertheless had periods of discouragement. Her letters, usually full of declarations of faith and hope, once in a great while hinted that she could find herself depressed by her nomadic life and its unending difficulties or awash in a sea of uncertainty. In the summer of 1835 when the project seemed to be at a standstill, she wrote resolutely to her mother and sister in Ashfield, "Whatever may be the result, I cannot regret that these things were not directed differently." But she had begun by saying, "I seem to be ever busy, and yet I accomplish nothing. I wander about without a home, scarcely knowing one week where I shall be the next." When arguments over the site postponed still further the first excavations, she wrote to Zilpah:

Sometimes I fear that I have so much of worldly expectation of comfort here, that it may be necessary to dash these hopes, by disappointing me in my plans of doing good. I do not know, that I uniformly expect much in this world, but ere I am aware, I find myself indulging the prospect that the present trying circumstances will be over, that in time I shall be settled down again in a pleasant field for doing good, where I shall not be constantly changing with no resting place, & constantly meeting with one obstacle after another. I always fear when I find my heart thus clinging to the hope of future good. Perhaps these are my best days this side the grave.[58]

Lacking the organizational structure that enabled solicitors for church-sponsored causes to plan ahead, she did on rare occasions feel that her hasty journeys were ruddlerless. In the late fall of 1836, after the cornerstone had finally been laid, her letters to Zilpah indicated both intense activity and uncertainty.

I have not entirely given up going to New York this autumn. I am thinking of going directly to New York from Boston. But it is almost impossible for me to predict my own movements. I spent last Wed. night at Belchertown, Thurs. night at Barre, Friday night at Amherst, & yesterday returned here [South Hadley]. I leave tomorrow on an excursion around on the hills for the sake of conversing with some individuals about our enterprize. I expect to get round to Belchertown the last of this week, on my way to Boston.

Two weeks later, writing from Boston, she was undecided at every point. She had two days before Mr. Hawks was to meet her in Boston—should she go to Andover or Norton? She was more unsure than she had been two weeks ago whether she wanted a cloak, a pelisse, a new shawl, or a fur cape, and she inquired again whether Miss Parsons could do her dressmaking if she came to Ipswich that week or the next. The crucial question was painfully familiar: was this the time to try a fund drive in Boston? If so, they would be "very still about it, so that a failure will not amount to much."[59]

The speed which she acted on a decision once reached must

sometimes have startled as well as cheered her co-workers. The "Address to the Public," an article she agonized over for more than a month early in 1836, was cordially approved by the trustees at their April 13 meeting and Mr. Choate and Mr. Hawks were named a subcommittee to see to publication. They may have encountered the editorial indifference or skepticism so familiar to supporters of the enterprise or they may not have yet begun making approaches by April 30. On that day Mary Lyon in a letter to Mr. Tyler about various problems included this report.

Since your suggestion in your letter of yesterday about cutting up my article for the papers, I have been almost inclined to yield, & let it go into the Recorder. If this is done, I am inclined to think it best to have it in the Recorder first, & afterwards collected in a pamphlet, if thought best. I have gone so far as to see Mr. Tracy today, & read him my article. He will insert it, commencing next number but one. I shall write to Mr. Hawks on this. I want to know your opinion. Would it be best to send it also to the New York Observer, & Evangelist? I have made important alterations in the manuscript, & I very much want to have Mr. Hawks see it.[60]

What made the periods of depression rare and brief, what sustained her, in addition to her energy and her ingenuity, was her certainty of God's help. She believed deeply that she was doing the Lord's work and that somehow or other He would enable her and her co-workers to determine the right location, to find assistance when it was desperately needed, to raise the money, to furnish the rooms. Practically every report of a new difficulty was accompanied by a declaration of faith. She repeatedly said in substance: "I know not what is before us. The Lord will direct. It is sweet to commend all to him." She kept on reminding herself that God was truly the only refuge. "May I be saved from depending on an arm of flesh," she wrote over and over again to her friends. Even in her account of the laying of the cornerstone, in which she rejoiced in almost feminist tones over what the gentlemen had conceded to the ladies, she made clear that it was truly the Lord's doing.

The stone & brick & mortar speak a language, which vibrates through my very soul. How much thought, & how much feeling have I had on this general subject in years that are past. And I have indeed lived to see the time, when a body of gentlemen have ventured to lay the corner stone of an edifice which will cost about $15,000,—& for an institution for females. Surely the Lord hath remembered our low estate. This will be an era in female education. The work will not stop with this institution. This enterprize may have to struggle through embarrassments for years, but its influence will be felt. It is a concession on the part of gentlemen in our behalf which can be used again & again.[61]

Mary Lyon had never been quick to take offense. When she first wrote Catharine Beecher in 1834 about her plans, hoping for both moral and financial support, she got in reply a lengthy proposition concerning Miss Beecher's textbook on arithmetic. If Miss Lyon would promote the adoption of the new edition, she could privately have a say as to the use of the profits on the sales she had stimulated. In the summer of 1836, when Miss Beecher was to be in Boston for a short while, Mary tried again. This time Miss Beecher addressed herself to what was wrong with the plans for Mount Holyoke and bade their author write out a defense and then come to talk over the issues. However, because of Miss Beecher's state of nerves at the time, strenuous conversation exhausted her. Miss Lyon must promise not to talk "in a very animated way" and come prepared to be "calm as a clock" and "not too interesting." There is no evidence that this modulated dialogue took place, but Mary, disregarding Miss Beecher's imperious tone, wrote out in full her reasons for the low tuition and therefore the low salaries for teachers, to which Miss Beecher seriously objected. The letter contains an interesting appraisal of the clientele from which the money was slowly coming in and a hint as to what Mr. Hawks and Miss Lyon must have been like as a soliciting team.

I thank you for your interest in my plans, expressed in the sincere way of criticism on one point. I think, however, you do not fully understand them.

The terms high, low, and moderate tuition mean very different things in different parts of the country. In the aristocratic south, where all the wealth is concentrated on large plantations, and in some of the speculating portions of the north, where wealth flows in as in a day, and in some of the most prosperous mercantile and manufacturing places, these terms are understood differently from what they are among the general community of New England. The latter, tilling a sterile soil, and uniting economy with prudence, are enabled, by the slow gains of patient industry, to provide comfortably for their children, and send them to school in their own neighborhoods, to sustain the ordinances of the gospel, and to reserve something to be cast into the treasury of the Lord, in order to send the gospel to the heathen, to raise up ministers, to build up colleges and seminaries at the west, and to supply the destitute of our own land, who are less able or less willing than themselves, with the sacred ministry.

Our plan is to place tuition at what will be regarded by the New England community, including the wealthy and the educated, with farmers and mechanics as moderate tuition. . . .

I have not been alone in considering it of great importance to establish a permanent seminary in New England for educating female teachers, with accommodations, apparatus, &c., somewhat like those for the other sex. Honorably to do this, from twenty to forty thousand dollars must be raised; and such a sum, raised for such an object, would form almost an era in female education. For years, Miss Grant and myself made continual efforts to accomplish the object; but all our efforts failed.

I am convinced that there are but two ways to accomplish such an object. First, to interest one, two, or a few wealthy men to do the whole; second, to interest the whole New England community, beginning with the country population, and in time receiving the aid and cooperation of the more wealthy in our cities. Each of these modes, if practicable, would have its advantages. The first, if done at all, could be done sooner and with very little comparative labor. The second would require vastly more time and labor; but if it were accomplished, an important and salutary impression would be made on the whole of New England. . . .

Again, we have held up to New England people the advantages of a teachers' seminary, with ample facilities for boarding and instruction, free of rent, of so superior a character that a supply of scholars could be secured without receiving those who were immature and ill prepared, and who are always a heavy tax on the time of teachers. We have shown that the same money will, in this way, do more to provide instruction for young women qualifying themselves to teach, than it would do in our country academies. After these professions, shall we ask for higher tuition, at the same time that we are asking for benevolent aid to carry forward our enterprise? . . .

I express myself with more confidence on this subject, because it has been with me, for two or three years, a matter of careful consideration; but further, because our laborious and indefatigable agent is of the same opinion, and all his intercourse with New England people has tended to confirm it. Having been wholly devoted to the enterprise for a year and a half, he probably knows more of the views of the New England community on this point than any hundred others. Careful in all his movements, he never has occasion to retrace a single step. Whatever may be thought of my sanguine temperament, he cannot be charged with being over-zealous. But his deficiency in zeal is more than made up by his unwearied labors, his never-ending patience and perseverance, his sound common sense, his careful observation of human nature, and his intimate acquaintance with New England people.

You speak of the importance of raising the compensation of teachers. In a list of motives for teaching, I should place first the great motive, which cannot be understood by the natural heart, Love thy neighbor as thyself. On this list, though not second in rank, I have been accustomed to place pecuniary considerations. I am inclined to the opinion that this should fall lower on a list of motives to be presented to ladies than to gentlemen, and that this is more in accordance with the system of the divine government. Let us cheerfully make all due concessions, where God has designed a difference in the situation of the sexes, such as woman's retiring from public stations, being generally dependent on the other sex for pecuniary support, &c. O that we may plead constantly for her religious privileges, for equal facilities for the improvement of her talents, and for the privilege of using all her talents in doing good![62]

Mary had to face criticisms much more unpleasant than Miss Beecher's. Some of her activities were unquestionably unconventional. Mrs. Cowles made an enlightening defense of the way she managed to plead her cause on her stagecoach journeys.

Travelling the road from Boston to the Connecticut often, she could scarce ride any ten miles of the route without being recognized by some fellow-traveller, whose cordial salutation would introduce her to the company. All felt very well acquainted with her, as soon as they heard her name, and she would soon be invited to detail the progress of the enterprise. Being infallibly certain that the object would commend itself to the good common sense and best impulses of true New Englanders, she improved every opportunity of unfolding its merits to any who seemed capable of comprehending them, whether acquaintances or strangers. She could make herself heard easily, although the road might be a little uneven, and would expatiate on the subject as freely as in her own parlor. She did not talk louder than many fashionably-dressed boarding-school girls do in public conveyances, the difference being that the latter inform the company of their own personal affairs, while she discussed principles as enduring as the human race, and as vital to human welfare as they are enduring.

She was not unconscious of the animadversion that such actions seemed to invite; "her familiar friends . . . found her fully aware that it would be in better taste to sit down in some secluded nook, and from its loopholes watch the movements and success of the agents; but she insisted that it was better to violate taste than not to have the work done."[63]

Mrs. Cowles, who must have seen more of Mary than anyone else did between 1834 and 1838, described succinctly her prevailing view of life: "Along with unbounded trust in God, she had a reasonable and intelligent trust in herself," and reconstructed the language of her rejoinders to friends who worried about her way of life.

"What do I that is wrong?" she would say to the friends who expostulated with her on the subject. "I ride in the stage coach or cars without an escort. Other ladies do the same. I visit a family where I have been previously invited, and the minister's wife, or some leading woman, calls the ladies together to see me, and I lay our object before them. Is that wrong? I go with Mr. Hawks, and call on a gentleman of known liberality at his own house, and converse with him about our enterprise. What harm is there in that? If there is no harm in doing these things once, what harm is there in doing them twice, thrice, or a dozen times? My heart is sick, my soul is pained with this empty gentility, this genteel nothingness. I am doing a great work. I cannot come down."[64]

The most abusive of the attacks in print was a five-page "review" in the April 1837 issue of *The Religious Magazine* of Mary Lyon's twenty-page pamphlet issued in February, "General View of the Principles and Design of the Mount Holyoke Female Seminary." The editor was Professor E. A. Andrews, a Yale graduate who had taught Greek and Latin at the University of North Carolina; since 1833 he had been head of the Mount Vernon School for Girls in Boston. Professor Andrews derided both the publication and the enterprise. He quoted sentences, correcting the grammar and mocking the sentiment at the same time. Ipswich Seminary, cited in the pamphlet as the exemplar for the academic program, also came under attack. He disapproved in principle of boarding schools for girls and of church support for any kind of higher education, and directed his bitterest scorn toward the character and attainments of the women heading the two seminaries. Most New Englanders, he maintained, would need to ask about Ipswich

what is the course of study there pursued, who are the persons, eminent in any department of learning, who direct the education at that school, and who is the Mrs. More, or the Madame Roland, whose splendid endowments, elegant manners, and extraordinary accomplishments, are to serve as models of imitation for the young ladies who resort to that seminary? Especially will they

*ask, "Who are the eminent individuals to whom are to be com-
mitted the various departments in the projected seminary?" A
thorough education will never be given by those whose own
education is strikingly deficient, and young ladies will rarely
become distinguished for delicacy of sentiment, or for refinement
and elegance of manners, by studying models presenting only
the more masculine traits of character.*

In succeeding paragraphs he extended and reiterated his denun-
ciations of female forwardness in pupils and teachers.

*The most remarkable instances however of even female self-
complacence which any age has witnessed, has [sic] been ex-
hibited, we believe, in our own day and country, by ladies
engaged in conducting "some of our most distinguished female
seminaries."*[65]

His grammar is of particular interest in view of his excoriating
attack on Mary.

Zilpah Grant and trustees and friends of Ipswich Seminary must
have been infuriated, especially those who themselves disapproved
of Mary Lyon's undertaking. In the May issue a brief note "to
correspondents" said that "no allusion was intended to the
principal of the Ipswich Seminary, towards whom the reviewer
entertained no other sentiments than those of respect and
esteem." This obviously did not suffice as apology. The August
issue carried a four-page letter defending Ipswich, written by a
"respected author" not directly connected with the seminary.
Professor Andrews was still unwilling to take back anything he
had said; he was publishing the letter "that in case any wrong was
done by the former article, the aggrieved may have an opportunity to be heard through the same channel." This defense was
literate, reasonable and dignified and nowhere said any word in
behalf of Mary Lyon or Mount Holyoke.[66]

No published reaction from Mount Holyoke has thus far been
discovered, nor any reference of any sort to the article by Mary
Lyon. But the college archives do contain a full-dress reply by
Professor Hitchcock, half again as long as the original article.

In a letter intended for the *Boston Recorder*, he condemned attack by innuendo and ridicule rather than reasoned discussion, and defended the Ipswich system, teachers, and graduates as well as the Herculean task performed by the founder of Mount Holyoke. After her death he recalled that he had found her unruffled by Professor Andrews's attack. He gave her his letter, ready to mail, asking her to do with it whatever she thought best—and that was the last he ever heard of it. Although she was not unaware of rebuffs and jeers, her faith in God and her confidence in her own ability to perceive and do His bidding seemed to free her from rage and resentment.[67]

During the years from 1834 through 1837, most of the available records focus so consistently on the struggle for funds and supporters that it is hard not to feel that Mary had a one-track mind. But there is fragmentary evidence that even then her interests did range and that her sense of humor did not desert her. She was always on the lookout for good books to use as texts. In 1834 before she had sponsoring committee or contingency funds, she was soliciting from potential supporters of the new seminary subscriptions for the reprinting of Jonathan Edwards's *History of the Work of Redemption* (75¢ retail; 62½¢ in quantity). These sermons, designed to be the foundation of a philosophy of history from before creation through the millennium and the last judgment, had been much admired by Joseph Emerson; no wonder Edwards's conception of design and order in men's affairs as documented by biblical history and prophecy and also by the course of recorded events seemed exceptionally valuable to Mary Lyon.[68]

When she was living with the Hitchcocks, she paid considerable attention to the four children. An exchange of correspondence early in 1836 when she was away for several weeks indicates that the three oldest, aged 7, 9, and 11, had been studying Latin with her. In her absence, they were reciting daily to their mother; they found Latin "a very pleasant study" and the verbs "very interesting as you said they would be."[69]

The most impressive educational extra she undertook while launching her own campaign was helping to establish Wheaton Seminary. A prosperous citizen of Norton, Massachusetts, Judge

9. Eunice Caldwell, later Mrs. John P. Cowles, was the first principal of Wheaton Seminary and the first associate principal of Mount Holyoke. She succeeded Zilpah Grant as confidante to Miss Lyon. Mount Holyoke College Library Archives.

Laban Wheaton, resolved to build a memorial to his only daughter, who died in March 1834, and was persuaded by his daughter-in-law to make it not a statue but a first-rate school for girls. Since Judge Wheaton was then 80, the detailed planning was handled mainly by his son and daughter-in-law, who sought Mary Lyon's advice on all sorts of matters. Whether it was a copy of her first printed appeal, issued in February 1834, that made the initial contact is not recorded. All parties must soon have discovered that Miss Lyon's own project had too many unusual features to be absorbed by the Wheatons but that her judgment of people and her skill at organization were highly valued. By the time Judge Wheaton was fully persuaded to go ahead with the school, she had a candidate for principal—none other than Eunice Caldwell. A gifted Ipswich graduate, Eunice had returned to teach immediately after completing the course in 1829 and had continued for four years. For a part of 1833–34 she had also taught at Miss Eaton's school in Philadelphia, and of course she would be Miss Lyon's associate principal when the new seminary finally came into being, but she had not yet taken complete charge of a school. When Mary Lyon first broached the idea, apparently Eunice had doubts about the high seriousness of the Wheaton intentions as well as her own capacity to cope with the administrative arrangements. Miss Lyon explained in a letter to young Mr. Wheaton.

Miss Caldwell wishes to devote herself to the business of teaching, not to promote mainly her own interests, and happiness, but to promote the present and future and eternal welfare of the rising generation. She does not wish to engage in any place, without knowing so much of the situation, as to know that it would be favorable for the promotion of these objects. If she should after further consideration, think favorably of the plan of laboring in your place, before any decision is formed, I think it will be advisable that she should visit your place, and learn what she can on the spot, which she could not learn in any other way. It will also be rather necessary that I should go with her, as she will depend on me so much to aid in making all preparatory arrangements.

When Miss Lyon wrote on July 8, she thought that she and Eunice might both get away for a visit while school was in session, but by the middle of August she realized that even she could not add anything to her burden in the four remaining weeks of the term, with the first meeting of her committee to be managed in the meantime. Apparently both of them went to Norton right after Ipswich closed on September 16; a contract drawn up by Mary Lyon and addressed to the trustees was dated September 25. It began by making clear her own role: "In compliance with a request from Laban M. Wheaton Esq., that I would furnish a teacher well acquainted with the system pursued at Ipswich Female Seminary, and that I would render what aid I could towards the adoption of a similar system in the school to be opened next spring in Norton, I have made the following arrangements." The course of study, which was to follow the Ipswich pattern, was to be determined by Miss Caldwell; landladies could charge for board and room no more than $1.75 a week and could assign only two occupants to one room; there would be four terms of eleven weeks and tuition would be $5 each term; Miss Caldwell was to receive the tuition for compensation and from it pay all expenses except for the school building, which was to be rent free.[70]

Mary Lyon continued to deal with practical problems as they arose. She composed the newspaper announcements for the impending opening, quashed a proposal to have more than two students share one room, arranged for Eunice Caldwell not to have to eat and sleep in a house full of students (and then changed her mind because, as she explained in a hasty note to Eunice, the alternative arrangement looked worse).

> *Ipswich, Feb. 25, 1834 [1835]. Wed. P.M.*
> *My dear Miss Caldwell,*
> *I have but 10 minutes to write but I want to send by this mail. At Norton I settled it that you were not to board with the scholars. But Mrs. Wheaton's particularity, & excessive fear of a speck of dirt, makes me afraid that you could not be comfortable. I have just been talking about it with Miss Grant, & she thinks it would be vastly more trying to you than to board in the boarding house, & I am nearly of her opinion. Now I will do what I can for you & will you have it now that you will board with the scholars. It must be known before the notice goes into the paper, & I want to hear from you by the very first mail. There will be room for only 16 scholars, in the house, & if you & I are there only 14. Miss Caldwell [sic] says the circumstances will be favorable & you will do well. I am inclined to think that we have made the subject more formidable of you boarding with the scholars. I am half inclined to think that I shall feel happier to leave you in the boarding house. Now will you be willing that Miss Grant & I should look this over & have you board at the boarding house if we think best.*
>
> > *Affectionately yours,*
> > *Mary Lyon*

Eunice, who was not so vigorous or extroverted as Miss Lyon—or Miss Grant, concurred reluctantly: "Miss Caldwell feels tried about taking so much on herself as she must to board in the boarding house, but she is willing to try, if I think best. On the whole, I think it best to try," Mary Lyon told the Wheatons, reiterating the importance of the special conditions attached. The landlady must agree that the teacher would have a room to herself with better furnishings and a bit more service, the right to choose which students would be resident in that house, and—after a reminder from Miss Grant—the privilege of having a guest with her at no extra charge.[71]

This last stipulation was important for all concerned. Mary had made clear her intention to help Eunice whenever she could. After the opening of school at the end of April 1835, she was frequently at Norton, sometimes to give the school a boost and sometimes to get on with her own business. Extracts from letters written by a student at Wheaton sometime in 1836 give one view of her activities. This young woman saw Miss Lyon as "going around establishing seminaries and looking after those placed in her care." Until Mount Holyoke should be ready a year hence, when she had "nothing but writing to do," she made Wheaton her home. What really exercised the student was Miss Lyon's role as visiting instructor at Wheaton:

About three weeks since, she came into the school room one morning and said she wanted the whole school to commence at the beginning of Arithmetic and see how long we would be in going over the first 50 pages, and we might say ourselves how long we thought it would take us. Some said one day, some two, and some a week. I was among those who said two days, but some of the girls in the house said one day, so I went to work and finished my 50 pages in one day and about ten more, making 60 pages in a day. After this she gave us lessons to get and sums to do and kept us all day long running out of one room into another, upstairs and down, till we have almost worn the shoes off of our feet. I wish you could have seen us running to and fro and her after us singing out quick, step a little quicker, and giving one a push and another a pull all over the room. I never went so quick in my life that I know of. This week we have been driven through all the rules as far as we have been and have had composition to write every day last week and every other day this week, besides reading, spelling and writing two hours each day and singing one hour.[72]

166

By no means all of Mary's time at Norton went into correspondence about Mount Holyoke, classroom exercises, or even the new Wheaton boarding house, which she "talked into being" the second year and then organized. She seized spare intervals, both at Norton and at Amherst, for further study. She explained to Zilpah her plans and the reason why she was saying little about them:

Considering that it must be at least two years before I can commence teaching at South Hadley, I think it is best to spend some time in study, though I should not think it wise at my age to give up active labor for study. The time being providentially thrown on my hands, the case is different. I should prefer not to say much about it, because I do not expect to make much progress, or to retain much of what I gain; but much more, because it seems ridiculous for a lady of forty to be trying to make over her education. What time I do devote to study, I can probably take much better this year than next, and I can find no better place than this. Here, no one inquires what I am doing, or how I spend my time.

Just how much she accomplished it would be impossible to say, but her letters indicate that she did find a number of occasions for adding to her general knowledge. The one volume on a political issue which she mentioned reading was William Ellery Channing's book on slavery; she made several references to textbooks, notably in algebra and chemistry, which she was reviewing closely. She was also regularly attending lectures and college sermons at Amherst. She found Professor Hitchcock's course in geology particularly valuable and, even though her travels were accelerating and the class met three times a week, she managed to hear many of his lectures.[73]

Being a member of Professor Hitchcock's household also brought her into daily contact with the tutors, who were then taking meals there. These three or four young men were in effect the instructors, supplementing the work of the six to eight professors. No doubt among the brightest of the recent Amherst graduates, they had been chosen "to teach Greek, Latin, Mathematics, and not a few miscellaneous studies to the lower classes, to occupy rooms in college and keep order among the students, and to bear a most important part in their general education and training." Many of the early tutors, according to Professor Tyler's history, were "men of rare talents and attainments." Although none of those on the staff while Mary Lyon was in residence became famous, they all spent their lives preaching or teaching. They "discussed literature, science and religion with each other and the Professor" and also on occasion "canvassed principles, plans and methods of education with Miss Lyon." Her standards of academic excellence had already evolved out of the instruction of Joseph Emerson and her years of teaching experience, but her two winters in Amherst attending college lectures and enjoying the play of mind of bright young college instructors may well have reinforced her determination to keep on raising the level of achievement at Mount Holyoke year by year.[74]

That the Seminary did open on November 8, 1837, was something of a miracle. In the preceding three months Mary had to call upon all her energy, all her faith, all her ingenuity. In early September she described to her mother the kind of life she was living.

I want you should let me hear from you often. Letters sent to this place will find me very soon; indeed, I must be here now most of the time. I have so much letter writing to do, that I seem not to have time for much else. And yet I have five times as much as I can do which I wish to do. But I must do what I can, and let the rest go undone. There is scarcely a mail which does not bring me a letter; yesterday's brought five. Most of them require an answer, and many of them will require two or three before I get through with them. Among all these letters, I should now and then like to receive one from my own dear mother. As for myself, my head is filled with such a variety, that I can write nothing except it is on business. Our building is going on finely. The seal to every thing about it must soon be fixed. My head is full of closets, shelves, cupboards, doors, sinks, tables, &c. You will think this is new work for me, and, indeed, it is.

A letter to Zilpah the following week, arranging to borrow money, likewise suggested both the pressure she felt and the zest with which she was rising to the challenge.

When I look through to Nov. 8, it seems like looking down a precipice of many hundred feet, which I must descend. I can only avoid looking to the bottom, & fix my eye on the nearest stone till I have safely reached it. I try to take the best possible care of my health. I have had more real sick days with head ache the last few weeks than usual, but on the whole I am very much sustained by a kind Providence.

She no doubt also considered it the work of a kind Providence that Mr. and Mrs. Joseph Condit, whose house stood just north of the Seminary building, invited her to share their home during those last three months. Her stay not only contributed to her comfort and health but also seems to have increased the mutual respect and affection of pastor and principal.[75]

The opening date must have been agreed upon by Miss Lyon, the trustees, and the builders by the beginning of August; paid newspaper announcements appeared in Boston and New York and locally between August 9 and 18. But it was not a foregone conclusion that the building would be habitable by the announced date. To Mr. Choate, rejecting a young woman he had recommended, she sized up the situation on September 21: "With great effort we expect to commence Nov. 8, but it will require the greatest possible effort. Some parts of the paint will be so fresh that we must use it with the greatest care, & some of the fixtures will not be done. If we can get the carpenters, masons, & painters all out of the building into the woodhouse I shall be glad."[76]

The shortage of furniture for student rooms continued to be desperate, and nearly every letter May Lyon wrote contained an urgent plea for gifts or loans of spoons, pillows, comforters, bed ticking, money. At the end of August she drafted a letter to the accepted candidates, asking them to borrow or beg bedding. She had enough copies made by hand for a general mailing but second thoughts about the risk of misunderstanding prevailed, and most of them were never sent. She was acutely aware that the number of admissions must depend on the number of rooms with sufficient furniture to be occupied. By the third week in September she had had more than a hundred applications, of which she had accepted 50, refused an unspecified number outright, and put the others on a waiting list. From members of this last category and even from late applicants, she proposed to accept those young women who could themselves round up money or furnishings for one of the empty rooms. This procedure brought at least one complaint. One young woman apparently felt compelled to purchase some of the bedding and thus to pay more for her education than others. Mary Lyon had to write still another letter saying that no injustice had been intended; if Miss Wheeler paid out more than the others who, like her, had been admitted because they could help with the furnishings, her tuition charges would be reduced. Even this letter ended by asking if, in view of all the admission applications from Hardwick, some lady in the town would not finish raising enough money to furnish the Hardwick room—or at least lend a bed. Applications kept pouring in. By November 8, when Mount Holyoke opened with 80 students, Miss Lyon had received close to 200 requests for admission.[77]

On November 8 "the doors were without steps; the windows without blinds; the wood-house was not covered; stoves were not set up; the furniture, delayed by storms, had not all arrived; and much of the bedding pledged had not made its appearance." Many of the 80 young women were impressed, as they long afterward recalled, both by these circumstances and by the people involved: memories of bleak walls and bare ground outside and entrance through a back basement door were balanced by memories of the dining room where on one table food was spread for travelers and at another a group of girls were stitching comforters, the kitchen where the elegant Mrs. Safford and Mrs. Porter were washing crockery, the big hall upstairs where Deacon Safford in shirt sleeves was tacking down matting. Strongest of all were the recollections of Miss Lyon, her face aglow, not in the least tired or worried or flurried by the struggles of the last three years. The first students in retrospect thought of her as full of abounding life, possessing winning dignity and cordiality, a born leader, almost a pattern of perfection. As one student said at the time, in a letter written to her mother after the first seven weeks when the difficulties of daily life had been most acute, Miss Lyon was "wonderfully calculated to make the best of everything and to lead others to do so."[78]

5
The Hazards of the Start

. . . all the building fitly framed

together groweth unto

a holy temple in the Lord.

EPHESIANS 2:21

It could well be called a miracle
—that almost completed five-story building and the 80 young
ladies, many of whom had traveled two or three days to reach
South Hadley by November 8, 1837. But even full enrollment, a
well-equipped building in nearly habitable condition, and trustees at
work in person to finish it off did not guarantee the future of
Mount Holyoke Female Seminary. Institutions for higher learning
founded in the first half of the nineteenth century faced many
hazards and were considerably more likely to perish than to survive. The tabulation made by Tewksbury for 16 of the 34 states
in the Union at that time shows that 516 institutions in these
states had opened their doors to students by 1860 but only 104
lasted into the twentieth century. Four out of five of the burgeoning colleges succumbed to some kind of misfortune. Mary Lyon
was spared one major threat—denominational in-fighting; unlike
the colleges for men, Mount Holyoke had received no financial
support from organized religion. But the Seminary was just as
vulnerable as any college to destruction by fire or epidemic, and
it was both unfinished and untried.[1]

The unfinished state of the building put special demands upon
everybody—students, faculty, trustees, and, most of all, Mary
Lyon. For more than a week after the opening day, the Porters
and the Saffords stayed on, putting in long hours of physical
labor. Deacon Porter speeded up the construction crews and, on
the side, taught Mary Lyon bookkeeping. Deacon Safford took
charge of unpacking and setting up furniture, helped by students
and young men from the village. Miss Lyon, on the job from
4 A.M. to 11 P.M., dealt with problems from every department
but concentrated on domestic operations where ingenuity and

system were urgently needed. Completing the building was to her not just a matter of corralling more furniture and finishing off exteriors. As she had been saying for at least a year, this was only "the first building," and she was probably even then urging trustees to plan for an addition to enlarge the enrollment and scope of the school. In the meantime, she still had to demonstrate that her unorthodox and exacting scheme would work at all. Could daily cooking and cleaning realistically be added to a demanding academic schedule? Would young women accustomed to the smorgasbord approach to education be able and willing to meet her rigorous standards for admission and sequential study? The first students encountered both skepticism and hostility in their home communities and even members of the educational and religious establishment who were in general sympathy with Mary Lyon's aims expressed doubts about some of her methods. Zilpah Grant continued to have strong reservations about the domestic work, and Catharine Beecher still opposed the low faculty salaries.[2]

Unquestionably the Seminary did go through some ominous periods, especially during the initial year of repeated trial and error; Miss Lyon's special gifts of organization and leadership were never more important. But within four years the Mount Holyoke system had been proven viable and remarkably resistant to shocks. The first of these shocks came at once and could have been lethal. After all Mary's protracted efforts to find the right person to superintend the domestic department, her choice was a mistake. Miss Peters, a former pupil of Joseph Emerson and then a teacher in his school, had the intellectual and personal qualifications Miss Lyon had particularly sought to give standing to the domestic department, but the intricacies of scheduling defeated her. "Everything seemed like a mountain to her . . . she had the headache, could not sleep nights." When Mary wrote on November 27, "My present cares are almost overwhelming," she had been arranging and supervising the washing, ironing, sweeping, baking, and dishwashing crews. She also gave special attention to making bread. Because the first batches were disappointing, she took her correspondence and account books to the baking room, where she spent several hours almost every day in order to discover by observation and experiment the operating secrets of the brand new Rumford

10. A wood engraving of the Seminary building before any additions or enlargements had been made. Probably executed in September 1838. Mount Holyoke College Library Archives.

oven from Deacon Safford. Within a few weeks she and her dedicated baking circles had achieved the excellent bread that was henceforth one of the hallmarks of the Seminary. The hope that Miss Peters could take over the supervision, once all such details of the system had been worked out, proved vain, but there is no indication of any reproaches. When after two or three months the poor woman "broke down completely, looking the picture of despair" and had to leave, one student recalled that "Miss Lyon comforted her." Mrs. Cowles reported that in addition to her salary as originally stipulated by the trustees, Miss Peters received when she left a personal gift from Mary Lyon of a sum almost equal to her wages.[3]

In spite of the initial difficulties, the domestic work turned out to be a success. The students of the first year rose to the challenge of incomplete facilities, uncharted operations, and constant change. Their letters suggest that many liked their assigned tasks, admired the general arrangements, and took pride in the results. Two days after the opening, Elizabeth Bull was predicting cheerfully that when they were settled, "we shall have every convenience that we can wish for our rooms; broom, dust pan and brush, hearth brush; tin pail, large pitcher for soft, and small for drinking water; two lamps, table and stand, basket for wood, bellows, etc., etc." Two weeks later, Nancy Everett, the heroine of the first Seminary romance, sent her family in Wrentham a detailed description of the building and the system as it had by then evolved.

There is just seventy-nine scholars, which with three teachers Miss Lyon, and the superintendant of the domestic department make a family of only eighty-four. You can hardly imagine what a formidable line we make going to church, or taking our daily walks. I believe if ever there was a happy family it is this! We are so independent; that is if we wish for anything or to do anything we are at perfect liberty to do or get it, without a parcel of Irish girls scowling upon us, or wishing us out of the way.

Perhaps you may like to know about the division of the labor, and this I will try to tell you. In the first place the bell rings at five o'clock in the morning to call up those who get breakfast, which consists of potatoes (very nice) and cream, white bread and butter. Sometimes for variety hasty pudding is substituted for the former. It takes fourteen to get breakfast—eight to set the tables, there being five to set—one to make the fires, in the stove, under the set kettles for dishwater potatoes and washing floors; and in the seminary hall, spaceway and dining room etc.—then five or six to peal the potatoes.

I rise at half past five every morning, together with Misses Lucy & C——Brigham, having an appointment from that time till breakfast time. If we fail of being down at the set time Miss Lyon sends up for us. I really do not know when she sleeps, for she is up the first in the house, sometimes before four, and once she rose at one thinking it was five! The bell rung—and we who heard it were in great consternation for a short time thinking the house was on fire. The mistake was explained and we once more betook ourselves to repose. After breakfast there is such a number for washing tumblers of which there is a host, all drinking cold water but five! so many for washing and scouring knives, so many for the crockery of whatever sort, and eight or ten for sweeping the various stairways, space-ways, etc. About the same number for dinner and supper, only different ones. Dinner is made up of roasted beef, codfish, and the like, and always a second course of dumplins, pies, or puddings. Supper of bread and butter, sauce, and cake or gingerbread. So you see we live well, yet all is plain. In the evening there is a circle of ladies that attend to making bread and pearing apples for dumplins and pies, washing potatoes for the next day and another in the morning for making pies and preparing the dinner.

I wish you could see the establishment and apparatus connected with it. It reminds me of "Uncle Chester's boarding house." Here every one is to be prompt to all engagements, knows her place, and is to do her work equal to "four" which is the highest mark. We have two splendid double parlors, furnished by the ladies that have attended Norton School, which are on one side of the front door, and the seminary hall is on the other which is the whole width of the building and half the length;—then there is a large reading room or library, a sitting-room, and lodging rooms occupied by Miss Lyon. These, together with the entry include the first story over the basement, the walls of which have the hard finish put on, the wood work well painted which makes it look perfectly in good taste—just like the one who gave directions, viz. Miss Lyon. The basement story consists of the dining room as large as the seminary hall, kitchen, ironing room, baking room, kneading room, pantry washing room, and five or six great closets. The other three stories are for the scholar's and teacher's lodging rooms, there being about sixteen in each story. Every chamber is provided with a large cupboard almost large enough for a bed, furnished with drawers, shelves and places to hang clothes. So we have as much room as we want. I had no idea of finding things so convenient.[4]

Frequent changes were inevitable, when, as Mrs. Cowles reported, "one plan was continually interfering with another" and Mary Lyon believed that shifts in assignments would be good for student morale. One of the student leaders who, under Miss Lyon's direction, "carried the institution safely through that most trying season" was Hannah Bailey of Amesbury, a former Ipswich student. She took on all sorts of tasks with equanimity. Her

11. Nancy Everett, later Mrs. John Dwight, and her year-old son Melatiah, painted by Joseph Goodhue Chandler. She attended the Seminary in 1837–38. It was on the opening day that she first met her future husband, who was one of the local youths helping the students settle in the still unfinished building. Mount Holyoke College Art Museum.

domestic work for the first ten weeks had been sweeping, but in late January she was making brown bread, mixing "nearly half a bushel of meal at once," and, with one other student, distributing, recording, and collecting for firewood, which was charged separately. There was a daily check-off, when each student came with her woodbasket, and at the end of each quarter the total sticks of wood each student had burned was multiplied by an agreed-upon rate in dollars and charged to the student. Hannah Bailey helped to do the computing, which, she wrote, was better than studying algebra. During 1837–38 the total number of sticks burned was 28,777, and at 208 to the dollar, $140 was collected.[5]

Many students, even the less robust, did more than their initially assigned tasks. Lucy Goodale, who entered March 10, three weeks before the end of the winter term, managed her daily work assignments with no trouble; by April 10 she was being shifted from crockery to pies. "After every dinner and supper cousin Elizabeth and I go to washing plates and I think you would laugh to see the piles of them. At dinner there are usually 200, at breakfast and supper not quite 100. But our happy circle of eight only laugh at them and they quickly disappear. Tomorrow E. and my-self are to leave this work for others and go to making pies. We are to make 15 every day excepting Mondays, Sundays of course and Thursdays." On the other hand the rigors of washday—scrubbing, wringing, carrying pails of hot water and the extra trips on the run up and down stairs—left her exhausted every Monday; in August she was still discouraged by her "lack of energy." Nevertheless, on a hot July evening, she was one of the volunteers when Miss Lyon invited "benevolent young ladies . . . after singing to take a walk with her, a walk to the garden for peas, but as the lightning was very vivid and it was late only eight of us went. And she gave each of us a row, herself taking one. We picked more than an hour, till nearly nine. Today others are shelling them. Then we have been favored with the exercise of pumping the well dry as the water was not good. Each enjoying the privilege only 5 or 6 minutes." There was apparently no choice about the five hours "of extra of extras" asked of every young lady for a major house cleaning in the midst of reviews and preparations for public examinations and com-mencement. Lucy's year-end assignment was indeed strenuous, but somehow she managed to survive it. On August 8 she wrote with justifiable pride "today I have done wonders. I arose at four, assisted in fixing my room, and performed my hours daily work before breakfast, then washed windows all the time till dinner, carrying them up and down 3, 4, or 5 pairs of stairs and all with-out breaking one, and now my part of cleaning house is done."[6]

Mary Lyon herself described the launching of the domestic operation in great detail in a letter written in July to the Rev. Theron Baldwin, head of Monticello Seminary, with whom she had had such interesting conversation the preceding September.

But your inquiries refer more particularly to the little appendage of our concern—the domestic department. With us this is entirely successful. The positive advantages of our plan are for us far greater than I anticipated. The difficulties & the immense labor or organizing were far greater than I anticipated. The final success is far greater than my most sanguine expectations. I found by experiment, that the qualifications for a lady at the head of the domestic department must be so various & so extensive, that it would be far easier to find all my teachers than one to fill this place. In this respect I was quite mistaken. Though the lady whom I had engaged would do well for many places, she could not sustain the amount of responsibility of the place. She spent a few months with us but I did not dare give her the direct responsibility of the department, lest it should be the means of making the whole unpopular.

In all such cases, you know there is but one course to be taken. We must do the work ourselves. When we have had an interest in planning, we can sometimes make up in zeal what we lack in skill. Since she left us, we have had no regular superintendant. I have the general direction, but the immediate care is taken by two young ladies, who are in this department like assistant pupils, devoting a part of their time to study & a part to superintending the domestic work. These we term "General Leaders." This plan I like much better than to have a regular superintendant, unless I can find one in whom I can have entire confidence as adapted to the situation. Everything is done better, & more pleasantly for the young ladies, & with much less care & solicitude on my part.

This failure in the domestic superintendant was a great disapointment, but it has not been without its advantages. Every part of the plan on which the young ladies are organized for their domestic work, is the result of personal observation. For many weeks I was engaged many hours every day about the domestic department— sometimes contriving about fitting of furniture, & cooking utensils— again planning for the division of labor, & for time & place, so that every thing could be done in season & in order without any loss to the young ladies, & with no interference with studies or recitations. I had several points to gain, & sometimes my whole energy was devoted to one, & sometimes to another.—One point was that a high standard should be established for the manner of having the work done—another that every department of the domestic work should be popular with the young ladies.

For three or four months I never left the family for a single half day. I then said to the young ladies, that I considered the family as organized, & that I wished to go to Boston to be absent two or three weeks that I might (besides finding a little rest) know whether the wheels which I had been occupied so long in arranging could move without my aid. On my return, everything was in

*perfect order, & there has not been a time since, when I could not
be absent or sick three months without any sensible loss to the
domestic department. Now I need not go into the kitchen once a
month unless I prefer, though I do love daily to pass around from
room to room in the basement story, & see how delightfully the
wheels move forward. I trust you will excuse this egotistocal [sic]
description of the organization of our domestic department, as
the object is to give you facts as they are. . . .*[7]

In this letter she specified three main advantages: daily exercise;
opportunities for sociability; increased concern for the welfare of
all. Her enthusiasm for the physical benefits suggests that she did
not realize the strain on girls like Lucy; otherwise her optimism
seems justified. She emphasized the character and dedication of
those pioneering first-year students; indeed, all her life she continued to pay tribute to their "conscientious faithfulness" and
"noble and generous spirit." Certainly they responded to her fundamental assumption that intelligent young women could get done
almost everything that was absolutely essential, and everybody
profited from her gift for discerning quickly what individual
students could do best. As Mrs. Cowles put it, she had "the skill
of a Napoleon in finding her generals and putting them in their
right places." This happy collaboration turned what might have
been a disaster into a triumph; the system evolved in 1837-38
helped to carry the institution through the administrative ups and
downs of the next half century.[8]

The academic program presented an entirely different problem
from the housekeeping operation; improvement in preparation,
extension of the curriculum, student persistence through a three-
year course—they could only be accomplished little by little.
Under any circumstances Mary Lyon, whose virtuosity at working
out complicated schedules had been proved at Ipswich, would no
doubt have paid close attention to the domestic organization. But
even with the crucial difficulties of November 1837, she would
probably not have relinquished so much academic responsibility
in the early months if she had not been able to transfer it to the
associate principal, Eunice Caldwell, her close friend and a gifted
and experienced teacher. Eunice, dedicated and brilliant, did not

181

have Mary Lyon's physical stamina, and she was tired when she came to South Hadley, having carried Wheaton through the summer term, against Miss Lyon's better judgment. Indeed, her nerves were sufficiently on edge that it was thought best for her to eat and sleep at the Condits' for a few weeks and to postpone some of the mathematics classes she was to give. Nevertheless, she shouldered a very full load. She worked out academic schedules; for a period she led morning devotions; she did much of the supervising of the other two teachers, Mary Smith and Amanda Hodgman, both Ipswich graduates, and the three undergraduate teaching assistants. For six months she took over Mary Lyon's correspondence. The academic standards that were established did everyone credit, but she finally succumbed to the cumulative pressure. In May she had to leave for nearly ten weeks of recuperation, returning just in time for intensive reviews and the public examinations. But before May 1 Miss Lyon knew that in succeeding years she would have to get along without Miss Caldwell altogether; on that date she announced to the school that their much loved associate principal had become engaged to John Phelps Cowles, outspoken professor of Old Testament literature at Oberlin and cousin to Zilpah Grant.[9]

Many of the young women who attended the Seminary some part of the first year were in their twenties, had taught for several years, and were motivated by high ideals of service rather than purely intellectual ambition. Even Mary Lyon, who was always sanguine about the qualities of the students she was then teaching, pointed out to Mr. Baldwin that she had felt it necessary initially to allow enrollment for only ten or twenty weeks. However, "more than half of those in the winter continued through the summer, & more than half of our present scholars will continue the next year." Her total applicant list for the 90 available places in 1838-39 was nearly 200, and she would henceforth be able to require for admission a readiness to attend for a full year. She had also made some exception in the preparatory studies required. The oral entrance examinations, calling for both exactly remembered facts and phrases in grammar, United States history, geography, and elementary psychology, and for rapid solving of arithmetic problems, presented major hurdles to some of the young ladies.

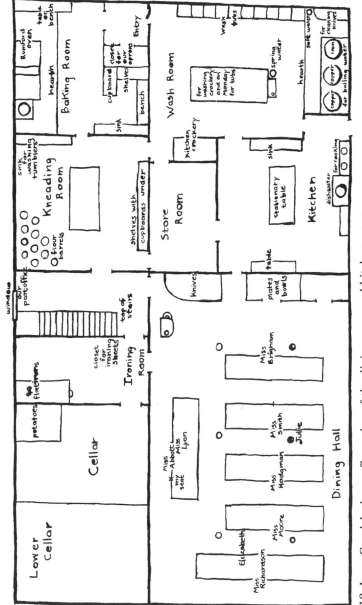

12. Lucy Goodale drew a floor plan of the dining room and kitchens soon after her arrival at the Seminary in March 1838 to help explain to her family her admiration for "the excellent design and arrangement" of the building. Plan copied by Catherine Casey. Mount Holyoke College Library Archives.

Review classes continued as long as necessary even though, as the catalogue reported, some had spent so much time on preparatory studies that they could not complete the work of the junior year by the end of the summer. The students seem to have approved this strictness. Harriet Wheeler, writing to her mother on December 28 that she felt she had better study a little more before she ventured upon the arithmetic examination, said, "They mean to have thorough work here in everything." That word echoed through the student letters. "It will take me at least three years to complete a thorough course of study," Harriet Hollister wrote her younger sister in Vermont. "They are very thorough here, more so than I expected. They will make us get our lessons and get them well. I thought I knew something before I came here, but, sometimes I feel as if I did not know anything," Nancy Everett wrote on November 26. She still had her own arithmetic examination to take, though she had been drafted to hear a review class recite in cube root and arithmetical progression.[10]

Classes were arranged on the Ipswich system: two or three major subjects pursued intensively for each "series" of six to ten weeks, and extras—including a weekly composition, calisthenics, and vocal music—continued throughout the year. It is not surprising that most students seemed to enjoy their academic work, even though learning was by rote, as it was throughout higher education then. Both Miss Caldwell and Miss Lyon, who in due course found time to return to the classroom, were exceptional teachers. Among Miss Lyon's classes, remembered long afterward with special enthusiasm, were those on Butler's *Analogy of Religion, Natural and Revealed*; Whately's *Logic*, which she was teaching for the first time with "eagerness and relish"; Milton's *Paradise Lost*; and chemistry. Lucy Goodale was one of many fascinated by the demonstrations and experiments.

The other day I stopped after the class was dismissed to look at some quick-silver, and she asked me if I should like to assist her, and glad I was of the opportunity. So I tied some zinc turnings together and she put them in a solution of acetate of lead and in a few days we had a beautiful lead tree. Then she told me I might make a looking glass. The first thing to do was to find some glass and for this I was sadly at a loss. At last I thought of a room where the window over the door was broken and went and begged a piece. I fixed the shape as well as I could, made an amalgam of mercury and tin and spread it upon tinfoil, making it very even. I laid it upon the glass and there was a perfect little looking glass.[11]

If the average pioneering student of 1837–38 did not quite equal her successors intellectually, some of those enrolled the first year were superior by any standard. Three of them turned out to be conspicuously able teachers and administrators, who were drafted by Mary Lyon immediately after graduation and played no small part in the success of the Seminary. Abigail Moore, daughter of Mary's oldest sister, Electa, came from Fredonia, New York, to Ipswich, thanks to her aunt's encouragement and financial assistance. (This, as with Mary's other nieces and nephews, included both gifts and loans.) Abigail had taught for three years in Virginia and had been her aunt's second choice for domestic superintendent. From the opening day she must have stood out—one of four seniors, one of three assistant pupils, an extra aide for Miss Lyon. From her graduation in August 1838 until her marriage eight years later Abigail was on the Seminary staff—from 1842 to 1846 as associate principal—and always a pillar of strength in practical matters. Mary Whitman, a member of the middle class, was exactly the kind of young woman for whom the Seminary had been conceived: an experienced teacher, dependent on her own earnings, who had been "waiting a long time" for such an opportunity and planned before entrance to spend two years at the Seminary, "As I wish to be very thorough." She was a kindred spirit and soon took Eunice Caldwell's place as Miss Lyon's friend and confidante. After her graduation in 1839 she was successively teacher, associate principal, and, for a short while after Mary's death, principal. Mary Whitman's successor was also a student the first year, a member of the junior class named Mary Chapin. Few would have guessed that this small, modest 17-year-old would be the one to steer the institution through a very difficult transition period and into a dozen years of growth and prosperity. Lucy Stone was also one of the early students at Mount Holyoke, but she was called home by the death of a sister after three months—too short a stay to get her name in the catalogue. In later life she recalled provoking a reproof from Miss Lyon about Garrison's *Liberator* and antislavery agitation. When, after four more years of teaching, Lucy Stone had saved up enough money to get her through college, she headed for the more congenial climate of Oberlin.[12]

Lectures on character, manners, and the amenities of group living were a regular part of the Seminary program, and, from the first, they were popular. Mary Lyon had a quick wit and a power of mimicry hard to get down on paper, but over the years many students were to agree with Lucy Goodale that "at the table we all love to hear Miss Lyon's little bell ring, we expect something from her." She gave a sample of the presentation of household information.

She said this morning, "I don't want any of you to feel bad because you have no room-mate for next term. I expect about 40 new scholars and I shall perhaps give you one, and I want you to show your hospitality and benevolence in trying to make her happy." She said, "I do not dread next term. The new scholars will have on sad faces,—they will not know as they shall want to go up so many stairs, don't know as they shall like to take care of the knives, or wash the dishes, and you will be merry as birds because you are acquainted here. Now I want you should lay yourselves out to make them so too."

Harriet Hollister reported that "Miss Lyon says when the sons of the prophets needed to have their house or college enlarged they did it with their own hands," adding, "There is not another Miss Lyon in the world; she is a pattern of perfection."[13]

This warmth of feeling seems to have engendered tolerance even of proposals that might well have been resisted. When the successive squads at the wash tubs Monday morning left the floor standing in water, Miss Lyon took immediate precautions against wet feet in winter. She purchased in Northampton enough india rubbers for the entire school, for which each student paid $1 a pair. Eventually arrangements for evaporation and drainage would make them unnecessary. In the meantime many of the young ladies must have agreed that "it would be presumption for us to get along without them this winter."[14]

Probably the rule that occasioned most individual opposition was the ban on tea and coffee. Almost immediately after the opening, Mary Lyon persuaded all but half a dozen students to get along without either beverage; within two or three weeks the holdouts had either given in or gone home. Julia Hyde long afterward recalled the grounds of Miss Lyon's initial appeal as economy, but she must also have celebrated the virtues of cold water. Temperance was then a great cause. In addition to total abstinence from alcohol, dietary rigor was being advocated by many, including Professor Hitchcock. In 1830 he delivered and published a series of lectures, *Dyspepsy Forestalled and Resisted*, urging moderation, especially in eating meat, and simplicity, that is, only one or two dishes per meal instead of many. Although in time he modified some of this advice, thirty years later he still believed firmly that "whatever may be necessary in poor health and in old age, for the young and the middle aged, pure water is all that is necessary, and best adapted to health and strength." Mary Lyon, who had flourished under the dietary regime of the Hitchcock household, held just as firmly to the superiority of cold water. Until after her death, tea and coffee were used in the Seminary only as two of the medicines prepared by the young women serving as nurses.[15]

But in spite of this restriction, many students wrote home enthusiastically about the food at Mount Holyoke. In most ways, Mary Lyon was not a follower of Sylvester Graham, although she must have known about the much discussed diet and regimen of that doctor from Northampton. At Oberlin, which was then following the Graham system to the letter, students and faculty were denied not only tea and coffee but most meat and fish, gravy, butter, pepper, mustard, oil, vinegar, and pies and cakes unless they were made of honey or maple sugar and graham flour or corn meal. Before Professor John P. Cowles married Eunice Caldwell, he ate at the Oberlin boarding house. When he "brought a pepper shaker to the table it was ordered removed by the trustees." And Fletcher points out, "His subsequent dismissal was not unrelated to this offense!"[16]

In spite of the late start and time-consuming difficulties of 1837–38, Mary managed to schedule some of the special events that subsequently gave variety to the school year. The first Thanksgiving was modest compared with later celebrations, but even in 1837 the young women who did not go home for New England's major winter holiday enjoyed a special dinner, given by Deacon and Mrs. Porter, and an evening of hospitality with South Hadley neighbors. The tradition of an unscheduled day's holiday for a trip to the top of Mount Holyoke was firmly established. In the summer term there were two excursions of about 50 students each, one on June 23 and a second on July 14, led by Professor Hitchcock, who had just been giving geology lectures at the Seminary; six months earlier, 25 hardy young ladies had got to the top on a fine day in January. Lectures like Professor Hitchcock's, from visiting faculty, ministers, and missionaries, soon became an important means of enriching the curriculum and extending the range of both students and teachers.[17]

Mary Lyon also set up student organizations on the principle followed at the Buckland and Ipswich schools: the students had a free choice of whether to join, but the purpose and organizational scheme were controlled from above. Of these, the most indicative of Miss Lyon's belief in the future of the Seminary was the Memorandum Society, which was an alumnae association. It was launched on March 10 with a detailed constitution drawn up by two of the seniors, Abigail Moore and Sarah Brigham; Miss Lyon was president. Members paid $2 for lifetime dues and promised to send information about themselves at least once in three years. The Society would send catalogues annually and issue an up-to-date directory of members once every five years.

Whatever was left over from the payment of dues would go to build up the library, another project for the future calling for community support. A reading room had been an essential part of the building design, but the trustees, in debt for bricks and mortar, had not budgeted anything for books. Contributions came from students, faculty, and friends. Julia Hyde, who reported that Mary Lyon had given $15 and Eunice Caldwell $20 to the collection taken up in the Seminary at the beginning of March, asked her impecunious minister father, "Come now do not you want to beg some money for our library?" Substantive gifts of books came from students and faculty at Amherst, who were formally thanked by the trustees in May. Mrs. Hitchcock donated a collection of minerals made by her brother, and Professor Hitchcock delivered his geology lectures gratis on the understanding that the young ladies would make a special contribution for a set of geology books. Mary Lyon's first purchases with the student contributions, recorded with approval in student letters, were weighty tomes—the many-volume sets of the Americana Encyclopedia, the Bridgewater Treatises (which showed how the order of nature supported revealed religion), the works of Josephus, first-century historian of the Jews.

Not all of the reading matter was ponderous. Miss Lyon had always encouraged her students to be interested in current events. Before there were any books on the shelves, the reading room tables contained a variety of newspapers and journals supplied by the students through another of her schemes. Anyone who wished to do so joined a Society of Inquiry by paying 12½ cents toward a school subscription, or by bringing in every week some periodical sent her regularly from home. The titles ranged widely: religious weeklies like the *Boston Recorder* and the *New York Observer*, the monthly *Missionary Herald*, *Youth's Companion*, the *Penny Magazine*, *Human Rights*, the *Emancipator*.[18]

Although each succeeding month brought increased stability and brighter prospects for the Seminary, toward the end of the year it sustained a major loss which Mary must have felt keenly. Eunice Caldwell's illness and absence for nearly ten weeks of the summer term created an immediate burden almost as heavy as Miss Peters's collapse at the opening. Writing in early August to invite Mr. and Mrs. Heard to the commencement exercises two weeks later, Mary apologized at some length for having failed to invite them to the dedication, which had finally taken place May 3.

How the mistake should have been, that we did not write to you, I cannot exactly tell. Certainly it was in my heart to do it. Besides it was on my memorandum, lest it should be forgotten. For to tell the truth, during the last year, much of the time, amidst all my cares about school, family, domestic concerns, obtaining furniture, setting up housekeeping, economizing our menues, & contriving how to do without what we cannot have, it has seemed as if I should forget everything, unless it was on my memorandum. But

*a few weeks about the time of dedication, was the most difficult.
Miss Caldwell's health failed, & she had many other things to
occupy her thoughts, & to take what little strength she had. For
several weeks, I was obliged to take most of Miss Caldwell's cares
in addition to my own. But we have been carried nearly through
the year with great kindness and mercy.*

It was the forthcoming marriage, of course, that was the heaviest
blow. Possibly Miss Lyon, too, privately viewed Professor Cowles's
visits, early in April, early in May, and again in August as overlong.
Unquestionably she had a strong sense of loss—for Eunice as well
as for Zilpah—when she wrote

*The intimate communion which continued between us for so
many years, I do not, I cannot forget. Sometimes former views,
and former intercourse, and former mutual duties and obligations, and mutual kindness and faithfulness, in contrast with
the present nonintercourse almost between us, come over me,
with an overwhelming power. I know it must be so. I know
you cannot come to see me, nor can I go to see you; and if I
could, I should not feel at liberty to tax your strength with
my visits. The same is true with regard to our writing. I am generally entirely reconciled. But occasionally, when I have heard
nothing from you for weeks or months, only as I do by the
by, as I do from any of my common acquaintances, I find myself
involuntarily saying, Is this that same friend with whom I lived
and labored so many years, with whom I had so much intercourse
from day to day, and with whom I have exchanged so many
letters? This is the changeableness of earth. How transitory is
everything here! It seems as if I could say of nothing that it has
long been, but only that it once was; or that it now is, and may be
a few days longer. Of all the changes that take place, the changing
of friends, of companions, of fellow-laborers, of fellow-travellers
through this pilgrimage, is the most painful. Rather let these
changes come year by year, and month by month, so that there
may be no tender and long-strengthened cords to be torn asun-
der—that there may be no train of recollection and former communion to add to scenes of desolation.[19]*

This state of mind was rare; she soon recovered her normal optimism. Even though Eunice had not returned when she started her long letter to Theron Baldwin, she began her appraisal characteristically: "On the whole, the success of our institution in every department is greater than I anticipated." Whether, if Eunice had stayed, Mary Lyon might in the long run have spent more time teaching herself or maintained a faculty of greater experience and intellectual sophistication, it is impossible to guess. Before too long she found in Mary Whitman a successor as friend and confidante.

The anniversary on August 23 went off in fine style. Public examinations were held Monday afternoon and Tuesday and Thursday mornings. Wednesday more than half the students attended commencement at Amherst College, while the rest stayed home to prepare for the 40 dinner guests—trustees, ministers, others—invited to eat with the students before the exercises Thursday afternoon. Mary Lyon had finally been prevailed upon to let the ceremony be held in the church; afterward she agreed that it was not unsuitable. The procession from the Seminary to the church was led by the trustees and the speaker, followed by Miss Lyon and the other teachers, the three graduating seniors, and the rest of the school. All the girls wore white, were bareheaded, and carried parasols. The address by Dr. Joel Hawes of Hartford contained "good common sense," although, Mary Lyon noted, it was "not quite as finished as I should have liked." The diplomas were presented by Mr. Condit, as secretary of the board, "in his neat, elegant manner"; these parchment evidences of achievement were in English, not Latin, and illustrated a favorite verse of Joseph Emerson which was also on the Seminary seal, "That our daughters may be as corner stones, polished after the similitude of a palace" (Psalms 144:12). Professor Hitchcock noted that the palace on the diploma had been modified by the engraver from a drawing by Mrs. Hitchcock to include domes and minarets like Brighton Pavilion, but he still felt that "the instrument" was "a very neat one."[20]

It is not surprising that Mary Lyon resisted anything that might be construed as public display in the ceremonies. From the beginning she had told the students "You must not call this Miss Lyon's school," not for fear of continuing skepticism or hostility but because her name might divert attention from the guiding hand of God at every point along the way. Nevertheless, to almost everyone in that crowded church, she was truly the dayspring and center of the Seminary in being. Even students who found the pressures and restrictions of daily life difficult to sustain treasured the remarkable quality of that first Seminary year. Although Julia Hyde found the wash-day-before-breakfast a torture every Monday, she shared in the tumultuous welcome in March when Miss Lyon came back after three weeks in Boston—laughing, crying, kissing, "as if my mother had returned." And the student delight was doubled by Mary Lyon's own. "Miss Lyon is so happy since she came home, she goes about the house and admires the works of her own hands." Lucy Goodale, who decided in August to spend a year at home before she returned for another year of Seminary tension, still admired the system.

I do hope that I shall not lose my love of order and system, when I get home but I do very much fear that my many good plans and resolutions, will be broken. How I do wish the things at home would go like clockwork as they do here, so much is accomplished, and every thing is cheerful and nice and "in good taste."[21]

For the next three years the Seminary appeared to be running smoothly in all departments, but the pressure on Mary Lyon slacked off very little. For one thing, money still had to be raised and furniture supplied. Although the admissions criteria became more exacting, Miss Lyon's acceptance letters continued to ask the young ladies themselves to round up and bring with them beds and bedding. One accepted candidate from Northfield offered to sleep on a straw pallet if Miss Lyon could find someone else as a roommate hardy enough to sleep with her on the floor; in any case she would bring ticking, pillows, and other bedding. The major money-raising effort, however, was for a capital sum sufficient to add on a wing.

By June 1839 Mary had made time to produce still another fund appeal, a 26-page pamphlet entitled *Female Education: Tendencies of the Principles Embraced, and the System Adopted in the Mount Holyoke Female Seminary*, asking outright for $20,000 for additional buildings and $5,000 for furniture, books, and laboratory equipment. Once again she enunciated her principles: a permanent endowment in the hands of independent trustees, and mature students, at least 16 years old, who could meet exacting entrance requirements and were ready to pursue advanced subjects in a sequential three-year course of study. She stressed the importance of "religious culture" and "cultivation of benevolence," placing them ahead of "intellectual culture" in her list of educational goals; she pointed out at length the advantages of the domestic work system; she reminded her readers of the need for well educated teachers to improve the quality of common schools as well as secondary education. Finally she specified in some detail the advantages of a large seminary.

In order that a lady may have the most thorough education, she should spend a number of years in close intellectual application, after her mental powers have acquired sufficient strength, and her physical system sufficient maturity, and after she has all the necessary preparation. This must be during the best part of her life, when every year is worth more than can be estimated in gold and silver. Facilities for success should be given her, which will be an ample reward for the sacrifice of so much time. She should have the benefits of a systematic course, and should pursue studies in their natural order, while she has the privilege of reciting in a class of a suitable number, and of similar improvement to her own.

Whoever has undertaken to organize a school, has had abundant evidence that all these points cannot be gained where the number is not large. This seminary is able now to secure all these advantages in some degree, but not so perfectly as it will, when the two hundred can be received. What is now done is effected by a great effort of the teachers, and a great loss of time, to which they will not then be subject. Library and apparatus, such as cannot be found in little schools, are as necessary for females pursuing a thorough course of study, as for the other sex. Perhaps experiments and illustrations are more important for them, as they have a less number of years for the pursuit, and as their time must be more occupied with other things.

She concluded by once more contrasting the long established habit of public support for the colleges for men with the neglect of institutions for women, and pleading for equality in giving. "Have not the friends of education another blessing to bestow, though they have already done so liberally in behalf of their own sex?" The pamphlet was unsigned; contributions might be directed to Mr. Hawks or Deacon Safford.[22]

For several years Mr. Hawks was out on the road a great part of the time. When in 1840 he proposed giving up his agency so that he could have more time at home, Miss Lyon "said she could not spare him this ten years." In addition to his best efforts, she saw the need of extra impetus to bring operations to completion. At a meeting of the board in April 1839, the trustees agreed to contract for bricks sufficient for a 50-foot addition, later extended to 75 feet, but it was not until August 1840 that, emboldened by some money "unexpectedly accumulated in the hands of the Steward from the receipts of the School," they authorized the borrowing of $5,000 and the start of operations on the south wing. The minutes of this meeting recorded their intention to build, when funds should justify it, a parallel northern wing to accommodate comfortably the 200 students that Mary considered the desirable number; but it was not until more than four years after her death that the second wing was ready for occupancy. When construction did begin on the south wing in the fall of 1840, she was still pushing hard. In December she wrote to ask if Mr. White would collect immediately as much as possible of the money due her, in order to facilitate a loan to the trustees, who had a large payment due the first of the year.

Be particular to tell him that I want he should not incommode himself as he is so good & faithful to attend to my business. You may also say, that if he finds it difficult to get it quite all collected that is in his hands till nearly the middle of summer, I can possibly do without a small part till then. I suppose that he might find it a convenience to himself to delay a part till then. He will not I presume mention this to those of whom it is to be collected, lest they should take the advantage & delay it till a later period. I shall then want to use every dollar I have, very much indeed.

13. This lithograph of the Seminary building was made by Nathaniel Currier from a drawing done by Persis Thurston, a missionary daughter from Hawaii who graduated in 1845 and taught in the Seminary for the next three years. The view shows the first major addition to the building, the south wing, which was completed in December 1841. Mount Holyoke College Library Archives.

In addition to making ready cash available when large sums had to be paid out in January and July, Mary devised another bit of financial encouragement: she would have her own furniture in the new rooms she was to occupy—in other words, she would pay for everything purchased out of her own funds. Even with these spurs to action, the addition was not ready until December 1841; for the preceding two months of school she had had to exercise all her ingenuity to fit more than 170 students into very crowded quarters.[23]

The special responsibility that she probably felt most deeply was religious leadership. From the first she had set aside considerable time for religious exercises; and she indicated in the 1839 fund-raising pamphlet the importance of "public worship, the Bible lesson, and other appropriate duties of the Sabbath; a regular observance of secret devotion, suitable attention to religious instruction and social prayer meetings." Although the schedule changed in details from year to year, virtually every student enrolled at Mount Holyoke during Mary Lyon's lifetime attended two services at the village church every Sunday, studied and recited a long Bible lesson over the weekend, spent a half hour in the early morning and another in the evening alone in private devotion, and received from Miss Lyon scriptural instruction at morning devotions and practical advice on conduct and morality at the general exercises in the afternoon. In addition, most of the girls joined one or more "social prayer" circles and attended at least one of the separate weekly meetings arranged according to the religious state in which students had classified themselves when they entered: as church members, as having no hope of salvation, or as somewhere in between. Then there were the "monthly concert," a meeting at the church to hear about and pray for the missionaries, and two yearly fast days, one at the new year to pray for the conversion of the world and one on the last Thursday in February for literary institutions—that is, the colleges and seminaries from which the religious leaders of the next generation would come.

Most of these services seem to have been either approved or tolerated by nearly all the students in the early years. The two daily "half-hours," for which the large, lighted closets had been designed to enable two roommates to have privacy at the same time, were popular even among the unconverted. Out of these occasions came "the sessions of special interest in personal religion" in which, every year after the first, a number of students were converted. In 1837–38 all but a dozen students were already "hopefully pious" when they came, and great extra effort was needed to make the institution go. Indeed, as Lucy Goodale wrote her mother in March 1838, although a revival was in progress at the South Hadley church, "owing to 'the presence of study' from the approaching examinations, Miss Lyon is unable to make as many arrangements as usual for her pupils to attend." They did manage to get to some of the hour-long prayer meetings held at sunrise every morning.[24]

During the second year the Seminary experienced a remarkable revival; according to a brief religious history written in 1846 by Mary Whitman, "every member of the school appeared to be deeply affected, and all but one or two indulged the Christian hope." There were about 30 hopeful conversions in 1838–39 and the same number in 1839–40; at the end of the latter year, as Miss Whitman reported in italics, "*all indulged the Christian hope.*" The fourth year revival was less spectacular; even so, "six or eight only remained, at the close of the year, without hope."[25]

It is difficult for readers today to realize the popularity of revivals in the second quarter of the nineteenth century, particularly in the colleges. The "appetite for self-examination and self-recrimination" that Perry Miller saw as part of the American character was certainly fed by the "religious excitements" that Charles Grandison Finney and other "New Measures" men created in New York state and then spread across the country. Oberlin, which opened in 1834, managed to get Finney himself as professor of theology and then president; in the words of Professor Fletcher, the "spiritual and moral heat generated by Finney's revivals had produced Oberlin," which, "without Finney certainly seemed unthinkable." And Oberlin was not alone. "Nearly every prominent evangelist," according to Timothy Smith, "gave time and raised money for a college which he hoped would train young ministers to follow in his steps. In this respect Oberlin was only in degree more significant than Amherst, Rensselaer, Rochester, Wittenberg, Connecticut Wesleyan, Ohio Wesleyan, Gettysburg, and Western

Reserve Colleges and Lane, Yale, Andover, and Union Theological Seminaries." At Amherst Professor Hitchcock in his last years could say, "The religious history of Amherst College is more important and interesting than everything else pertaining to it," and point with pride to 14 major revivals between 1823 and 1862, supplemented by "many other seasons of special interest."[26]

A revival in a college was usually conducted by its president, perhaps assisted by some of the faculty and a visiting evangelist, all probably ordained ministers. Before the Civil War a sizable proportion of college faculty members and eleven out of twelve presidents were clergymen. Mary Lyon, who relied on God's blessing as transmitted through her and some of the young teachers at their regularly scheduled religious meetings, was always humble about her own powers. A few months before her death, at a time of "special religious interest," she asked Mrs. Porter to pray for her. Before meetings she was to conduct, she would be "weighed down with fear and trembling and anxious solicitude"; if there seemed to be some response, she felt "overwhelmed with gratitude, and with a view of my own unworthiness." Indeed, she wrote, "None but God knows how the responsibility of giving religious instruction to those candidates for eternity weighs on my heart." What particularly impressed Professor Hitchcock, who played a major role in the Amherst revivals, was the quietness of the conversion process at Mount Holyoke.

A person might live for weeks in the seminary, during one of these revivals, and yet see nothing unusual, save a deep solemnity and tenderness during religious exercises. Those exercises would not be much multiplied, nor would the literary exercises be suspended or diminished, unless in individual cases of deep seriousness. Both teachers and pupils would seem to be deeply engrossed in their studies, and would be, in fact during the hours appropriated to study. Nor would the subject of religion be obtruded upon the visitor, or introduced, unless he manifested an unusual interest in the state of the school . . .[27]

Although there seemed to be none of the drama that marked most revivals, on campus and off, the proceedings at the Seminary were of great interest to most students and their families. Elizabeth Hawks was Nancy Everett's most faithful correspondent in the two and a half years between Nancy's departure from the Seminary and her return to South Hadley as John Dwight's bride. Elizabeth enjoyed gossip, but she also dealt in sentiments of piety and considered the revivals major news.

You have doubtless heard of the interest, at the seminary, upon the subject of religion. The work has indeed been wonderful. All but three in school, are indulging hopes. Those three, are, Miss Woods, Miss Clark from Amherst, and Miss Lucy Spencer, sister of Julia, and Eliza. Several professing Christians have given up their hopes, among whom were Misses Miranda Smith, Bass, and several others, I believe these are the only ones, with whom you were acquainted. Twenty one are indulging hopes. Among the number are, Misses Henry, E. Spencer, Penfield, Hitchcock, and Baldwin. I think I never saw any person so entirely altered as Miss Hodgman. She is very much engaged, goes from room to room, talking with the young ladies. We are now *indeed a happy family. Oh how I wish you could be here. But God is everywhere present with his children, and it is not necessary that we should be in the midst of a revival, to* feel *his presence. I am very glad to learn, that you feel so much interest in the subject, (and indeed you always do) and that you feel so much, the importance of living to the glory of God.*

One of those converted in 1839 was Caroline LeConte, who came from farming country in the Finger Lakes region of New York and stayed straight through three years to graduate in 1841. Her description of her conversion was very impersonal. After summarizing Miss Lyon's talk on the love of God and His plan for the redemption of rebellious man, she devoted a paragraph to the spring revival.

Yesterday we set apart for fasting & prayer for the convertion of the impenitent of this Institution; the Holy Spirit appeared to be indeed amongue us, in his reviving and quickening influences on the hearts of his professed people; and his convicting influences on the hearts of the impenitent—it is indeed a searching time—some who have been professors for years have given up their hope, and are now seeking anew. Since the commencement of this revival twenty one have, as we humbly trust been born again—Shall we not bless the Lord for his goodness toward us! and shall we not be encouraged to open our mouth wide that he may fill it—shall we not ask that he would glorify himself by the convertion of every soul in this Institution?

Lucy Goodale, who had joined the church at 15, kept reporting to her family successive stages in the 1839-40 revival. Like other professing Christians, she was aware of the danger of backsliding; one letter suggests how an intensity of religious feeling could be sustained even after every one of the impenitent had achieved at least a trembling hope.

It is indeed a great privilege to be here while the Savior is so near and the influences of the Holy Spirit are enjoyed. The interesting state of feeling continues. All have expressed a hope that they have passed from death unto life. What great cause have we for gratitude for such blessings. We pray that they may not be deceived. We fear for them when they return to the scenes and temptations of the world, for it is comparatively easy to live near to God in these consecrated walls. Our morning prayer meetings are continuous; they are good seasons. We meet in circles for prayer on Sat. evening. At the same time those who have indulged hope this term meet one of the teachers and the rest who have not made a public profession meet Miss Lyon in her room. Three have united with the church and another is now propounded.[28]

The effort most important to the future of Mount Holyoke—and of higher education for women—was the steady rise in academic expectations. Every catalogue and every appeal for funds carried the reminder that standards would go up as soon as circumstances warranted. One of Mary Lyon's first lines of attack was examinations. In the fall of 1838 oral examinations were required not only of the entering juniors but also of the returning middle class and seniors, who had to demonstrate their precise recall of what they had learned the preceding year. Sarah Brigham, one of the first three graduates who had all returned to teach, described the system to Nancy Everett, who was still considering coming back for another year.

Review & examination—review & examination have been the principal words & afforded the principal employment of both, teachers & pupils, since we came together. The plan of examining Miss Lyon proposed last term, has been adopted—Everyone is examined in all she studied during the last year—Classes from ten to fifteen are formed & questioned till all the teachers, who are present, are satisfied, with regard to the amount of knowledge the scholar possesses of the study examined. I do regret exceedingly that you have been absent these few weeks. I do not think a greater amount of school business was ever accomplished in four weeks.

Classes have been examined in Polic. C. Boo.—Physiology, Blair's & Newman's Rhetoric, Ancient Geog. Men. Philosophy, History, Chemistry, Astronomy, Euclid, Algebra, & Grammar. The last three are now on hand, but will be finished this week—also Eccle. His. & Smellie's Phil. of Nat. History. Almost all of the new scholars have entered the Junior Class—A new class in Phys. & Rhet. will finish the book this week—& the Senior Class have been through Alex. Evidences of Christianity—Chemistry is commenced next week & a class in Milton this week or next.

Nearly all the Senior Class complete their reviews this week & then will take Whately's Logic—You perhaps may say you are glad you have not been here, to be driven at such a rate. But if you are coming back, this year, I am very sorry—& I write now to urge you to come just as soon, as you possibly can, after the reception of this. It is not probable, that there will be another class in Logic during the year—& it would be impossible for you to study it in your room. I told Miss Lyon today that I was going to write you, & enquired what I should say—She says, "tell her to come immediately, if she thinks of coming this year—for if she delays till next term, I fear she will not complete the course . . ."[29]

Not everyone rose to the hurdles. One of Nancy Everett's roommates, who had returned for a second year, left in early March 1839 for a teaching job. Her name was omitted from the 1838-39 catalogue because "she would not be examined in those studies to which she had attended, and therefore could not be admitted to the middle class. She said when she left that she *ought* to have been a member of the *senior class*." But Miss Lyon seems to have gauged the capacities of her students pretty accurately year by year. In the fall of 1839 Lucy Goodale reported cheerfully enough upon examinations still going on a month after the Seminary opened.

It is nearly five weeks since school commenced and I have yet to be examined in Algebra, Abercrombie and Rhetoric. Miss Lyon said those whose reviews and examinations were not completed in four weeks would be considered tardy but I am not very badly off, for you know "Misery loves company" and nearly half the school is mine. However I have succeeded beyond my expectations, History, Chemistry, Philosophy and Political Class book are disposed of. In the last mentioned study, in reciting the qualifications of a voter, I said he must have resided in the town for a year, but answering one question partly wrong does not prevent our being marked "4". Philosophy, Mr. Albee had made me understand so well that it caused me little trouble. You know I studied Blake's Astronomy at the same time. I think I shall venture upon that to be examined in Wilkin's.

The next day she received "4," the best mark, "in all the Algebra imposed upon the Junior Class, i.e. 10 sections."[30]

The start-of-the-year tests did not take the place of the public examinations conducted as part of the commencement ceremonies or the intensive reviews that preceded them. By the end of the third year Miss Lyon had scheduled afternoon examinations straight through a nine-day period. Interrogation proceeded by sections and was interspersed with calisthenics drills, choral music, and the reading of student compositions; even so, all of the 120 students must have had several chances to recite before an audience. Outsiders were present every afternoon after the first; on the final days and the afternoon planned especially for children—mainly calisthenics and music—the Seminary Hall was crowded. This expansion of the examination period was never repeated; it was inevitably connected in everyone's mind with the devastating typhoid epidemic which followed. But Miss Lyon kept on putting her mind on all the examinations and year by year shifting the arrangements to make them if possible less strenuous but certainly more searching. The students who wrote home that the examinations they had just been through were harder than the ones they had taken a year ago were probably right. The applicants for admission were specifically warned that they must be better prepared. A circular on admission printed in the summer of 1840 declared that "probably any indulgence hereafter relative to preparation will be unnecessary and inexpedient." Examinations would be rigorous. Those in doubt that they were prepared to pass demanding examinations were advised to consult their most recent teachers. Withdrawing an application for admission would be less painful than having to withdraw from the Seminary.

Miss Lyon never lost sight of the importance of intellectual maturity to the kind of institution she was evolving. Her reluctance about a dubious candidate who was the daughter of missionaries showed the nature of her concern.

South Hadley, Mar. 2, 1841

Rev. Mr. Hallock,
Sir,

I have received yours making application for the admission of your niece into the seminary. I have great doubt what I ought to say on the subject. Our number for the next year is nearly filled out. Still I think we must receive her, if it is best for her. Of this I have great doubt, after reading your frank description of her character. Our institution is adapted to scholars of great maturity. The instruction we give is general, insisting much on great principles, leaving those instructed to adapt & apply it to themselves. On scholars with the maturity of ours, I think the immediate practical effect quite as great, as the influence on their principles of action, & on their future character & conduct much greater than any other course. We give but little of that personal care, & that individual instruction so essential to the improvement of persons of but little maturity, & especially of those possessing prominent & radical defects to be rooted out. It is true we could

203

give much attention to an individual. But then, if it is seen to be no part of the general system, it loses a great part of its influence. If she could be placed in a small family school for one year, under the care of a lady of just the right character & skill, it would be vastly better than for her to be in our seminary, I have no doubt. Perhaps it may be said of those who come here, that unto every one that hath it shall be given, & she shall have abundance, but from her that hath not, shall be taken away even that she hath.

It is farther essential for her improvement here, that she be thoroughly prepared for admission. Without this preparation, she could not go on with profit with our scholars. With her character, this point would need special attention. She will be in danger of professing to be prepared when she cannot bear an examination.[32]

The curriculum was another point of attack. Miss Lyon was determined to add Latin to the prescribed course of study just as soon as she could manage it. In fact, Latin was taught as an extra, sometimes by an undergraduate "assistant pupil," every year from the first, and was promoted in every catalogue as a desirable addition to the studies required for entrance. She must have begun early in the general exercises persuading students who had never considered it before that they really did want to study the subject. In November 1839 Mary Burr wrote urgently to her family in Connecticut for their permission to take Latin: "before long a knowledge of this branch will be required of almost any select school teacher. In two or three years Miss Lyon will require one year of Latin of all who complete the course she says." Lucy Goodale was another of the students Miss Lyon steered into Latin, "though I should never have studied it of myself, at least not at present. But as it is assigned to me, I have only to accept it with pleasure." Encouraged by the caliber of the applicants and the response of the students, Miss Lyon ventured to print in the 1839-40 catalogue her hopes for a fourth year and for Latin as an integral part of the curriculum.

There is a regular English course of study, occupying three years. Some devote a part of their time to Latin, and continue more than one year in the same class. This is very desirable for all who expect

*to complete the regular course. It is contemplated that the course
of study will embrace four years to give a regular time to Latin. It
is hoped that the improvement of the pupils, and the expectation
of friends will soon justify such an addition.*

As it turned out, Latin was not required for graduation until
1846, and the course was extended to four years only in 1861.
But Miss Lyon's continuing expectations affected both students
and teachers and energized the whole academic program.[33]

There were other kinds of enrichment, some initiated by Mary
and some by students or the local community. In addition to
visiting missionaries and ministers who practically always led one
of the regular religious services, occasional academic lectures
opened new vistas. In the spring of 1840 the students heard a few
talks on architecture by Professor Snell of Amherst and in the fall
a series on the philosophy of history by the Rev. John Lord,
nephew of a former president of Dartmouth. In politics both the
town and the school were mainly conservative—that is, Whig; but
the presidential election of 1840 and the continuing conflicts
among antislavery groups provided opportunities for some coun-
tervailing minority opinions. An abolitionist spoke at the church,
which was later the scene of a big Whig rally. The table in the
reading room carried the *Emancipator, Slavery as It Is* and the
Abolitionist, along with the *North American Review* and the
Biblical Repository. In December 1839 the students had voted
how to spend the $120 they had collected for New Year gifts to
their teachers. The result was that Miss Lyon was made a life member of the Home Missionary Society (which took $30), Miss Moore
and Miss Whitman were made members of the Tract Society, Miss
Torrey and Miss Reed of the Seaman's Friend Society, Miss Humphrey of the Sunday School Society. Before the final votes some
students suggested the Anti-Slavery Society. It was voted down by
a large majority; nevertheless, Miss Lyon was achieving a range of
backgrounds and assumptions, conceivably more than she knew.[34]

Financially sound, besieged by applicants, raising academic
standards, rising in public esteem, the Seminary at the end of the
third year looked to be in fine shape, and Miss Lyon herself, if
harder pressed than ever, seemed indestructible. Suddenly she

received a shocking blow. The commencement exercises had been particularly satisfying. Mark Hopkins, president of Williams College, had delivered the address to an overflow audience that, according to one student count, contained more than 30 clergymen. The young ladies not only finished their nine days of public examinations with distinction but provided an ample dinner for upward of 200 and suitable refreshments for an evening party for all the students and their guests. Twelve young women had received diplomas and for the next year there was in prospect an excellent senior class of 16 (including Lucy Goodale) to set the tone for an even better school. By mid-August the trustees were finally ready to have work start on the new wing; in another year nearly twice as many new students could be admitted.

Then word began to come of the critical illness and death of Seminary students from typhoid fever. During the nine-week vacation some 40 of the 120 students enrolled were seriously ill; nine died. No clue to the cause has emerged. At a time when typhoid and typhus were indistinguishable to most doctors (the terms were used interchangeably in contemporary accounts of symptoms and procedures) and the standard treatment included emetics and purgatives, no one was trying to track down contaminated water or milk—or a typhoid carrier. A carrier was one possibility, if not a probability: former teachers and students came back to help out with reviews and domestic operations—this year Miss Lyon had invited Sarah Brigham Kittredge, a bride of two weeks, and her minister husband to come and work—and special guests were sometimes entertained for several nights in student rooms vacated for the purpose. Since the incubation period is two weeks, the infection must have occurred more than a week before the concluding anniversary service on July 30. Lucy Goodale, who died August 26, according to her mother's recollection had her first symptom, a severe headache, August 3. Direct contact was certainly the means of transmittal in the family of Fidelia Fiske, who was critically ill but ultimately recovered. Her father and sister were both infected and died, Deacon Fisk on September 24 and Hannah on October 17.[35]

Though medical knowledge of the disease was limited in 1840 (the typhoid bacillus was discovered in 1880), there was general agreement that typhoid—or typhus—fever stemmed from uncleanness; it was epidemic in crowded towns and in areas near decomposing animal and vegetable matter. For Miss Lyon's spotless Seminary, where the linen, the crockery, the pots and pans, the tables and floors were scrubbed to a fare-thee-well, this was a bewildering indictment. Even worse was the popular interpretation of the tragedy: the young ladies had died because they had studied too hard and were "kept in too close." Mary Lyon felt first of all the personal loss. As she afterward told Fidelia Fiske, "When my pupils were dying one after another, I was afraid to take up a paper lest I should see some new name added to the deceased, and not have strength to meet it. I was afraid to ask a question, or even listen to conversation, lest I should not find myself prepared for what I might hear." She wrote Zilpah Grant, "None but my heavenly Father knows how great a trial this was to my heart." She was concerned about the physical cause and also the divine purpose; she felt she "ought particularly to inquire about the moral cause, and to seek to know what the Lord would have us learn from his dealings with us."[36]

Whatever the cause of the epidemic, the consequences were widely felt. When school reopened October 1, there were only 80 students on hand; only half of those expected to make up the middle and senior classes had returned. Mary Lyon recruited from her waiting list to such good effect that in a month the total enrollment was up to the original target of 120. She was able to tell Rufus Anderson, secretary of the American Board of Commissioners of Foreign Missions, that there had been "no excitement" among the students about the epidemic, only increased conscientiousness, "and though they all felt the loss in the number and standing of our higher classes," the "junior class is the best we have ever had." Among those most critically ill, who were unable to return for a year or two were both Fidelia Fiske, who was to pioneer as a missionary, and Mary Chapin, who was to become principal of the Seminary. Prevention was on everyone's mind, and good health became the recurring theme of the general exercises for the whole year. At least once Mary spoke out in defense of the Seminary. In mid-October she told the students that she and the teachers had not been able to place a finger on anything important to safeguard student health that should be changed and suggested that, although they were "grieved by the ridiculous reports circulated," they could afford to wait in silence for God "to vindicate his own acts."[37]

There is no doubt that word of the tragedy spread. A former Ipswich student teaching in Georgia, to whom Mary Lyon had proposed a teaching post at Mount Holyoke, wrote back to explain that she did not want to leave after all, because Miss Lyon's offer had so improved her own situation—more assistants and more time off. She mentioned with sympathy the sickness and the deaths. One of the middle class of 1839–40 who did not return had been trying to raise money in her home town, New London, Connecticut, to furnish a room; she wrote that the $10 she was about to add to $20 sent earlier would be the last. "The recent death and sickness of so many connected with the Institution seems to have left an unfavorable impression . . . on the minds of our friends." But in spite of such reactions the standing of the Seminary seems not to have been permanently affected either by the loss of so many students or by the stories in circulation about what had happened.[38]

Arrangements for care of the sick had been very much on Mary Lyon's mind from the first, and a pattern had been well established before the summer of 1840. Rooms on the second floor were set aside as "sick rooms," a teacher and some of the students were assigned infirmary duties and equipped with the standard home remedies. Sometimes volunteers were invited to carry wood and water and sit with the invalids during meals. For the seriously ill, young women experienced in family nursing were recruited to watch round the clock and paid for this service by the sufferers or their families. The South Hadley doctor was immediately available and other doctors were called in on serious cases. Deaths did occur within the Seminary walls—perhaps about one a year. The first happened in the spring vacation in April 1839 and the second the following November when Adeline Hawks, niece of Roswell Hawks, died a sanctified but painful death, harrowing to many of the students until Miss Lyon's encompassing faith transformed the experience. From time to time bad colds or influenza did sweep through the school, but there was never afterward anything to compare with the severity of the 1840 epidemic. Considering medical practice at the time and the gravity of the illnesses and accidents coped with, the sanitary procedures and the general care seem to have been remarkably good.[39]

Mary Lyon by mid-winter had found a personal lesson from God in the epidemic—He was preparing her to meet the deaths of her sister and mother. Jemima, the older sister who lived in Ashfield, had died early in 1838 and Freelove, the youngest sister, had married her brother-in-law. In late September 1839, when the typhoid news was at its worst, Freelove died, probably of complications following childbirth. Two months later, on November 25, Mary Lyon's mother died at the age of 75. This was a prostrating blow. As she wrote Zilpah Grant,

alone I followed my dear mother to the grave. Her prayers, which I have daily had for so many years, I shall have no more. She, to whose comfort I have been expecting the pleasant privilege of administering for years to come, as almost the only child left her, will need nothing more. I feel my family loneliness; but with it eternity seems very near, with all its precious privileges, purchased by the blood of our glorious Savior.

The immediate personal consequence was a physical collapse that took her out of circulation for two months and limited her activities for weeks afterward. Her letter to Zilpah gave some details.

The last stroke touching my health has been to me scarcely a trial. As I have been obliged to give up many labors to other hands, and some weeks nearly all, I have felt that I have nothing to say and scarcely any thing to ask, but that God might be glorified.

After about a month's active labor in organizing the school, I began to find my strength very weakness. I tried to rest, but all seemed only to reduce me still more. I have had but little disease, but a general prostration. For several weeks I could not read much, nor write, nor think, nor feel, nor talk. For about two months I did not go out to church. Now I can go half a day, and do several things of the lighter sort.

I want to tell you many things about our school, and how kind

Providence has been to us, and how the way was all prepared beforehand for me to be laid aside. But I must wait till I write to you again.[40]

It was Deacon Safford who helped her to recover completely. She was finally persuaded to leave the Seminary for about six weeks, visiting the Saffords and then traveling west with them on a trip partly intended to improve his own health and partly to help out an impoverished relative living in Michigan. Mary Lyon went as far as her brother's home in Stockton in western New York, arriving dramatically just in time to save the farm from foreclosure. She returned July 15, all set to prepare for public examinations lasting only three days (half the classes had been examined in an earlier series at the beginning of May) and braced to fit a larger school into new quarters not yet completed.[41]

On the whole the Seminary came through its trial by pestilence very well. Repeated emphasis on the rules of sound health—sensible diet and clothing, exercise, seeing a doctor promptly, not studying in recreation hours—was surely all to the good, even though the day-to-day pressures were essentially unchanged. As in every other year Mary Lyon made some minor changes in the daily and weekly schedules; the modifications in the final reviews and examinations seemed to make a real difference, at least to Julia Hyde, who found them "very much better than the previous arrangement." Even so, as Julia herself had observed six months earlier, the "system includes the feeling of pressure as one important means of improvement. Sometimes I cannot help feeling she carries this principle rather too far—but it is not very easy to dissent from one so much beloved and revered as she is." Quite a few of the students who were particularly intelligent and idealistic also had great energy and found the crowded daily schedule stimulating. Antoinette Hubbell, a New York City girl in her first year at the Seminary, described with unmistakable zest the exigencies of her daily program.

At present I study half an hour before breakfast, from 5½ till 6. From ¼7 till 7¼ is one of my precious half hours for secret retirement. At 7½ I join one of the classes for calisthenics, 15 min.

*At ¼8 we meet in the Seminary Hall for family devotions. Imme-
diately after leaving the hall I go out for exercise in the open air,
and visit "young Niagara" or go through the orchard to follow
the meanderings of our little nameless streamlet or ascend Prospect hill, or—. The remainder of the forenoon is occupied with
study and recitation. Some of the classes in calisthenics practice
15 min. before 12. I usually devote them to reading.*

*We dine at 12, after which I spend the time until 1½ on French.
This little share of attention given to French (Mon. and Thurs.
only) does not promote my advance much in the acquirement of
the language, but merely assists me to retain the slight acquaintance I have of it. We are translating one of Racine's tragedies,
Esther. I study Latin for the succeeding day till 2. Between 2 &
3 Mon. and Thurs. sing, with a choir of 25 or 30, while most of
the others are drawing. Tues. I am employed that hour folding
sheets and table cloths, with one other, Miss Charlotte Hyde.*

*At 3 we assemble for sectional exercises, 15 min., the school
being divided into 3 sections, one meeting in the Hall, another in
the reading room, and the other in the chemical room. The exercise consists principally of giving in daily accts. (you are sufficiently experienced in teaching to have an idea what they may
be) but the division of which I am a member is generally so free
from exceptions on the points that we are requested to observe
that we find about eight min. to spare which are agreeably spent in
repeating items of intelligence, missionary, political, scientific,
grave or merry, wise or silly.*

*At 3¼ Miss Lyon meets us all in the hall, taking for herself half
an hour to instruct us various subjects; —today, (Tues.) she has
just finished that of health, upon the various branches of which
she has spoken for several weeks past. We then go to our rooms to
study 3/4 of an hour till 4½. I spend it analyzing, parsing, etc. in
Young, Mon. and Thurs., Tues. & Fri., preparing my chemistry
or Latin. The remaining 3/4 of an hour till the bell rings for the
close of study hours at 5¼ is passed Mon. and Thurs. in the grammar class (which seems more interesting to me than any other
grammar class I have ever been in unless it was Miss Clark's);
Tues. & Fri., reading, upon a plan similar to that of Professor
Bronson, whom you may have heard in New York.*

The interval till tea time, at 6, is variously employed in social intercourse, sewing, writing, procuring wood and water for our rooms, etc. For the last few weeks many of us have spent a portion of it in social prayer. During the recreation hour on Tues. I am with the circle who sorts clothes, as I have no domestic work Mon. At 7 the bell rings for study. From 7½ to 8 secret devotion,—recess, 15 minutes, then mental exercise again untill the retiring bell at 9¼. Truly I think we demonstrate the possibility of putting the motto "Early to bed and early to rise" in practice, I will not attempt to say whether the consequent "health, wealth, and wisdom" as certainly follow, unless it be health, which I enjoy in a most excellent degree.

There are no recitations on Wed., writing, reading and hearing compositions, and ironing form the order of the day, though in these as in all our employments there is perfect system. If you should occasionally turn your mind's eye towards me the hours immediately after tea, Fri., you might catch a glimpse of me over the wash tub, not a large brass-bound cedar washing tub, but a neat stationary shaker contrivance in keeping (not in size, but in convenience) with all our domestic apparatus. I have not mentioned any particular hour for my daily exercise in house work, as being one of the accommodating miscellaneous circle, I am called upon at various hours & for various things.

And, now, Caroline, that I have written out this sketch of my engagements, I fear that it will seem to you more like a labyrinth than anything else. By it you will only know how I, insignificant I, am engaged during almost every hour in the week, while it gives you but a partial view of the manner in which the more advanced are making increased accessions to their present attainments.

While I am just picking some of the twigs from the tree of knowledge, they are weaving for themselves a wreath of its fair flowers, or gathering some of its fruits. —But I have forgotten to say anything of Sat. or Sun. They are both short, short, yet happy days. I wish that you could feel the interest in this institution which is felt by its friends—knowing the benevolent principles upon which it has been founded, & upon which all the plans in connection with it are based,—I wish that I could express them to you, as I would but I see that I shall not have room to enlarge

*upon them at present. . . . You will see two reasons why we are so
contented here. We are constantly employed; (and oh, how much
happiness, right kinds of employment impart:) there is also much
variety with great regularity in our engagements which always
gives interest.*[42]

One of the special features of the 1840 commencement was an
address in verse to the senior class by one of its members, Sarah
Browne, whose occasional pieces in galloping tetrameters were
much admired by the whole school. In 20 stanzas she pictured the
possible destinies of her classmates—wives, teachers, home or
foreign missionaries—all marked by self-sacrifice and heroism. Her
concluding tribute to Mary Lyon and charge to the class was a
challenge to conquer the world.

*By all that ye owe to her pruning skill
By the mental void she was striving to fill
By the holy light to your pathway given
From a mind whose lamp was a spark from Heaven
By the plighted truths of your soul sincere
Oh!* honor *her name* by your bright career.

As they entered the "God-like race" she adjured her fellow seniors

*Be your course right on as the eagles fly
Right on—to a glorious destiny.*

Sarah Browne's poem probably did represent some of the romantic aspirations of many young women who attended the Seminary
in its first years, but the language was too high-flown for most
pupils of Mary Lyon, who talked to them of high deeds in simple,
humble terms. At the opposite pole were the phrases of Caroline
LeConte, a farm girl from upstate New York, who devoted a
considerable part of one letter to her mother to explaining why
she was getting a liberal education and what she would do with it.

*You wish to know what I will do for a living when my personal
property is used up. As to my personal property, I hope it will last*

213

*me next year out & be sufficient to carry me home, (if my life &
health are spared). I have not thought any thing further about it.
I guess that this was not just what Ma ment to ask. Did you not
mean to say—What are you agoing to do with your learning or so
much learning? or how do you intend to employ your time? I
shall have been to school some time, and as I hope learned something, but my mind works slowly, (you know my hands used to,)
so I acquire knowledge very slowly.*

*Then, there is another thing, my memory is not very retentive,
then to I am often in want of words to express my ideas in, with
all these disadvantages you must not expect that I will be so won-
derous wise when I return home—here you may ask what is the
use of my going to school then? It is my duty to improve, or to
use the talents which God has entrusted to me—My mind has been
so much taken up in the acquisition of I was agoing to say, knowledge—you may put any word you like, I mean studying or getting
lessons & writing compositions etc.—(by the way one of my compositions was read at examinations, the day before the last, so I
think I must have improved some in writing)—that I have not
thought much about how I shall use it when I get home.*

*I will teach if there seems to be an opening, or a place where I
am thought to be needed or perhaps I shall be needed at home,
that is if Mr. ―― takes Mary. I hope I shall be needed some
where and be directed to fill that place which providence shall
provide for me. I should love very much to stay at home, at least
one short year, and learn to do house work & spin and all such
things, and rest too, I suspect that I shall need about one years
rest,—Margaret advises me to get married the first good chance,
this of course I intend to do—but when I read in your letters of so
many marriages, I think I shant want to take up with every body
elses leavings, so I shall grow up an old maiden like the rest of my
sisters. If I have my health which is very good now when I get
through I think I ought to support myself by my own earnings,
don't you think so?*[43]

There were other signs of the growing prestige of Mount Holyoke. Demands for teachers multiplied. Requests for advice came
from those heading up other schools, including the future president

of Vassar College who urgently wanted Miss Lyon's architectural plans for a female seminary about to be started in Alabama. Notable guests attended the anniversary exercises. In 1839 Mrs. Lydia H. Sigourney, the popular poet and moralist, brought her ten-year-old daughter up from Hartford for the public examinations as well as the commencement address. But what the students wrote and told their families and friends probably contributed most substantially to the widening understanding of what the Seminary was already doing and what it was hoping to attempt.[44]

It is possible that the epidemic did have some long-term consequences: it may have retarded the tempo at which the curriculum offering and the standards of academic performance were advancing. Without this rebuff at the hands of the Lord, Mary Lyon might have sooner been able to push and coax the essentially conservative board of trustees into requiring Latin and lengthening the course to four years. Both possibilities had looked reasonably near to her when she wrote the copy for the 1839-40 catalogue. In any case her students knew, as their letters and notebooks repeatedly testified, that her expectations would continue to rise. When she recommended that all students should take one hard study like Latin or mathematics straight through the year and get a thorough grounding in both before they went on to the science and philosophy studied by the upper classes, she was apt to conclude with a confident look toward the future. "There is no reason why ladies should not faithfully pursue such studies as well as gentlemen. Our course of study embraces much, but probably fifty years hence it will appear quite limited."[45]

6
In High Gear

That our sons may be as plants
grown up in their youth;
that our daughters may be
as corner stones, polished after
the similitude of a palace.

PSALM 144:12

Mary Lyon's years as head of Mount Holyoke were briefer than anyone had expected; she died quite suddenly March 5, 1849. But she had close to a decade of unquestioned success. From 1841–42, when the Seminary opened with 170 students accepted in anticipation of the new wing (ready for occupancy three months later), through 1848–49, the yearly enrollment averaged just over 200. This number, which was the exact size she had been planning for from the first, was achieved with plenty of margin. Many applicants were turned away every year; for the fall of 1847 when the total enrollment crept up to 235, to the strong disapproval of some trustees and supporters, Mary Lyon had received more than 500 applications. Steadily rising popularity could not then be taken for granted by even the best known and best endowed colleges. During the same eight-year period, Amherst and Wesleyan were encountering fiscal difficulties; the Amherst yearly enrollment averaged 135 and Wesleyan never exceeded 125 students.[1]

To what extent any given Seminary student was taking work of college level is difficult to estimate. In the early years even some of the seniors might be spending part of their time on studies needed to fill in gaps in their earlier training. At the same time many students were caught up by Miss Lyon's intellectual intensity and her steady drive for higher standards; regardless of their individual programs, they shared her perception of Mount Holyoke as a college-in-the-making. Professor Fletcher of Oberlin spelled out the curricular pattern of virtually all United States colleges in the middle third of the nineteenth century: "liberal doses of Greek, Latin and Mathematics in the freshman and sophomore years (the classics predominating in both years but

Mathematics occupying more time in the second), courses in sciences in the junior and senior years (Mathematics and Classics being continued, but much less time being devoted to them), and Mental and Moral Philosophy in the senior year." Less than half of this offering was available at Mount Holyoke, which provided no Greek, limited Latin, and about half the mathematics required of young men. But the remaining 35 to 40 percent of the standard curriculum, including nearly everything the young men studied in their junior and senior years, formed the basis of the Seminary sequence of studies. Miss Lyon continued "maturing" the academic schedule as indefatigably as the domestic arrangements; her system of four or five "series" instead of three units of study coinciding with the fixed terms of the school year allowed for many shifts and may have made it easier to continue the pressure for high standards.[2]

A much corrected schedule for 1846–47 in Mary Lyon's handwriting gives a good idea of how the time was distributed. Most students took only two principal studies in a series. In addition, they were required to take Bible study, weekly composition, and calisthenics, and many in the course of a year had two or three extras, such as drawing, botanical terms, reading aloud, choral music, and French. Out of each 40-week year 4 weeks were set aside for review and examinations, leaving 36 for classroom recitations. Juniors spent the first 10 weeks on algebra and English grammar. (Even strict entrance examinations in grammar did not fulfill the obligation Mary felt to give prospective teachers reasonable command of the English language.) The remaining 26 weeks in the junior year were devoted to ancient and modern history and to a math-science sequence: geometry, 13 weeks; algebra, 6 weeks; physiology, 7 weeks. But those entering inadequately prepared in Latin, which had just been required for admission, might recite in Latin as long as needed and postpone the math and science. Some juniors were allowed to take three major subjects; some appear to have substituted botany for the last 10 weeks of the history sequence. Members of the middle class started off with 3 weeks of "double lessons" (two recitations a day) in rhetoric, followed by Latin for 33 weeks and a second sequence: grammar, 7 weeks; geology, 7; chemistry, 9; astronomy or botany, 10.

Middle class girls weak in Latin, many of whom had entered before the language was an absolute requirement, might substitute "English" studies: Smellie's *Philosophy of Natural History*, Marsh's *Ecclesiastical History*, Alexander's *Evidences of Christianity*. The senior class started with 3 weeks of double lessons in Paley's *Natural Theology*, followed by two parallel sequences: (1) physics, 9 weeks; logic, 7; moral philosophy, 7; *Paradise Lost*, 10; and (2) solid geometry, 12; mental philosophy, 13; Butler's *Analogy of Religion, Natural and Revealed*, 7.[3]

The textbooks used at the Seminary were usually those most popular on college campuses; when Miss Lyon chose versions by less favored authors, the contents seem not to have been dissimilar. The Amherst and Mount Holyoke catalogues for 1841 to 1849 list 12 texts used in common: Day's *Algebra*, Playfair's *Euclid*, Cutter's *Physiology*, Olmsted's *Natural Philosophy* (physics) and *Astronomy*, Silliman's *Chemistry*, Hitchcock's *Geology*, Smellie's *Philosophy of Natural History*, Whately's *Logic*, Whately's *Rhetoric*, Wayland's *Moral Philosophy*, and Butler's *Analogy*. Of course it took more than the listing of college texts to guarantee that a female seminary was offering study at an advanced level. Thomas Woody tabulated the 36 subjects offered by the largest number of seminaries for young women in a study of the catalogues of 162 schools in existence at some time between 1749 and 1871. The 107 schools that were functioning between 1830 and 1871 appear to have offered most of the subjects taught in the junior and senior years of college: three out of five listed logic, nine out of ten offered chemistry and physics, and four out of five listed mental philosophy (psychology) and moral philosophy (mainly ethics). Most of these schools spread out for their pupils a wide range of studies, including spelling, painting, and ornamental needlework, and made no claim to the continuity or the rigor of a college course. Some historians, including Woody, considered a legally professed intention an essential qualification for the first college for women. He gave considerable space to Georgia Female College, chartered in December 1836 and opened in 1839, because it sought and obtained the power to grant degrees; in the end he rejected its claims to primacy as a college because the entrance age was 12 and the president himself felt the institution did not meet college standards. Woody dismissed without discussion consideration of such "high grade seminaries" as Emma Willard and Mount Holyoke because "in their incorporation there was nothing to suggest they were to make an effort at collegiate education"—that is, they did not apply for a charter to establish a four-year course and grant a degree at the end. Even if Mary Lyon had not encountered bitter scorn of "female greatness," it is impossible to imagine her consenting to such claims in advance, no matter how determined she was to raise academic standards as fast as possible. She would have been as offended as Harriet Martineau by the pretensions of a gentleman Miss Martineau met on her western travels in 1835 who was "vice-president of an educational establishment for young ladies, where there are public exhibitions of their proficiency, and the poor ignorant little girls take degrees."[4]

The caliber of the academic program then as now depended primarily on the intellectual ability and previous education of the students and the faculty. Mary Lyon never relaxed her efforts to make admission more and more selective. She held to the 16-year age requirement with very few exceptions; beginning in 1846-47 the catalogue read, "None are admitted to the Seminary under sixteen years of age, and it is generally better that they should not enter under seventeen or eighteen." In the fall of 1845 one youthful junior wrote a friend that most of her fellow pupils were between 20 and 30 and looked even older; not more than 20, she feared, were under 17. In the first years Mary seems to have had meager data about applicants except for age and, sometimes, acquaintance with family or sponsor. Many of the surviving letters of application were written not by the candidates but by their ministers, teachers, fathers, older brothers or sisters, or former Seminary students. By 1847 Miss Lyon had evolved a two-page printed statement, explaining why she was reluctant to take girls whose families felt they were not strong enough to negotiate the stairs to the fourth story or the most strenuous domestic work assignments. This sheet asked about seven qualifications, including scholarship, health, and reliability in caring for clothes and money.[5]

The admissions process was fraught with uncertainty, for Mary as well as the young ladies. Just like any contemporary admissions director, she had to guess how many accepted candidates would

14. Louisa Torrey, a student in 1844–45, later became Mrs. Alphonso Taft; her oldest son was William Howard Taft. Mount Holyoke College Library Archives.

fail to appear on opening day. From the records she kept for three successive years, 1845–46, 1846–47, 1847–48, it seems that about 30 percent of the new scholars never came or left within a few days and nearly as many of the old scholars who had made written applications to return were also "late failures." Either they had received and accepted a recommendation from Miss Lyon that they stay out for a year to mature or they simply did not come back. Although she hoped that many members of each entering junior class would complete the three-year course in sequence, Mary knew that some of the students she admitted would not have the time or means—or perhaps the capacity—to finish. What she did require was agreement to attend for one full year; in the prevailing state of education for women, it took pressure to maintain the one-year rule. In the spring of 1844 Louisa Torrey, who had been admitted to the middle class in the fall, wrote about her pending spring vacation, "It will have been nearly eight months since I left home . . . I little thought of staying so long when I came." In spite of her dislike of Seminary rules, she approved of the course of study, in which she was "making very good progress," and added, "Sometimes I feel as if I should want to come back and graduate next year."[6]

There were some dropouts during the year for reasons Miss Lyon considered legitimate: a family emergency, marriage, the offer of a particularly suitable job teaching—or dismissal for breaking rules. Although in November 1847, as Emily Dickinson reported, "The school is very large & though quite a number have left, on account of finding the examinations more difficult than they anticipated, yet there are nearly 300," by the time the catalogue was printed the following spring, the total enrollment was down to 235. To compensate for dropouts in years when the enrollment was below capacity, Miss Lyon quietly admitted a few candidates during the year; they were frequently the friends of students then enrolled, who might help to make the transition to Seminary system easier. On March 19, 1842, Maria Savage, a senior, wrote a long letter to her friend in Connecticut, Rhoda Roys, reporting that she could enter the Seminary either the ensuing fall or that spring.

Miss Lyon has kindly invited me to answer the application you made to become a member of this seminary which I now do with great pleasure . . . She says you may come at the commencement of the next year, which will probably be in Oct. The commencement of the year is the regular time for the admittance of all, & it is expected that they will continue the whole year, unless something unforeseen prevents; which includes forty weeks of term time. She wished me to tell you that she has put your name among the list of candidates for the next year and if she hears nothing from you she shall expect you.

The present year will close the last of July or first of Aug. so there are yet seventeen weeks besides two weeks vacation which will commence seven weeks from next wednesday. Miss Lyon said that if you wish you may come this year, and now, as soon as you like, but she supposes you will not probably wish to come until the next. If you come this year, you can enter without being examined in any thing, as the commencement of the year is the time for examinations. We are now rather in the middle of a series of studies, but shall commence a new series next term, so it will be

*like commencing a new term of an academy, though the schollars
are all the same.*

*The next term will commence nine weeks from next Thursday
and will continue ten weeks. I do not know as the studies will be
those that you will like to persue. I expect to study Paley, and
Butler's Analogy, and pay some attention to Botany, if you never
have studied these, I presume you would like to come & attend to
them next summer. Perhaps there are some other studies that will
be taught during that term that you would like to attend to, but
I do not know what they are. The expenses of those that stay only
a part of the year are two dollars per week, including board and
tuition, & for others it is sixty doll. for the whole year.*

*I will send you a catalogue that will state many particulars
respecting the qualifications for admittance to the sem. & also
to the different classes. If any one can be examined in all the
junior & middle studies or anything in the course equivalent to
these, they can be admitted to the senior class. The examinations
are quite rigid and are a good test of the scholarship of all that are
admitted. Several left this year because they could not pass
examinations in the preparitory studies. I presume you will be able
to enter the senior class without difficulty. But it requires the very
first-rate scholars to be able to do this. The manner of instructing
is very thorough indeed. I would like to dwell a long time upon
the excellences of this sem. but have not time now.*

Maria sang the praises of the school and of Miss Lyon, "one of
the most devoted christians with whom I was ever acquainted. I
am continually reminded of the faith, holiness & active zeal that
characterized the apostles, when I see the untireing efforts of this,
our dear teacher to promote the spiritual interests of all under her
care, & to advance the cause & interests of Christ her Lord &
Master." Maria urged Rhoda to come right away so the two of
them could be there together, described the revival then in progress and had a good word for domestic work.

*We all room board in the same building do our domestic work
which is done in finest style, & occupies from one to one hour and*

15. This daguerreotype of Emily Dickinson was taken in South Hadley during 1847–48, when she was a Seminary student. Amherst College Library; by permission of the Trustees of Amherst College.

a half a day. No one can conceive of the regularity of the system who is unacquainted with it. It exhibits the greatness of the mind who planed it which is Miss Lyon's. The building is very splendid indeed. Very much the finest & largest that I ever saw for the purpose of a seminary, & it is exactly calculated for the purpose for which it is employed.

Rhoda did decide to come at the beginning of the summer term but whether the examinations waiting in the fall were daunting or some other difficulty arose, she did not return, at least not long enough to get her name in the catalogue.[7]

The entrance examinations were intentionally formidable. They were mainly oral and called for historical data, solutions to problems, and grammatical rules given with speed and in the words of the textbook. Those who failed the first time could try again; review classes were usually scheduled for two or three weeks, but, as Emily Dickinson explained, "if we cannot go through them all in a specified time, we are sent home." No wonder that, though she finished within three days and promptly started reviewing the studies of the junior class so that she could be examined in them and enter the middle class, she declared of the entrance exams, "I never would endure the suspense which I endured during those three days again for all the treasures of the world." Year after year most of the entering students might well have echoed this sentiment and at the same time also have taken pride in knowing that once again "Miss Lyon is raising her standard of scholarship a good deal." Mary felt personal concern for the girls who had to be dismissed for failure. She encouraged some to study on their own and try another year; for others she found places in preparatory schools that would help them make up their deficiencies. The preceptor of Westfield Academy in January 1843 discussed in detail the capacities and achievements of eight young women she had placed in his care.

You have doubtless wished to receive some report from me long before this concerning the young ladies in my charge—but the truth is I have found my time so fully occupied that it had seemed an impossibility for me to be alone long enough to do so. Our half Quarter closed last Sat. and perhaps the fairest representation of what each young lady has done may be made by giving her average mark for recitations during that last half term. I should say, perhaps, that 10 is considered by us in marking a perfect recitation—is our highest mark. They stand on the general average as follows—

Miss Alling 9.60/100 Miss Crane 9.60 Miss Riggs 9.45 Miss Kirby 9.20 Miss Richards 9.10 in class No. 1 or among those whose number is 9 & above. Miss Hinman 8. or class No. 2. Miss Hill 7. Miss Smith 7.80—Twenty six of our Scholars stand above Miss Alling, & 90 above Miss Hill.

Miss Alling & Miss Crane are about on an equality both good Scholars & very faithful & will have accomplished all that could be expected in the time. Miss Riggs has been very studious & made considerable progress but needs to review considerably before she will be prepared for examination. All of them except Miss Alling & Miss Crane are exceedingly deficient in Arithmetic.

Miss Kirby has been studious but does not learn as easily as the three just named. She will go over the ground, but will not retain what she learns as well. Miss Smith has tried to do too much. She

227

went thru Simple Equations in October but was obliged to leave it last week. She has made a beginning in Latin also. Miss S. is ambitious to do much, but does not strike quite so deep as she ought—inclines to be superficial. Miss Hill does as well as she can—but is slow to comprehend & finds it difficult to express what she knows—is well disposed. I hardly think you will be disposed to receive her at the close of our Term. Miss Richard—ahem—what shall I say—She is unique! A good scholar & a poor one—a good disposition sometimes, sometimes not so good, but at all times needs a watchful eye—We found very soon it was necessary to tell her in plain New England language (i.e. with much decision & kindness) what must & what must not be done. I cannot begin to describe the course she pursued until her track was marked out. Now however I am happy to say she appears to be very well disposed—is much more even in her temperment—studies quite well & on the whole doing well. She rooms with Miss Kimball which is all in Sarah's favor—

Miss Hinman—for whom you expressed considerable anxiety—is the most hopeless of the whole. She seems so decidedly opposed to everything that appears like effort either bodily or mentally that I think we have reason to expect little from her. She went on with the Arith. class a little farther than she had been before & then quit & said she wd. do anything but study Arith. What I shall do with her I hardly know. She says she intends to go home with her father who is to be here in 2 or 3 weeks. Says she did not want to go to S.H. in the first place— & much less now. I asked her if there was anything in particular that she disliked there—She replied "there was more work required than she expected." She is a young lady of pretty good mind naturally but needs exceedingly the very exercise & discipline she so much dislikes. I have just written her father stating the circumstances of her case & asking him to advise me immediately what course it will be best to adopt. I shd. have written you first—but with her present feelings I knew it wd. do no good, as you could do no more than write her father.

The young Ladies are very faithful in their studies, but are very much concerned lest they shall be rejected on another examination.

Our School is quite full & very laborious to me but pleasant—
Shall we not see you here while the young Ladies are here. Shd. I
hear from Mr. Hinman I will inform you.

I am yours truly—
A Parish[8]

Mary Lyon continued to make room both for mature self-supporting young women whose desire for more education, like hers,
had been whetted by their employment and also for very bright
girls who had already on their own or with special instruction
completed part of the Seminary course of study. Each year she
admitted perhaps twenty candidates for advanced standing who by
examination qualified for the middle or even the senior class.
When in the spring of 1848 she started working on admissions for
what turned out to be the last time, she predicted accurately that
the increase in the Latin requirement would sharply reduce the
size of the senior class: to qualify as seniors, students must have
completed the first four books of Virgil. At least two of the
twenty-three seniors in the 1848–49 catalogue (only half the number graduated the year before) were new scholars. The Wingate
sisters from southern New Hampshire near Concord passed with
ease examinations in all the subjects of the junior and middle class
curriculum. It was Sarah Wingate who in February contracted the
fatal case of erysipelas that precipitated Miss Lyon's final illness.
Among the members of the junior class entering that September
was Lydia Shattuck from backwoods northern New Hampshire,
who at the age of 26 had already taught 18 terms of school. She
managed the preparation for Mount Holyoke partly through the
assistance and encouragement of former Seminary students and
their families. Lydia, who joined the Seminary faculty upon
graduation in 1851 and spent her whole life in its service, became
distinguished as a teacher of science and a botanist, maintaining
the teaching tradition Mary Lyon established and extending
Mount Holyoke's range in the scientific world.[9]

The quality of instruction at Mount Holyoke Female Seminary
must be considered in the light of practice on the campuses of
colleges for men. A considerable amount of rote learning prevailed,
especially in the first two years. Professor Rudolph, deploring the

16. A daguerreotype of Lydia Shattuck, who as a student helped nurse Miss Lyon in her last illness. She graduated in 1851 and spent her whole life on the Seminary faculty, winning scientific recognition as a botanist. Mount Holyoke College Library Archives.

influence of the Yale Report of 1828 and other expressions of academic conservatism in delaying curriculum reform until after the Civil War, found much of what went on "more and more superficial, more and more a matter of daily recitations on elementary material, more and more deadly and deadening." Of course some of the teaching was admirable; the system tended to perpetuate other kinds as well. [10]

The teachers at the Seminary, like the tutors at Amherst, were hand-picked recent graduates and, like them, were conspicuously good students, devoted to the institution and able and willing to do a great deal of hard work. Mary surrounded herself almost immediately with some exceptionally competent and dedicated co-workers, on whom she was soon depending a great deal. Abigail Moore, her eldest sister's third daughter, was 25 when she started on what turned out to be an eight-year term on the faculty. She regularly taught French and physics and proved to have organizing skill almost as remarkable as her aunt's. From 1842 to 1846 she had the title—and the burdens—of associate principal, along with Mary Whitman, another of Mary Lyon's main supports. The kind of business entrusted to Abigail and the extent to which she contributed to curricular change and household improvements are suggested in a letter written in the summer of 1845 about purchasing laboratory equipment.

You recollect I asked you if I might spend a little money in purchasing apparatus. I arranged matters to stop in Boston a little while, boarding at Mr. Bliss'. I went to Mr. Wightman's & looked over what he had. I should like much to buy a few articles of no very great value mostly on optics. I will just enumerate the articles with their prices.

Brewster's Kaleidescope	*$5.00*
Phantascope	*2.50*
Tissue figure	*1.25*
Tellurian	*1.50*
Pistol house	*6.00*
Spider	*.25*
Star	*1.75*
Image plates	*2.00 or 3.00*

Perhaps I might find a few more little things the whole of which might amount to nearly $20.00. There is a polariscope, which has a good deal of interest, but I should like to see Prof. Snell before I decide to ask for it. It costs $35.00. I saw microscopes & telescopes there, & think that we very much need a Solar microscope. The one I saw was $120 & the telescopes from $75.00 to $300. But we need the microscope first. Mr. Wightman gave me a book describing all the animals exhibited on those slides you bought. And now I am in as much doubt as before what to do. It does not belong to the class in Nat. Phi. to go through a course of Nat. History. I have thought a little course of instruction on Nat. Hist. to the junior class might be well in connexion with exhibiting the plates. I will undertake it if it should be thought best, but it must be short. Say two hours a week for one series perhaps the grammar series. I think there may be something of a call for it as Smellie has so much gone out of the school. I speak of it that you & Miss Whitman may bring the best of your wisdom to bear upon it. It is only a thought which may be worth nothing.

Will you tell Miss Whitman I bought a book for the school which will be of more service to her than to me. Davis manual of magnetism, containing a description of all the apparatus he has for sale & might be used as a text book. Some valuable experiments are detailed which are appropriate to Nat. Phi. I should like to purchase of him the following instruments to illustrate the magnetism of the earth.

A magnetic needle on a brass stand	*$1.00*
Dipping needle	*3.00 to $6.00*
Case of bar magnets	*2.50 to 5.00*

Some little things such as a circular piece of iron—Star of iron bar of iron & wire for making experiments there would cost only a trifle. I can leave here early in the morning & without spending a night in Boston have them put up & take them with me. Will you write by return of mail that the answer may reach me before I leave here. I shall stop in Monson on my way back. I thought you might be the more willing as I had spent nothing for French.

I called at the mission house to leave directions about the heralds & annual reports. Dr. Anderson remarked that a few days before a gentleman of great respectability & discernment expressed concern about their receiving so many at the seminary. He said he took the ground that the last year was only an accidental thing which would not be likely to occur again. The gentleman said if it were once admitted that the teachers approved of increasing the school so much, its popularity would decline at once, & he thought the friends of the institution ought to look to it. Dr. A. thought the remark was a just one, that we could not do for so large a number what we otherwise could. At Dea. Saffords Mr. Gale asked after the size of the school. I told him the building could accommodate about 200. Deac. Safford says & you have 250 so adds Mr. Gale you can accommodate 200 & have 250. I thought these remarks properly belonged to you & I would transmit them. I expect the publick will be looking at the school very critically the coming year.

Will you tell Mr. Hawks I have the germ of a good plan in my mind for fastening the newspapers. Can he not engage a carpenter to make them after I come back say Sat. or Monday. I want them finished before the school commences. I am sorry to trouble you with so long a letter & did not intend it. Mrs. Coggin sends her love & she wishes you would come & see her. Mrs. Kittridge wishes the same.[11]

When word of Abigail's engagement and pending departure got round, everybody asked the same question: "What will Miss Lyon do without her?" There seems no doubt that Abigail's leaving did affect Mary and the whole Seminary; one of the hardest hit was her fellow associate principal, Mary Whitman. Like Abigail, Mary had stood out among the dedicated students of 1837–38, had taught from the day of her graduation—Mary finished in 1839, and had become associate principal in 1842. She was also Mary Lyon's confidante. Miss Whitman seems to have been the closest of any of the teaching staff to the kind of specialization achieved by professors in the colleges for men. Mary Lyon had confidence that her teachers could handle all the subjects they had studied as undergraduates and varied both the regular teaching assignments and the extras that were always cropping up. Miss Whitman no doubt had her share of extras, but she seems to have taught science—especially chemistry and geology—most of the time. She spent the summer term in 1846, just before Abigail left, at Professor Hitchcock's home in Amherst, attending lectures and demonstrations and studying scientific literature. In the summer vacation the year before, she and Mary Lyon had joined Professor and Mrs. Hitchcock, young Edward, and Professor Adams of Middlebury on a two-to-three-week geological excursion into Vermont. But such intervals were not enough to save her from exhaustion when there was no other associate principal to share the load, especially during Mary Lyon's periods of illness. By the start of the 1848–49 school year, she was in a state of nervous collapse and took leave to recuperate by travel. When she was called back five months later by Mary Lyon's death, she was only partially recovered. She was the obvious choice as successor, but within a year her health had given way completely again and she had to resign.

Another niece joined the teaching staff early. Lucy Lyon, second daughter of Mary's only brother, entered the Seminary in the fall of 1838 and graduated in 1840. At the beginning of the summer term in 1841 she was invited back for what turned out to be five years; in the summer of 1846 she, too, became engaged to a

17. Lucy Lyon, Mary's niece, graduated in 1840 and taught in the Seminary five years, then married an intending missionary, Edward Lord, and went with him to China. Mount Holyoke College Library Archives.

minister-missionary. Lucy may have had the quickest mind—and the strongest ambition—of any of the young teachers. She seems frequently to have been assigned the advanced subjects that her aunt would have taught if health and other responsibilities had permitted: Butler's *Analogy*, logic, *Paradise Lost*. While she was teaching more than one section of one or two of these subjects, she might also be giving a course in physics or psychology; one year her extras included supervising all the junior class sections of algebra and geometry and reading 25 to 50 senior compositions every other week. It was she who originated the journal letter for Fidelia Fiske and, until her own departure for China, wrote the running account of Seminary daily life and saw that it was copied and distributed.

Among the other teachers Miss Lyon particularly depended upon were Susan Reed and Susan Tolman. A member of the middle class and an assistant pupil in 1837–38, Susan Reed came from Heath; she was another of the hill-town girls who made the Seminary go that first hard year. She joined the faculty immediately after graduation and served nearly five years; she left to

18. Susan Tolman, one of six sisters who all attended Mount Holyoke, graduated in 1845 and taught at the Seminary until her marriage in 1848. She and her husband, Cyrus Mills, worked together as missionaries in Ceylon and later as co-founders of Mills College. Mills College Library; by permission of Mills College Archives.

prepare for the marriage that would take her as a missionary to Ceylon. Susan Tolman, who graduated in 1845, was the fourth of six sisters to attend Mount Holyoke; she taught at the Seminary for three years and left to marry the Rev. Cyrus Mills, and likewise head for Ceylon. After fifteen years in the missionary field, husband and wife returned to California and together built up what became Mills College. Both Susans seem to have been particularly successful teachers. Both were devoted to Mary Lyon.

But any selection seems invidious when so many of the young women on the faculty were remarkably dedicated—even those whose terms of service were short. One third of the forty-three teachers on the Seminary staff during Mary Lyon's twelve years as principal taught only one year. Most of those who chose to leave departed not because of long hours or modest pay but because of declining health or impending matrimony. Mary refused to accept more than $200 a year plus board and heat, so that became the maximum, paid to Miss Emily Bridge during her four years as superintendent of the domestic department and to Miss Whitman and Miss Moore when they became associate principals. The other teachers seem to have received board and from $100 to $140 a year, depending upon their experience and their assignments (those in charge of a section received $40 more). These wages were "respectable," in Mrs. Cowles's judgment, but not princely. The size of the paycheck appears to have been no more of a consideration with her teachers than it was with Mary Lyon, who celebrated benevolence and self-denial almost every day of her life.[12]

The heavy work load did prove too much for some of these eager young women; several had to withdraw entirely or absent themselves for weeks because of illness. But although some fell by the wayside, Miss Lyon's unquenchable confidence in their physical stamina as well as their capacity to learn and to teach seems to have produced remarkable results year after year. A "Book of Duties," probably begun in 1842, suggests the elaborate opening procedures—house cleaning, registration, examinations, and the even more arduous concluding weeks when Miss Lyon invited in two or three volunteers because she herself saw the teachers were too hard pressed. A week of intensive review and preparation for oral examinations before an audience was only the beginning. Someone had to schedule and rehearse the singing and calisthenics, select compositions to be read, find and rehearse suitable readers, since modesty forbade that the author read her own work in public. Other responsibilities included "completing certificates, preparing bedding for company, inviting company, deciding rooms for guests, taking their names as they arrive, lighting them to their rooms, looking after their wants, care of preparing their rooms, & having them cleaned daily, providing a seat in the stage for them when they leave, preparing copies of the order of exercises during the examination in sufficient numbers, & putting one apiece into each of the rooms of the guests, and writing out the order of the procession on Thurs." Domestic chores took teacher time throughout the year. Most did their own washing and ironing; they presided at table, enforced quiet at bedtime, periodically inspected student rooms and graded the condition of the furniture on the examination scale of 4 to 1. In addition to all the meetings for students, which they were no doubt expected to attend, there were regular teachers' meetings every week. In the fall of her senior year, Julia Hyde as an assistant pupil was included in the instructional sessions.

19. A daguerreotype of Lucinda Guilford, who graduated in 1847. She had been a paper mill worker in Dalton; after graduation she went to Cleveland, where she became a notable teacher. Mount Holyoke College Library Archives.

"But there is not much ease to be had Saturdays—for what with Family Meeting and Table Meeting and Teachers' Meeting and Section Meeting and Gen exercises and a few other inexpressible things—the guide people cut up time into slices as thin as wafers."[13]

In spite of the stress, there were real rewards for those strong enough to keep up the pace. They were teaching brighter and better prepared students and more advanced subject matter than they could expect in other positions open to them. The learning, by unanimous testimony, was thorough. Not only was four weeks out of the school year set aside for review and examination; every week the fourth and final recitation was a review of the new material covered in the first three recitations. Although in general teachers and students stuck pretty close to the textbooks by which the courses were denominated, recitations were not necessarily dull. When Maria Savage was advising her friend about credits for advanced standing, she explained that although for examinations teachers confined themselves to Worcester's *Elements*, the announced textbook in general history, for class recitations "the scholars consult a large number of textbooks to attain a very thorough knowledge." Mary Lyon was a very skillful teacher. In the 1840's she spent little time in academic instruction, but her example at general meetings and her wise advice must have been illuminating. Indeed, the quality of the classroom performance by Mount Holyoke Seminary teachers may well have compared favorably with that at Amherst or Williams. Dozens of student letters convey enthusiasm for the subjects studied and the teachers. Lucinda Guilford, later head of a school in Cleveland and biographer of Mrs. Banister, was bright, quick to criticize, and passionately eager to learn; she expressed herself with vigor. When, in the middle class, she was studying geology and physics, she declared, "A new world has opened before me." As a senior taking solid geometry, psychology, and French, she wrote, "My studies this year are well springs of delight."[14]

Mount Holyoke in Mary Lyon's time had no equivalent for the required declamation exercises or the extracurricular debates of the student literary societies that proved so stimulating to many of the ablest young men attending college. A diary kept by William Hammond, who graduated from Amherst in 1849, shows how the literary societies could extend intellectual interests and reasoning power—and intensify the fierceness of the competition for top rank at graduation, which was one kind of pressure the young women escaped. Even without such spurs, even with crammed daily schedules, the society of the Seminary was congenial to young women bent on intellectual self-improvement. Some students and faculty did read for pleasure, most often during vacations. Julia Hyde, studying at home, wrote Lucy Goodale at the Seminary of the five Shakespeare plays she was reading on her mother's recommendation; she had already been urging Lucy to find time for Shakespeare, a few good novels and the poems of Cowper, Mrs. Sigourney, and Mrs. Hemans. When Emily Dickinson had to spend a month of the school year at home, recovering from a bronchial infection, she kept up her studies and went through four popular novels as well as Tennyson's *The Princess* and Longfellow's *Evangeline*. On young Hammond's first meeting with Nelly Holman, the Seminary student he kept returning to visit, their mutual appreciation of Longfellow's *Hyperion* helped to cement the friendship.

Mary Lyon disapproved of novels on principle. She warned students against the fiction and other kinds of trivia in the popular miscellanies known as annuals, in which ideas were "scattered so sparsely over the pages, it is almost impossible to find them," and added "Penny things are good for penny minds." But she did advocate reading after graduation, recommending history, travels, and poetry. At least once she urged all the teachers to follow some plan for self-improvement. In the winter of 1844-45 one group of four, including Mary Whitman, managed to set aside a half hour during the day for reading aloud to one another, starting with Macaulay's *Miscellanies*. Other teachers enrolled in courses they had not been able to take as undergraduates, particularly Latin and French; those who persisted would have encountered such classics as *Télémaque* and the *Aeneid*.[15]

What the young teachers had not attained in knowledge and perspective was provided in part by some of the supplementary lectures that were standard fare at the colleges for men. Professor Hitchcock was generous with his time and energy, driving over the Notch and bringing his equipment with him; he seems to have come every year during Miss Lyon's lifetime except when he was away on a long trip. He regularly gave series of lectures on geology, chemistry, and physiology and periodically preached at the village church or led Seminary devotions. One sermon, the Coronation of Winter, a spontaneous upwelling of feeling after a spectacular ice storm, was repeated and justly admired on both sides of the Notch. References to his lectures are frequent in student letters. Louisa Torrey wrote her mother after his lecture on galvanism, "I have left several of the young ladies in the hall taking electrical shocks," and explained that she had bought, not rented, the geology text because it was "a fine work" written by "one of the most distinguished [geologists] in the United States." Lucinda Guilford was properly awed by the prospect of being publicly examined on geology "before the man that WROTE THE BOOK."[16]

The series of twenty-five lectures on physiology that were illustrated by a life-sized manikin and skeleton (purchased for $700 by

Professor Hitchcock out of his own funds) made a very strong impact when they were first given in 1844. Miss Lyon, having warned the young ladies in advance "not to be finicky and silly about it," canceled the Wednesday missionary meeting in favor of the opening lecture on January 31 and arranged for all the teachers to take sections afterward so that every student could recite on what she had been seeing and hearing. Midway through the series Lucy Lyon called them *"exceedingly* interesting." Marietta Sherwood, a junior just over 16, was fascinated by the way the manikin, made of flesh-colored papier-mâché, came apart to show every muscle, vein, and bone separately. So was Mrs. Elijah Grant, Zilpah's sister-in-law, then staying at the Seminary to care for her daughter Martha, dangerously ill of typhoid fever. Mrs. Grant was equally impressed by the movable organs and the cost, which she had heard was $1,000. Another Amherst faculty member who gave sequential lectures for more than twenty years was Professor Ebenezer Snell. He reinforced the teaching of physics not only by his own lectures and demonstrations but also by his assistance in purchasing, setting up, and repairing apparatus at the Seminary. At least twice he also gave talks on architecture, which some students found very revealing.[17]

Addresses and sermons by visiting dignitaries were common from the beginning; tight as the daily schedule was, Miss Lyon could always adjust it on short notice for something she thought the students ought not to miss. The anniversary speakers were notable; all were clergymen and some were also college presidents, like Heman Humphrey and then Edward Hitchcock of Amherst and Mark Hopkins of Williams. At the sixth commencement in August 1843 the speaker was the famous Lyman Beecher, then president of Lane Theological Seminary, who was accompanied by Mrs. Beecher and one of his well-known sons, Edward, then president of Illinois College. When Catharine Beecher came in the spring of 1846, she was in the throes of her campaign to organize support for supplying teachers to the West. She stopped by, on crutches, en route to a water cure at Brattleboro, accompanied by her younger brother Thomas, who had been delivering the addresses that she wrote.[18]

Many of the visiting clergy were missionaries of some sort, soliciting money and personal interest for the good causes to which they were devoting themselves. Students heard about the hazards and triumphs of missionary effort but many talks focused on the geography and the daily life of the Sandwich Islands or Burma or China—and also the western frontier and the Kentucky backwoods. In the spring of 1842 the Rev. and Mrs. Justin Perkins brought with them from Persia one of their converts, by then a bishop in the Nestorian church. Dr. Rufus Anderson, secretary of the ABCFM, came with Mrs. Anderson in the summer of 1844 right after his return from inspecting the Congregational missions in the Middle East. Firsthand reports were brought even from Canada and central Europe where evangelical Protestants were fighting "popery." It was an account in 1845 of the Waldensees then living in the Piedmont Valley that made Abigail Cowles exclaim, "How many more of such good things abound here than in our part of Conn."[19]

Not all the visitors from the larger world to South Hadley came under Seminary auspices. The village church was then blessed with an admirable pastor, the Rev. Joseph D. Condit. A Princeton graduate coming from a family of ministers, he had many acquaintances in and outside of New England and arranged first for pulpit exchanges and then, as his health grew feebler, for substitutes. His own sermons, popular with Seminary students and teachers as well as his parishioners, sometimes touched on current events or problems: the shipboard explosion that killed the Secretaries of State and the Navy, the "wicked aggressive" Mexican War. During the week the church was hospitable to benevolent and secular enterprises—lyceum lectures, concerts, political rallies. Mary Lyon vetoed student attendance at the appearance of a mesmerist and gave few permissions for two talks by a runaway Virginia slave, but approved going to temperance lectures. When the reformed drunkard John B. Gough lectured in South Hadley in May 1846, he was not quite 29, but his power over the most diverse audiences as he described his fall and struggles for restoration was already making his name a household word. Both faculty and students were much moved. Lucy Lyon was spellbound by his almost-two-hour performance and found his autobiography *"intensely thrilling."* Elizabeth Bell, a 17-year-old member of the middle class, concluded a lyrical account: "May he, as he wished in the last clause of his discourse, die with the Bible in one hand and the temperance pledge in the other."[20]

Mary Lyon kept telling her students each year just how much more she would ask of the entering juniors and of the graduating seniors in the year ahead, and the students kept writing their relatives and friends about how the standards were being raised. But relatively little public mention was made of the continuing academic advance of this already advanced institution. The attention of the general public was attracted to other achievements of the Seminary: the domestic work system, the support of foreign missions, and, most immediately noted, the continuing conversion of nonbelievers in the student body. Although in the 1840's interest in revivals was receding somewhat and the Seminary in 1841 doubled its size and thereby afforded proportionately fewer of the personal contacts on which individual conversion was often based, Mount Holyoke efforts to save souls continued unabated throughout the decade. At the end of his life Professor Hitchcock took special pride in the Amherst record of revivals: up to 1863 "no class has passed through College without also passing through a marked revival. Indeed, fourteen revivals in forty years, makes one every three years." Mount Holyoke's record under Mary Lyon was still more remarkable. In every year of her administration except for the first, the Seminary had a revival of "a thoroughness and extent almost unheard of in the modern history of the church." After quoting a dozen of her letters conveying the intensity of her concern for the saving of souls, Professor Hitchcock analyzed the nature of her achievement. He found "the true secret of the extraordinary exhibitions of divine grace" in "the uniform and systematic fidelity of the instructors." He pointed to the unusually high proportion of converts and commended the restraint with which the revivals were conducted. "And how free have these seasons been of all extravagance and enthusiasm!"[21]

The revival in the spring of 1843 was particularly memorable. It was triggered by Fidelia Fiske's departure on March 1 as a missionary to Persia, after six weeks of suspense that had stirred the whole Seminary and especially Mary Lyon. In Boston for the sailing of this much loved young teacher, Mary spent a week with the Saffords in "spiritual refreshing" through continuing private prayer. When she returned, her sense of urgency spread to both teachers and students; with examination and vacation periods not too far away, she knew there was little time—perhaps four or five weeks—in which to work for nearly 60 souls still without hope. So it was indeed remarkable that "in about three weeks, all but six expressed some hope that they had found the Savior." The half dozen letters written by Mary during this three-week period to the Saffords and Mrs. Banister show not only her emotional involvement—and her increasing susceptibility to bad colds and "lung fever"—but also her skill at avoiding public display. With courtesy and tact she deflected a proposed visit by Dr. Edward N. Kirk, a widely admired evangelist who headed the newly formed Mount Vernon Church and would for the next quarter century be one of the leading preachers in Boston. She wrote the Saffords, strong supporters of Dr. Kirk:

You recollect Mr. Kirk's vivid description of the difference between passing through the deep valley and rising up into a revival, and leaping immediately into the sympathies of a revival. We need experience of his first to fit us for the varied and important remaining duties of the year. On this account, I have some query whether it may not be better that Mr. Kirk's visit should be deferred a little longer. If he could stay two or three full weeks, I would as soon that he would come to-day as ever. But if he cannot stay but one week, and possibly even less, it is very important that he come at the right time, and expend his power in the best way. His fear that he could not stay long enough is my great fear. It seems to me like a very desirable thing that certain minds, certain difficult cases, should come under the influence of a powerful and warm heart, like Mr. Kirk's, and we all need some stirring means; but my own will has ever been graciously kept in an even balance concerning this thing. I am prepared to rejoice or to acquiese as soon as the will of the Lord shall be made known.

She concluded by beseeching both Saffords and Dr. Kirk to pray for the Seminary every day.[22]

In subsequent descriptions of the process of conversion, she reported that "Our studies go forward, as usual, with all their regularity"—except for one Monday given over, by common consent, to fasting and prayer. Although she managed to summon strength and voice to conduct an extra meeting for the impenitent every day, she felt that the role of the other teachers was very important, in the small prayer meetings held at recess and other intervals and in private conversations with individual students. The close attention given to the emotional state of each student is suggested in Mary's request to Mrs. Safford for specific prayers for some "difficult cases." One student

retains her hope, but something in her character revolts from every thing social in feeling or action. I cannot find that an individual in the house has been able to approach her successfully in the least degree on the religion of her heart or life. I have met minds in a similar state, and, as a matter of judgment in her case, have avoided meeting her on the subject, hoping that some door might be opened in her behalf before the year closes. Many things may be done and said in time of a revival that cannot be done and said at any other time. This may be the favored time for her. I have approached the subject gently, and hope I may have the privilege of doing something more. I think it not best that she should know that the subject passes between us. But I hope you will really pray in her behalf.

We have some individuals that seem among the most hopeless. They are among the righteous towards men. They have passed seasons of conviction, and perhaps indulged hope once or twice. Here they are clothed now in the self-righteousness of not being deceived this time. Do pray for them.

Miss Lyon rated the 1843 revival high not only for the number of converts and the "unparalled rapidity" but also for the stillness with which it was conducted. So did the students. Lydia Pomeroy, a junior from Stonington, Connecticut, and a Christian when she entered, wrote her mother about what had happened and recorded a high resolve "to live more for the glory of God."

I have some good news to tell you. We have been enjoying a revival here. The spirit of the Lord has been in our midst, and many have been brought to his saving knowledge. Out of sixty impenitent young ladies, at the first of the year, only five are left who do not express hope. Such a time I never saw before. There was no excitement, the work was going on silently, and surely. We have had prayer meetings every afternoon, and evening, and two or three days, were given up entirely to this object. Last Monday was appointed as a day of fasting, and prayer, and on that day five individuals found as we trust joy and peace in believing.

Among the number, are Lydia Ann (she appears well, and our cousin N. Taylor, she was very wild before. Some others are the most wonderful cases I ever saw, so opposed they were to religion, and so gay, and thoughtless. Now they are so gentle and humble, and it seems that their very natures are changed. We have some of the best teachers here, they have been faithful for the salvation of souls, visiting from room to room and conversing and praying with the inmates. Miss Lyon of course has entered with her whole heart, and soul into the work. I do believe she is one of the best ladies that ever lived.[23]

One of the converts, Rhoda Perkins, the daughter of a minister, described her experience to her parents.

I could not wait to receive an answer from home, to my last letter, before I write that, which I trust will gladden your hearts. And can it be, that I too do hope in that same mercy that my dear sisters and brothers do? I feel as if I could, and hope that I have found Christ precious to my soul. Since I wrote to you that Miss Lyon said she did not think there would be a revival here this year, it seemed as if all the christians aroused from their slumber, and the fervent prayers that were offered by them were answered. Though there were sixty of us who were not pious only four remain unconverted. I never saw any thing before like it.

Knowing that you would like to know the particulars concerning myself I will try to write them. Ever since this term commenced Miss Lyon has had inquiry meetings and there have been more or less that attended every evening. As my feelings were in the first part of the term I thought I ought not to attend them, and did not, more than one or two. It was but three weeks last Sabbath evening when Elizabeth and I were conversing upon the subject of religion, that I told her that if any one would tell me that I might go home, or become a christian immediately, I should rather go home. Oh, wicked indeed, and I have thought since what a wonder that the spirit did not leave me, never to return.

In a short time one of the teachers came in to talk with me upon the subject of religion and my feelings were very much altered. I thought it my duty to attend the inquiry meeting, which was that evening. Such a room full I never saw, not a dry eye could be seen, and as the question was asked them, what above all things they desired most?, The responsive answer of each was to become a christian. On Monday my feelings increased and I thought I would give any thing to see my Father or Mother to converse with them. I knew not what to do. Some of the young ladies came in to talk and pray with me, but I felt no different. Tuesday night I think I felt entirely changed, but I cannot tell just when I hope I gave up all to him I had so long treated with such neglect. If I have truly consecrated myself to God how thankful ought I to be that I have such praying parents. Had I not been the child of many prayers it seemed as if there would have been no hope for such a guilty creature as I was.

News of the remarkable results of the Seminary revival had already reached her parents in Weymouth, through a Seminary visitor, before Rhoda mailed her letter, begun on April 5. On April 8 she added a postscript apologizing for distressing her parents, who could not know until she told them that she was no longer one of the unhappy few still without hope.

Although revivals declined in the 1840's, there was still interest in the high moments and the number of souls saved in a "season of refreshing"; both secular and religious newspapers sometimes carried reports from distant towns or colleges. It seems likely that the results of Mount Holyoke Seminary revivals were frequently spread not only by word of mouth but also by small news items reprinted from one paper to another. The *Tri-Weekly Post* of Springfield on January 26, 1847, carried a paragraph taken from the *Boston Traveler*, which credited the figures to a letter written from someone in the Seminary to a friend in Boston. It reported that more than 90 had entered in October as impenitent. Three months later more than 60 of them were expressing hope; 50 of them had been converted within a ten-day period. Of the 14 seniors who had been impenitent at the beginning of the school year, ten were indulging hope and the other four were deeply interested.[24]

In the revival of 1846–47, begun in mid-December, Miss Lyon was recovering from serious illness and could do relatively little, though she did conduct at least one meeting every day. It was in good part the students who generated the community feeling necessary to set off this form of group response. Susan Tolman, in her second year of teaching, recorded a day-by-day account in the journal letter. On the second day she noted that those so far converted were mainly from the middle class. "The interest seemed rather to commence there with a few praying hearts." One was surely Susan's younger sister Julia, practically the first to indulge hope. Susan described both the immediate exultation and the inevitable reaction afterward. On December 14 she reported, "During meals scarcely a word is spoken, & many there are, who cannot eat because of deep feeling. The whole house is as still as on the Sabbath. Every footstep is light, & every voice hushed. During recreation hours, in going to different rooms, or to the public rooms, we see two or three quietly conversing together, one perhaps a christian, the other an awakened sinner inquiring the way to Jesus." Five days later she found that "the interest today does not seem to be equal to what we have witnessed for several days preceding" but thought that this was "more a reaction than a feeling. Many have felt so long, & deeply as to become almost exhausted & sick." On January 7, the eve of the two-week winter vacation, she was worrying about the danger of backsliding during this "trying time." She quoted some of the converts, "Oh, I dread vacation, I fear to go out into the world," but concluded that the test ahead might be "needed to sift the chaff from the wheat." Every year a few of the converted did fall by the wayside but, apparently, not many. What everybody seems to have remembered best about this revival was "that precious middle class," more than half of whom returned the next year to graduate as the class of 1848.[25]

In other years the process of conversion was not so intense and was spread out over a longer period of time, but whether it was swift or gradual, the central action was free choice by each student. In 1847–48 the efforts for salvation of souls were so "silent and obscure" that Mary Whitman thought they could not properly be called a revival. Nonetheless, religious interest was evident in the winter term; conversions occurred at intervals in December and January and then continued into April at the rate of one a week. By the end of the year more than fifty of the impenitent had expressed hope. Among the thirty young women who remained without hope was Emily Dickinson. In spite of the claims of some biographers, there is no evidence that she—or any of the other unconverted—was badgered or defiant. Even when extra religious effots were most concentrated, students could—and did—choose to refrain. Some chose to disregard a day of fasting and prayer on December 24, 1847, that had originally been so designated by the village church and then adopted by Mary Lyon after she had taken soundings of student opinion. Such special days were in addition to the two nationally observed days of fasting and prayer fixed by the church: the first Monday in January for the conversion of the world and the last Thursday in February for the colleges. The strong stress in the Seminary observance of fast days was on private prayer; students were encouraged to do as they liked about abstaining from food. Indeed, in 1845 one student thought it worth recording that on the fast day for the conversion of the world, more than half the young women had not gone down to meals.[26]

There were, during revival periods, extra meetings in Mary Lyon's room—always designed for a particular group of individuals who would signify by note in advance if they wished to attend. On December 27, 1847, the invitation was to "all those who felt anxious for the salvation of their souls and were willing to answer questions," on January 10 to "all those who had a fear, who felt pained at the thought that this work might cease & they be passed by," on January 17 to "all who had decided that they would today [sic] to serve the Lord and those who had today felt an uncommon anxiety to decide." Emily Dickinson was one of the seventeen who chose to attend this last meeting. Even though her mind was not changed by the persuasions of Mary Lyon or of her cousin and roommate, Emilie Norcross, who had been converted the year before, she certainly did not sound resentful or scornful of these efforts in her behalf. On the day of Miss Lyon's meeting, she wrote her school friend Abiah, "I love this Seminary & all the teachers are bound strongly to my heart by ties of affection" and mentioned in a postscript the strong religious interest, adding, "I have not yet given up to the claims of Christ, but trust I am not entirely thoughtless on so important & serious a subject." In May she was writing again to Abiah: "I regret that last term, when that golden opportunity was mine, that I did not give up and become a Christian. It is not now too late, so my friends tell me, so my offended conscience whispers, but it is hard for me to give up the world."[27]

Readers attempting today to assess this kind of religious pressure must remember that the regular business of the Seminary—study, recitations, domestic work, even some recreation—went on during every revival. Lydia Pomeroy, who wrote in an exalted state of mind about the 1843 revival, included in her letter a description of a sleigh ride the preceding Saturday and mentioned that the students had for several nights been watching the comet (a remarkable one, visible even in daylight, then at its most brilliant). Early that same March, when Mary Lyon returned after her week of prayer in Boston, she seemed completely caught up in the tremendous personal effort it took to get a revival started, but she still found time to deal briskly with an unsatisfactory student. The letter she wrote to the father, asking him to come and take his daughter home, has not survived but his reply suggests that Miss Lyon was a shrewd appraiser of parents as well as young women and that she did not expect a revival to remedy intellectual incapacity or indifference.

Hartford, March 11th, 1843

Dear Madam.

I received a letter from you last evening, stating that you have from the first acquaintance with my daughter, thought her unfit-

ted in discipline and maturity, to be a profitable member of your School;—besides being unqualified in her studies;—and you think we have been deceived by her teachers in regard to her attainments;—and that you have now come to the conclusion to send her home.

I regret exceedingly to hear this account of her, and of the decision that you have come to, and particularly so at this late period, after commencing on her second term,—when if you recollect in the letter I wrote you in regard to her staying, I made a particular request, that if you did not retain her through the year, that you would let her come home, at the close of the first term. I should have been satisfied if that course had been pursued, and thought it perfectly right.

I do not wish her to stay in the School through the year, under present circumstances, but should be glad to have her stay until the first week in April, on account of the weather, and bad travelling etc, as she is very subject to violent attacks of inflamation in her throat, upon the slightest cold.

In regard to her abilities, and our being deceived by her teachers, I will only say in reply, that she has always attended the best of our private Schools, where the teachers have been in the habit of sending to the parents very often, of the obedience and progress of their children;—so far from her being of a disobedient or an indolent scholar, she has always been a particular favorite with them, and this is the first time that we have ever had any complaint sent us, about her in any respect. I think Madam, that the opinion you have formed of her, cannot be from your own personal acquaintance with her, but from the representations of others, who may have some prejudice against her, and have made the case as bad as they could.

She is a girl of a gay and volatile disposition, frank and open in her manners, and if she has been guilty of any indiscretion, I am persuaded that it has proceeded from mere thoughtlessness, and not from any disrespect to her teachers;—she is young, and has never been from home before;—she is extravagantly fond of reading, so much so, that her mother has been obliged to limit her books, when at home, and the greatest thing we feared when she went from us was, that she would read so much, that she would

*neglect her studies, and her failures in this respect, I presume origi-
nates from this cause, and not from indolence, or any defect in her
abilities or intellect.*

*I would now ask as a particular favor, in view of her youth and
inexperience, that you will pass over her failings as charitably as
possible, and whenever she leaves the Seminary, that you will not
expose her to the School, nor let them know the cause;—if you will
Dear Madam comply with this request, you will confer a lasting
favor upon her parents, and receive the heartfelt thanks of,*

*Your obedient servant,
Henry Francis.*

*Miss Mary Lyon
Ps. I shall be much obliged to you, if you will not charge extra, for
the time my daughter has been with you, as I do not feel able, nor
willing to pay more than the regular tuition price. H.F.*[28]

There is no doubt that in her last years Mary put increasing effort
and time into the salvation of souls. Students, teachers, and trustees
were all aware of her mounting concern for the impenitents and in
the main approved her increasing stress on the process of conversion. Mrs. Porter recalled with admiration that when Miss Lyon
arrived in mid-January 1849 to spend what was to be her last winter
recess in Monson, she had said, "O, when I come before those
young immortals to teach them eternal truths, I am borne down
with a sense of its importance as never before . . ." It turned out
that in the pattern she had set, even conversion could be carried on
without her physical presence. With the support of the teachers—
all participants in revivals as students—and the approval of succeeding generations of students and their parents, the Seminary continued until after the Civil War to win souls to Christ. In 1848-49,
the year of Mary Lyon's death, when events precluded a regular revival, before the final examinations sixty young women were indulging hope. In his twenty-fifth anniversary address, Dr. Kirk, then
president of the board of trustees, gave some figures about the number of conversions in the first quarter century of the Seminary. Out
of 3,400 students he guessed that about 1,000 had entered without
hope. Of these 1,000 at least three fourths must have been converted during their stay in the Seminary; the total number certainly

exceeded the 739 tabulated in the twenty years for which accurate records were available.[29]

The reputation for piety of the young ladies at Mount Holyoke was no doubt enhanced by the attention given to foreign missions. Next to the Seminary itself, this was the cause closest to Mary Lyon's heart. Foreign missionaries had been her particular heroes since childhood. Year by year, as she welcomed those home on furlough to speak at the Seminary, she enlarged her personal acquaintance with the men and women in the field—and with the often undisciplined daughters they wanted her to educate. She followed closely the operations of the American Board of Commissioners of Foreign Missions, frequently attending the annual meeting; she encountered some of the criticism beginning to be voiced within the Christian community. But she never lost her admiration for this kind of self-denial nor her faith in the power of such dedicated men and women to convert the world. Among other staunch supporters of foreign missions were two of Mary's ablest and most discriminating friends, Reverend Condit and Professor Hitchcock.

One quality Mary Lyon wanted to strengthen in all Mount Holyoke students was benevolence. She expected them to devote their lives to the general good—as teachers, as wives and mothers, as devout and generous supporters of the church. She believed in the need for instruction in the art of giving—and for plenty of practice. She also felt that the Seminary had a special obligation to support the missionaries. As she told a group of former students gathered around her at one of the ABCFM meetings: "The seminary was founded to advance the missionary cause. I sometimes feel that our walls were built from the funds of our missionary boards. Certainly much of the money expended upon them was given by those who hold every thing sacred to the Lord, and who, probably, would otherwise have devoted it to sending the gospel directly to the heathen." In preparation for the collection of the annual missionary contribution, Miss Lyon regularly gave a series of talks which lengthened year by year. Her injunctions were partly Biblical, partly pragmatic. The directness of her approach is shown in entries in the journal kept by Antoinette Hubbell, a senior, in February 1844:

25th [February 1844]

Miss L. told us the reasons for taking a miss. contr. in this family. Practice will make a more lasting impression on the mind, than any amount of instruction. Wherever we are, we should consider our miss. contr. a part of our expenses, and plan accordingly. We have some control over our money and it is our act, though it is true we should regard the feelings of our parents, but many do not estimate the benevolence of their parents high enough. If she had a daughter, she should wish her to do as her heart desired, and then come to her for her opinion. Miss L. spoke of the deep interest and anxiety she feels every year in this subject, the trial of giving the little she has, is nothing in comparison, and probably it will be one of our most important duties hereafter, to lead others to give as they ought. Am. Board, Home, Tract, and Bible are the cornerstones of all the other soc. but our efforts will here be more united for the first two only.

26th

Miss L. spoke to us on the subject of economizing for the sake of giving. This is not mean, but noble. Many are poor because they have not enough, and do not know how to be economical. Economy consists in making the least amount accomplish the greatest good. Dress is our present problem, and in this we are to save the most, particularly by two methods; by being careful of clothes, wearing suitable articles, as gloves, or shoes, for the occasion, with neat repairing, and etc, by delaying a seemingly important purchase. But always with never an exception, appearing in good taste, and thus you may gradually lower your standard of dress.[30]

The results were remarkable. A letter written immediately after this appeal shows how Mary Lyon's mixture of precept and example affected one student.

Yesterday a subscription paper was passed in behalf of the missionary cause. Miss Lyon is the most interested person in this cause I ever saw. It seems to be her chief desire and prayer that she may cultivate to a high degree the same spirit in all under her care. Her efforts have been greatly successful. Her scholars are scattered all over the world as missionaries and in other fields of usefulness. Her heart and hands are ever open to do good. She certainly possesses a rare vein of benevolence, such an one as very few possess.

Take this as an example: she pays annually ninety dollars for the missionary cause. Perhaps you might say, well she might for she probably has a large salary and obtains it in an easy way. But tis quite the opposite she has been pressed by the Trustees to accept of $800 pr year but she does not receive but 200: and as to her easily obtaining it that too is as contrary. Her days and nights are those of care and anxiety. Her teachers all pay as much or nearly as much in proportion to their income. Last year the sum raised by them in connection with the young ladies was $950. This year exceeds that, how much is not yet quite known.

Perhaps you ask how much is my donation. I have thought much of the subject and finally concluded to pay about 4.50. This undoubtedly seems quite extravagant, but I will tell you how I have been thinking I would manage to have it not really so. You know we talked before I left home that I might get me some sort of a bonnet in the spring, and perhaps a dress, but I have concluded to get along comfortably without them and appropriate of that sum 4.50 in this way. Do pardon me if you think this wrong. Very many of the young ladies pay 5.00, some 8.00 and I believe some 10.00.

The total turned out to be $1,130, over $200 more than the preceding year. The subscription book for 1843–44, open for all to see, revealed that almost 40 percent came from Mary Lyon and the dozen teachers. These young women received salaries in cash (apart from board and room) that averaged less than $150 a year; their average missionary contribution was almost $30. From 200 students the average gift was $3.50, and for some, who had barely been able to collect the $60 for the year's fees, the gift was a sacrifice. Between 1842–43 and 1848–49, the year of Miss Lyon's death, the annual gift from the Seminary to foreign and home missions averaged $1,000 a year.[31]

Mary Lyon's conviction of the need for sacrificial giving and the importance of supporting foreign missions first also found expression in the one book she wrote, *A Missionary Offering*. This slim little volume of a hundred pages was produced at white heat over a few days in May 1843 when the emotions stirred by Fidelia Fiske's departure on March 1 and the revival that reached its climax in April were given a new direction by news that missionary gifts were falling off. In a letter to Fidelia afterward, Mary explained what had happened.

. . . my spirit was so stirred, and my heart so burdened, that I wrote as fast as possible, without inquiring how I wrote, or whether I had time to write. In the month of April, the scenes of the revival, the prospect of our next missionary subscription, the falling off of the missionary receipts, all combined to give me an unusual current of emotions in view of certain subjects. I was preparing a connected series of topics to present to the school, the substance of which you will find, to some extent, in the first three and last two chapters. I had just commenced before the monthly concert in May, to which reference is made. After reading the affecting circular, which I heard with deepest interest, in behalf of all our school, who were present as well as myself, Mr. Condit invited a young minister, just commencing preaching, to make some remarks. To Mr. Condit's disappointment, and to my distress, instead of following out the subject, he just attempted to make some strictures on our missionary operations, alluding to slavery, and speaking of the want of economy at some of our stations. The defect of the young man was more in the head than the heart. All agreed that his remarks were, at least, ill-timed. But, among other results, they gave existence to the little book. It was scarcely two days before most of the materials were gathered together.[32]

The book began by celebrating the missionary movement, especially the ABCFM and its annual meeting at Norwich, Connecticut, the preceding September, which had justly been called a little heaven on earth.

If I am permitted to enjoy but one more scene of nature's sublimity, I will not ask to behold the wonders of other lands, and of other climes, I will only ask to taste once more of the delights of our own Niagara's scenes. So if I am permitted to behold but one more public scene of moral sublimity, let that be another annual meeting of the American Board. I ask not to visit the splendid halls of [t]he old world, and listen to the eloquence of those master minds, whose praise is in all the earth, from the equator to the poles. Whatever may be those sublime delights, I only ask to witness again the simple, the modest, the unpretending grandeur of one of the annual sessions of the American Board.

An admirer of Jonathan Edwards, she dealt with the pains of hell and the agonies of judgment day for those who failed in Christian sympathy and personal responsibility for the heathen. The human being whom she pictured as observing and suffering all these agonies was a "timid sensitive female." In the procession of those trying to justify the meagerness of their gifts to convert the world, this "delicate female" stood out; she had had to spend considerably on her own needs and comforts to satisfy the demands of "necessity, respectability, and deference to superiors."[33]

Mary Lyon's heaviest irony was directed toward Covetousness, whom she envisioned as a sophisticated young man, in a series of Miltonic encounters with "good" New Englanders whose excuses she knew well.

He could transform himself into an angel of light, and he could put on every garb, from that of Milton's cherub youth, to that of the highest, and boldest archangel before the throne. He was a friend of every cause, and he could become an agent of every enterprise. He now appeared as an advocate of Foreign Missions. . . . His public appeals in behalf of Missions were warm and spirited. His censures on the apathy of the church, were loud and vociferous. He made an eloquent speech on the extravagances and luxuries of the age, and on the vast imports and expenditures of the nation. He entered into a labored and exact calculation of the ability and resources of the church. He proved to the entire satisfaction of his hearers, that there was wealth enough in the country—that the work could all be accomplished without the least self denial of a single individual. Just look, he said, at the vast amount worse than thrown away on our Congress, on our State Legislatures, and on our navy, and in every other department of government. Just look at the sums expended annually on the articles of rum, wine, and brandy—of tea, sugar, and coffee—of silks, laces, and ribbons, and of a thousand other things, a mere fraction of which, would sustain the whole cause of Missions. . . . I saw this same advocate for Missions come into an assembly composed entirely of men, who were discussing this subject. There he was very eloquent in praise of female sympathy, female piety, and female benevolence. Woman, he said, was last at the cross, and first at the sepulchre, and she had ever been first in every good work. There was scarcely a female in the land, who was not now either knitting, or sewing for the cause. Woman was fruitful in invention; what she undertook, she always accomplished. While the Board had so many warm hearted, faithful friends, there was nothing to fear. Man had only to go forward in the even tenor of his way, and give about as he had done. All that was extra, he might safely commit over to the industry, the ingenuity, and the benevolence of the other sex.

Again I saw him seated in a circle of females. They were relating, one by one, the various difficulties in their missionary efforts, and comparing their condition with the more easy lot of the other sex, who had all the money under their own control. With all their toils, and all their self-denying zeal, the little sum, which they could raise, would avail nothing in so great an enterprise. It was a serious question, whether it would not be wise to give up their efforts, and commit the whole work over to the other sex. Just at that moment, he proffered his kind advice. He should not favor so rash a step as was last proposed. The cause of Missions needed female sympathy, and female prayers. It would be well to sustain their sewing societies, and to endeavor to keep up an interest. Woman ought in some way to do a little— just enough to open her heart, and secure her prayers. But no one ought to look to her to meet extra calls.[34]

Although *A Missionary Offering* could not be called a feminist tract, its expectations for women were high. Among the truly generous persons pictured in contrast to the followers of Covetousness, there were as many women as men. Praise went to the good managers, like the minister's wife, a woman of "intelligence and superior education . . . of refinement and taste." Her husband wisely turned over to her the administering of all the household funds and she provided for both "the comfort of the household" and "the treasury of the Lord." The most fully sketched of all the liberal women was her own widowed mother, lovingly pictured from childhood recollections. In memory she had sustained her children abundantly and still, out of her little means, "always had room enough and to spare to a more restricted neighbor."[35]

Part of the difficulty in getting support for foreign missions was the opposition of many abolitionists. That Mary Lyon, apolitical and averse to controversy, should consider a plea to free the slaves a specious argument suggests the extent to which the church in 1843 was already torn over the issue of slavery. The sophistical rhetorician of *A Missionary Offering*, no doubt modeled on the young minister at the South Hadley concert, addressed working people informally.

He gave some gentle hints against learning, and learned men. He made some remarks of doubtful meaning about the salaries of ministers, and their power over the people, and about the payment of agents. He introduced some ambiguous insinuations concerning the management of the missionary enterprise, and the mode of expending money on some of the stations.

To a learned audience he was more polished: "His whole discourse was so learned, and his composition so beautifully finished, that I found it difficult to remember much of it, and I shall find it still more difficult to relate it. I shall only attempt to gather up a few of the leading thoughts, leaving behind all the learning, and all the beauties of style." Into the ear of "warm hearted benevolence" he whispered "in behalf of the slave." He did not need to make a frontal attack if he could separate close friends simply by raising the issue. "He well knew, that a house divided against itself cannot stand."[36]

In subsequent years this kind of antislavery pressure increased. In the fall of 1845 an activist from Springfield tried by letter and personal interview to persuade Miss Lyon, as head of what claimed to be a religious and benevolent institution, to persuade the trustees to do what he had read in the newspapers that Dartmouth was going to do—accept colored students on the same basis as whites. In the spring of 1846 a one-time pupil made a passionate plea that the students should be encouraged to develop benevolent concern for "the enslaved heathen of our own land" as well as for those on foreign soil. She criticized the missions operation only by implication: "I am not about to call in question the character of the Missionary Board, nor pain your benevolent heart with a single word to its disparagement. I sincerely hope it will emerge from the clouds of controversy in which it is now involved as pure and spotless—as beautiful and radiant with heavenly light, as any one of its most enthusiastic admirers may believe it to be." Such appeals may only have strengthened Mary Lyon's mistrust of abolitionist zeal and her conviction that foreign missions must come first. In March 1848 she was still telling the young ladies "the church that will give for the conversion of the world, will give for the salvation of her country."[37]

The brief closing chapter of *A Missionary Offering* pleads with every Christian for the "last farthing"—the utmost that he can possibly give. Even an excerpt may convey something of the intensity of her feeling and the rhetorical nature of many of her addresses to students.

No one knows to whom the balancing power may be given, which shall determine this great question in the court of heaven. The balancing power was given to Achan, and with his wedge of gold, he could trouble the whole camp of Israel. The deciding power was given to Phineas, and with javelin in hand, he was able by a single act, to stay the plague, and save thousands from a speedy death. Let no one say, therefore, that the little which he can do, will have no avail. When God, in the court of heaven, shall weigh the offerings, which shall decide this great question, he may say, "This poor widow hath cast in more than they all." On the other hand, let no one, feel, that he can afford to consume treasures on himself, because he has already done so much for the cause. The little, that remains in his hand, which he can give, and which the

Lord requires of him, may be the balancing power, which shall decide the whole case.[38]

Mary Lyon went about achieving publication with characteristic energy and thoroughness. She consulted Mr. Hawks; Dr. Anderson, corresponding secretary of ABCFM and editor of the *Missionary Herald*; Mrs. Banister; and the Saffords to such good effect that by mid-July the little volume was off the press and being distributed. Miss Lyon gave one copy to each student at the Seminary, and Mrs. Banister took thirty-two copies for her friends and acquaintances. At the author's insistence, the book had been published anonymously, but the authorship was no doubt an open secret to Mary Lyon's friends and must have strengthened the connection in many minds between Mount Holyoke and the missionary cause.[39]

Among the pioneering students who attended the Seminary its first year, four went almost immediately to missionary posts. Charlotte Bailey, who stayed so briefly that her name was not listed in the catalogue, married Reverend Aldin Grout in November 1838 and was in Natal, South Africa, in May 1840, launched on a lifetime of helping her husband work with the Zulus. Mary Avery, the oldest of the three daughters of Deacon Avery who attended the Seminary, in the spring of 1839 was stirred by an appeal for a teacher for the Cherokee Indians, made by Miss Lyon. She apparently often used the general exercises to present challenging opportunities to the whole school. Mary was accepted immediately and for five years taught with great success in Arkansas; she returned home to recover her health and later married a missionary to the Creek Indians in Florida. Emma Bliss in 1839 married an Amherst classmate of her oldest brother, Reverend Henry J. Van Lennep, and sailed with him for Smyrna. There, after three months, she died; she was just 20. Prudence Richardson, the only one of the four to complete the course, had taught for some years and was 28 when the Seminary opened. She also married an Amherst graduate, Reverend William Walker, in November 1841 and they sailed almost immediately for Cape Palmas, West Africa; within three months she, too, was dead.[40]

Neither personal sorrow for such losses nor fear of a similar fate seems to have diminished the interest of Seminary students in young men bent on missionary careers. The stories of the martyr wives in early expeditions were well known and often retold not only in the Seminary but in churches throughout New England. In any case, early in 1843 a new possibility stirred up the whole institution, the young faculty quite as much as the students. Reverend Justin Perkins, who had grown up about five miles from South Hadley, and graduated from Amherst, had founded a mission in Oroomiah, Persia, in 1833. He and Mrs. Perkins returned on furlough in 1842, accompanied by an able convert, by then a bishop in the Nestorian church. They were immediately made welcome at the Seminary, where they gave talks and attended the concluding public examinations in August. When Mr. Perkins came in mid-January 1843, six weeks before their departure for Oroomiah, he was seeking two young ladies to go with them and to conduct a school for Persian girls. This was a surprise to Mary Lyon. She had encouraged her students to take difficult posts in the South and West, but in a foreign mission the odds against an unmarried woman seemed great. Indeed, she had just been saying that most young ladies could do more at home than in a foreign field. Nevertheless, this appeal won her warm endorsement. When she invited notes from those who wanted to consider the possibility, she received forty within an hour, including one from a member of the faculty to whom Miss Lyon was particularly attached.

Fidelia Fiske, an 1842 graduate from Shelburne, had known and admired Mary Lyon from childhood; an older sister had been converted at her Buckland school in 1826. After six years of teaching district school, Fidelia had entered the middle class in October 1839. The Fisk family were principal victims of the typhoid epidemic of 1840; Fidelia was so ill she was unable to return to the Seminary for a year and her father and a younger sister both caught the infection from her and died. It was Fidelia whom Mary Lyon, prostrated by the typhoid tragedy and the deaths of her own sister and mother, had invited to come and convalesce with her at the Seminary. She was giving up a devoted friend as well as an able and dedicated teacher when she pushed through Fidelia's acceptance. On the first try, the strong objection of the Shelburne pastor and Mrs. Fisk's reluctance had made Fidelia turn down the offer, in spite of her own ardent desires. Then Mr. Perkins found one qualified young woman elsewhere, and the second Seminary candidate withdrew because of family objections. Mary Lyon drove thirty miles with Fidelia through snowdrifts to Shelburne; her mother's consent was won on February 19. Within a week Fidelia had said her farewells at home and in the Seminary; the young ladies had sewed furiously to provide her an adequate outfit; and she was on her way to Boston, accompanied by Miss Lyon, who attended her embarkation for Smyrna on March 1. No matter what her previous doubts, Mary was thrilled by this opportunity to serve on distant soil. "This was the great object . . . for wh. the Institution was built—to prepare laborers for Christ's cause," she had told the students when the final decision was pending. Letters from Fidelia about Oroomiah and from Mr. Perkins about her success both as a teacher and as a member of the missionary community helped sustain the heightened interest in missions everywhere.[42]

Fidelia Fiske's success did not of itself open the way for numbers of other single women. The sponsoring board members and most of the heads of missions were conservative clergymen who preferred their established practice of match-making by judicious introductions of young men and young women who had applied separately for overseas assignments. Mount Holyoke was not nearly so much involved in this kind of pairing off as legend would have it, but there were a few documented instances, especially among Seminary teachers. It is not surprising that the teachers perceived the glamour as well as the dangers of missionary life. They were constantly reminded of the high value Mary Lyon set on foreign missionary service; having responded year after year to her rising expectations, they were prepared to fill their days very full, meet a succession of domestic and intellectual challenges, and submerge their concerns in the common good.[43]

In the summer of 1845 a young Englishman named Edward Webb, who was studying at Andover, came to South Hadley. He was a friend of William Howland, who was about to marry Susan Reed and head for India. Webb had also been tentatively accepted for the Indian mission but needed a wife. Within two weeks he was engaged to one of the most charming of the young teachers,

20. Abby Allen, a student at the Seminary for two years, married Samuel B. Fairbank in 1846 and went with him as a missionary to India. Mount Holyoke College Library Archives.

Nancy Foote. Lucy Lyon, whose eagerness to become a foreign missionary had been mounting ever since Fidelia Fiske left, tried for an independent assignment. In the spring of 1846 as a Baptist she made formal application to the Baptist board to be sent out unmarried to start a school for girls. She spent the last week in May in Brooklyn, attending the annual missionary meetings and being interviewed. Whether she would have overcome the reluctance of the executive committee cannot be guessed; before the end of the week when they would have had to make a decision, she was listening sympathetically to overtures of a Baptist theological student at Hamilton (later Colgate) who was expecting to be sent to China and was actively seeking a wife. It took six weeks of sustained correspondence and a visit to South Hadley for Lucy and Edward Lord to be officially engaged; Lucy felt the need of explaining to Fidelia, "I did not accept his hand *merely* because he was to be a missionary." When Reverend Cyrus Mills first called on Susan Tolman in South Hadley in the summer of 1847, they had both indicated to the ABCFM that they wanted to be missionaries, but they refused to be hurried into matrimony. After they became engaged, it was, by their own choice, more than a year before they married and left for Ceylon. At least one other Seminary graduate, Mary Rice, class of 1846, did go out in Mary Lyon's lifetime as an unmarried teacher, but she was not really breaking new ground. Her destination was Oroomiah, where she would assist and then succeed Fidelia Fiske.[44]

The impetus that Mary Lyon gave to foreign missions lasted long after her death. There is no doubt that Mount Holyoke sent out a remarkable number of young women to foreign service straight through the nineteenth century. When she died in March 1849 the number was 35; ten years later there were 60 on the rolls of the ABCFM. At the semicentennial ceremonies in 1887 it was reported that of the women then serving under the ABCFM, 261, more than one fifth, 56 in all, had been educated at Mount Holyoke. A bronze plaque recording all the foreign missionaries from the first 50 classes contained 178 names; by the time of the centennial in 1937, the total number on the honor roll, all carefully recorded and tabulated, was nearly 400.[45]

The scores of young women who went out from the Seminary across the continental United States as teachers and home missionaries received far less attention than their counterparts in foreign lands, though their numbers were far greater and their long-term influence more widespread. In making such a comparison it is essential to keep in mind the remarkable organization of the ABCFM, which gathered and stored all sorts of personal data about the men and women it sent out and published reports of their activities. For the home missionaries there was no comparable major source of information among dozens of agencies that recruited ministers and their wives and also single women for service in city slums and frontier settlements. About the teachers who were not missionaries, accessible data was rare indeed; employment was a function of local school boards, public support varied from town to town and year to year, private school jobs and private schools could vanish overnight.

Mary Lyon, who knew the stumbling blocks for women teachers, understood the long-term value of accurate records and set about getting her own data as soon as possible. The Memorandum Society (alumnae association), which she had organized when the Seminary had been in operation only four months, published its directory as promised at five-year intervals. Membership was voluntary, cost $2.00—the lifetime fee—and was urged upon graduating seniors; probably about half the young women who attended the Seminary enrolled. From the Society records, carefully compiled for over half a century, it is obvious that more than half of this self-selected group of alumnae did go into the classroom after they left the Seminary. By 1887, the Society had enrolled 3,033 members, of whom more than 2,000 had taught after leaving Mount Holyoke. Even in the early years, when finding good teaching jobs could be difficult for able young women, the figures were a source of pride to Mary Lyon; in 1847 the Society had 593 members, and 279 were teachers.[46]

How many of them held hardship posts in the West or South it is hard to guess. Filling such jobs took not only idealistic and resourceful applicants but also skilled assistance in placement. Catharine Beecher, sustained by the Beecher family name and support and also by her own considerable powers as a publicist, spent four years collecting funds for what became the National Board of Popular Education, organized to send adequately prepared young women to teach in the West. When Governor William Slade of Vermont completed his term of office in 1846, he joined the enterprise as full-time paid agent. Even though Miss Beecher soon withdrew over a policy disagreement, the organization continued to enjoy considerable public attention. In the decade of its existence starting in 1847, it sent about 450 young women to the West as teachers. Some of these had been recruited by Mary Lyon, but not many. In her response to one of Miss Beecher's circulars, she explained her reluctance. Although she approved the undertaking, she found Miss Beecher's arrangements too indefinite to assure young recruits a minimum of physical and fiscal safety.

. . . there is a difficulty as to my immediate success in furnishing teachers for your enterprize. For young ladies must not only be willing to go, but must also gain the approbation of father, mother, or, perhaps, brother or sister, or sister's husband.

As the enterprise now is, it will be difficult to satisfy very careful friends. Just write to me of a particular place by name and that a teacher can have proper assurance of her paying expenses and a salary of say only $100, and I have little doubt that I can send you a good teacher with full consent of friends as soon as I can find a safe escort.

But if I can only say I wish to send a teacher to Miss Beecher to spend a few weeks at Cincinnati in preparing for an unknown field with an unknown salary, and to be under obligation to an unknown donor, the case is different.

You will not understand that I disapprove your mode of commencing *your work. After your enterprise has made farther advance I hope to do more than I can do now. You will excuse me if my suggestion [sic] are borrowed from my own experience the last ten years. Having had many obstacles thrown in my own way, I anticipate them for others, and having been blessed with more success than I ever hoped, I am prepared to expect success for others as I do for you.*

Writing a little later to a young minister who had asked for teachers for a poor area of South Jersey, Miss Lyon had again been explicit about the need for reasonable community support before volunteers arrived on the scene:

For such destitute regions as you refer to, I think there may often be found female teachers with the needed benevolence and self-denying spirit, and yet very much is necessary to prepare the way in all such cases. Ladies cannot go out alone and unprotected like gentlemen. They can work as hard and with no more in return, and perhaps less, but they must have a home and counsellors and

definite work laid out for their hands. There have been some cases,
where ladies have been sent out with too little definiteness and
have been expected too much to lay out their work for themselves.
This I have no doubt that you will look after. Reports have come
to me that Miss Beecher's operations are defective in the particular
to which I have referred. I hope the report has no good foundation
for my heart has been greatly interested in her work, and labor of
love to which she has given herself so zealously and disinterestedly
and some upon whom I look almost as my own dear children I
have encouraged to go out under her banner.[47]

The mounting demand in established schools for teachers educated at Mount Holyoke was partly a phenomenon of an expanding educational system but also a tribute to the caliber of those
already at work and to Mary Lyon's expertise at placement.
Though she encouraged young women to accept arduous work for
low pay, she insisted in their behalf on clear financial arrangements in advance. Her knowledge of schools was comprehensive,
her appraisals of individual talents and limitations were penetrat-
ing; she could recommend with warmth and candor not only the
top students but also those less successful academically. In the
summer of 1846 she wrote in confidence to Reverend Charles
Beatty, head of a well established seminary in Steubenville, Ohio,
to whom she had begun to recommend prospective teachers in
Ipswich. Her note concerned a young woman of 28 who had spent
two years at Mount Holyoke without making sufficient academic
progress to be listed in the catalogue either year.

Rev. & dear Sir:
I take the liberty to write you a few lines relative to Miss Cornelia
Martin. She has received a letter from Miss Condit inquiring
whether she would be willing to take the place of governess in
your school & family. I will just say that I should regard her as
admirably qualified for such a situation. She has much dignity &
decision, with much affability & kindness, & a very large share of
benevolence. She has a great desire to do good, & had in view a
situation of more self denial than her friends would consent to
have her occupy. While her heart was tried by their refusal, Miss

Condit's letter came to comfort her, as she hoped the way might be open for her to do good. She has written to her friends & they would be pleased to have her go to Steubenville. As her family are making a remove it is more convenient for her to remain here till the question is decided. She has studied most of the English branches in our course, but owing to early mental training, & other causes, I have thought that as a teacher of classes simply, she would not take that high stand that would be expected of a lady of her dignity & character in other respects. On this account, I have not attempted to recommend her as I otherwise should have done. [The two preceding sentences are marked "Confidential."] I have expected that Providence would provide her some field of labor corresponding with her large heart, & large soul. I write this on my own responsibility without her request. But if you will just drop me a line on the subject I shall regard it as a favor.

Respectfully yours,
Mary Lyon

If Miss Martin goes to Steubenville she will need directions about the best route to make her journey.

Mr. Beatty apparently made the appointment by return mail. Two weeks later Mary Lyon sent a follow-up note, again praising her as "a lady of great worth," mentioning her family background—her father, a Southerner, was an army doctor of limited means in poor health, and including her travel plans and projected time of arrival.[48]

Miss Lyon took it for granted that her "daughters" would continue after they left the Seminary to ask help from her in finding jobs; for most teaching posts the tenure was brief and advancement came by moving elsewhere. Placement was a year-round activity; it usually reached a climax in the already crowded anniversary weeks. In 1847 Miss Whitman had to preside on two of the three days of public examinations because Miss Lyon was too busy interviewing students and writing employers even to come into the Hall; on August 3 ten of the 44 seniors were already engaged as teachers. When a special opportunity arose, Miss Lyon had no hesitation in inviting a qualified young woman to leave the job she had already accepted, on the clear understanding that Miss Lyon herself would find an acceptable replacement.

In August 1846 she made such a suggestion to Lydia Bailey, class of 1845, who had taken a job at Peacham, Vermont:

I have an application where they want a teacher who can teach Latin, French & Greek. As this is so rare a request relative to a female teacher, I thought you might be glad of the interest as you can teach all three. Would they not release you at Peacham if I could secure a good teacher to take your place, at the time you left? I mean to have you leave immediately, just as soon as you can get another letter to you [sic] after I receive yours. The school is about 45 miles from Albany. They have given he says, from $10 to $12 a month & board. If you should succeed well, I think they would increase the compensat. It is under the care of a gentleman. The school commences two weeks from Monday next, so that the teacher must arrive as early as two weeks from tomorrow. I have written to a lady, inquiring, if she will be willing to go immediately & take your place. If you want the place, I think best for you to ask for a release. I must hear from you without the least delay.

Just after I wrote you last, I received your letter containing the welcome offering for Miss Butler. Many thanks for this token of love to her & myself too.

Lydia chose to stay at Peacham; four years later she joined the Mount Holyoke faculty. A similar suggestion had been made that spring to Sarah Bonney, class of 1843, when the decision did not have to be reached in such a hurry.

As you have been sometime at Jacksonville, I have thought that you might like a change, & perhaps Mr. Williams would not object to the change, provided your place could be well filled. I have therefore thought of recommending you to another place. As I have an application on hand now, I thought that I would mention your name. The situation is at Cincinnati. It is an important situation & I should think a very pleasant one. I have communicated with Mr. Williams' brother on the subject, & he will write to him. If you have the invitation you will of course do as you prefer

about leaving your present situation. If you have not that invita-
tion, & would like some other, please let me know.

Sarah left Jacksonville in 1846; she went not to Cincinnati but to
Greenwich, Connecticut. Whether she obtained this post directly
through Miss Lyon, there are no records to show.[49]

The multiplying requests from Mount Holyoke alumnae in good
positions for colleagues and assistants received close attention.
When Susannah Fitch, an 1847 graduate, wrote after a year of
teaching in Hamilton, Ohio, seeking an experienced assistant who
could teach music, Miss Lyon had no clear candidate but suggested
five possibilities, noting which ones had been in the Seminary with
Susannah and undertaking to sound out the two most promising
alternatives right away.[50]

Mary Lyon's conviction that in the right circumstances the
majority of Mount Holyoke students could—and should—teach
well was unshakable. She rejoiced as year after year a new crop of
young women went out to fill more classrooms and year by year
increased the demands on her for replacements and reinforcements.
This steady infiltration through individual contact made no headlines but had a strong cumulative effect. For the fiftieth anniversary celebration in 1887 Mary Chapin Pease selected out of a long
list of possibilities the names of sixty-two alumnae who had
headed educational institutions in thirty states and territories. Her
list included heads—who were not infrequently also the founders—
of kindergartens, high schools, normal schools; of boarding schools
like Abbot, Dana Hall, and Monticello; of the women's divisions
of coeducational colleges like Knox, Grinnell, and Whitman; of
the "daughter" colleges for women, including Wellesley along with
Mills, Lake Erie, and Western. This list did not make headlines
either; even in 1887 top billing by the Seminary itself went to
foreign missionaries. But it does suggest the extent of Mount
Holyoke influence and provides an interesting gloss on Mary's
prophecy at a grim moment in 1836: "In the many hundreds, if
not thousands, of teachers which it will send forth, it will doubtless be an instrument of good, far beyond the present grasp of my
feeble comprehension."[51]

Another of the nonacademic achievements that drew public

attention to Mount Holyoke in the 1840's, along with the effectiveness of the revivals and the number of young women going out
to foreign missionary service, was the domestic work system. This
was the feature least understood and most widely opposed in the
original plans for the Seminary; at the start most of Mary Lyon's
supporters had doubts about the principle, or objections on the
grounds of impracticality. To be sure, there was no miraculous
reversal of all opposition once the Seminary was open; occasionally
parents of prospective students protested, some girls who came did
complain. Mary Lyon never found the kind of superintendent she
had envisioned; after the collapse of Miss Peters the first year she
did not appoint a successor until 1841. Miss Emily Bridge seems
to have fitted into the scheme reasonably well but when, after
four years, she left, she was not replaced. Some of the responsibilities were shared among teachers and students and Mary Lyon
herself continued to be more and more involved in the operation
each year of her life. But in spite of its flaws, two years after Miss
Lyon's death, Professor Hitchcock could truly call the whole
system an "extraordinary and uninterrupted success."[52]

After the first two or three years, objections to housework as
menial seem to have been rare. In one interchange with a friend of
the family of a candidate from Norfolk, Virginia, in June 1842,
Miss Lyon dealt briskly with detailed inquiries revealing the young
woman's reluctance to be committed to "cooking, washing, etc.,
which are here considered menial occupations." She focused on
the ability to adapt to unfamiliar circumstances. "An educated
lady, who expects to be useful, should have her mind so enlarged,
that she can adapt herself to different states of society & to the
customs of different parts of the country. She should be prepared
to travel in foreign lands, without making the customs of her own
home the standard for every thing she meets." She also gave an
explanation for the popularity of domestic work that student
testimony throughout the 1840's bears out: "Many young ladies,
of noble, elevated & truly independent feelings, enjoy as they
would engaging in a new enterprize the attempting to do what
they never did before." Much to her surprise, her letter provoked
a quick withdrawal through the intermediary, who made it clear
that both he and Miss Nelson felt rebuked. Mary Lyon thereupon

drafted an apology, explaining that she had not in the least resented his original inquiries, from which "I should consider it unpardonable in myself to receive any offense." She took full responsibility for the misunderstanding, saying "I would not willingly wound the feelings of a stranger" and "I must have been very unfortunate in my language" and concluding, "By what you say of Miss Nelson, I presume she would be a very cheerful happy member of our community." By way of fuller explanation she cited earlier reactions to the system and her own determination not to let it assume major importance:

For a few years while the establishment of this institution was in contemplation, & for two years in its infancy, I received a multitude of serious & rather apprehensive inquiries about the domestic work, as though this was the main thing. I regarded it as a mere appendage, as a matter of no prime importance any way. I was anxious that our warm friends, who thought it an excellence, would last see it in its real light as a very small one, & strangers who might fear it to be a defect would feel it to be one easily submitted to. With this object in view I think I have formed the habit of passing over inquiries rather slightly, & of dealing in general principles on the subject, not sympathizing much with warm commendation, or attempting to vindicate. [53]

Of course students inevitably did talk and write about a feature which was so unusual and made such a difference in their daily routine. While there are recorded complaints, both the letters written at the time and the recollections put down a half century later indicate that most young women approved—and many enjoyed—the jobs assigned them. In mid-October 1843 three new students from different backgrounds, writing home about their first impressions, reported favorably on the work they were doing. A fashion-conscious young woman from Ohio, Elizabeth Wolcott, who noted that all the teachers dressed "middling plain," asked for work of moderate difficulty. Students that year were spending 1, 1¼, or 1½ hours a day, depending on the strenuousness of the task. She was put at washing potatoes and liked it. Louisa Torrey from Millbury, Massachusetts, started out with reservations. Her first reaction to Mary Lyon was disappointment: "I should not suspect that she was intellectual in the least from her looks; and indeed I do not believe she is very much so." But the domestic work was "not as much of a hindrance as I expected"; she praised the system and the physical arrangements. On the bread-making crew, she molded ten loaves a day. Lydia Baldwin from nearby Southampton, notably well prepared and also expert in household operations, had already been drafted in the midst of the examination period to spend several days nursing a sick student. She was pleased with her regular assignment: two days washing tablecloths, two days ironing tablecloths, two days of supervision, overseeing washing circles one day and ironing circles the other. She thereby got 15 minutes a day for herself and "everything is so arranged that it is not hard work."[54]

One reason for such general acceptance was the wide variety of jobs. Those who were too frail to scrub and inept at cooking might mend towels or trim lamp wicks or collect and distribute mail or make fair copies of Mary Lyon's business letters. Miss Lyon seems to have been ready to make changes; student assignments might be shifted three or four times within a single school year. Almost any student who did not like what she was doing could look forward to relatively speedy relief. Another attraction was sociability; in a school of 200, with every minute of the day accounted for, new students sometimes found little time to make friends and welcomed the camaraderie of the small circles. "The girls with whom you have washed dishes, or tablecloths, or been with on the baking circle, could not ever be far away from you again," Lucinda Guilford declared at the end of her life. Even on wash day, when seventy girls had to rub, boil, rinse, and hang out their own clothes in short order and the rules forbade speaking above a whisper, community feeling was generated; they had "real fun," "merry times." Even solitary workers scrubbing the floors of their own rooms might sing on the job; the corridors on "recreation" morning sometimes echoed to the strains of "Sweet Home" and "A Life on the Bounding Wave."[55]

As Mary Lyon had observed, many students took pride in their own jobs and also in the Seminary standard of housekeeping, almost as far above average as the academic achievement. Some girls enjoyed developing a special skill, like dividing a large roast into equitable portions for tables seating fifteen or more. Others liked doing simple tasks with care and dispatch. One circle leader writing to a friend in Ohio specified what she and the other five in her group accomplished by working not more than one hour and ten minutes apiece: after each meal they cleared the tables, scraped the plates, shook and folded the tablecloths, and swept the dining hall. Miss Lyon's skill at job analysis was enviable. The changes from year to year in enrollment and academic program might seem small, but she kept on adjusting her work assignments to fit every fluctuation in numbers and schedule and also to take advantage of the abilities of her principal leaders. She seems to have put as much thought on selecting these young women as in choosing candidates for major teaching opportunities, and sometimes had filled the top domestic work places before she had settled on the new faculty for the coming year. Her method of keeping a high level of performance was certainly not arcane. Every circle leader checked her own crew and was herself checked by a student supervisor, a teacher assigned to double check and, very likely, another teacher whose responsibility it was to supervise the supervisors. In any case Miss Lyon kept an eagle eye on the whole operation. She was the one who summoned a delinquent from the fourth floor to hang up a forgotten dish towel, who encouraged a novice trying to scour knives and showed her the way to go at it, who helped out a hard-pressed dinner circle by herself making the thickening for soup, perfectly smooth and ready to blend.[56]

By putting her mind on every step in each housekeeping process, Mary Lyon detected not only carelessness but also inadequacies in space and equipment, which she also remedied promptly. In 1837 the domestic hall was already a wonder to many, with kitchen and kneading, baking, washing, and ironing rooms supplied with appropriate stoves, sinks, tables, and closets, and the needed implements. In 1843 Lyman Beecher, who delivered the anniversary address in August, found the whole building eminently suited to its purpose. His bon mot was passed on by students: "he said he wished four angels from heaven would take this building and remove it to Cincinnati," where he was president of Lane Theological Seminary. Nevertheless, Mary Lyon kept seeing possibilities for improvement. In summer vacations when carpenters and masons regularly came in to make repairs, she sometimes called for structural alterations as well. During the two-week spring vacation in May 1847, when she was the only faculty member on the premises, she managed rather extensive changes, even though there were fifty students in residence who had to be organized to feed and keep house for themselves and find their own entertainment, outdoors and in. Susan Tolman recorded the results: "The outside door, & copper boiler have exchanged places. The two south rooms in the end of the hall occupied by young ladies are entirely shut off from the hall by a narrow passage. The cellar door is where the large closet used to be. The store rooms too have been somewhat changed. Miss Lyon is pretty well, though rather fatigued."[57]

In comparison with other residential schools and colleges, Mount Holyoke standards for food, cleanliness, health care, and safety were high. Mary Lyon was determined to buy only the best food and supplies and counted on all the assistance in purchasing that the trustees were able to give her. Deacon Avery engaged a winter's supply of butter from the best butter makers in Conway and rejected dried apples not up to Seminary expectations. Deacon Safford, who purchased and shipped from Boston everything from tea cups to secondhand pianos, selected and had sent a variety of foodstuffs: herrings, tongues, dried beef, rice, molasses, nutmegs, raisins, lemons. Most of the cooking seems to have been expert, to judge from Mary's accumulated recipes and culinary hints found in her hastily scrawled lists and in some student journals and letters. Different foods must be washed differently—rice and beans in two waters, rubbing the grains hard between the hands; dried apples in cold water, being thorough but quick and gentle so as not to lose the juice. A succulent deep-dish peach pie could be made by wiping the peaches carefully and putting them in whole. Pies being taken out of the oven should be carefully inspected for wood ashes and, if necessary, wiped with a cloth before being put away.[58]

By modern nutritional standards, Seminary meals were overloaded with bread, pies, and cakes and short on fruit and vegetables, but considering what was available and customary, the range was commendable. Students were permitted fresh fruit between meals but often had difficulty getting it; sometimes they could buy apples from the teacher in charge of cooking operations. Miss Lyon included extra fruit when she could. One summer a gift of blueberries enabled all to have bowls of blueberries and milk; another summer there were enough currants for currant pies and currants and sugar for supper. Fruits that were delicacies—oranges, peaches, raisins, grapes—figured at the Thanksgiving party and also at gatherings of teachers and entertainments for students staying over a vacation. These special purchases were often paid for by Mary out of her own pocket. Vegetables were infrequently included in student descriptions of meals, but her lists indicate that not only potatoes but beets, squash, turnips, parsnips, peas, greens, string beans and cabbage were regularly on the menu in season. Tea and coffee were banned except as medicine during her lifetime, but milk was an acceptable alternative to cold water. In 1847 the milk drinkers numbered almost one quarter of the student body and filled four tables. Many students rejoiced in boxes from home, usually containing fruit, pie, cake, and other "eatables." In spite of repeated warnings against them, the contents do not seem to have been confiscated if permission was requested of the proper teacher.

Some students did indeed complain—institutional food has been a universal target through the years—but there was also positive enthusiasm for Mount Holyoke food. Even students like Sarah Wingate who had just arrived and were still homesick and bewildered by the rules and the bells might enjoy the meals. "They never have only two kinds at a time, but it is good & there is plenty of it. The first night we had for tea baked apples, raised bread and butter and sweet cakes, plum cake I think. We have meat only for dinner, cold water entirely," she reported to her parents on the third day of the fall term. A lively young woman from near Rochester, New York, in the middle class, was halfway through the school year when she sang the praises of the fine white linen tablecloths on the sixteen dining room tables. She was equally pleased by "food that would not be obnoxious even to an Epicure, *roast beef*, soups, fishes of many kinds, roast & stewed

fowls, in short, every nice thing, then comes the 'Second Course'
at dinner of pies & puddings & sometimes a dessert of fine apples."
Most students were less ebullient. On balance, Emily Dickinson's
reaction seems to have been not unrepresentative. After a month
at South Hadley, she wrote a school friend:

*You have probably heard many reports of the food here & if so I
can tell you, that I have yet seen nothing corresponding to my
ideas on that point from what I have heard. Everything is whole-
some & abundant & much nicer than I should imagine could be
provided for almost 300. girls. We have also a great variety upon
our tables & frequent changes.*

About the same time she sent, in a letter to her brother Austin, a
"Bill of Fare" for a regular weekday dinner, written out menu
fashion.

Roast. Veal.
Potatoes.
Squash.
Gravy.
Wheat & Brown-Bread.
Butter.
Pepper & Salt.

———

Dessert.
Apple-Dumpling.
Sauce.

———

Water.
Isn't that a dinner fit to set before a King.[59]

Health care at the Seminary probably compared favorably with
what students had received at home. From the first Mary had put
stress on a sound daily regime, with plenty of fresh air, exercise,
and warm clothing; after the typhoid epidemic of 1840 this advice
was redoubled. The building was always kept immaculately clean.
The original arrangements for the care of the sick seemed to work

well and were maintained: infirmary space was provided, a South Hadley doctor lived near by, teachers and students experienced in family nursing were detailed to care for the seriously ill. These sick-room crews had to deal with major medical problems: tuberculosis, typhoid, influenza, pneumonia, rheumatic fever, spinal meningitis, scarlet fever, chicken pox, a fractured skull, broken bones, and scalded limbs. In view of the nature of these afflictions and the state of medical practice in the 1840's, the early Seminary health record seems good—in spite of the typhoid epidemic. During Mary Lyon's lifetime there were no other such outbreaks. In the winter of 1845 several cases of scarlet fever developed in a mild form; Miss Whitman caught it but was back teaching in a few weeks. Colds, bronchitis, and influenza did spread, especially in the spring. In April 1846 influenza became so prevalent that thirty to forty students were sent home before the spring examinations in order to recuperate; there were no fatalities. The following year spring examinations were advanced to mid-March and successfully concluded without any rash of colds or fevers either then or a month later. Smallpox was two or three times reported in the neighborhood. When cases occurred in Hadley in March 1846, Mary recommended that everybody be vaccinated. In April 1848 a rumor was spread in South Hadley that there was smallpox in the Seminary; the selectman who called to investigate was soon convinced that the young lady in question had measles.[60]

The threat of fire was omnipresent. When every room had its own wood stove, every firemaker had to be always vigilant. Indeed, considering the number of potential sources of trouble, it seems a miracle that the original building survived without major damage until the fire of 1896, when it was razed. The degree of responsibility that Mary Lyon instilled in individual students and the effectiveness of the system of supervision are indicated in the near misses of the 1840's. Of the four episodes, only two could have been caused by student disregard of the fire laws: a blaze in a student room was started in November 1846 and another in February 1848 when sparks from the stove flew up and lit on the bed. A chimney defect caused the fire in January 1844 that burned through the ceiling of the dining hall and into the floor of the library. Lightning struck the building in July 1845 and was conducted to the metal racks for drying dish towels over the oven in the domestic hall. The entire cupboard was immediately ignited and burned a hole in the Seminary hall floor. In every instance, prompt organization of student bucket brigades from the cisterns to the conflagration and the assistance of nearby townspeople enabled the fire to be quickly extinguished, and the damage was minor.

The domestic work system as administered by Miss Lyon called for a rigorous daily schedule and stringent enforcement of the kind of rules that seminaries and colleges were then accustomed to prescribing. On first encounter even the equable young women who would soon be performing domestic tasks ungrudgingly and approving the food and the household arrangements were apt to find the daily pressures overwhelming. Many students recovered rapidly from the initial shock. "The first four or five days the excitement was very great in my brain; I could compare the feeling in my head to nothing else than a wheel rapidly revolving, but now I am getting used to these scenes, and enjoy myself well," wrote one such new student in the fall of 1848. A classmate wrote to a friend in December with approval: "I never knew the value of time as I do here—every moment needs to be employed in order to make our duties meet." But there were some who went on feeling exhausted or oppressed by having to keep such a succession of appointments, marked by bells practically every half hour from five in the morning till ten at night, by having to run up and down stairs to keep from being late, by finding only scraps of time to write letters home or visit another student or read a book. Miss Lyon kept on "maturing" the daily schedule, along with every other part of the Seminary operation, and some of her changes did reduce the need to hurry; but as academic improvements also continued, bits of free time were apt to be occupied.[61]

The existence of seventy rules, dictated into student notebooks and printed on a single sheet, must have exacerbated the sense of pressure. The major requirements were perfect attendance and absolute promptness at every recitation, every study hour, every meeting, every job, every meal. Other rules enjoined quiet—keeping completely silent during study hours and devotional periods, speaking only in whispers in the halls and domestic work rooms,

RECORDED ITEMS.

Absence from School Exercise,
Absence from Table,
Tardiness at School Exercise,
Tardiness at Table,
Tardiness in Retiring,
Tardiness in Rising,
Absence from Domestic Work,
Tardiness at Domestic Work,
Entering Rooms,
Communications of the first kind,
Communications of the second kind,
Failure in Walking,
Absence from Church,
Delinquency in Composition.

UNRECORDED ITEMS.

Spending time with others when it is not time for entering
Delay in the Space Way,   [Rooms,
Speaking loud in Space Way,
Interruption in Half Hours,
Specified time on Lessons,
Absence from Rooms in Study Hours,
Fire Laws,
Money Locked,
Rooms in order,
Entering or delaying in the Basement,
Silent Study Hours,
Closing Doors,
Loud Speaking after the Retiring Bell,
Conversing in Reading Room or Sem. Hall,

WEEKLY ITEMS.

Throwing things from the window,
Marking the Building,
Purchasing Eatables,
Setting or lying upon the Quilts,
Making things warm in Rooms,
Riding without permission,
Taking company to Rooms without permission,
Broken Crockery,
Calling at the Rooms of those not able to go to the Table,
Taking Tea out without permission,
Making calls without permission.
Exchanging Chamber Furniture or Bedding,
Taking any not given,
Lamps burning after retiring,
Sleeping with door closed,
Sending papers without permission,
Boxes of food,
Debts,
Rising before the Rising Bell,
Exposure of health,
Wardrobe in order,
Account Books balanced,
Time devoted to composition.

WASHING ITEMS.

Speaking above a whisper in the wash room,
Doing five minutes' work, or offering to do it,
Tubs rinsed,—Wash-boards in place,
Using pumps properly,
Changing circles without permission,
Omitting Washing without permission,
Passing over wet floors.

IRONING ITEMS.

Tardiness at the close of Ironing,
Putting flat on the Ironing Board,
Speaking above a whisper in the Ironing Room,
Carrying Holder and Duster,
Exchanging articles.

21. "Recorded Items" headed the list of rules on each of which every student was asked every day to report her own conduct. Mount Holyoke College Library Archives.

visiting other students only in approved hours. Another set of rules called for care of Seminary property—no marking on walls, breaking crockery, lying on top of a quilt, exchanging school furniture with the girls next door. There were rules about a student's own possessions, which she must keep safe and in good order—her wardrobe tidy and mended, her cash locked up and properly accounted for. Health and safety were not neglected; the seven fire laws stressed essential precautions about fenders, matches, live coals, and lamps, and one sweeping prohibition forbade "exposure of health." Only half a dozen of the seventy items dealt with student contacts with the outside world. These were not banned, but permission was necessary to go for a ride with friends, to take visitors to student rooms, to pay calls or take meals at homes in the village, or to correspond with anyone except relatives and old friends.[62]

Enforcement at the Seminary continued to be based on the elaborate system of self-reporting, in essence the one that Zilpah Grant had devised for Joseph Emerson at Byfield. Sections of fifteen to twenty-five students met daily; the section teacher not only noted every admitted omission or violation but also was responsible for the general conduct of her group, gave them special permissions, and checked on their health. Once a week at a meeting of the whole school the major "recorded items" were checked off again and the violators left standing exposed before all the students and teachers. This scheme had its limitations; at least one graduate in the class of 1848 remembered long afterward that some students cheated. "It was hard to be quite honest in the face of the whole school." But Mary Lyon never thought of relying on self-reporting alone to achieve order and harmony in the daily life of 200 young women, most of whom were living for the first time in a group larger than the family. She checked up on everybody. The roll was called in classrooms and section meetings, and absentees were sent for. Absence was just as identifiable at meals, at church, and in all Seminary Hall meetings, since everyone had assigned seats, often in alphabetical order. In group entrance examinations students were seated so that they could not copy. At night, after the last bell, some of the teachers patrolled the corridors to guarantee quiet and make sure that everyone was in bed with door ajar, lamp out, fender in place.[63]

In addition to daily and weekly reports by each student and daily checks by the staff, Miss Lyon continued to depend on frequent talks to the assembled young women to discourage misdemeanors. She used her native wit to make reproof and warning entertaining; there is every evidence that the students looked forward to these sessions. Many girls mentioned them in letters, often regretting that they couldn't get down in words the effect when she was speaking. Excerpts from a letter by Persis Thurston, missionary daughter from Hawaii, suggest the nature of Mary Lyon's points of departure.

Sometimes Miss Lyon gives us a description of a beautiful young lady, who always walks very lightly & quickly, she always has her hair combed neatly, she always looks cheerful & happy, she is always in the proper place at the proper time, & when she is at work, she does it in the best way. When she is skimming milk, she never spills a drop of cream. Her room is always in order, & when she sits down to study, she studies with all her mind. Some young ladies take a book, & read over a paragraph, & think, & t-h-i-n-k, and t-h-i-n-k, and then they hardly know what they have been thinking about. . . . Another time she talked to us about punctuality, when we were all assembled in the Seminary Hall waiting for three or four tardy ones. She gave us a sum in arithmetic & when we found the answer we rose, & she asked us what it was. It was this. If there are 180 young ladies in the school, & they wait two minutes for somebody that is tardy, how many hours of their precious time is consumed. Six hours was the answer. If they wait five minutes before we are ready to begin business, Fifteen hours. And then she would tell us that if [we] waited so long every day, it would soon be as long as a man's lifetime. When the tardy ones came in, she said, "Ladies we are only talking a little about punctuality. We were trying to calculate how much time was lost by waiting two or three minutes for you." Miss Lyon knows how to make any body feel ashamed of doing any thing wrong. I wish you could hear her say it in her own words, & in her own animated way.

Ann Webster, who graduated in 1842 and taught at the Seminary for two years, could still recall after nearly half a century the line of argument leading to a particularly skillful anticlimax:

she started off with a short talk on comparative anatomy. The scientist, in exhuming animal remains, may find but one bone or one tooth, but from that alone he forms the entire animal and tells us whether it ate grass or flesh, whether it was gentle or ferocious. So little things indicate character. Knowing one trait of a person, whether they do or fail to do some little thing, the whole individual is revealed. You need know no more. If Domitian would amuse himself by catching flies and piercing them through with a bodkin, it was to be expected that he would kill Christians. The great principle was developed in a masterly way. It was so far a magnificent lecture by itself, but the initiated knew there was "something coming," that the argumentum ad hominem would soon be apparent. It came at length. The descent was easy, but by no means ridiculous, in fact it was solemn. It seemed that much to Miss Lyon's satisfaction the ironing room had been nicely refitted. The coverings were white and dainty. But on the inaugural day these were badly discolored, some showed the imprint of the iron, while a few had been burned through. We do not think Miss Lyon cared so much for the spoiling of the goods. She took that joyfully. But it did pain her that any of her dear family should evince a carelessness akin to recklessness. It was the moral tarnish she feared. It might be a straw but it showed the way of the wind.

Mary Lyon even managed to elicit anonymous criticisms of student behavior from other students which she could expatiate upon with few hurt feelings.[64]

Serious offenses, which occasioned no levity at all, were dealt with summarily and the offenders and sentences reported to the whole school immediately. Expulsion might follow any kind of unapproved involvement with a young man; the theft of money or food was also a serious matter. No figures are available, but it seems possible that two or three students were expelled nearly every year, apart from those sent home for poor health or inability to keep up with the recitations. On the whole Miss Lyon's judgments seem not to have been thought severe; indeed, teachers and students sometimes found her too lenient. Several times sizable amounts of money disappeared. A graduate in 1845 at the end of her life remembered one such episode particularly for Mary Lyon's sympathy for the culprit: "In one unfortunate case of theft . . . I remember how much I was impressed with her love and sympathy, and yet the justice she manifested towards the unfortunate one. How thoroughly she impressed it upon us that we should so care for our money and valuables as to place no temptation, and never speak unnecessarily of the incident." A junior reporting thefts totaling thirty dollars in the Thanksgiving vacation of 1844 was deeply impressed by the power of Miss Lyon's exhortation to the whole school about the remorselessness of conscience; in a few days the missing cash was secretly restored to the trunks of the owners. In June 1846 two young women violated both the rules and the social code. One was caught at night climbing out a window—in the back buildings; the other was reported missing at 10:00 P.M. She turned up at 8:00 the next morning, all innocence, with the story that she had been ill in the night, had to go to the out buildings, and, being too unwell to climb back up the stairs, had spent the night in one of the sleeping rooms downstairs, full of beds. Mary Lyon's verdict was that neither girl might return the next year but that both could stay through the summer term provided they did not see each other at all and left the building only before breakfast (for the required walk) or with an escort assigned by Miss Moore. But many students, some of whom, it turned out, had seen strange men outside the Seminary signaling, urged the greatest severity. They persuaded Miss Lyon to reverse herself, and the older of the two culprits, in the middle class, was sent home the next day under escort; she was not even allowed to wait for her father to come for her.[65]

Even at their most severe, Mary Lyon's punishments were meted out with sorrow and concern. Mrs. Stow found much evidence of the effect this warmth of feeling had on the sinners. "Often those who had grieved her most became her warmest friends. When for her own good or that of the rest it became necessary to send one away, it was done with the same tenderness with which she had been received . . ." One graduate who as a junior was almost dismissed years later thought of Mary Lyon's "look of yearning love" and "those words of reproof" as "among my dearest memories." Even so, the bells and the rules did vex a number of vigorous and law-abiding students. Entering juniors headed their letters "Convent of St. Lyons" or wrote about "this nunnery." A member of the middle class after six months in South Hadley was still exclaiming: "O I shall be so glad to get home where I can speak above a whisper and not have to move by a line and plummet." A 19-year-old senior wrote her father, "I don't know but I shall run out of the church with my diploma in my hand & down to the cars without waiting for the rest. I am in such haste to get away." What now seems remarkable is not the resistance but the large measure of assent for so rigorous a standard of daily performance. In part students must have been moved by Mary Lyon's genuine affection and selflessness; in good part, surely they were rising to her confident expectations for them. The assumption that virtually every young woman there could achieve so much—in study, in domestic work, in daily routines, in religious devotion—must have been exhilarating to a group already self-selected for intellectual ambition and dedication to the service of others.[66]

Many students discovered relatively soon that Mary Lyon not only enjoyed life herself but wanted them to have extra pleasures when opportunities arose. In the letter in which Emily Dickinson described entrance examinations, her daily schedule, and the food, she also observed, "One thing is certain & that is, that Miss. Lyon & all the teachers, seem to consult our comfort & happiness in everything they do & you know that is pleasant." The immediate vicinity provided various attractions, both for "recreation day" excursions of a few hours and all-day jaunts for the young ladies spending a one- or two-week vacation at the Seminary. In South Hadley Center and at the Falls three miles away there were a number of small manufacturing operations which students seem to have been encouraged to inspect: paper mills, woolen mills, a tannery, pearl button factories. On an excursion to Northampton, students might shop and also visit the cemetery where missionary martyrs were buried, or drive around the empty buildings of the Round Hill School for boys, which had been run by Professor Bancroft, or pass the quarters of the Gothic Institute for young ladies. At Amherst the chance to inspect the college buildings and science collections and to attend a social gathering at a faculty home attracted groups of young ladies even when the Amherst students were absent, being also on recess. Although Springfield was less accessible, shopping trips were possible and the Springfield Armory, with its "beautiful steam engines" and other machinery on display drew enthusiasm from both students and faculty escorts.[67]

Traveling groups of singers occasionally gave concerts in the village. On one occasion Miss Lyon refused to cancel evening study hours for the public performance at night but arranged the next morning's schedule so that the Hutchinson family could give an hour's private concert in Seminary Hall. At least once she arranged that those who wished might see a traveling menagerie, with Mr. Hawks as escort. She even tolerated visits to the itinerant daguerreotypists who set up shop at intervals in the village, provided their patronage would not reduce individual contributions to missions. But for one of these entrepreneurs she had to withdraw permission, except for those who had already made appointments, because some of the young ladies being pictured had been tardy to or absent from regular Seminary appointments. Some special events won Miss Lyon's strong approval. When Professor Hitchcock was inaugurated president of Amherst on April 15, 1845, all the teachers and sixty students were present. When, in November 1848, a scale model of Jerusalem was on display in Northampton, she arranged for the trip and, when it snowed in the early morning, postponed both "recreation day" and the excursion until the following day. All the teachers (herself excepted) went, as did Reverend Laurie, who knew the city at first-hand, and almost 200 students. They were no doubt glad of the improved weather, since they had to walk nearly two miles to the river, where the ferry took them across to the railroad station only ten minutes from Northampton by train.[68]

Perhaps the most unexpected of all the traveling exhibits arrived in Cabotville (now Chicopee) for two days in December 1845—the complete skeleton of a mastodon dug up in the lower Hudson River Valley the preceding summer. That Mary Lyon allowed some of the students to take a precious evening for the trip was in itself memorable. Some students recorded facts about size and origin; others, like Lucinda Guilford, were inspired to parody.

I took a sleigh ride to Cabotville to see the greatest NATIVE AMERICAN in the country. He has but lately become known to the public and is exerting a tremendous sensation wherever he goes. At Cabot where he remained two days, crowds of ladies and gentlemen called to pay their respects, and, among them, the greater part of the Lyon-ites. He has a noble and commanding figure, but I should think was troubled with absence of mind. You have no idea how inferior I felt when introduced into his presence, but we did not have the opportunity of hearing him speak. I was not surprised at this, for it is generally understood that he was travelling "incog" an eminent example of persons of very obscure origin jumping at once into notoriety. Yes, I have seen a Mastodon, whose skeleton was twenty feet long and twelve feet high and six feet wide.[69]

The pleasures of the countryside could be enjoyed with a minimum of organization and regulation. In winter, sleigh rides were always popular. Mary Lyon had one of the teachers organize the party and collect the cost; each student paid for her own recreation, and Miss Lyon saw to it that charges were not excessive. Participation in all such extras was voluntary, and a number of students did prefer to stay home and "enjoy the solitude finely," as Emily Dickinson did when the menagerie came. In spring, summer, and fall some girls found time and energy for walks, in congenial company, of some length—to the pine woods, to the river, to the foot of the mountain. They came back with wild flowers in profusion, rock specimens, chestnuts. One young woman brought back a tortoise. The wild flowers, garnered for pleasure and also for botany notebooks, receded so rapidly that in June 1848 Mary, to save the arbutus and hepatica and potentilla from extinction, ruled that within a three-mile radius of the Seminary no one was to pick any flowers for ornament or to collect more than one specimen of a kind for pressing (except perhaps one other for a dear friend)—or ever, unless directed by a teacher, to gather batches for class identification. For several

22. A view of the South Hadley Center Common as seen from the Seminary building, painted by Joseph Goodhue Chandler in 1876. The Congregational Church on the right, which stood from 1844 until it burned in 1875, was regularly attended by Mount Holyoke teachers and students. Mount Holyoke College Art Museum.

years some students worked in the garden plots into which the front yard was for a time divided. Others with green thumbs had plants in their own rooms—cactus, umbrella plants, althea, gilly-flowers, lemon trees. The view from the windows facing the Mt. Tom range to the west was universally admired, and several girls were moved by the effect of bright moonlight on the graveyard below just across the street. The whole school turned out several times at night to admire the sky—when the aurora borealis was particularly striking or the comet of 1843 at its most brilliant.[70]

Mountain Day was the occasion for at once celebrating the name of the Seminary and enjoying for a full day the beauty of the immediate surroundings. Nothing was allowed to interfere with this event sometime in June or July. Although Mary Lyon seldom went, most of the teachers and students, with high enthusiasm, every year headed in platoons of carriages for the foot of Mount Holyoke. Rebecca Fiske's sketch of the activities at the top, written for the missionary readers of the journal letter, might have been equally evocative to alumnae for the next century.

There the ferry boat hastens across the river, now the car-whistle sends up its brisk notes from the other side of the river—Now our second company have reached the Holyoke Hotel—Where they are leaving their carriages—Now a little cluster of songsters that [we] took with us are vieing with the feathered ones above them in their melody—They are seated on that rock overlooking North-ampton, just now they sung "When up the Mountain Climbing," then "The Silver Moon," and now "Love Not." One group of 20 or 30 are eagerly looking for a blank in the record books, where they may leave their names to fame. Others are strolling with Botany in hand in pursuit of flowers—one little circle are on the roof looking through the spy glass which just now they have directed towards Amherst to get a peep at the new observatory. Another still are rolling stones down the precipice to gain a novel kind of music, and a few have sought places, each to be alone, & enjoy their own thoughts.[71]

Professor Hitchcock, who loved the mountains and wanted others to enjoy them, twice turned the Seminary holiday into a coeducational enterprise. In 1845 he felt the need of better access to the top of Mount Holyoke and managed to enlist the senior and junior classes at Amherst to hew out a "horse path." Mary volunteered to have the young ladies provide a picnic dinner for all, and the undertaking went off with éclat. The path was finished before noon, and the picnic fare was accompanied by suitable toasts and elegant speeches by Professor Fiske, who taught Latin and Greek, Professor Shepard, who taught natural history, and Professor Hitchcock himself. Then he led the way to "the columns," a rock formation at the foot, where the whole company was saluted by a brass band from Northampton. The next year Professor Hitchcock accomplished a like feat for the tallest mountain in the range. Norwottuck was named by him and christened before the assembled students and faculty, after the young men's heroic accomplishment in road building and just before the feast brought by the girls from Mount Holyoke. These grace notes enhanced but did not supersede enjoyment of the climb and the view:

Northampton, Amherst, Hadley, and here and there smaller villages lay spread out upon their surrounding meadows, while miles of forest variegated the scene, more beautiful than any thing I had ever imagined. A small rude tower, 20 or 30 feet high, had been erected and standing on the top of this there was nothing to obstruct the view which must have comprehended one third of the state. Mt. Monadnock in New Hampshire could just be seen. The Connecticut showed itself here and there in its windings, shining like burnished silver in the emerald around. I spent three hours constantly gazing upon this splendid panorama, first from one point and then from another. It seemed to me I could so pass days and weeks.

The first address was the formal naming of the summit by the Amherst valedictorian. It was appropriate and eloquent. As he pronounced the Indian name NORWOTTUCK a red flag bearing the word was run up beside the stars and stripes that already floated at the top of the tower. President Hitchcock and Professor Shephard then addressed us. After a while came the following toast. "Mt. Holyoke Seminary in the Connecticut Valley. An apple of gold among pictures of silver." A son of one of the Trustees

*responded in a beautiful speech on behalf of the young ladies of
the Seminary. Then we adjourned to the tables which were loaded
with everything necessary to constitute a true picnic. Music and
toasts followed and the old woods rang to the sweet strains of
harmony and the loud cheers sounded out after some brilliant
sentiment. But I could not help turning from it all to look again
and again at the sublime show beneath us.* [72]

Contact with young men was not really a rarity at the Seminary,
despite public opinion to the contrary. Mary Lyon was the spirit
of hospitality. After her long years of homelessness she took
unqualified pleasure in welcoming her family and friends, the
friends of friends, the near and dear of trustees, teachers, and
students to the "house" of which she was so proud. The procession of visiting ministers and missionaries who addressed the
Seminary included not only fathers but also fiancés and a few
young men hoping to find a helpmate. But most of the young men
visitors were themselves studying in the vicinity. Brothers, cousins,
and acquaintances of Mount Holyoke students attended Amherst
or Williston Academy, across the river in Easthampton, in numbers;
there was a good deal of coming and going apart from organized
excursions. Miss Lyon encouraged her nephews as well as her
nieces to get an education by giving them loans and good advice
and also by inviting them to come for vacations. In May of 1847
she entertained the sons of three different sisters, Stukely Ellsworth from Yale, William Putnam from Williams, and Mason
Moore from Williston. For visitors who came on recreation day,
there was little difficulty in seeing friends, to judge from an
account of how William Hammond, a free-wheeling Amherst
sophomore, met the sister of some young ladies he knew.

*Rang the bell in great terror, for fear of Miss Lyon and the assis-
tant dragonesses; a very plain young lady came to the door, and to
my great astonishment on asking for Miss Holman I was shown
into the parlor without any inquisition preparatory! This was a
huge apartment, sumptuously furnished with a rusty stove, cherry
table, and multitudinous cane-bottomed chairs.*
Never having seen Nelly, I feared some embarrassment, but my

fears vanished like the wind when she entered with a smiling face, hands outstretched, and "So this is Willy!" Was even unexpectedly pleased with her. She is very pretty, lively, and intelligent: more piquant *and original than her sisters, yet not deficient in grace and sweetness. There was not the slightest embarrassment or reserve. We were at once old and intimate friends, and for an hour and a half both* Willy *and* Nelly *rattled on most wonderfully. We talked of Gardiner and Gardinerites, college and the seminary, study and reading, and a score of other interesting topics. Was much pleased with her literary taste. She admired Longfellow, whose* Hyperion *she was just reading, loved the German enthusiastically, and read it with ease; we could have talked hours on such subjects without weariness.*

She got a teacher to accompany us through the building, that being the requisition: rather an agreeable plain young lady, S. Fiske's sister. We saw all that was to be seen: the pleasant recitation rooms, the pleasanter chapel, or what corresponds to such, the little library and reading room, where all but the strictly religious periodicals are carefully put away from Saturday till Monday, the huge dining room, with its all but score of tables, and huger kitchen, where the young ladies of the seminary all labor an hour daily. We went through the long space-ways, meeting any number of plain young ladies and catching sly peeps into their little boxes of sleeping rooms; said "beautiful" at every eligible window, and did all the other things right and proper in viewing the building.

In the fall of 1848 two cousins from Needham were visited on recreation day by a young man from home who drove them over to Williston to see a cousin there. Because the friends stayed overnight in a South Hadley hotel, the girls managed half an hour more of visiting by jumping up at the five o'clock bell and being at the hotel by six—a perfectly acceptable procedure as long as they were back at the Seminary in time for breakfast.[73]

There was also interchange with neighbors in the village. Some students already had relatives or acquaintances in the area when they came; others found friends among the families who boarded a few young ladies for modest fees during vacations. Some of the more social families entertained their young guests by making and receiving calls, attending sewing society meetings, or arranging sleigh or carriage rides; in the evenings guests and hosts might join in singing, parlor games, charades, or tableaux. Former students who had married and settled down in the vicinity were apt to entertain the teachers periodically. Martha Scott, whose home was in North Hadley, graduated in 1845 and taught in the Seminary for the next ten years. In 1846 she acquired as a stepmother a Seminary student named Dorcas Hapgood. The new Mrs. Scott's stay at the Seminary had been too brief to be recorded in the catalogue, but her repeated hospitality to the Seminary teachers seems to have been welcome.[74]

Mary Lyon probably liked best of all entertaining the students and the community together. The great social affair occurred on Thanksgiving, which in the Seminary was celebrated with features that students from less puritanical parts of the country were already associating with Christmas or New Year's Day; neither of these days was observed at the Seminary with any festivities during Mary's lifetime. The Mount Holyoke Thanksgiving in 1848 was described at length by a young woman from northern New York state who was impressed by every step of the operation. On Wednesday everybody not needed for preparations in the kitchen spent the day making artificial flowers and evergreen wreaths and decorating the public rooms with bunches, sprays, and swags. Some of the pink and white paper roses were shaped into letters to form mottoes displayed upon the walls: "Sweet Home" and "We are a band of sisters." On Thursday, when the students "had the privilege of sleeping as long as we wished to in the morning provided we were ready for breakfast at eight oclock," Helen Graves, who had risen at five and spent two and a half hours helping Mrs. Hawks make mince pies, had reason to enjoy the "nice broiled chicken" served for breakfast. Everybody went to church; dinner, served at 2:00 to students and visiting trustee families, featured roast turkey, cranberry sauce, squash, mince pies, and tapioca pudding. The special treats for supper included biscuits and jelly with cream.

It was the evening party for friends and neighbors of the Seminary that particularly impressed Helen Graves. After extended socializing in the much decorated and "brilliantly lighted" parlors, the whole party adjourned to Seminary Hall, rearranged for the occasion. The center of the room was occupied by a table "with a large vase of flowers in the middle and one on each end, and apples, grapes, raisins, walnuts and almonds in abundance." When the refreshments had been distributed by the appointed young ladies, student entertainment followed: piano selections, choral singing, a fifteen-minute demonstration of calisthenics performed to music. The affair concluded with a hymn, a chapter from the Bible, and a pastoral prayer, and the young ladies retired, Helen with the feeling that she had "closed the day more pleasantly than I had ever passed a Thanksgiving before."[75]

Over a decade the only significant changes in the pattern of Seminary hospitality were in the loads carried by individual teachers, who directed every step of the process. As Sophia Hazen and Mary Chapin noted in the journal letter, this was the first year that the whole occasion had been engineered without the sustaining guidance of either Mary Whitman, who was traveling for her health, or Abigail Moore, whose absence, after two years, was still felt. That everything went off so well was no surprise to Mary Lyon. She had chosen this year, with Miss Whitman away, to double the number of invitations to the community; in the evening they entertained 70 to 80 instead of 30 to 40.[76]

No matter what the special academic or social events, at Mount Holyoke—as at most colleges and seminaries—the climax came at the very end of the year. Three days of public examinations were followed immediately by the commencement ceremonies. This was the occasion when every student, no matter now nervous she might be about her own performance, wanted her parents and friends to be present. Accommodations in the village had to be reserved ahead; families coming just for the day were reminded that "South Hadley time is half an hour faster than time elsewhere." Student interest was no doubt heightened by the presence of dignitaries—the speaker, the trustees and their wives, specially invited guests; Mount Holyoke's bountiful and ordered hospitality might include their entertainment for two or three days at the Seminary and certainly meant sharing the company dinner carefully prepared in advance to be served after the anniversary address Thursday noon. Part of the excitement no doubt came from the size of the crowd. For the examinations in Seminary Hall, which started on Tuesday and finished on Thursday morning just before the commencement procession to the church, the audiences were large. They included not only notables and relatives but also the friendly and the curious from several nearby towns, encouraged by announcements sent from the Seminary to the local papers.[77]

That accounts of the Mount Holyoke examinations are highly laudatory is not surprising. Available published comment on examination performance at all sorts of colleges and seminaries and even "select" schools of widely varying excellence was always lavish with praise. When the principal mode of recitation was verbatim recall of appropriate parts of the textbook, one kind of perfection was within relatively easy reach. Although the New York and Boston papers that gave extensive coverage to the commencement activities of two dozen colleges for men seldom mentioned Mount Holyoke's anniversary, the Connecticut Valley newspapers in the 1840's indicated considerable local pride in the South Hadley seminary. Although the *Springfield Republican* writer in 1843 was in some respects meagerly informed—he thought that Mount Holyoke taught domestic science as part of the curriculum, he did not hesitate to declare that "the extent and perfection to which the education of females is carried in this institution surpasses anything to be found in any other Ladies Seminary in our land," and to speculate that "as much interest was felt and manifested at this anniversary as at the Commencement of any College for young men." One of the most informative descriptions of the examinations was written in 1847 by the bright Amherst sophomore, William Hammond, who had been calling on Nelly Holman all summer:

After dinner, Father and I went over to South Hadley to witness a part of the examinations there. After a very pleasant ride, got there a little after two, and found South Hadley filled as I never saw it before. Arrived at the hall, they put Father in one of the chief seats of the synagogue. I found a place among some students, near Pomeroy, and also quite near Nelly H., though I had to content myself with gazing at her in silence. A class in Virgil were on the floor when I came, and the little I could catch was highly creditable to their scholarship. Then the first four books of Euclid; very well done; the teachers gave out the captions, and then the girls drew their own figures and demonstrated them without the use of letters. Then a class in botany, of which Nelly formed a part, very interesting to me and honorable to herself; then history and one or two other things of the kind, very good and very dull; then calisthenics, in which Nelly ought to have taken a part, but to her own great joy, and my sorrow, was excused. All very much as when I saw them before; everyone dressed in white, with green wreaths for this especial occasion. Then music from the piano, and singing: very fair. Then five compositions: very good, indeed, though rather for style than ideas: even in the style it was often easy to detect traces of some popular author. Then more music, and the performance closed.[78]

At these exercises Mary Lyon's public role continued to be a modest one. The principal actors were the young women who taught and the young women who learned and, at the end, the ministers who conveyed official recognition of their achievement. According to Professor Hitchcock, Miss Lyon's examination questions and the answers they elicited were impressive. He recalled her handling of Butler's *Analogy of Religion, Natural and Revealed*, which by tradition was taught to college seniors by the president.

At one of these examinations, when the senior class had just recited to Miss Lyon in Butler's Analogy, we happened to overhear the conversation between two presidents of colleges who were on the platform. Says one of them, "How is it that these young ladies recite in Butler so much better than our senior classes?" "I do not know," was the reply, "unless it be that they have a better teacher."

But she did little classroom teaching in her last years, and during these days of widest public exposure she was not very much on center stage. Nevertheless, her presence was memorable. One young woman who attended a friend's graduation just before she enrolled in the Seminary herself recalled long afterward the way

Mary Lyon had looked to her in August 1846. She was "radiant in silk and lace," her eyes "alight with enthusiasm and benevolence," her voice "low but distinct," her words "few and dignified"; indeed, her face and features "expressed both goodness and greatness." The *Springfield Republican* account of this occasion did not focus on Mary Lyon but gave its praise in terms that she must have approved. This "highly useful" institution "is doing a vast amount of good" by educating so many young women "in the most thorough manner" at very low cost. The concluding assessment might well have been echoed by most of the audience crowded more tightly than ever into the South Hadley church: "The prospects of the institution were never brighter."[79]

7
From Generation to Generation

*And the rain descended, and the
floods came, and the winds blew,
and beat upon that house;
and it fell not: for it was
founded upon a rock.*

MATTHEW 7:25

In August 1846 the Seminary was unquestionably flourishing, but a change impended which those who knew the institution well recognized as major. Abigail Moore, Miss Lyon's niece, was leaving to become the second wife of Ebenezer Burgess and go with him to his mission station in Ahmednuggur, India. When Abigail had graduated in 1838 and immediately afterward joined the Mount Holyoke faculty, she was 25 years old and had had years of classroom experience. In the ensuing eight years she proved versatile as a teacher, carrying the instruction in French until a native speaker could be obtained and taking on history, botany, logic, and physics as circumstances demanded. But her special strength was organization, and she turned out to be physically able to carry almost as heavy a load as her aunt could. In 1839 the new faculty members included another particularly capable and dedicated graduate, Mary Whitman, who was then 30. With these two mature, resourceful, earnest young women to supplement her own remarkable talents, Mary Lyon quickly built up a first-rate administration. By the fall of 1842 both Miss Moore and Miss Whitman had the title of associate principal and the same salary as Miss Lyon ($200 plus board); by all accounts together they shouldered a substantial share of the whole operation. As Mary wrote: "Everything is systematized, and Miss M. and Miss W. urge forward the wheels so beautifully that all seems more than ever like clockwork. I enjoy very much having every thing done better by others than it can be by myself." Abigail's withdrawal was a surprise and also a "severe stroke to the Seminary."[1]

Even Mary's faith that the Lord would provide did not prevent her from feeling the blow. She wrote about the change to Fidelia

Fiske in Persia in terms reminiscent of the way she had met setbacks in her initial struggles for funds:

The first question generally is, "What does Miss Lyon think of it?" I have nothing to say in all these things, only to ask that the will of the Lord may be done, and to submit to all the dispensations of Providence, whether with means or without means. This is certainly a great event to us, and especially to me. My only wish concerning it is, that it may be for the furtherance of the gospel. We know so little of the great plans of God, that it is wisest, and safest, and sweetest, to leave all with him.

In characteristically forehanded fashion, Abigail gave almost a year's notice of her departure, but her aunt did not use the time to find a qualified replacement or even to increase the number of teaching faculty. Even when it turned out that her other niece, Lucy Lyon, after five years of gifted teaching, had also got a missionary husband and would leave at the same time, Mary did not arrange for replacements as such. Instead she put her mind to still further reorganization, transferring some duties to other teachers and dividing a large portion between herself and Miss Whitman. Mary was of course committed to the concept of rapid faculty turnover, since she had designed the Seminary to prepare for short-term teaching careers before marriage; as she grew older and more tired, she seems to have become less ready to entrust to beginners the intricacies of scheduling and supervising.[2]

Most observers on the scene counted Miss Moore's departure a principal cause of Miss Lyon's serious illness in the winter of 1846–47, which kept her housebound for several months. In view of the pattern of illness now apparent in the last ten years of her life, this conclusion could be argued. But there is no doubt that Abigail's leaving contributed to Mary Whitman's nervous collapse. Beginning in September 1846 Mary was the only associate principal and had to shoulder many of her erstwhile partner's duties as well as all the unexpected extras which they had formerly shared. During Mary Lyon's illness these extras were considerable. As Mary Lyon's close personal friend, Mary Whitman was naturally concerned with nursing care at the same time that she was assuming

23. Mary Whitman, later Mrs. Morton Eddy, joined the Mount Holyoke faculty when she graduated in 1839. From 1842 to 1849 she was associate principal; for most of the year after Miss Lyon's death she was principal. After Miss Caldwell left, she had in turn become Miss Lyon's confidante. Mount Holyoke College Library Archives.

or passing along those of Miss Lyon's responsibilities that could not be postponed. But when she began to recover, Mary Lyon went back to devising new arrangements, and the pace for Mary Whitman scarcely slackened. In May 1847 she took on supervision of the new landscape plans for the Seminary front yard. In July, without a fellow organizer, she had to confront the multiplicity of commencement activities and an added feature—a reunion. By July 14 she had 50 beds in readiness for the classes of 1844 and 1845. When the climactic days of public examinations arrived, it was Mary Whitman who presided; Mary Lyon was too busy interviewing seniors about jobs and writing placement letters to take her accustomed place on the platform.

Mary Lyon's unquenchable confidence in the capacity of her dedicated followers to absorb more and more work got remarkable results up to a point, even with a high-strung young woman like Mary Whitman. But there began to be warning signs that her limit was near. In July 1847 Susan Tolman recorded a revealing little item in the journal letter.

Miss Whitman feels the cares that are coming upon her much. As Anniversary approaches these increase. She told the teachers a few days since when she asked them for a list of their classes preparatory to reviews, that she hoped they would bring them promptly, for if every body was not prompt, she did not believe she should live through the next four weeks. She said it in her own peculiar way that made us all laugh.

Mary Lyon's increasing reluctance to delegate detail worried Mary Whitman as much as the extras. A letter to Mrs. Porter, who was vacation hostess and personal friend to Abigail and Mary Whitman as well as to Mary Lyon, indicates a growing sense of helplessness.

Miss Lyon has enjoyed unusual health since the commencement of the term, I have not seen her possess so much real vigor for several years. So deeply does she involve herself in every thing in both school and domestic matters that I think she must be exhausted by vacation. I would it were not so, and it need not be, but it cannot be helped. There is I think an increased desire to see to every thing herself, certainly much less willingness to commit things to others than formerly. I would have her take things more gently and preserve her valuable life, and let her intellect take its wonted vigor in giving instruction, but the expression of the desire is unavailing and I am quiet.[3]

By July 1848 Mary Whitman's health was seriously in question; in a note inserted in the journal letter she spoke of frayed nerves, of "exhaustion of spirit, & discouragement of heart attendant upon such exhaustion," of her loss of "mental elasticity." In geology and mental philosophy, the courses she had been teaching, the public examinations had to be canceled because she was not well enough to conduct them. The ensuing eight-week vacation did not restore her to normal health; at the beginning of the new term the doctor, Mary Lyon, and Mr. Hawks agreed that she must take an extended leave—six months to a year. The recommended cure was travel, and Mary Whitman set out in October for Ohio and way points, planning visits to Mount Holyoke classmates and friends en route. The trip and the cure were broken off five months later by the news of Mary Lyon's death. She got back to South Hadley at the end of March to take up the reins as best she might.[4]

Another major loss to Mary Lyon, comparable to Abigail's departure, was the death in September 1847 of Mr. Condit. As a young man of 31, physically frail but intellectually gifted and devout, he had come from a Long Island parish to the South Hadley church in 1835. Very soon he had become a warm friend and supporter of Mary, whom he admired despite what Mrs. Cowles called her "rather uncourtly exterior."

To any playful remark on her energetic movements, he would pleasantly say, pointing to the seminary, "If she were more of a woman, she could not have done all this." In case of any difficult question of duty, as when he was offered a professorship at Amherst, he would say, "I think I shall see the way of duty; Miss Lyon is praying for me."

His contributions to the Seminary were of great value: he was one of the five trustees who applied for the charter in 1835, secretary of the board from the time it was organized in 1836, a member of the executive committee, along with Mr. Hawks and Deacon Porter, from 1838. This last post was especially important because the full board met only once a year, and the difficult issues that arose in the 1840's seem to have been settled in this committee. The Condit hospitality was generous—to Mary Lyon, who had lived in the household for several months before the building was finished, and to individual members of the Seminary and their friends. Mr. Condit's acts of generosity included personal sacrifice. When Mary Lyon was seriously ill in November 1846, he took her place on three successive Thursday evenings to talk to the Seminary on Christian responsibility, although by then his own health was deteriorating noticeably. As a pastor he was remarkably successful. His sermons were admired by the teachers and students and also by parishioners who frequently disagreed with each other; while he was minister, factional arguments within the congregation seem to have been few.[5]

Mary Lyon missed him both as a friend and as a man of God; his death was "a very great loss, and to myself a personal affliction."

24. The Reverend Joseph Condit, painted by Joseph Goodhue Chandler. He was minister of the South Hadley Congregational Church from 1835 until his death in 1847 and also secretary of the Seminary board of trustees. His sermons were admired by parishioners and students. Mount Holyoke College Art Museum.

Deacon Avery had predicted that South Hadley could not possibly secure a successor with "the deep piety, the talent, the wisdom and the prudence" of Mr. Condit. It turned out that the church took until May 1848 to find any successor at all. This meant that the substitutes who had filled in during the last months of Mr. Condit's life were followed by a long series of supply ministers of varying rhetorical skill and fervor. Of this lot Mary Whitman wrote with unusual vehemence: "I do not think that there could have been a succession of sermons from evangelical ministers less calculated to convert a sinner than those we have had this term." It is no wonder that Mary Lyon felt keenly the absence of Mr. Condit in the pulpit, especially when a revival was in prospect or in progress, or that in her last two years she was weighed down more than ever before by the religious responsibilities she had assumed.[6]

Statistically considered, longevity in Mary Lyon's family was uncertain. Her mother lived to 75 and her brother to 81; on the other hand, her father died at 45 and four of her five sisters had died before her, three of them still in their thirties. Whatever her actuarial chances of a good old age, she inherited remarkable physical energy and endurance. After the heroic labors of bringing the Seminary into being, her vigor was undiminished. Between 1837 and 1840 she seems neither to have slacked off nor to have experienced unusual exhaustion. But in the winter of 1840–41 after the typhoid epidemic she was prostrated for two months and recovered slowly, not being her usual self until midsummer. She attributed her illness to the shock and grief of the student deaths and the subsequent loss of her sister and mother; it seems probable that what she had experienced, physiologically speaking, was the onset of tuberculosis. For the rest of her life she suffered from a succession of colds, often accompanied by swelling of the face, and, at varying intervals, periods of prostrating respiratory illness.[7]

The longest of the severe attacks occurred in the winter of 1846–47. After a summer when her health had been less good and her exertions, preparing for Abigail's absence, more strenuous than usual, she started the school year "tired out." Her hearing, which had been declining for several years, became markedly poorer; by mid-October she was suffering from a "severe cold" which "settled upon her lungs." For most of the next three months she was seriously ill; intervals when she made some improvement were followed by relapses. On Thanksgiving day she was able to go into the dining room for dinner and as the revival got underway in December she managed to speak to small groups of students in her room. Gradually the relapses became briefer. In early February she felt ready to begin her series of talks to the whole school on giving to missions at the regular morning devotions. By the end of February she was able to visit the Porters for five days; she spent her fiftieth birthday in Monson. In mid-April she managed a five-day business trip to Boston, taking with her in her trunk the physics apparatus which had to be repaired. She returned from this trip with so much of her old vigor that she sent off for the two-week spring vacation all the teachers and assisting students— who had had a strenuous winter—and herself took sole charge of the fifty girls spending their vacation in the Seminary. At the same time, eager to put into operation the new domestic plans she had evolved in convalescence, she called in masons and carpenters to make structural alterations in the domestic hall.[8]

In spite of the inroads of disease, Mary's habitual movements

25. This ferrotype of Mary Lyon may have been copied from a daguerrotype taken in 1845. Neither this nor any other of the portraits now in existence seemed a good likeness to the students under Mary Lyon who lived on into the twentieth century. Mount Holyoke College Library Archives.

and the pace at which she worked in the last five years of her life still conveyed to most observers a sense of abundant energy. In November 1845 a student wrote: "Miss Lyon causes everything to be interesting in which she takes an active part. I wish you could be here and hear her talk; she will become so engaged as not to be able to sit in her chair, but she must get it all out; she is 48 years old." In January 1847 when Miss Lyon was up after being in bed much of the preceding three months, a senior listed some of her regular duties—conducting the senior section meeting, morning devotions and afternoon exercises and overseeing considerable domestic work—and added, "It is a daily *wonderment* to me how she can perform so much *actual labor* besides having a care of every thing connected with the school and boarding." Even Mary Whitman, who in December 1847 was worried by Mary Lyon's excessive attention to detail, believed that her general health was then good. It is no wonder that her death came as a shock to the Seminary as well as the outside world.[9]

Evidence abounds that Mary herself had a sense of physical decline. After the first onslaught of the 1846–47 attack, she made

her will. Reaching the age of 50 seemed to her a portentous mile-
stone. "How solemn that I have lived half a century. How few my
remaining days," she wrote Susan Reed Howland in Ceylon. "Of
my active life I took leave on my fiftieth birthday," she told some
former Buckland pupils she chanced to meet in Springfield, and,
unexpectedly willing to talk about herself, elaborated in characteristic metaphors: "It is evening with me now. . . . I gather up the
odds and ends and keep the machine in motion. . . . I have laid
aside my armor . . ." In her last year nearly all her letters contained some reference to feeling ill or tired. In May 1848 at the
end of an emotional letter of welcome to the new minister, Mr.
Thomas Laurie, she apologized for its length, explaining that she
was almost sick and lacked the energy to write the short note she
had intended. In June she recommended to Mrs. Banister the book
of religious biography and counsel she was reading. "It is just what
I need to feed and refresh me when I am so tired that I can do
nothing with strong meat." In August when she belatedly acknowledged money received from a former student and teacher (probably
in repayment of a loan), she mentioned that she had been experi-
encing extra "anxiety & care, when I feel little able to bear it."
But even when she was so often weary and aware of the shortness
of life, Mary could not stop planning for the Seminary and for her
own future. Her last letter to Abigail, written six weeks before her
death, combined her sense of mortality with her habitual optimism
and continuing expectations. Even with Mary Whitman away, the
year 1848-49 had thus far been easy and her health relatively
good, but "at all times, whether I have more or less strength, I
feel that I am fast hastening to my eternal home, my home of rest
in the bosom of my God, as I hope." And then the next sentence
made clear her confidence in her own immediate future: "Still, I
trust I may have a little more work to do on earth."[10]

The second term started off briskly February 2. Everybody was
assigned a new seat in the dining room and at church; a major
shift of rooms and roommates was speedily completed. Miss Lyon
launched the seniors on *Paradise Lost*, the first class she had taken
in four years. Visitors who addressed the school included a missionary couple recruiting teachers for the Choctaw Indians, and
Reverend Harris from Conway, a new trustee. Then a senior fell ill

of a particularly alarming disease, erysipelas. This acute strepto-coccus infection of the skin and subcutaneous tissue was conta-gious and could be fatal. By February 21 it became apparent that Sarah Wingate would not recover; her father arrived from New Hampshire just before her death two days later. Miss Lyon, who had been suffering from influenza as well as the glandular swelling of her face, roused herself to reassure those who feared contagion and help all the students to focus not on Sarah's suffering but on her joyful reception in heaven; this appearance in Seminary Hall on February 23 was Miss Lyon's last. She soon showed symptoms of erysipelas—intensified, the teachers believed, by word that a nephew who did not believe in Christ had committed suicide. Within a few days, the acute infection seemed to be subsiding, only to be followed by the most distressing phenomenon of all— three days and nights of delirium when she talked continuously and refused all medicines and liquids. Rebecca Fiske's account to Fidelia suggests how agonizing this must have been for the teachers and the few trusted students who were taking turns at the bedside.

While she suffered so intensely for a drop of water, she could not be persuaded to take it. No one knew but her Savior how much she wanted it, she would say, but she had all those days the strong impression that her Savior had forbidden her taking it—and all her friends were combined with Satan to tempt her to sin and destroy herself.

At least Rebecca had a crumb of comfort in one partially lucid moment when Miss Lyon had called her by name and seemed to respond to a hymn she recited. Finally the raving lapsed into semiconsciousness. Although in her last hours she was too weak to say more than a single syllable, she indicated by signs that she did feel an all-encompassing love of Christ. She died about 8:30 Mon-day evening, March 5.[11]

This was a devastating blow, most of all to the teachers. To these eleven young women who had been coping heroically with the emergencies of the preceding three weeks, her total disappearance must indeed have been "like the blotting of the sun out of the heavens at midday," especially without the consolation of a deathbed blessing or even a hint of faith triumphant. The funeral, as described in the journal letter, was simple and moving. It was held on Thursday afternoon, starting at the Seminary, where the students filed past Miss Lyon's open coffin for the last time before forming the procession to the church. Only three relatives walked behind the coffin, Elisha Wing, a brother-in-law; his son; and one nephew, Mason Moore, brother of Abigail. They were followed by the school in anniversary formation—the trustees, the teachers wearing pieces of black crepe on their bonnets, the seniors, the underclassmen, guests. The sermon, which "gave a just view" of Miss Lyon's character, was preached by Dr. Heman Humphrey, former president of Amherst; prayers were offered by two trustees, Mr. Harris and Mr. Swift, who "were afflicted in our affliction and knew how to meet our feelings." Then the procession moved to the grave on Seminary grounds south of the orchard, where it could be seen from most of the rooms facing east. There Mr. Laurie spoke briefly. When the young women returned to "this desolate house," he told Miss Hazen and Miss Chapin, who until Miss Whitman's return were perforce in charge, "She is with Christ and Christ is with us."[12]

All the trustees and many of their wives attended the service; Deacon Porter stayed at the Seminary several days during Miss Lyon's illness and immediately after her death. Themselves shocked and grieved, the trustees comforted the teachers "by their sympathizing and prayerful spirit" and left them with a mandate to "carry out as fully as possible all Miss Lyon's principles and plans." To an astonishing degree the teachers succeeded, not only in the spring and summer of 1849 but also during the trials and uncertainties of the next three years. At breakfast March 6, Miss Hazen told the school that Miss Lyon had died and announced that the regular Tuesday class schedule would be kept. Some of the students were scandalized, but the teachers knew perfectly well how Miss Lyon would have wanted them to use that time, with the funeral two days later. Mary Whitman, on whom everyone was counting to take the major responsibility, did not arrive until March 28. The news had reached her in Ravenna, Ohio, and the return trip had to be made overland in mud season, since the lake boats had not yet started up after the winter. Two weeks before she reached South Hadley, the teachers had to close ranks again when one of their number, Lucy Curtis, was called home to see her dying father. More tragedy lay just ahead. One week after Lucy got back to the Seminary, she suffered a massive hemorrhage of the lungs; before the end of April she also was dead of tuberculosis.[13]

Everybody seemed to rise to the first crises. Mr. Hawks, who as steward was living in the building, took over the morning devotions three days a week, even launching the appeal for missionary funds which had been peculiarly Miss Lyon's own. He also undertook by himself an ambitious landscaping project—setting out hundreds of seedling forest trees to line a walk from the Seminary building to the brook. Martha Scott managed single-handed the whole domestic work schedule, to which Miss Lyon had always given so much time and thought, and also supervised the sick rooms while other teachers took over her recitations. After Lucy Curtis's death, Margaret Mann, a graduate in 1842 who had taught at Mount Holyoke four years and was about to take charge at Wheaton, was able to come for the summer term and somewhat reduce the extra pressure on the other teachers.[14]

The students, who had their own grief to struggle with, perceived the heavy responsibility resting on the teachers, especially on Miss Hazen and then Miss Whitman, and responded by "faithfulness and good conduct." In time, of course, lapses from perfection were inevitable, but for the rest of the year the sins were relatively few and the sinners quickly contrite. The student reaction that particularly stirred the teachers was the number of conversions. With a minimum of scheduled meetings and special seasons of prayer, nearly 60 of those who had been impenitent at the beginning of the school year by the end of July expressed hope that they had found the Savior. The memory of Mary Lyon's energizing faith was reinforced by the power of religion that seemed to be sustaining the young teachers so nobly. One senior wrote of Mary Lyon, "everything we do seems to bring her right before us" and of Miss Hazen, "it seems to me no one could doubt the truth of religion to have been here, & witnessed all her trials . . . & then see the lovely spirit she has manifested through all."[15]

Most of the usual extras were preserved intact, including Mountain Day and Professor Snell's lectures on physics and architecture. There were a few compromises; for instance, calisthenics, choral music, and student compositions were omitted from the examination programs in the spring and at the anniversary. At the spring examinations, which were held early in May, the trustees organized themselves into committees, one attending each day's sessions. The results for this series were "never better," the journal letter reported. A special project of the trustees was the monument that marks Mary Lyon's grave. Contributions were promptly collected, and by May 21 Deacon Safford and Deacon Porter, who with Mr. Hawks constituted the committee, arrived with the finished stone. They not only supervised the installation but themselves did some of the digging; the whole operation was executed with the utmost care and thoroughness. The shaft of Italian marble, suitably inscribed, rested on a block of granite placed squarely over the coffin, which had been enclosed in a stone vault so cemented as to be completely waterproof. Even the posts for the iron fence around the enclosure were made of granite and sunk four feet into the ground. It touched the young teachers to see "these men who labored with Miss Lyon so faithfully" in founding and supporting the Seminary "building her tombstone with their own hands."[16]

The trustees were no doubt concerned; they spent more time in South Hadley in the spring of 1849 than at any time since the Seminary opened. But they did not hesitate to settle the major responsibility at once upon Mary Whitman. Three weeks after she got back from her interrupted journey of recuperation, the board met to name her principal and Sophia Hazen associate principal for 1849–50 at salaries of $300 and $250 respectively. They must have seemed the only possible successors; it is not surprising that the trustees failed to inquire into the uncertain state of Miss Whitman's health or into Miss Hazen's need of a break. An 1841 graduate, Sophia Hazen had been teaching consecutively for eight years and Miss Lyon had promised her a year's leave of absence, starting in the fall of 1849. The other teachers and the students were anxious, particularly about Miss Whitman, recognizing her personal loss as well as the heavy burden she had to assume and noting that her health, though improved, was "not as good as we

313

hoped a five month absence would make it." Perhaps no woman of 40 as reserved, intense, and conscientious as Mary Whitman would have been likely to make a full recovery from protracted nervous exhaustion under such circumstances. Nevertheless, she started out resolutely and sensibly. She systematically tackled the spring and summer extras—admissions, placement, examinations, hospitality; she even distributed mementos from Mary Lyon's personal effects; and she managed to take regular rides, morning and evening, as prescribed by the doctor. For the first few months it looked as though she might win out. At the end of July, though oppressed by the heat, she seemed better than at the beginning of the term. She was probably sustained at the start by the dedication of so many students and the teachers to Mary Lyon's goals. Mary Whitman's brother, who visited the Seminary at the end of May, was impressed to see that not only his sister but all the other teachers acted on the conviction that Miss Lyon's place must be filled even "by instrumentality as weak as ours." It was the teachers who day by day were aware, in Mary Chapin's words, that "ours is a loss which no Arithmetic can calculate."[17]

The year 1849-50 proved to be the critical one for Miss Whitman and her staff. As in all previous years, when classes started at the end of September new scholars outnumbered those returning for a second or third year. Fewer than half the 200 plus young ladies had lived under Mary Lyon's influence or even known her by sight. The number of teachers was increased to fifteen, but seven were brand new to the rigors of Seminary teaching and five of the fifteen were engaged for only part of the year. It is not surprising that Mary Whitman wanted to be sure of experienced assistance in guiding this collection of students and teachers. Early in the fall she was worrying about the health of Miss Hazen and also Miss Chapin, the other teacher on whom she felt she could rely for strong administrative support. As the year wore on, more worries emerged. Discipline was difficult. Two students were caught in pathological purloining of food; they had fifty pieces of cake sequestered in bureau drawers and admitted to having earlier taken thirty-nine pies. A group of three defiant young women repeatedly made trouble; by the time, close to the year's end, that they were finally expelled for breaking the rules about gentlemen callers, everybody wished Miss Whitman had dismissed them at their first transgression. In mid-winter Sophia Hazen became engaged to a missionary; no matter how much her health improved in the immediate future, she would not be at the Seminary the following year. Mary's own state of health, about which she had been optimistic in the fall, gradually declined. She continued to miss Mary Lyon, "my chief earthly dependence and dear friend, my only one," all the more, probably, because she had been collecting material for the section she still hoped to write of the joint biography being organized and edited by President Hitchcock. As early as the end of December she foresaw the possibility that she might again "have all the billows come over me."[18]

What turned out to be the last straw is not on record; whatever the immediate cause, early in April Mary Whitman resigned. Her four-page letter to the trustees conveyed distress and disorganization. She offered the trustees a choice: either her resignation to take effect August 1 or her appointment as a kind of visiting consultant for as many years as it would take her to recover completely. In any case her health was then so poor that she would have to be absent for most of the rest of the year. She considered Miss Hazen and Miss Chapin also in such uncertain health that she had already suspended the spring reviews and examinations and she proposed canceling the commencement exercises and all but one day of the final public examinations. Indeed, she even suggested the possibility of closing the Seminary three and a half weeks early. At the emergency meeting of the board on April 23, the trustees did not accept any of her alternatives. They voted her a year's leave of absence with pay, starting August 1, 1850, and said simply that reviews, examinations, and anniversary exercises for the current year were to continue as usual. In addition, they set up a committee to look for a successor; obviously they were not really expecting her to recover even after a year's leave, nor intending to find an immediate substitute.[19]

Although precise facts concerning this crisis are scarce, it seems probable that Mary Whitman was at the Seminary only briefly after the end of April. Some of the trustees helped out. The Swifts took her into their home in Northampton for a while, perhaps so that she could be near one of the doctors she was consulting. The

Willistons had planned to drive her in July to Saratoga, but after ten days back at the Seminary preparing to leave, she was so exhausted that when she did depart July 9, she felt able only to go to the home of relatives in Bellows Falls, Vermont. Mr. Hawks and his daughter Elizabeth, who, like Mary, had been a Seminary student in 1837-38, made the trip with her. She was unable in the ensuing months to write any of her section (covering the years from 1837 to 1849) of the joint biography. But she did seem by degrees to recover and to enjoy reasonably good health for most of the remaining twenty-five years of her life. In November, when she wrote a long letter to some of the teachers about her health, she was in Cambridge under the care of her uncle, who was a doctor. In March 1851 she became engaged to Deacon Morton Eddy of Fall River; the following July they were married.[20]

Once again the teachers collectively rose to heroic demands in the middle of a school year. In some ways the disappearance of Mary Whitman was harder to face than Mary Lyon's death. With no obvious successor in view there was no indication of how long they would have to manage without firm administrative guidance and the faith in each of them individually that had made their work exhilarating. Miss Hazen, who had taken much of the brunt the preceding year, could not again shoulder such a load. Because of poor health she was absent well over half the 13-week summer term which started in early May; she did manage to come back and help out with the final examinations. Mary Chapin, who had always been a modest second to Sophia Hazen, perforce assumed general charge; as interim caretaker she continued to avoid center stage when she could. The other teachers took on additional responsibilities as need dictated. The entire staff must have been involved in the discipline problem that had been smoldering all year and finally erupted, affecting the whole school and occasioning much talk outside. The three principal sinners were finally told their parents had been summoned to take them home for "violation of the rules of propriety & good order" in entertaining gentlemen callers. But the culprits, instead of concealing their misdeeds and punishment, spread their own version of events through the school. They won so much sympathy that before the teachers could expose their misrepresentations, six followers had associated themselves with the ringleaders and also had to be dismissed. The discussions accompanying this second set of expulsions apparently cleared the air, won back student support, and enabled teachers to get through the last strenuous days in good order. Distressing as it must have been to have various versions of this episode spread abroad, the effect on enrollment figures was negligible. The list of students for 1850–51, well along when Miss Whitman resigned in April, was complete in mid-July; it contained more than 300 names, allowing for at least 50 dropouts. The teachers who handled admissions had refused more than 100 applicants.[21]

More alarming than any immediate disciplinary difficulty to those who knew the Seminary well was the possibility that Miss Lyon's steady pressure to raise academic standards might not be maintained. One young woman from New Hampshire who had been a junior in 1848–49 and then left to teach wrote anxiously in August 1850 to a classmate still enrolled. She had heard from another student that the examinations just concluded had covered only the subjects studied in the summer term (no doubt the best that could be managed under the circumstances) and feared that this must have retarded the progress of the institution. She also wanted light on a question of intense interest to both students and teachers—who would succeed Miss Whitman? By late summer of 1850 the rumor had reached her that the trustees were looking for a man.[22]

Teachers for the year 1850–51 seem to have been recruited without too much difficulty; of the thirteen, including Mary Chapin, only five were new and had yet to experience at first-hand the cumulative demands made upon every Seminary teacher. Like their more experienced colleagues, the new teachers were Seminary graduates who had known and deeply admired Mary Lyon. No one could question the dedication of this faculty, but few of the close friends of Mount Holyoke—or the teachers themselves—would have predicted that they would steer the Seminary so successfully through the year without the appointment of any successor to Mary Lyon. At the start of the first term in October, the teachers' hopes were high. A candidate for principal, accompanied by her ten-year-old daughter, was on the scene in order to become acquainted with the system and test out the desirability of the arrangement to all concerned. Mrs. Harvey A. Sackett, then in her mid-forties, had been principal of Le Roy Seminary in New York state and, with her minister husband, was shortly to become a central figure in the group that spurred the founding of Elmira College. She had been recommended to the Mount Holyoke trustees as "mighty in the Scriptures" and on first acquaintance seemed to the teachers "calculated to command respect and love." But almost at once, according to the journal letter kept by Helen Peabody, doubts began to rise. By November 8 an entry questioning how much longer Mrs. Sackett would stay minced no words: "The appendage of a husband would render her permanency impracticable did she possess other qualifications." When she did leave at Thanksgiving, the final judgment was equally unsparing. Whatever may have been the indiscretions the young teachers could not forgive, it seems obvious that she had never assumed even a fraction of the daily workload that everyone else took for granted.

She had nothing but the Sab. & Tues. evening meetings and the compositions of the Senior class. Highly as we esteemed her as an individual, the developments of a few weeks convinced us that she lacked the discretion, the system and the ability to take broad and comprehensive views of things, so essential to the harmonious, successful and profitable operation of the vast and complicated machinery of this consecrated Institution. I will not enter into detail. Suffice it to say that we are again left with nothing to cling to but the Omnipotent arm.[23]

In Mary Whitman's letter of resignation to the trustees she had declared: "The experiment of the year [after Mary Lyon's death] I consider of great value. It has fully proved the excellence of Miss Lyon's plans, and their practicability by common minds." The half dozen young women who did the most to keep Mount Holyoke thriving during the two years that elapsed before the trustees finally made a definitive appointment were not exactly "common minds." But they did represent one kind of graduate for whom Mary Lyon had particularly planned the Seminary in the beginning. They came from New England villages and small towns, they had

26. A daguerreotype of Mary Chapin, later Mrs. Claudius Pease, successor to Mary Lyon. She graduated in 1843, was a teacher from 1843 to 1850, acting principal from 1850 to 1852, and principal from 1852 to 1865. Mount Holyoke College Library Archives.

long been eager for more education, they had already had experience as teachers or surrogate mothers and household managers when they entered the Seminary, and they were usually older than many of their classmates.[24]

Mary Chapin was 28 when Mary Lyon died, 30 when the de facto general direction of the Seminary descended upon her. Her father, a Williams graduate, believed in education and took young men into his home in Somers, Connecticut, to prepare them for college or for business. At home Mary had learned a variety of skills young; at 13 she was called back from Abbot Academy in Andover by her mother's death to help keep house for her father, two brothers, and sister. She also learned to copy deeds and documents and keep business records for her father. A small shy girl, Mary was 17 when she entered the Seminary in February 1838 in the middle of the first year. She did not complete the course until she was 23, having caught so severe a case of typhoid in the 1840 epidemic that it took her two years to recover fully and be ready to finish up. Immediately after graduation in August 1843 she returned as a member of the faculty. She seems quickly to have become a success in the classroom—she particularly liked teaching mathematics—and as general assistant to Miss Lyon. Long afterward she recalled how the shift in responsibility had seemed to her.

I had always been with Miss Lyon a great deal from the first. I was feet to her, eyes to her, anything to help her; and so I understood all the kinds of work that the principal had to do, and when there was no one else to do it, I did it; and as one after another gave out, I had to keep on. I was twenty-eight, but I never had thought of myself as anything but a little girl.

All her life she was unassuming and avoided the limelight. Report has it that Mary Lyon only a few months before her death had named Mary Chapin as competent to be her successor—a perception it took the trustees some time to achieve.[25]

The other teachers who kept the Seminary moving ahead during the years of uncertainty included Martha Scott, class of 1845, from nearby North Hadley, where she had obviously been a tower of strength in the household to her widowed father and younger sisters. She carried the responsibility for both domestic work and the sick rooms through the crucial transition years until colleagues could learn to cope with the special complexities of the organization that had always taken so much of Miss Lyon's time. Two of the teachers, both slightly older than Miss Chapin and readier at public speech, were members of the class of 1846 who had had considerable teaching experience both before and after their years as Seminary students. Harriet Johnson of Sturbridge, who was 28 when she graduated, returned to her alma mater to teach in the summer of 1848. Sophia Spofford from Thomaston, Maine, graduated at the age of 27 and was called back to the Seminary from a school in New York state in the fall of 1851. Emily Jessup of Norwalk, Connecticut, class of 1847, was serious but a bit angular as a student. Mary Lyon tried her out as a teacher for a single term in 1847–48, and she met the challenge so satisfactorily that the appointment was continued throughout the year, the beginning of a long teaching career, first at Mount Holyoke and then at Western. Helen Peabody, a farmer's daughter from Newport, New Hampshire, and the youngest of fourteen children, managed to get through the Seminary with the help of some brothers and sisters. She graduated in 1848 and immediately joined the faculty, where she soon demonstrated her aptitude for extras, from working out class schedules to keeping the journal letter.

These young women were not necessarily the Seminary students singled out by their classmates as especially brilliant, nor were they necessarily the most immediately successful or popular teachers when they first joined the staff. What they all had was an overriding conviction that Miss Lyon's plans must be carried out and that it was up to them, as she had so often said, to do what no one else would do. This conviction was an abiding force in their lives; after the interregnum they all went on to make contributions to the successful operation either of Mount Holyoke or of one of the "daughter" institutions that sprang up where Mount Holyoke graduates or admirers were stirred by a perceived need.[26]

Records of the two years when the trustees were making up their minds are meager, but they do suggest esprit-de-corps on the part of the staff—as if Mary Lyon's faith in their capability was still an activating presence. The Thanksgiving celebration in 1850 was more elaborate than ever, incorporating the second marriage of Mr. Hawks's widowed daughter Elizabeth. The young ladies produced a seven-tier wedding cake (the bottom two layers being constructed of a tin pan and napkins) and other special refreshments, and the evergreen and tissue paper decorations were particularly elaborate. All but one of the teachers stayed in the Seminary for this occasion and, as usual, divided up the responsibility for preparations: Miss Scott and Miss Jessup saw to "gastronomics," Miss Peabody and three new teachers supervised the decorations, Miss Chapin directed the singing. For the two-week vacation starting January 17, 1851, the 80 students who stayed were looked out for by Miss Johnson, Miss Jessup, and Miss Peabody. In March, Miss Chapin went to Boston for two weeks to see Sophia Hazen Stoddard and her husband off for Persia, to visit Mary Whitman, and to purchase the hundred books for the library that were to be the senior class gift to the school; Miss Johnson took charge in South Hadley. At the completion of the spring examinations in May, everybody fell to on the new schedules required for the 244 students: Miss Chapin and Miss Peabody worked out the new series of studies; Miss Johnson and Miss Jessup arranged room changes; Miss Scott redid the domestic work assignments.[27]

The regular anniversary events were concluded in 1851 without apparent trauma, and the following year started off briskly with a full complement of sixteen teachers, nine of them experienced in Seminary instruction, all but one of them students under Mary Lyon. Teachers' assignments were shifted as Miss Lyon had so often done. The domestic department was split up and spread among six teachers, two new and four experienced. A major extra responsibility, the Memorandum Society catalogue—the directory of alumnae addresses and occupations published once every five years—was assumed by Harriet Johnson. Both teachers and students seemed to take the vicissitudes of the school year in stride, including the deaths, within a month, of two particularly gifted and admired juniors.[28]

It was the trustees who turned out to be in disarray. Some of the trouble came from a factional fight in the South Hadley church, which had left the minister's salary so far in arrears that Mr. Laurie had sought and been granted dismissal by the Council of Ministers early in 1851. There was inevitably a struggle over finding a replacement; some of the parish were demanding that the Seminary pay part of the minister's salary. The brunt of this pressure was felt by Mr. Hawks as president of the board and, a Seminary resident, the only trustee on the scene every Sunday. Mr. Hawks was also the focal point for disagreement within the board itself. His combination of services was unusual: permanent fund-raiser and building steward as well as president of the board and member of the three-man executive committee (along with Mr. Condit and Mr. Porter) which made important policy decisions in between the annual meetings of the full board. As long as Mary Lyon had been principal, the arrangement worked well; her steady drive for enlargement and improvement balanced any extra trustee pressures. But after her death his influence increased markedly. He was elected by his fellow trustees to the four committees set up to deal with the emergency. Two of these committees were central to the survival of the institution: the one on instruction included Mr.

Hawks, Mr. Swift, and President Hitchcock; that on a successor to Miss Whitman included Mr. Hawks, Mr. Swift, and Deacon Safford, who soon resigned and was replaced by Deacon Porter. Although the Mount Holyoke trustees were in general politically and theologically conservative, they would never have served at all if they had not been men of considerable independence of mind. It was natural that when they were no longer confronted by Miss Lyon's conviction and urgency, they should find themselves in sharp disagreement. The rift seems to have been particularly deep between Mr. Hawks and Mr. Swift, the young Northampton minister who had succeeded Mr. Condit as secretary of the Seminary trustees and was being considered as successor to Mr. Laurie in South Hadley.

Little by little Mr. Hawks acquired more say in the day-to-day operation of the Seminary, especially on problems of discipline and community relations. Mary Chapin, always self-effacing, was so sure that she was only a short-term caretaker that she declined to identify herself in the catalogue as "acting principal" during the two years she was so designated by the trustees. It is not surprising that she sometimes deferred to his age, learning and long service to the Seminary, nor that he began to feel his presence indispensable. In June 1851 he got word of the death of his son in a drowning accident in South Carolina, but he would not leave to visit the young man's friends and business associates until he had found a deputy to stay in the Seminary during his absence. Whether he and his fellow trustees were pleased with the role of the young Dr. Leonard Humphrey is not recorded, but the students and teachers apparently enjoyed his four-week sojourn. He was probably involved in the administrative decision not to allow Seminary students to go either to Springfield or Northampton to hear Jenny Lind sing. He was certainly the prime mover—and chronicler in the *Springfield Republican*—of a July 4th entertainment for the students and the village. The occasion had all the Thanksgiving party features, including calisthenics, elaborate refreshments, decorations with pyramids of roses and a large motto over the platform: "Liberty and Union." The program, presented entirely by men, combined patriotic sentiments and the reading of the Declaration of Independence with satire on the women's movement.

The high point was the reading of an "Amazonian Declaration of Independence," parodying the declaration of the 1848 women's convention, and a series of toasts in similar vein. Whether any of the young women found these sentiments less than hilarious, there is no way of telling; not a single student letter describing the occasion has turned up so far.[29]

By fall some of the trustee disagreements came to a head. An invitation to settle in South Hadley as minister was extended to Mr. Swift on September 5, but he knew there was still hostility in some quarters and took more than two months to respond. In the meantime President Hitchcock had finished seeing through the press the biography of Mary Lyon, which had taken his sustained efforts for the past year, even with assistance from Zilpah Grant Banister and Mary Whitman Eddy in collecting materials, and from Hannah White and Eunice Caldwell Cowles in writing the first two sections. When he turned his attention to the Seminary's immediate future, he was roused to action. On October 10 he, Mr. Williston, and Mr. Harris addressed a formal request to Mr. Hawks to call a meeting of the full board as soon as possible to deal with the settlement of a South Hadley minister and also to discuss student health, improvement of the building and the grounds, and the appointment of a principal. Ten days later, apparently in response to a reply from Mr. Hawks, President Hitchcock was more explicit about what was wrong.

Dear Sir

Allow me to say something more in relation to the Sem [Mount Holyoke] & a meeting of the Trustees.

You suppose that I depended upon "the outdoor remarks." I will tell you how I got my information not merely concerning the settlement of Mr. Swift but a great many other things relating to the Sem. In the first place either by letter or personal conversation I have learned the views of all the Trustees except those of Mr. Bowdoin & Dea. Safford who has not replied to the letter I wrote him several weeks ago. I next went to the teachers of the Sem & conversed very plainly with them; & then I conversed with some of the leading men of S. Had. During the year past I have travelled a great deal & met with very many individuals of all classes of the community & have thus learned extensively the views of men concerning certain things connected with the Sem.

Now it is in view of all the information thus attained that I came to the conclusion that unless something be done speedily the Institution must suffer deeply & I fear go down. Such is now my settled conviction. I should hope that a meeting of the Trustees would prevent the mischief. But I think if delayed long it will be too late.

You fear that if we meet now "a new element" (divisions I suppose you mean[)], will be introduced among us. I assure you that it already exists to an alarming extent; & if something be not done to cure it it will soon be past remedy. Many of the trustees feel deeply wounded by the course of things for a year or two past. They feel as if they have been used merely as automatons:—(I use the language of others—) & that they might as well stay away from the meetings as go [to] them. They feel as if they had been deprived at the annual meetings of the opportunity of expressing their views, & that the public view imperiously demands some changes at S. Hadley. Now it was to try to cure this state of things that I & others have wished a meeting. Suppose we do differ on some points? Cannot Christian men agree to differ? Is it not better freely to view one anothers opinions & to pray over them than to suffer their differences to grow larger & more inveterate in private?

I do not suppose that we could now secure the Settlement of Mr. S. at S. Had. if we should come together. But I think we could do something to soften the asperity of feeling by a meeting. If nothing is done (I speak the universal opinion of all classes in this region not connected with the Sem.) the effects will be very disastrous. The only resort will probably be for the Sem. to have separate worship. Rumour indeed says that the Trustees are soon to have a chapel. As to this resort I can only say I should consider it a death blow to the Institution: & often having been an Instructor for thirty years I ought to know something as to the business of education how such a measure would operate upon the youthful mind. If it be adopted that is my view now and I should feel compelled publicly to disavow all participation in the measure. In my memoir of Miss Lyon I have stood forth as a defender of the Sem. in all its great features. I could no longer defend it, or recommend it, if such a measure were adopted & therefore to be consistent must disavow it.

Now I believe that these threatening evils might in a great measure be prevented, or at least greatly alleviated by a timely meeting of the Trustees. I believe they are inevitable without such a meeting. I have felt constrained therefore to take the lead in requesting such a meeting. I take the lead because I am the oldest man probably in the Board; not because it is a pleasant task nor because I have time to attend to it for I am overwhelmed with labours at home. Other Trus. are equally anxious for this meeting: but we shall not press it contrary to the strong wishes of yourself & others unless I see new reason to forward the petition. The responsibility of not having a meeting does not now rest on us. I would not for the world take that responsibility. But I doubt not you are equally conscientious in preventing a meeting & are willing to assume the responsibility. The result only will show who is in the right.

Freely do I excuse the freedom of your remarks, as I trust you will pardon the frankness & decision of mine. I trust also that we shall both remember that altho our views differ on this subject, they agree on almost every other point of importance, & therefore our differences are no reason for interrupting our personal friendship. In one thing we shall agree I think which is, that if God do not guide us all we shall make fatal mistakes & ruin the beloved Holyoke Seminary. May He save that whatever becomes of us.[30]

Mr. Hawks did not call a special session; the board next assembled at its regular meeting date after the anniversary exercises in August 1852. Nevertheless, President Hitchcock's criticisms seem to have had some effect. Mr. Swift was somehow sufficiently mollified that on November 18 he wrote the South Hadley church that he felt it would be unwise just then to accept a permanent appointment because of "circumstances which need not be named." But he made a counteroffer, which was promptly accepted, to take the pulpit for a single trial year at a salary of $700, paid quarterly, and three or four Sundays of paid vacation. When the annual Seminary trustee meeting did finally occur on August 5, the agenda was full of specific problems. The board authorized immediate work on the new plumbing system that had been investigated three years earlier; set up a new committee on grounds; voted to give $80 to the parish toward the painting of the church and $100 to the school library for books to be chosen by the teachers; and agreed to split the profits on the Hitchcock biography of Mary Lyon between the Seminary and the collaborators. Most important, the board voted to invite Professor Albert Hopkins of Williams College, brother of Mark Hopkins, to be principal and instructor in physical sciences. His specialty was astronomy, and he had managed to have built at Williams one of the early observatories in the United States. That the choice of essentially conservative trustees was a man is scarcely surprising; certainly there was no other woman just like Mary Lyon. The teachers had known for some time that it was a gentleman for whom the search was taking so long. Some of them might have applauded the selection of Professor Hopkins. His series of lectures on physics at the Seminary the preceding May had been found "delightful," and the religious services he conducted during the two and a half weeks he and his wife spent in South Hadley seem to have been acceptable. In any case, after six weeks of reflection, Professor Hopkins declined politely but firmly. He noted in his letter of refusal that the trustees themselves had not been overeager to conclude arrangements, judging by the interview he had had with Mr. Hawks at the Seminary commencement exercises or the one he had been led to expect afterward with Mr. Harris, which never took place.[31]

This refusal was followed by considerable activity. Mr. Swift, who had received a second invitation by almost unanimous vote to settle as South Hadley minister, on October 9 accepted; for the next six years he served as minister to the Congregational Church and as secretary to the Seminary trustees. President Hitchcock drew up a list of objections to the Seminary, which he no doubt conveyed to Mr. Hawks in some form. His principal complaint was too much pressure: a daily schedule so crowded that it prevented the enjoyment of leisure and endangered student health. In this reaction he may have been influenced in part by the experience of his youngest daughter Jane, a junior in 1851-52 who did not return to complete the course, but he was surely speaking entirely in his own right when he emphasized the long delay—by then three and a half years—in providing a successor to Mary Lyon. Mr. Hawks himself must have felt the urgency. He called a special meeting on November 18, at which Mary Chapin was named principal and Sophia Spofford associate principal. (They also voted to proceed with construction of the much-delayed north wing that Mary Lyon had long ago planned on.) No records exist as to the size of the vote in favor of Miss Chapin, or, indeed, as to which of the trustees had initiated the earlier votes of thanks passed in August 1851 and again in August 1852 expressing appreciation to the acting principal and the teachers for "the able & satisfactory manner" in which they had conducted the Seminary and asking them to continue on the same principles. Whatever the doubts may have been, when the decision was finally made, everybody seemed to be satisfied—even Miss Chapin herself, once she had got over the shock.[32]

The extent to which Miss Chapin had been keeping the Seminary moving when she was only acting principal is hard to ascertain because she was so self-effacing. As one alumna put it, "She was one of those rare souls who are content to work out of sight, allowing others to have the credit of the results . . ."; among the developments that after her death were attributed to Miss Chapin's energy were the actual building of the north wing, the enlargement of the library, the extension of series of science lectures by visiting professors from the colleges for men. Certainly these improvements, like the increase in Latin and the lengthening of the course, Mary Lyon had long had in mind and talked about frequently to teachers and students. Pressure for stronger preparation had been an essential part of the academic program from the beginning. Mary Chapin and the other teachers were unquestionably following Mary Lyon's principles when they kept on making it virtually impossible to be admitted directly into the senior class by examinations at entrance. Mary Nutting, who ultimately became Mount Holyoke librarian and historian, explained the system soon after she entered.

If candidates for advanced standing were allowed to pass an examination, instead of reviewing, as was the custom until of late; it would be easy to go through in one year. But as it is, no one has

*done it for two years past, at least; and no one, that we can hear
of, since the regulation about reviewing was made. Last year there
were eleven that tried to go through in one year, but not one succeeded, simply, as I said before, because the reviews occupy so
much time. These "rapid reviews" are anything but rapid; every
fourth lesson is a review of the three preceding ones, and when a
book has been finished, we review from the beginning.*[33]

Similarly, when she was still thinking of herself only as a caretaker, Mary Chapin did not hesitate to announce in the catalogue
appearing in the spring of 1851 that Cornelius Nepos, then being
taught to the junior class, would henceforth be required for
entrance. This meant that by the spring of 1853 it was possible to
announce that Latin must be studied in all three years of the
Seminary course instead of two, including both Virgil and Cicero;
in another two years Latin prose composition was announced as a
regular part of the course. These successive steps did ease the way
for the final shift in 1861 to a four-year course, more than twenty
years after Mary Lyon had published in the 1839–40 catalogue her
hope that "the improvement of the pupils and the expectation of
friends will soon justify such an addition."

Hard as it was for the trustees and many contemporary observers
to perceive in 1850, the perspective of time suggests that Mary
Chapin, for all her diffidence, had some of the same talents as
Mary Lyon. Though not as gifted as her predecessor at devising
new systems, Miss Chapin had considerable executive skill; she
understood and could apply Miss Lyon's complicated organizational schemes, and she was a good manager of funds. As a disci-
plinarian, she was reported to be consistent, patient, and kindly.
Although she avoided the public platform whenever she could
and lacked Miss Lyon's quick wit, she had a lively sense of humor,
personal warmth, and enthusiasm. She seemed to have little
difficulty in winning the support of the students as well as her
fellow teachers.

Though the long delay in settling on a successor to Mary Lyon
had distressed those most closely involved, it seems to have had no
effect on the Seminary's standing in the larger world. Thanks in
part to the alumnae scattered over the United States and in

27. Mary and Harriet, the two younger sisters of Lucy Goodale, who had died in the typhoid epidemic of 1840, both attended the Seminary. Mary came for a year in 1849–50 and Harriet completed the course in the class of 1855. Mount Holyoke College Library Archives.

foreign missions, esteem for Mount Holyoke continued to spread in the years immediately after Mary Lyon's death. Although many applicants were refused each year and a few failed the entrance examinations or dropped out, the school was still crowded. In 1850–51 there were 244 students; in 1851–52 there were 252; in 1852–53 258 girls from seventeen states and territories and three foreign countries. Visitors flocked to South Hadley. In August 1851 the Seminary doors had to be locked to prevent overcrowding at the public examinations. Faculty from Williams and Amherst lectured on science and matters of general interest. President Hitchcock gave talks on Mary Lyon, perspective drawing, and his recent trip to Europe and, in the fall of 1851, brought the entire senior class over from Amherst to see how excellently the Seminary building had been designed. Professor Haven of Amherst gave a stirring eulogy of Daniel Webster and a series of lectures on psychology to the seniors. The regular chemistry series were delivered by Professors Lasell and Chadbourne of Williams and Adams of Amherst, the physics series by Professors Snell of Amherst and Hopkins of Williams. The most picturesque in the procession of missionary speakers was a little Chinese girl who recited the Lord's prayer and the ten commandments in her native tongue. Catharine Beecher spent several days in the spring of 1852 at the Seminary with her friend Miss Mortimer, promoting a teachers' convention for women the following September. She had wanted to stage it at South Hadley, but there is no indication as to how she expected the guests to be fed and cared for when the Seminary students and teachers were away on their long vacation.[34]

The demand for Mount Holyoke–trained teachers continued high. Recruiters came from Oregon and Texas; the Texan was so pleased with the response at South Hadley, where he got the names of seventy potential candidates, that he was planning to cut down his visits to other seminaries. At least one opening must have been tempting to Mary Chapin herself. In the spring of 1852 Ellen Whitmore wrote about a head for the new Cherokee Indian Female Seminary in Oklahoma territory, which she and a fellow Mount Holyoke alumna would be leaving soon for marriage. The young woman chosen should be mature, energetic, gracious—like Miss Chapin herself or Miss Johnson. To be working head of a government-sponsored institution modeled closely on Mount Holyoke, under an able and sympathetic Indian chief, would have meant serving the missionary cause under agreeable circumstances —and an annual salary of $800. Mary Chapin chose to stay in South Hadley, although in March 1852 she had no expectation of becoming the permanent head of Mount Holyoke. Harriet Johnson accepted.[35]

From the first, one of the best indications of the Seminary's power to endure was student morale. Although there were some familiar discipline problems—stolen money, improprieties involving young men—most of the students in the early 1850's were cooperative and enthusiastic. For a whole term the thirty-one seniors in the class of 1852 managed not to break a single one of the seventy rules on which they reported daily in their section meetings. Without any dramatic revivals there was nevertheless serious concern about nonbelievers and more than thirty hopeful conversions each year. Students volunteered in numbers for the rigors of rooming on the fourth floor and for stitching up the long seams in the new Seminary Hall carpet. Many contributed not only to the annual missionary subscription but also to gifts for the school—books for the library, a new coverlet for the piano, a pair of solar lamps for the high desk on the platform.[36]

The foundation of student support in 1850 was just what it had been in 1837—delight in the intellectual challenge and in the order of a system that enabled so many young women to accomplish much more than they had thought possible. When Mary Nutting discovered that she would not be able, as she had hoped, to enter the senior class her first year, she wrote her father not to complain but to approve.

I value the advantages of learning to be systematic, punctual, industrious, etc. in any thing, in short the advantages which are common to all who are here—quite as much as those which I hoped for, in being in the Senior class. Instead of fretting because I cannot do all I hoped to, I am glad, more and more, every day, that I am here at all. I should not think the expense of my being here by any means thrown away, if I should do no more than finish the Middle studies, nor would you, dear father, if you knew all the privileges we have here.[37]

A young woman in the middle class in January 1852 wrote a long account of the Seminary to a friend in Maine. Her description of the building and the program seems indistinguishable from similar letters from her predecessors writing during the twelve years of Mary Lyon's administration. Susan Lennan was particularly impressed by the rigor of her studies.

At first it seemed very strange here indeed, and I thought I should never get used to the rules, and that I could do nothing without breaking them, but I soon got accustomed to them, and I am perfectly contented and like here very much indeed. Many of the girls were very homesick, but I see no tears now at thoughts of home and I dare say, they will cry as heartily next fall to think they must go away, as they did at first to think they must stay. One can get along pretty easy here if she chooses, but if you want to excel,—to graduate in less than four years, you must study for it. There are some here, now, who entered last year, and were obliged to study some of the preparatory studies, who are now behind me, although I have been here but a term. They care no more for their books than to get rid of them the easiest way possible. These will be obliged to stay four years.

This term I have finished a whole course of History, which includes Worcester's Elements, Goldsmith's England, Rome and Greece, and Grimshaw's France, and before the week closes, shall have finished and thoroughly reviewed Robinson's Algebra. And, Emily, as an encouragement if you ever come here, I will say, of all things that I ever got hold of, this Algebra beats them all. I never thought Algebra was very hard till I studied this. We girls have declared if we ever meet Professor Robinson, we will very nearly make him take his exit from this mundane sphere. But I don't care about it now, as long as I shall say good-bye to him this week, and it has done me the most good in the way of thoroughly exercising my brains, of any thing I ever studied. And grammar, I have been obliged to study that. No one can enter here without studying Mr. Green's Analysis. I thought I should lay my grammar on the shelf for the future, but I find I shall be obliged to use it oftener than I anticipated. This Analysis is different from anything I ever met with. Weld's is nothing more than the Alphabet compared with it. It is an excellent work.

Like her predecessors straight back to 1837, Susan found the key to all academic progress in the thoroughness required of every student:

Next term I shall take Euclid. I expect I shall find it pretty hard, but hope to like it. I hope to enter the middle class, and think I may, but am not certain. My Latin is the only thing that I build my hopes upon. If I had not happened to have Latin for two years, I should think my case hopeless, but as it is, I shall be greatly disappointed if I do not. It is more of an undertaking than I anticipated, and it is much harder than formerly. . . . If any one wants to get a thorough education, *come to South Hadley, I say. You cannot fail of* being thorough. *Every fourth lesson is a* review. *When you have completed a study, you go all over it and* review *it, and then every* fourth lesson *is a review. Before you are examined in the summer, all these studies must again be* reviewed *for examination. The teachers are competent and faithful. You have a good library (which is a great thing if a body could only get time to read!) and all apparatus that is necessary for explanations of the different studies.*

The domestic work did not seem to be a burden nor did most of the rules.

As for the work, we can almost always do what we like. If the work we prefer is light, we must work an hour and a quarter, if harder, only an hour. You can change at almost any time if you wish. The first of the term, I used to weigh the bread *for the morning's breakfast, and make thickning for toast. I changed in a little while, and now I build the* morning fires, *which is pretty hard but I like it as I* gain time. *I get all my work done for the day an hour and a quarter before breakfast. I get up at a quarter of four! and if we chance to oversleep, every thing is hindered through the day. One morning we did not wake, till a whole hour and a quarter after we should, and breakfast was delayed a whole hour and everything else. The girls gave us a vote of thanks for this nice nap. . . . You must not leave your* fire without putting up the fender. *(All the stoves are the open Franklin stove). You must not leave wood on the Zinc or hearth; nor matches out of box, nor must you carry fire unless in a fire pan. These are the fire laws and the only laws we have in school, all the others are* rules. *You see there is nothing that is not necessary in a family of more than two hundred and fifty pupils.*

If we did our work only when we pleased, you see we should all starve to death,—and there would be no system about the arrangements. As it is, every thing goes on regularly. Every one has her regular portion to do and is expected to do it. On Wednesday morning, the Seminary is cleaned from cellar to garret. Each one must do half an hour's extra work. It is not very hard to wash down a flight of twenty stairs all painted or to wash with a handled mop, a space of painted floor as large as a small bedroom, and this is the floor mopping at South Hadley, that I have heard folks make so much talk about. If any one is a mind to think it is very hard here, they can persuade themselves that it is, but I think any one with quite delicate health might go through a whole course here, and go away with better health than she entered. I know I should laugh if I were at home, to start out before sun rise and walk a mile in the keen cold wintry air, but I do it here quite often and think nothing of it. I am not obliged to walk before sun-rise, but as it is most convenient to do so, I often do it.

After a long description of the daily schedule and the building, Susan explained the system of assigning rooms:

It is rather hard to room in the fourth story. I roomed there the first four weeks. After those 4 weeks, we move. Each one writes a note to the teacher, telling with whom and in what story, not what room, she would like to be put. If they can possibly accommodate you, they commonly do, unless they think two wild ones want to get together, when they try to put a wild one and a steady one together. I now room in a double room, in the third story of the wing. I have three room-mates, very pleasant girls—one from New York—one from Vermont and one from Gardiner, Me.

She was reassuring about entrance examinations but when she urged her friend to enroll, Susan emphasized the constantly rising academic standards.

If you have never studied Latin, you are expected to take it up at once, and you will not be so high in rank, as it is a preparatory study. Every year they raise the standard of the school and it grows harder and harder each year. I have heard, but I could not give it as truth, that it is the intention to introduce Greek, and have the whole course occupy four years—the same as a collegiate course. Within a year or two, they have changed from Day's Algebra to Robinson's, which is much harder. —from Weld's Analysis to Green's, —and next year—every one must to begin the studies of the Junior year, have studied Nepos, else they will be studying the first part of the term only preparatory studies, which will give them no chance to enter the middle class. Within five or six years, Latin has been introduced. If you come here (and I will apply for you if you wish it) I would advise you to take Latin at once, and Algebra. Those things will carry you a long way in this Seminary.

I think you would be delighted here,—at first you would be a little homesick perhaps—but you would soon get over it,—and be as happy as I am, which is saying a great deal. If you do not come, if ever you come within twenty miles of the place, come and visit the school—you would be astonished to see how conveniently every thing is arranged—the domestic hall—the recitation hall— every thing about the whole building—and you would wonder as I do, that one woman could have planned it all.[38]

The fall of 1852 brought some changes that impressed the students. The most dramatic was the provision of hot and cold running water in the basement and living quarters on all four stories. With two bathrooms on each floor, there were accessible without going up or down a single stair not only bathtubs, white inside and green outside, and "large enough almost to go swimming in," but also water closets, and basins at which pails could be filled with hot or cold water. Eliminating so many trips up and down stairs—to the outhouses, to the basement to empty slop pails or get hot water for scrubbing—made life less strenuous, especially on the fourth floor. Even in the domestic hall the difference was appreciable. No young woman any longer had to spend five minutes on wash day lugging pails of water to keep the great copper kettle on the stove filled or would henceforth be asked to take a turn at the hand pump when the cisterns got low. It is not surprising that student letters described the arrangements in enthusiastic detail—even to the dam in Stony Brook, the water wheel, the pumphouse, the boiler, the cisterns in the attic.[39]

The other major development of the fall of 1852 was, of course, the naming of Miss Chapin as principal and Miss Spofford as associate principal. Students did write home about the event when it was reported to them by Mr. Hawks after the November 18th trustee meeting—but without surprise or excitement. This reaction had nothing to do with the feeling of the students for Miss Chapin as a person or administrator; it meant that they had taken it for granted that she *was* the principal. It was the idea that she had been only acting head that was "something entirely new to all of us." Certainly the Seminary seemed to be running with the kind of order Mary Lyon had created against odds. Although the school was over full—the catalogue count was 258—Julia Tolman could report in the journal letter with justifiable pride that, after only four weeks, thanks to the band of dedicated teachers led by Miss Chapin, "all the wheels seem to be in steady uniform equable motion." Like the teachers, the students responded to a system that was working and direction that was both mild and steady. As she had done in the two years just past, Mary Chapin in the thirteen years of her administration yet to come was to steer a straight course, with her eye fixed not only on what Mary Lyon had already done but also on what she was resolved to do the minute she saw the chance.[40]

In some ways Mary Lyon was very much a part of her time. Like many other New Englanders, especially those in the hills of western Massachusetts and western Connecticut, she found the center of her existence in evangelical religion. The puritans of the nineteenth century were individualists who had to achieve for themselves the state of mind in which they could commit themselves to God. They were also pragmatic idealists; many professing Christians spent energy on good works that could hasten the coming of Christ's reign on earth. It was the great age of the revival and of foreign missions—to the young women in the Seminary as well as to Mary Lyon. Her religion was strenuous but not grim. Although she was an admirer of Jonathan Edwards and a believer in eternal damnation as well as eternal salvation, Miss Lyon talked to the students much less about the pains of hellfire than the sadness of being left out of heaven and the exhilaration of life animated by faith:

Suppose one of you for whom many have prayed. A thousand years hence you are not in heaven. All those pious friends are there; but there is no lack. You will be forgotten. God will not miss you, your friends will not. The mother might lose an infant, & mourn exceedingly for that child. But twenty years pass, & she feels differently. Your name must never come to pollute heaven. You will be forgotten. It will seem to your dearest friends that heaven is filled.

Total commitment to God could transform daily living. "In every step [of] body & mind glorify God. When you don't study as you ought, you don't glorify God." And conversely, "I consider bread-making of so much consequence, that, in giving attention to it, I am confident that I am serving God."[41]

The Christianity celebrated by Mary Lyon engendered benevolence that was all-encompassing and heroic:

Every one we see seems to desire something of honor, ease, pleasure or improvement that will make something more of himself. We ought to turn the current of feeling towards others & it will branch out into a thousand streams. How much happier you would be to live in a thousand beside yourself, rather than to live in yourself alone. This throwing out the whole soul in powerful, vigorous, disinterested action for others, no matter how self-denying, will make you receive a hundred fold in return.

Mount Holyoke had been designed to enable young women to spread their benevolence to the farthest corners of the world. "You should be educated to go among rich or poor, in the country or village, to live in N. England, in the West or in Foreign Lands." Miss Lyon challenged the delicate as well as the sturdy, the modest as well as the self-confident:

Be willing to do anything & anywhere. Be not hasty to decide that you have no physical or mental strength & no faith or hope.

Think not too much of your weakness, or self-indulgence. May every one of us give more & find more for our heart & more for our hands to do & find more to suffer.[42]

In the first half of the nineteenth century many churchmen and laymen perceived the need to provide better education for women. It was during Mary Lyon's lifetime that local communities throughout the country came to accept fiscal and organizational responsibility for maintaining district schools for the early education of both boys and girls. Female seminaries and coeducational academies multiplied; though many were short-lived, the availability of good secondary education for girls was increasing. Some of the leading citizens who had found Miss Lyon's plans impractical and imprudent declared themselves in favor of higher education for women in the course of time. Mary Lyon differed from such advocates not only in her overriding sense of urgency but also in the way she managed to communicate her own love of learning. She commended the students who had found delight in using their minds and urged them to protect themselves against family demands that might extinguish the spark:

There are three classes of ladies, who ought to consider well, about striving to gain a superior education. 1st The few who have studied enough to love to study. They ought to beware how they form plans that will interrupt and break off their love for study. 2nd Those who have the elements of this love but have never had full opportunity to develop them. The social feelings they possess ought to be considered a talent to be used for good and with a superior education what might they not accomplish! Twenty years of life would be worth more with it than forty without it. 3rd Those that can learn if they try long and hard. Their genius, like gold, will shine if they hammer it long enough. But ladies are turned aside by a thousand things, wh. never interrupt gentlemen, and if they would build high, they must not be satisfied with laying the foundation.[43]

She tried to spur on all the students to discover for themselves the satisfactions of learning how to classify and to make abstractions. "Not all young ladies have a proper conception of how great a study Grammar is. To understand the nature of language & the foundation of language requires a philosophical mind." She distinguished between little minds which "come down to particular things" and great minds which "embrace a great deal like God." Indeed, at Mount Holyoke the intellectual challenge sounded as loudly as the call to self-sacrifice:

Your mode of existence is as far above the pleasure-seeker, as an archangel above an infant. If you have as much intelligence, energy and enterprise as you ought to have, you are doing much—and making much of yourselves. The hardest marble will take the finest polish. I would rather have a lady of hard marble than one of soap-stone.[44]

Mary Lyon was not a feminist in the ordinary sense of the word. There is no indication that she ever referred to the women's rights convention at Seneca Falls in 1848 and it is inconceivable that she would have approved the methods of Lucretia Mott and Elizabeth Cady Stanton. Nevertheless she was acutely aware of male assumptions of superiority. Her tribute to Joseph Emerson contrasted his genuine respect for women's minds with the attitude of most of his contemporaries:

The tendency of the course he pursued, was to inspire ladies with a modest *confidence, not only in their own individual powers, but also in the native abilities of the sex; and to give them those just views of their* real *worth, which are so suited to lead them to dislike and avoid all mean* pretensions *to knowledge, genius, and greatness; and which are suited to do away the assumption that females were never designed to be literary or scientific, and that they cannot be without injury to themselves and others. . . . In conversation with him, ladies generally had a feeling of being regarded like equals as well as friends. There was no needless gallantry—no apparent consciousness of stooping—or of condescension. His sincere and unfeigned regard for the sex, was told far less by words than by his cordial, familiar, and unaffected manner.*[45]

Miss Lyon did not waste the time of Seminary students proving scientifically that the intellectual ability of the sexes was equal; she took it for granted. If she did compare the sexes, she was apt to be noting the extra burdens women had to assume. At the weekly teachers' meeting she more than once observed "that it requires more discipline of mind to be a lady, than it does to be a gentleman. He has little of the minutiae to be attended to, & can get up in the morning & dive right into his business without interruption. But 'tis not so with the lady, nor would I have it so." And she repeatedly talked to the students about the social pressures that kept Mount Holyoke's academic standards from rising as rapidly as she would have liked. "The only reason why we do not put four years in, is the narrowness of means & views of those who would find it too much. Young men are required to prepare much longer; but young ladies are admitted without excuse. The Trustees object to adding another year. They design to make the three years' course more rigid. We would take a leap, but cannot & expect to advance gradually."[46]

Although Miss Lyon was anything but an agitator, she must be reckoned among the forces in the mid-nineteenth century which changed women's lives. Her means was faith: an unshakable belief in the capacity of young women to rise—physically, intellectually, spiritually—to the most arduous demands society would make. There was nothing sentimental in this faith. She perceived limitations in character and intellect; indeed, her appraisals of the students she had taught were unusually acute. Miss Lyon felt in every fiber of her being that many young women who were strongly motivated and encouraged could transcend their limitations. The same talents that had enabled her to bring the Seminary into being—her wit and wisdom, her remarkable energy, her administrative genius, her dedication to the Lord's work—were employed to make Mount Holyoke year by year a better instrument for enabling students to achieve more than they imagined they could.

For some, including ardent admirers, her soaring expectations were destructive, especially to young teachers who were high strung or not robust. Mary Whitman's collapse was probably the result of too much pressure. But many young women, including a considerable number who attended the Seminary only one year, found Miss Lyon's faith both stimulating and sustaining and left South Hadley ready to accept difficult challenges and serve where need seemed greatest. New students not infrequently began to respond almost as soon as they got over being homesick. An earnest diary kept by an entering middle-class member was full of inchoate but burning aspiration. After some months, one entry read:

My desires to rise are very, very *great. I want to be prepared for any station. I want to do every thing possible to improve my mind that it may be thoroughly disciplined. Ohmstead is very interesting—I want as I proceed to make the articles for exp—Oh how much happiness it would afford. I do long to do some thing of the kind. I must rise &* be nothing no longer.

A more verbally gifted contemporary, also entering the middle class, was able to be more explicit about the early effect on her of Mary Lyon's expectations: "I do mean to improve all I possibly can. I mean to be as wise, as consistent, as energetic, as 'planning' as sedate, as thinking, as thorough, as Miss Mary Lyon's beau ideal of a lady can be, or I should say, as Miss L. T. Guilford's capacity will allow her to be." Some parents sensed and approved these high hopes. The mother of twins attending the Seminary in 1848–49 wrote them in words they might have heard from Miss Lyon herself. "In fact, I want you to be strong minded, efficient young women—not volatile butterflies of a day, but prepared to act your part in life with energy & perseverance, and above all as Christians."[47]

The Mount Holyoke experience did make a lasting impression upon many students, as their work and their words bore witness; their families, their own students, their friends testified long afterward to their dedication and also to their veneration for Mary Lyon. Antoinette Brown Blackwell, the first Protestant woman minister ordained in the United States, at the end of her life recalled the Mount Holyoke students she had known at Oberlin, where she was a member of the class of 1847: "Some of Miss Lyon's pupils came to Oberlin to study further. I think she encouraged them in this. They were fine women, always quoting

Miss Lyon. We heard so much about her! They quoted her more than anybody else." Miss Lyon's power to reach so many of these young puritans stemmed partly from her faith in a just and loving God and partly from her close knowledge of students and her strong affection for all of them, even the frail and the flighty. Her warmth was personal and selfless; she thought about their individual circumstances and needs. In the early summer of 1847 although demands on her were already heavy, Miss Lyon found time to write a letter to send on shipboard with Mary Rice, who was going out to join Fidelia Fiske in Oroomiah, Persia. It was delivered upon her arrival, when everything around her was still strange and she could not help being aware that she might have said farewell to her home and family forever.

South Hadley, June 17, 1847

My dear Miss Rice:—

When Miss Fiske shall hand you this little note, you will be far, far away. Kind Providence preserving your life, I trust this will find you in your new, your chosen, your adopted home.

Your eyes there will look on the same glorious sun, the same beautiful moon, and the same sparkling stars that ours do in your own native land. Will it not be pleasant, when you are removed from all which once met your eyes, to look up to the heavens, and think that the eyes of your father and your mother may be looking at the same things? But nearer than this can we come together, when we approach the mercy seat. You will be no farther from that precious place of resort, no farther from your God, no farther from your last and best home in heaven. My dear, dear friend, be thou faithful unto death, and thou shalt have a crown of life.[48]

In assessing Mary Lyon's achievement, it is important to note the degree to which she continued to be on her own. Even when Mount Holyoke became a conspicuous success, she received scarcely any organized support from the established agencies for social and religious improvement. While individual ministers applauded her efforts and the ABCFM depended on her help, many clergymen who knew something of the Seminary withheld judgment or damned with faint praise; publications like *Godey's Lady's Book,* which frequently sang the praises of Emma Willard, hardly mentioned Mary Lyon. The idea that presidents of men's colleges might consider her an equal would have seemed preposterous. Apart from her sex, she had neither college nor divinity school degree and, as President Hitchcock knew by his own experience, "the prejudice among graduates toward the self-taught" was very strong. Even Catharine Beecher's activities seldom promoted Mount Holyoke. In June 1847 the brother of a Seminary student attended a meeting at the Park Street Church in Boston of the Ladies Society for Promoting Education at the West, a Beecher group formed with the help of Mrs. Banister. Young Mr. Whittemore wrote his sister that neither Mark Hopkins, president of Williams, nor any other of the reverend gentlemen who spoke said a word about Mount Holyoke. Mary Lyon's virtuosity in managing money as well as raising funds was probably not fully appreciated even by close friends during her lifetime. The Hitchcock biography in 1851 revealed that although in her twelve years as principal she had regularly given away at least half of her annual salary of $200, her personal estate, left mainly to the ABCFM, was almost $2500. By 1851 the Seminary had received gifts for land, buildings, and furnishings to a total of $68,500, all debts had been paid, and the trustees had in hand $1800 that could be invested. The annual academic and domestic operations, for which Miss Lyon had from the first assumed both fiscal and administrative responsibility, were still covered by the student fee of $60 for the 40-week year.[49]

Mary Lyon's personal qualities were partly responsible for the selective nature of the public attention she received. A country woman born and bred, she had both dignity and warmth but lacked elegance; many people needed a second look to perceive her excellences. These externals, however, were relatively unimportant; what made the difference was her inner self. She was not jealous, she did not hold resentment, she did not seek for herself the credit she was always ready to give her co-workers. She had that rarest of attributes, genuine humility. She would never under any circumstances have been willing to call the institution Miss Lyon's Seminary; that would have obscured the permanence for which she had fought so hard. She had no false modesty about the remarkable achievements through which the Seminary had been founded and sustained, but, as she repeatedly told the young ladies: "All resulted . . . from a combination of circumstances directed by God." It was He who bridged the impassable gulfs, she would say when she was explaining that her role in the resolution of successive crises was a secondary one. This way of recounting the events of her life was not apt to attract editorial attention. Hearers who knew Miss Lyon made their own translations, like the one Rebecca Fiske wrote in the journal letter: "After *all*, Miss Lyon must allow us to think, she has had *something* to do with Hol. Seminary. While we admit that the Lord has built it, we must know that he used *instruments*, and among these, Miss Lyon has not been the *least* nor the weakest."[50]

In spite of establishment skepticism and Miss Lyon's indifference to immediate fame, she was held in high esteem in much of the academic world. Mrs. Blackwell and her friends at Oberlin had thought Mount Holyoke "the highest of any woman's school in the country." A member of the committee set up to found Beloit and Rockford wrote for "a particular and correct idea" of every aspect of the Seminary, which he considered a model to be studied. Mount Holyoke in time attracted some of the socially prominent. One of the sophisticated Boston ladies who had once pronounced Mount Holyoke suitable for farmers' daughters entertained her salon by describing with pride the effect of the education received in South Hadley by the daughter of a good friend. The Hitchcock biography, published two years after Mary Lyon's death, was immediately popular. The demand continued over the next ten years; between 1851 and 1860 twelve editions appeared.[51]

It was probably after her death that Mary Lyon's impact on United States education was strongest. The proliferation of colleges for women in the second half of the nineteenth century, which she had enthusiastically predicted, and the general improvement in the quality of preparatory schools were, of course, the result of many efforts, to which Mount Holyoke alumnae contributed an important share. In 1887 Mrs. Stow listed ten "daughter" institutions, including Mills, Lake Erie, and Western colleges and schools in Persia, Spain, and South Africa, founded on Mount Holyoke principles with the aid of Mount Holyoke graduates. An accurate estimate of the number of Mount Holyoke Seminary students who presided over classrooms would require a full demographic study; the percentage is surely large. Records that are available show that a minority of Miss Lyon's young women went where no one else would go and did what no one else would do, and the great majority, scattering across the country as the frontier moved west, lived full and useful lives.[52]

The contributions to society of Mount Holyoke Seminary students and of many other young women whose opportunities for higher education developed after 1837 should establish Mary Lyon's place in nineteenth-century history; personal records of students and friends bear evidence to the intensity of felt life so often experienced in her presence. The obituaries and tributes carried after her death in religious newspapers in Boston, New York, Philadelphia, and elsewhere appear to have been written by longtime friends, nearly all ministers. The language of these tributes suggests that she had won the affection and admiration not only of the young women she taught but also of able and discriminating men of affairs. The first notice in the *New York Observer*, which did not hesitate to call Mount Holyoke "a female college," declared: "For enterprise, energy, and the successful inculcation of the principles of science and religion, she was the wonder of those who knew her." President Hitchcock, who had been a friend and supporter for nearly thirty years, gave as the commencement address in 1849 a full and carefully reasoned tribute to Mary Lyon, whom he placed "among the most remarkable women of her generation." At the end he maintained that her sudden death, distressing as it had been, occurred at the right time, "with her armor on and yet bright." The Seminary was in condition to be taken over by someone else and of late her health had been declining seriously. So, he concluded,

I cannot wish to call her back. But I do feel,—and many who hear me I doubt not feel it too,—I do feel a strong desire to be borne upward, on an angel's wing, to the Mount Zion where she now dwells, and to hear her describe, in the glowing language of heaven, the wonders of Providence, as manifested in her own earthly course, as they now appear in the bright transparencies of heaven. Yet further, I long to hear her describe the still wider plans she is now devising and executing for the good of the universe and the glory of God.[53]

Bibliography

Holograph and typed copies of letters and documents are identified in the footnotes by writer, recipient, place of origin, and date. Most of these holograph documents are in the Mount Holyoke College Archives; for those not at Mount Holyoke the footnotes give the location.

Allmendinger, David, Jr. *Paupers and Scholars: The Transformation of Student Life in Nineteenth Century New England*, New York, St. Martin's Press, 1975.

[Andrews, E. A.]. "General View of the Principles and Design of the Mount Holyoke Female Seminary," *The Religious Magazine*, new ser., 1 (1837), 184–189.

Beecher, Catharine E. *Educational Reminiscences and Suggestions*, New York, J. B. Ford, 1874.

Beecher, Lyman. *See* Cross.

Blackwell, Alice Stone. *Lucy Stone: Pioneer of Women's Rights*, Boston, 1930.

Cole, Arthur C. *A Hundred Years of Mount Holyoke College: The Evolution of an Educational Ideal*, New Haven, Yale University Press, 1940.

Cowles, Eunice Caldwell. "Notice of Miss Mary Lyon," *The Massachusetts Teacher*, 2, no. 4 (1849), 113–128. *See also* Hitchcock.

Cowles, Rev. John P., "Miss Z. P. Grant – Mrs. William B. Banister," *Barnard's American Journal of Education*, 30 (1880), 611–624.

Cross, Barbara, ed. *The Autobiography of Lyman Beecher*, 2 vols. (Cambridge, Harvard University Press, 1961), Vol. 2.

Dickinson, Emily. *See Letters*.

Dwight, Timothy. *Travels in New-England and New-York*, 4 vols. (New Haven, 1822), Vol. 4.

Emerson, Joseph. *Female Education: A Discourse Delivered at the Dedication of the Seminary Hall in Saugus, January 15, 1822*, Boston, 1823.

Emerson, Ralph. *Life of Rev. Joseph Emerson*, Boston, Crocker and Brewster, 1834.

"Female Education," *American Annals of Education*, 7 (1837), 219–222.

Fisk, Fidelia. *Recollections of Mary Lyon, with Selections from Her Instructions to the Pupils in Mt. Holyoke Female Seminary*, Boston, American Tract Society, 1866.

Fletcher, Robert Samuel. *A History of Oberlin College from Its Foundation*

Through the Civil War, 2 vols., Oberlin, Ohio, Oberlin College, 1943.

Frear, Mary Dillingham. *Lowell and Abigail: A Realistic Idyll*, New Haven, Conn., Yale University Press, 1934.

Gilchrist, Beth Bradford. *The Life of Mary Lyon*, Boston, Houghton Mifflin, 1910.

[Grant, Zilpah], "The Ipswich Female Seminary," *American Quarterly Register*, 11, no. 4 (1839), 368–375.

Guilford, L. T. *The Use of a Life: Memorials of Mrs. Z. P. Grant Banister*, New York, American Tract Society, n.d.

Hammond, William G. *Remembrance of Amherst: An Undergraduate's Diary 1846-1848*, ed. George F. Whicher, New York, Columbia University Press, 1946.

Haywood, Charlotte. "A Scientific Heritage," *Mount Holyoke Alumnae Quarterly*, 43, no. 3 (1959), 122–125.

Hitchcock, Edward. "A Chapter in the Book of Providence," *Twelfth Anniversary Address before Mount Holyoke Female Seminary, August 1, 1849*, Amherst, Mass., published by the [Mount Holyoke] Trustees, 1849.

Hitchcock, Edward. *The Power of Christian Benevolence Illustrated in the Life and Labors of Mary Lyon*, Northampton, Mass., Hopkins, Bridgman, 1851. This went through frequent reprintings to a twelfth edition in 1860; only one contained textual alterations. The edition of 1858, labeled "A New Edition," removed Hitchcock's name from the title page; the unsigned abridgments and revisions were made by Eunice Caldwell Cowles, and the volume was published by the American Tract Society.

Hitchcock, Edward. *Reminiscences of Amherst College*, Northampton, Mass., 1863.

Howes, Frederick G. *History of the Town of Ashfield, Franklin County, Massachusetts, from Its Settlement in 1742 to 1910*, Ashfield, Mass., n.d.

"The Ipswich School," *The Religious Magazine*, new ser., 1 (1837), 320–324.

James, Elias Olan. *The Story of Cyrus and Susan Mills*, Stanford, Calif., Stanford University Press, 1953.

Kendrick, Fannie Shaw. *The History of Buckland, 1779-1935*, Town of Buckland, Mass., 1937.

The Letters of Emily Dickinson, ed. Thomas H. Johnson and Theodora Ward, 3 vols., Cambridge, Mass., Harvard University Press, 1958.

"Location of Female Seminaries," *The Religious Magazine*, 2, no. 5 (1835), 232–235.

"Location of Female Seminaries," *The Religious Magazine*, 2, no. 7 (1835), 326–328.

[Lyon, Mary]. *Candidates for Mount Holyoke Female Seminary*, [July ?], 1847; minor revisions by February 1848.

Lyon, Mary. ["Circular to Ladies"], n.d. [probably November 1836], n.p.

[Lyon, Mary]. *Female Education: Tendencies of the Principles Embraced, and the System Adopted in the Mount Holyoke Female Seminary*, South Hadley, Mass., 1839.

[Lyon, Mary]. *General View of the Principles and Design of the Mount Holyoke Female Seminary*, Boston, Mass., February 1837.

Lyon, Mary. Letters and Documents. Volume 1, Letters 1825-1839; Volume 2, Letters 1839-1849, Documents 1821-1843. A selection of the holograph and typescript letters and papers in the Mount Holyoke College Archives, bound in two volumes.

[Lyon, Mary]. *A Missionary Offering, or Christian Sympathy, Personal Responsibility, and the Present Crisis in Foreign Missions*, Boston, Crocker and Brewster, 1843.

[Lyon, Mary]. *Mount Holyoke Female Seminary, Preparation for Admission*, South Hadley, Mass., September 1840.

McLean, Sydney R. "Emily Dickinson at Mount Holyoke," *New England Quarterly*, 7 (1934), 25-42.

Magnusson, Margaret L. "'Your Affectionate Mary,' A Vermont Girl at Mount Holyoke," *Vermont History*, 31, no. 3 (1963), 181-192.

Martineau, Harriet. *Retrospect of Western Travel*, 2 vols. (London, Saunders and Otley, 1838), Vol. 2.

Mary Lyon Through Her Letters, ed. Marion Lansing, Boston, Books, Inc., 1937.

Memoir of Mrs. Lucy T. Lord of the Chinese Baptist Mission, Philadelphia, American Baptist Publication Society, 1854.

"Memorabilia of Mary Lyon," ed. Amelia Woodward Truesdell, n.d. A collection of oral and written reminiscences gathered between 1905 and 1908; typescript.

Miller, Perry. *The Life of the Mind in America from the Revolution to the Civil War*, New York, Harcourt, Brace and World, 1965, Books One through Three.

"Monticello," *The Echo*, Monticello Seminary, 9 (1898), 3-7.

Morison, Samuel Eliot. *Three Centuries of Harvard, 1636-1936*, Cambridge, Harvard University Press, 1936.

"Motives to Study in the Ipswich Female Seminary," *American Annals of Education*, 3, no. 2 (1833), 75-80.

Mount Holyoke Alumnae Association. *One Hundred Year Biographical Directory, Mount Holyoke College, South Hadley, Massachusetts, 1837-1937*, ed. Mary C. J. Higley, South Hadley, Mass., 1937.

Mount Holyoke Committee of 1834. Records of the Committee September 6, 1834, to October 9, 1835.

Mount Holyoke Female Seminary. *Memorial: Twenty-Fifth Anniversary of the Mt. Holyoke Female Seminary*, South Hadley, Mass., 1862.

Mount Holyoke Female Seminary. *Third Annual Catalogue of the Officers and Members*, South Hadley, Mass., 1839-40.

Mount Holyoke Seminary. *Semi-Centennial Celebration of Mount Holyoke*

BIBLIOGRAPHY

Seminary, 1837–1887, ed. Sarah Locke Stow, South Hadley, Mass., 1887.

Mount Holyoke Trustees. Records of the Trustees of Mount Holyoke Female Seminary March 2, 1836 – February 26, 1913, 2 vols.

Norton, Helen. *Memorials of Mary W. (Chapin) Pease and Lydia W. Shattuck,* Boston, Beacon Press, 1890.

Notable American Women 1607–1950: A Biographical Dictionary, 3 vols., Cambridge, Mass., Harvard University Press, 1971.

Pierson, George Wilson. *Tocqueville and Beaumont in America,* New York, Oxford University Press, 1938.

Rudolph, Frederick. *The American College and University,* New York, Alfred A. Knopf, 1962.

Safford, Mrs. Ann E. *A Memoir of Daniel Safford by His Wife,* Boston, American Tract Society, 1861.

"Seminary for Female Teachers, at Ipswich, Mass.," *American Annals of Education,* 3, no. 2 (1833), 69–75.

Sewall, Richard. *The Life of Emily Dickinson,* 2 vols. (New York, Farrar, Straus and Giroux, 1974), Vol. 2.

Sklar, Kathryn Kish. *Catharine Beecher: A Study in American Domesticity,* New Haven, Yale University Press, 1973.

Smith, Timothy L. *Revivalism and Social Reform in Mid-Nineteenth-Century America,* New York, Abingdon Press, 1957.

Stow, Sarah D. Locke. *History of Mount Holyoke Seminary, South Hadley, Mass., during the First Half Century, 1837–1887,* South Hadley, Mount Holyoke Seminary, 1887.

Tewksbury, Donald G. *The Founding of American Colleges and Universities Before the Civil War,* New York, Teachers' College Press, Columbia University, 1932.

"To Correspondents," *The Religious Magazine,* new ser., 1 (1837), 239.

Tyler, William S. *Autobiography of William Seymour Tyler,* privately printed, 1912.

Tyler, William S. *History of Amherst College,* Springfield, Mass., 1873.

Waters, Thomas Franklin. *Ipswich in the Massachusetts Bay Colony,* 2 vols. (Ipswich, Mass., Ipswich Historical Society, 1917), Vol. 2.

Woody, Thomas. *A History of Women's Education in the United States,* 2 vols., New York, Science Press, 1929.

Young, Andrew W. *History of Chautauqua County, N.Y.,* Buffalo, N.Y., 1875.

Notes

Seven works frequently cited in short title form are:

Fisk, *Recollections.*
> Fidelia Fisk, *Recollections of Mary Lyon, with Selections from Her Instructions to the Pupils in Mt. Holyoke Female Seminary* (Boston, American Tract Society, 1866).

Guilford, *Use.*
> L. T. Guilford, *The Use of a Life: Memorials of Mrs. Z. P. Grant Banister* (New York, American Tract Society, n.d.).

Hitchcock, *Mary Lyon.*
> Edward Hitchcock, *The Power of Christian Benevolence Illustrated in the Life and Labors of Mary Lyon* (Northampton, Bridgman and Childs, 1852).

Letters and Documents.
> A selection of Mary Lyon's holograph letters and papers in the Mount Holyoke College Archives, bound in two volumes: Vol. 1, Letters, 1825–1839; Vol. 2, Letters, 1839–1849, and Documents, 1821–1843.

Memorabilia.
> A typescript collection of oral and written reminiscences collected between 1905 and 1908 and edited by Amelia Woodward Truesdell, n.d.

Missionary Offering.
> Mary Lyon's only bit of published autobiography appears in her unsigned book *A Missionary Offering, or Christian Sympathy, Personal Responsibility, and the Present Crisis in Foreign Missions* (Boston, Crocker and Brewster, 1843).

Stow, *History.*
> Sarah D. Locke Stow, *History of Mount Holyoke Seminary, South Hadley, Mass., during the First Half Century, 1837–1887* (South Hadley, Mount Holyoke Seminary, 1887).

1. Knowledge by Handfuls

1. Mary Lyon to Freelove, Ipswich, August 26, 1834. Hitchcock, *Mary Lyon*, pp. 121, 122.

2. Fidelia Fisk, *Recollections*, pp. 11, 14. Her name is usually spelled with a final "e" in college records and in general reference works. Hitchcock, *Mary Lyon*, p. 2. The first section of *Mary Lyon* was written mainly by Hannah White. See *Missionary Offering*, p. 60, for reference to the funeral.

3. *Missionary Offering*, pp. 58–59.

4. Fisk, *Recollections*, p. 30.

5. Fannie Shaw Kendrick, *The History of Buckland, 1779-1935* (Buckland, Mass., 1937), p. 57, for details about cooking. Frederick G. Howes, *History of the Town of Ashfield, Franklin County, Massachusetts, from Its Settlement in 1742 to 1910* (Ashfield, Mass., n.d.), pp. 337-338. The recollections of candle-making, spinning, and weaving were written down at the age of 90 by a retired Ashfield teacher who had been born in 1817.

6. Howes, *Ashfield*, pp. 335-336.

7. Hitchcock, *Mary Lyon*, p. 253.

8. Ibid., p. 8.

9. See the inventory of Aaron Lyon's estate—signed May 31, 1803, in Northampton Probate Court—found and copied by Sydney R. McLean. The inventory listed 150 items, including a toasting iron worth 12 cents and a pair of shoes worth 17 cents, but no books. For the trip to church see *Missionary Offering*, p. 59.

10. ML's was "a family which is known to have excelled in intelligence and scholarship," according to Hannah White (Hitchcock, *Mary Lyon*, p. 7). For sermons, ibid., p. 9 and Fisk, *Recollections*, pp. 32-34.

11. Fisk, *Recollections*, pp. 159-160.

12. *Missionary Offering*, pp. 58-59.

13. Kendrick, *Buckland*, pp. 225-226. These reminiscences by Joseph Griswold, 75, a local manufacturer, were part of the address he delivered at the Buckland Centennial, September 10, 1879.

14. Joseph Griswold to Miss Julia Ward, Griswoldville, October 9, 1879.

15. See Guilford, *Use*, pp. 13-14, and a letter from Eunice Caldwell Cowles to Lucinda Guilford, Ipswich, March 7, 1884. In persuading Miss Guilford to minimize this procedure in the biography, Mrs. Cowles observed, "She was but fifteen years old and had not probably then known there was any other way of managing a refractory child." ML's reminiscence comes from Fisk, *Recollections*, p. 36.

16. Hitchcock, *Mary Lyon*, p. 37.

17. At Sanderson, Burritt must already have been at work on his first textbook, *Logarithmick Arithmetick*, published in September 1818. His major work, the astronomy text *Geography of the Heavens*, was much used in schools and colleges for a generation; by the time he had it ready for the press, Mary Lyon was one of the selected teachers whose approval he sought in advance; see his letter to her from New Britain, August 3, 1832. Also Hitchcock, *Mary Lyon*, pp. 261-262, 26 and Stow, *History*, p. 16.

18. Quoted by Amanda Ferry Hall, the daughter of Amanda White, from an unidentified letter. This reminiscence was probably written after 1900.
19. Howes, *Ashfield*, p. 223.
20. Most of the early descriptions of such difficulties go back to Amanda; cf. Hitchcock, *Mary Lyon*, pp. 15-16, and sketches long afterward by two of her daughters, Amanda Ferry Hall and Mrs. H. W. Jones. A later comment on her appearance is made by Mrs. Cowles (Hitchcock, pp. 283-285). Two men whose acquaintance with her covered a span of years tended to minimize these limitations. President Hitchcock of Amherst said, "The idea that Miss Lyon was gross in her manners, and negligent in her dress, after she became a teacher, is not true" (*Mary Lyon*, p. 467). Joseph Griswold, the manufacturer with the long memory, declared, "I never saw her when she was not dressed neat and tidy, and good enough for the position which she occupied" (Kendrick, *Buckland*, p. 232).
21. Hitchcock, *Mary Lyon*, p. 13.
22. ML to Polly Newhall, Buckland, April 7, 1818.
23. Andrew W. Young, *History of Chautauqua County, N.Y.* (Buffalo, N.Y., 1875), p. 558, has data about the migration.
24. Hitchcock, *Mary Lyon*, p. 37. Also ML to her mother, Londonderry, N.H., September 25, 1825; ML to Zilpah Polly Grant, Buckland, December 26, 1825; Hitchcock, pp. 44-46. Later on she explained to the students at Ipswich how she acquired this command: "if we were unhappy, it was probably because we had so many thoughts about ourselves, and so few about the happiness of others. She asked us to call to mind an unhappy day, and inquire whether we, during that day, had had large desires for the conversion of the world. She also said that, at one period of her life, she used to be dejected and unhappy; but she came to the conclusion that there was too much to be done for her to spend time in that manner. Since that, she had experienced but little unhappiness" (Hitchcock, *Mary Lyon*, p. 89).
25. Amanda White to ML, letter dated Ashfield, July 16, 1818, broken off, redated January 31, 1819; uncatalogued. The version of Mrs. Cowles (Hitchcock, *Mary Lyon*, p. 254), is not corroborated by Fidelia Fisk, *Recollections*, p. 45, who thought Mary left home "with her parents' approbation"; but it seems to be supported by the undated reminiscence about the horse, by Mrs. H. W. Jones, daughter of Amanda.
26. ML to her mother, Byfield, May 13, 1821. Hitchcock, *Mary Lyon*, p. 18.
27. Ralph Emerson, *Life of Rev. Joseph Emerson* (Boston, Crocker and Brewster, 1834), p. 246.
28. ML to R. Emerson, April 12, 1834. R. Emerson, *Joseph Emerson*, pp. 420-423.
29. Ibid., p. 162. ML to her sister Rosina, Byfield, July 30, 1821. Hitchcock, *Mary Lyon*, p. 22.
30. Ralph Emerson to Dr. Bela B. Edwards, Wethersfield, Conn., October 26,

1826; and ZPG to R. Emerson, Ipswich, April 1834. R. Emerson, *Joseph Emerson*, pp. 306-307, 432.

31. Hitchcock, *Mary Lyon*, p. 16. ML to her mother, [Buckland], July 21, 1821. Hitchcock, *Mary Lyon*, p. 20.

32. ML to her mother, [Buckland], July 21, 1821. Hitchcock, *Mary Lyon*, pp. 19-20.

33. Joseph Emerson to R. Emerson, Beverly, November 12, 1807, when the latter had just been accepted at Yale. JE to his wife, Williamstown, July 2, 1812. R. Emerson, *Joseph Emerson*, pp. 161, 202.

34. Ibid., pp. 259, 38, 301-312.

35. Ibid., pp. 331-334.

36. Letters from Amanda, one in 1821, one after ML's death; Hitchcock, *Mary Lyon*, pp. 15-16.

37. The nature of the excisions and "improvements" can be seen in the letters that did survive in manuscript form. The most substantive alterations were probably in the early letters. See, for example, a letter to Hannah White from Londonderry, N.H., July 2, 1824, which is virtually rewritten in Hitchcock, *Mary Lyon*, pp. 30-31, and a letter to Zilpah Grant from Ashfield, February 28, 1827, where the version in Hitchcock, *Mary Lyon*, pp. 52-53, omits two thirds of the original, including all the names and personal messages: it is not Mary but Zilpah who has failed to write; Hannah White is improving as assistant; will Zilpah buy nine yards of gingham and trimmings for Mary's bonnet?

38. ML to her mother, [Buckland], July 21, 1821. ML to Rosina, Byfield, July 30, 1821. Hitchcock, *Mary Lyon*, pp. 18-21, 21-22, 7.

39. JE to Dr. Leonard Woods, Wethersfield, Conn., March 31, 1833. R. Emerson, *Joseph Emerson*, p. 402. Joseph Emerson, *Female Education: A Discourse Delivered at the Dedication of the Seminary Hall in Saugus, January 15, 1822* (Boston, 1823), pp. 32-33.

2. A Throne of Her Own

1. ML to Hannah White, Londonderry, N.H., July 2, 1824; the version in Hitchcock, *Mary Lyon*, pp. 30-31, has been extensively rewritten. "The intelligence which we receive of the work of grace in Dartmouth College is refreshing. I hope the students from Ashfield share in the work." ML to her mother, Derry, N.H., May 20, 1826; Hitchcock, *Mary Lyon*, p. 47.

2. His religious concern never abated. He exchanged the pastorate for the professorship in 1825 only because he felt his health was not up to the demands of the ministry. He considered natural theology the most important subject he taught and was a central figure in a number of Amherst College revivals. See Edward Hitchcock, *Reminiscences of Amherst College* (Northampton, Mass., 1863), pp. 287-292.

3. ML to ZPG, Ashfield, December 1, 1823; Hitchcock, *Mary Lyon*, pp. 26-27.

4. ECC to Lucinda T. Guilford, Ipswich, March 7, 1884.

5. *North American Review*, 143 (1886), 329-344. Beth Bradford Gilchrist, *The Life of Mary Lyon* (Boston, Houghton Mifflin, 1910), p. 13. Rev. John P. Cowles, "Miss Z. P. Grant-Mrs. William B. Banister," *Barnard's American Journal of Education*, 30 (1880), 611-624.

6. JE to ZPG, Saugus, May 8, 1822. R. Emerson, *Joseph Emerson*, p. 261; this eloquent appeal for her services concluded, "I hope no lion will be in the way of your coming." JE to ZPG, Wethersfield, Conn., June 19, 1830. R. Emerson, *Joseph Emerson*, p. 337. Ibid., pp. 375-376.

7. ML to Miss C. (Hannah Chickering), Buckland, February 21, 1825; Hitchcock, *Mary Lyon*, p. 41. ML to ZPG, Buckland, February 2, 1829; Hitchcock, *Mary Lyon*, p. 69. Sometime after Adams opened, the town of Londonderry divided and the section where the school was located was called Derry. Some letters and contracts use the old term, some the new.

8. ML to Amanda White Ferry, Londonderry, N.H., September 26, 1824; Hitchcock, *Mary Lyon*, p. 33.

9. ML to Hannah White, Londonderry, N.H., July 2, 1824. The version in Hitchcock, *Mary Lyon*, pp. 30-31, differs in many details.

10. Hitchcock, *Mary Lyon*, pp. 139-140. Guilford, *Use*, p. 111.

11. ML to Amanda White Ferry, Londonderry, N.H., September 26, 1824; Hitchcock, *Mary Lyon*, p. 35.

12. ML to ZPG, Ashfield, February 28, 1827. ZPG to ML, Derry, N.H., February 6, 1828; Guilford, *Use*, p. 94.

13. ML to Mrs. Pettibone, Londonderry, N.H., June 24, 1825; portions of words supplied where sheet is torn off.

14. ML to Hannah Chickering Briggs, Londonderry, N.H., June 1, 1827; letter owned by Norwood, Massachusetts, Historical Society.

15. L. and A. Woods to ZPG, Andover, July 16, 1827.

16. ZPG to ML, Derry, N.H., February 6, 1828; Guilford, *Use*, pp. 93-94.

17. ML to Freelove Lyon, Londonderry, N.H., October 25, 1826; Hitchcock, *Mary Lyon*, pp. 50-51.

18. Ibid., p. 50.

19. ML to Hannah Chickering Briggs, a fellow teacher at Derry, Buckland, February 21, 1825; Hitchcock, *Mary Lyon*, pp. 40-41.

20. ML to ZPG, Buckland, December 26, 1825; quotations are from a copy made by Professor Sydney R. McLean of excised portions of the letter in Hitchcock, *Mary Lyon*, pp. 44-45. Zilpah had apparently warned Mary against employing Hannah White, and Mary was apologetic: "I know this seems a little like not taking your advice, but when I tell you all, I believe you will think I could not do better" (ML to ZPG, Buckland, January 1, 1830); Hitchcock, *Mary Lyon*, p. 75. For student accounts of mealtime conversation, see Maria Cowles to Henry Cowles, Buckland, November 25, 1829, copy obtained by Professor McLean; also Lydia Farnham to Samuel Fletcher, Ipswich, January 5, 1833.

21. ML to ZPG, Ashfield, January 6, 1828; Hitchcock, *Mary Lyon*, p. 58.

22. Barbara Cross, *The Autobiography of Lyman Beecher* (Cambridge, Harvard University Press, 1961), 2: 45.
23. ML to ZPG, Ashfield, March 18, 1828; Hitchcock, *Mary Lyon*, p. 64. ML to Rosina Lyon Ellsworth, Buckland, March 9, 1830; Hitchcock, *Mary Lyon*, p. 76.
24. For visitors see ML to ZPG, Ashfield, February 28, 1827, Buckland, March 2, 1829; Hitchcock, *Mary Lyon*, p. 71. Also Fisk, *Recollections*, p. 69. Also Susan —— to Abigail Tenney, Buckland, January 30, 1830; and Mary Dillingham Frear, *Lowell and Abigail: A Realistic Idyll* (New Haven, Yale University Press, 1934), p. 13.
25. Susan —— to Abigail Tenney, Buckland, January 30, 1830, in Frear, *Lowell*, p. 13. Buckland School, 1830: "Questions on Intellectual Philosophy," in bundle so labeled in ML's handwriting.
26. Maria Cowles to Henry Cowles, Buckland, November 25, 1829; copy obtained by Professor McLean.
27. ML to Amanda White Ferry, Buckland, February 20, 1826; Hitchcock, *Mary Lyon*, p. 46. ML to Rosina Lyon Ellsworth, Buckland, March 9, 1830; Hitchcock, *Mary Lyon*, pp. 76–77. Fisk, *Recollections*, p. 67.
28. She acknowledged another kind of love, "displeasing in the sight of God," and prayed for the right kind. ML to her mother, Londonderry, N.H., September 7, 1825; Hitchcock, *Mary Lyon*, p. 42. ML to Freelove Lyon, Derry, N.H., August 22, 1827; Hitchcock, *Mary Lyon*, pp. 53–54.
29. ML to Hannah Chickering Briggs, Ipswich, September 3, 1828 (owned by Norwood Historical Society), and September 26, 1828 (owned by Wheaton College Archives). James Melledge to ML, Boston, October 8, 1828. ML to ZPG, Buckland, February 2, 1829; Hitchcock, *Mary Lyon*, p. 69.
30. ML to ZPG, Londonderry, N.H., July 25, 1826; ML to Freelove Lyon, Londonderry, N.H., July 30, 1826; Hitchcock, *Mary Lyon*, pp. 49–50.
31. ZPG to ML, Dedham, February 29, 1827; Guilford, *Use*, pp. 22–23, also p. 87.
32. ZPG to ML, Derry, N.H., January 7, 1828 and February 6, 1828; Guilford, *Use*, pp. 90, 91–94. Zilpah must have felt triumphant in 1830 when the Adams executive committee asked her to come back to run the academy in her own way. By that time Ipswich had outdistanced Adams at its best.
33. ML to ZPG, Ashfield, November 26, 1827, December 10, 1827, December 26, 1827, January 8, 1828; Hitchcock, *Mary Lyon*, pp. 54, 55, 56, 59.
34. ML to ZPG, Ashfield, January 19, 1828, February 12, 1828; Hitchcock, *Mary Lyon*, pp. 59, 60.
35. ZPG to ML, Ipswich, January 11, 1829; in edited form it appears in Guilford, *Use*, pp. 138–139.
36. ML to ZPG, Buckland, January 22, 1829; Hitchcock, *Mary Lyon*, p. 129.
37. Guilford, *Use*, pp. 143–144, 142.
38. Catharine Beecher to ZPG, place unspecified, n.d. [summer 1829] ; Guilford, *Use*, p. 142.

39. Hannah White to Mrs. Thomas White, Ipswich, August 7, 1829; copy in Professor Sydney R. McLean's notes. ZPG: "Arguments *for* & *against* Miss Grant's uniting with Miss Beecher," n.d.

40. Catharine did not find any other co-head or get the endowment money or escape the physical collapse she had warned of. Within two years she resigned as principal of the seminary. Early in 1832 she went with her father to Cincinnati, where she again started a school, but her major impact on the education of women came through her writing, lectures, and organizing activities, not through classroom teaching.

41. ZPG to ML, Ipswich, Thurs. P.M. January 21 [1830]; a brief edited excerpt appears in Guilford, *Use,* p. 150. In spite of the tone of this letter to Mary, Zilpah probably was not irritated by the offers from Franklin County or by one she mentioned that was pending from Andover; she took care that word of all such proposals reached the Ipswich trustees in good season.

3. Trial Run

1. ML to ZPG, December 9, 1829; Hitchcock, *Mary Lyon,* pp. 130-131.

2. At both Unitarian Harvard and Calvinist Amherst attempts were made in the 1820's to break the stranglehold of Greek and Latin on the curriculum. At Harvard, Ticknor succeeded in building up a modern language department in spite of entrenched faculty resistance. At Amherst a "parallel" course, strong in science and modern languages, was voted by the faculty in 1826 but failed to attract students. Samuel Eliot Morison, *Three Centuries of Harvard, 1636-1936* (Cambridge, Harvard University Press, 1936), pp. 228-238. William S. Tyler, *History of Amherst College* (Springfield, Mass., 1873), pp. 170-173.

3. Notebook of Lydia Fletcher Clark, student at Ipswich October 30, 1833, to April 22, 1834, entry of February 20, 1834.

4. ZPG to ML, Ipswich, Thurs. P.M. January 21 [1830]. ML to ZPG, Ipswich, January 29, 1832; Hitchcock, *Mary Lyon,* pp. 81-82.

5. "Motives to Study in the Ipswich Female Seminary," *American Annals of Education,* 3, no. 2 (1833), 75-80.

6. ML to ZPG, Buckland, January 20, 1830, Ipswich, March 18, 1832; Hitchcock, *Mary Lyon,* pp. 76, 82. ML to Miss Cole, Ashfield, March 20, 1830. ZPG to ML, Ipswich, February 5, 1829.

7. ML to ZPG, Philadelphia, July—, 1833, and Detroit, September 18, 1833; Hitchcock, *Mary Lyon,* pp. 98-99, 107.

8. Mrs. E. C. Cowles, "Notice of Miss Mary Lyon," *The Massachusetts Teacher,* 2, no. 4 (1849), 123-125.

9. Hitchcock, *Mary Lyon,* ed. 1858, p. 90.

10. Eight of these 11 names did appear in the list of 19 seniors published in the next catalogue; of the three who did not achieve diplomas, one had fallen ill and died.

11. Hitchcock, *Mary Lyon,* ed. 1858, p. 200.

12. Guilford, *Use*, pp. 136–137, 151.
13. ML to ZPG, Ipswich, November 9, 1832; Hitchcock, *Mary Lyon*, pp. 88–89. Ibid., p. 153.
14. Letters and Documents, 1:15–18.
15. Susan Smith to ML, Chillicothe, Ohio, May 8, 1831.
16. Susan Smith Little and Rev. Henry Little to ZPG and ML, Oxford, Butler County, Ohio, November 9, 1831. Obadiah Smith to ML, Hatfield, April 21, 1832.
17. He soon got a job in Tennessee teaching Latin and Greek, and Eliza joined him there. They had two sons before her death in 1835. He continued to make a name for himself and served as president of Middlebury College from 1840 to 1866.
18. E. P. Labaree to ML, Oxford, Ohio, December 12, 1831. The advent of the Beechers was widely discussed in 1831. Lyman Beecher had been elected head of the new Lane Theological Seminary in October 1830 but was slow in making up his mind. After the election was repeated in January 1832 he finally accepted; he and Catharine arrived in Cincinnati for an exploratory visit in April. Catharine got the Western Female Institute going in 1833, but she too encountered a lack of public concern, and this school lasted less than five years.
19. Henry and Susan N. Little to ML, Oxford, Ohio, March 5, 1833.
20. Delia Allyn to ML, Chillicothe, Ohio, June 18, 1833. Mr. Pomroy was not mentioned; final decisions seemed to be made by Sarah Stearns.
21. ML to Rev. Charles C. Beatty, Ipswich, February 6, 1834.
22. Louisa Packard to ML, Palmer, July 7, 1829, and Philadelphia, September 25 - November 22, 1834. No other letters from Louisa survive; she died of consumption in 1841 at the age of 34.
23. Harriet Fairchild to ML, Derry, N.H., June 22, 1832.
24. Louisa Billings to ML, Buckland, December 15, 1830.
25. Abigail Tenney Smith to ML, Union Village, N.Y., October 24, 1831. Her tenure was brief; a letter of October 6, 1832, described her marriage to the Rev. Lowell Smith and the imminence of their departure as missionaries to the Sandwich Islands, i.e. Hawaii. She had obviously been in touch with Ipswich in the meantime; along with pieties suitable to her new estate, she sent thanks for the gifts of clothing the girls had made for her to take with her.
26. Eliza Adams to ML, Mount Vernon, Ohio, September 17, 1833, November 28, 1833.
27. Guilford, *Use*, pp. 154–155. Hitchcock, *Mary Lyon*, p. 158.
28. ZPG and ML to the Trustees of Ipswich Female Academy, Ipswich, February 17, 1831; Hitchcock, *Mary Lyon*, p. 159.
29. ML to Professor Hitchcock, Ipswich, February 4, 1832; Hitchcock, *Mary Lyon*, p. 161.
30. The five whose zeal flagged were the Rev. Warren Fay of Charlestown, who did join Mr. Felt and Mr. Heard in signing a printed appeal for funds;

William Heard, Ipswich shipbuilder, who did take the trouble to attend the dissolution meeting; Ralph Emerson, Zilpah's former pastor and professor of ecclesiastical history at Andover Theological Seminary; William Reed of Marblehead, merchant, former member of Congress, and philanthropist serving on the boards of Dartmouth, Andover, and several benevolent societies; Rufus Choate of Salem, noted lawyer and orator then serving his second term in the House of Representatives.

31. ML to Professor Hitchcock, Ipswich, February 4, 1832; Hitchcock, *Mary Lyon*, pp. 162, 164.

32. Guilford, *Use*, pp. 160-165.

33. Ibid., pp. 160-165. See also ML, Letters and Documents, "Explanation of a plan of buildings," 2:347-356. Zilpah may have seen and approved a draft of the 1832 prospectus. She apparently spent the summer within reach—near Boston—and she obviously wanted to be included. A copy of the circular among her papers bore the handwritten notation "In this plan Misses Grant and Lyon were associated." As to the organization and phrasing, there seems no reason to question Mrs. Cowles's testimony in Hitchcock, *Mary Lyon*, p. 167: "This circular bears strongly the imprint of Miss Lyon's mind and hand."

34. ML to J. B. Felt, July 3, 1832; Thomas Franklin Waters, *Ipswich in the Massachusetts Bay Colony* (Ipswich, Mass., Ipswich Historical Society, 1917), 2:555. ML to ZPG, Ipswich, November 29, 1832; Hitchcock, *Mary Lyon*, p. 168.

35. ML to ZPG, Boston, February 4, 1833; Hitchcock, *Mary Lyon*, pp. 171-172.

36. ML to ZPG, Ipswich, February 24, 1833; Hitchcock, *Mary Lyon*, pp. 174-176. Rev. Daniel Crosby to ML, place unspecified, February 20, 1833; Hitchcock, *Mary Lyon*, p. 173.

37. ML to D. Crosby, n.p., n.d., in Letters and Documents, 1:33-34.

38. ML to ZPG, [probably Ipswich], April 6, 1833; Hitchcock, *Mary Lyon*, p. 183. ML [to ZPG?], from Amherst, April 25; ML, place unspecified, "six weeks later;" Hitchcock, *Mary Lyon*, p. 166.

39. ML to Hannah Chickering Briggs, Ipswich, May 14, 1833; Hitchcock, *Mary Lyon*, p. 95.

40. Guilford, *Use*, p. 155.

41. Hitchcock, *Mary Lyon*, ed. 1858, p. 97.

42. She mentioned Mary Lyon's succession of close friends, "with whom she loved to talk over her own affairs, opinions, and feelings, and to whom she confided a thousand little interests, which concerned nobody but herself"—without even hinting that she herself had been such a friend. Professor Hitchcock took pains to make the identification in the section he wrote. Hitchcock, *Mary Lyon*, pp. 257, 292.

43. ML to ZPG, [Ipswich], December 9, 1832; Hitchcock, *Mary Lyon*, pp. 168-170.

44. ML to ZPG, Ipswich, March 1, 1833; Hitchcock, *Mary Lyon*, pp. 176-182.

45. ML to ZPG, [Ipswich] , May 2, 1833; Hitchcock, *Mary Lyon*, p. 182.
46. ML to ZPG, Rochester, N.Y., October 12, 1833; Hitchcock, *Mary Lyon*, p. 109. Sydney R. McLean, "Grant, Zilpah Polly," in *Notable American Women 1607–1950* (Cambridge, Harvard University Press, 1971), 2:75. One striking example of Zilpah's pique was the ten-page history of her seminary in Derry and then in Ipswich, printed in the final Ipswich catalogue dated April 1839 and also published in the *American Quarterly Register* for May 1839. In this detailed account of her educational theory and practice over fifteen years there is no mention of Mary Lyon by name nor any reference to the existence of an assistant principal.
47. ML to Abigail Moore, Ipswich, n.d.; Hitchcock, *Mary Lyon*, p. 92.
48. ML to ZPG, Ipswich, January 23, 1833; Hitchcock, *Mary Lyon*, p. 94. Account of death of Sarah Jane Kingsley, September 19, 1832, with penciled attribution to Nancy Emerson, probably written by M.G.; see ML to ZPG, Ipswich, September 15, 1832; Hitchcock, *Mary Lyon*, p. 86.
49. *American Annals of Education*, 3, no. 2 (1833), 69–75. In this article neither Mary Lyon nor Zilpah Grant was mentioned by name; references were made to "the superintendent" and "the two principal teachers" without any indication that one was absent. Jacob Abbott to ZPG, place unspecified, n.d., but endorsed in her handwriting August 1833. Abbott was well known in New England as principal, editor, and prolific author; among his 180 volumes were the 28 in the Rollo series for boys.
50. Eunice Caldwell, 1832 Notebook October 31 – November 21, entry for Thursday, November 15.
51. Lydia Farnham to Samuel Fletcher, Ipswich, January 5, 1833.

4. The Great Work Accomplished

1. Hitchcock, *Mary Lyon*, pp. 96–109.
2. Ibid., pp. 99–100.
3. Ibid., p. 106.
4. From ML's travel notebook in the section headed "June 1833. General memorandum of journeying." Apparently homemade, the notebook has no cover or pagination; 29 of the 84 pages are blank.
5. The three who saw ML were Charles Larned, Di Garmo Jones, and Eustis P. Hastings. They had met with the other incorporators of a society for the promotion of female education on March 18, 1830, and were elected officers on March 24. Information from Mrs. Alice C. Dalligan, Chief of the Burton Historical Collection of the Detroit Public Library. ML's comment is in Hitchcock, *Mary Lyon*, p. 123.
6. ML to ZPG, Amherst, December 23, 1835; Hitchcock, *Mary Lyon*, pp. 219–221.
7. George Wilson Pierson, *Tocqueville and Beaumont in America* (New York, Oxford University Press, 1938), pp. 381–382. His conversation with President Josiah Quincy took place September 20, 1831.

8. ML to EC, South Hadley Canal, March 9 [1836]. The 4,000 word article on which she was then working was not accepted by a magazine, as she had been hoping, nor was it issued in pamphlet form, but it did appear in three installments in the *Boston Recorder,* 31, nos. 20, 21, 22, for May 13, 20, 27, 1836.

9. ML, Letters and Documents, 2:389-392. Manuscript corrections have been silently incorporated into the text. The manuscript is undated but was probably written in 1833; it may have been composed while there was still a faint hope for the New England Seminary for Teachers.

10. ML to Hannah White, Ipswich, August 1, 1834; Hitchcock, *Mary Lyon,* p. 199. As she went on speaking and writing, she found still other advantages. The pamphlet she prepared in February 1837 made no mention of saving money and stressed the value of domestic work in freeing students and teachers from "servile dependence on common domestics."

11. This printed letter carried the salutation "Brethern and Friends," was signed by John Todd, Joseph Penney, Roswell Hawks, Committee to Address the Public, and had a Northampton date line. Even these enlightened supporters of the cause used some phrases Mary Lyon must have winced at. In talking about the plan for domestic work, they explained the purpose, "that its pupils may learn those duties and acquire those habits of domestic economy," when she had just been saying, in "School for Adult Females" among other places, "It is no part of the proposed plan to teach young ladies domestic pursuits."

12. This pamphlet, entitled "Mount Holyoke Female Seminary" and dated South Hadley, September 1835, must have occasioned severe struggles over composition. The front page says in parentheses "Not Published," and a note at the end asks recipients "to make no more use of it than they would of a written communication." An urgent note from Mary Lyon to one of the committee members wanted to make sure that the "article" would not be printed before she had time for further verbal alterations; she had sent it to members of the committee for preliminary consideration. ML to Rev. William Tyler, Ipswich, September 5, 1835.

13. The three installments were carried, without any indication of authorship beyond the label "For the Boston Recorder" or any mention of Mary Lyon in the text, in the *Boston Recorder,* 31, nos. 20, 21, 22, for May 13, 20, 27, 1836.

14. The letter was signed "Mary Lyon," and had the salutation "Dear Madam" and space for dates of writing and of requested reply. A notebook endorsed "Printed letters sent away" contains 110 names to which copies were sent between November 28 and May 11.

15. Hitchcock, *Mary Lyon,* p. 298. This was the publication that precipitated a most ungenerous attack in *The Religious Magazine.* In spite of that unpleasantness, the pamphlet must have been effective; at their meeting on April 12 the trustees voted a second edition of 2,000 copies, which were printed in May. Mary Lyon's name did not appear in either edition.

16. ML to ZPG, Boston, February 4, 1833; Hitchcock, *Mary Lyon,* p. 172.

17. The first members were Rev. Daniel Dana, Newburyport; Rev. Theophilus Packard, Shelburne; Rev. Edward Hitchcock, Professor at Amherst; Rev. Joseph B. Felt, Hamilton; George W. Heard, Ipswich; Gen. Asa Howland, Conway; David Choate, Essex.

18. The charter (below), approved February 10, 1836, lists as trustees William Bowdoin, South Hadley Falls; Rev. John Todd, Northampton; Rev. Joseph D. Condit, South Hadley; David Choate, Essex; Samuel Williston, Easthampton. The minutes of the meeting of October 7-9, 1835, in South Hadley, show that Mr. Heard was named to the third ad hoc subcommittee to determine the number and names of trustees to be submitted on the charter, the first subcommittee having failed and the second declined to serve. Mrs. Cowles's observations about Mr. Heard are recorded in Hitchcock, *Mary Lyon*, p. 205.

Commonwealth of Massachusetts.
In the Year of our Lord one thousand eight hundred and thirty-six.
An Act to incorporate Mount-Holyoke Female Seminary.

Be it enacted by the Senate and House of Representatives in General Court assembled and by the authority of the same, that William Bowdoin, John Todd, Joseph D. Condit, David Choate, and Samuel Williston, their associates and successors be and are hereby incorporated by the name of the Trustees of Mount-Holyoke Female Seminary, to be established in South-Hadley in the County of Hampshire, with the powers and privileges and subject to the duties and liabilities provided in "Chapter forty-fourth of the Revised Statutes passed November fourth in the year one thousand eight hundred and thirty-five," and with power to hold real and personal estate not exceeding in value one Hundred thousand dollars, to be devoted exclusively to the purposes of education.

House of Reps. Feb. 10, 1836.
Passed to be enacted.
Julius Rockwell Speaker.
In Senate Feb. 10, 1836.
Passed to be enacted.
Horace Mann, President.

Council-Chamber 11th February 1836
Approved
Edward Everett

19. Tyler, *History of Amherst*, pp. 24, 59, 369. In spite of these activities, Williams conferred a D.D. on him in 1824.

20. ML to ZPG, Buckland, December 9, 1829; Hitchcock, *Mary Lyon*, p. 131. Theophilus Packard to ML, Boston, March 26, 1834.

21. T. Packard to ML, Shelburne, May 13, July 5, 1834. ML to ——, September 8, 1834; Hitchcock, *Mary Lyon*, p. 201. J. Felt to Edward Hitchcock, Boston, December 23, 1851.

22. He was named a trustee in 1836 and elected president of the board from 1838 to 1858. From 1844 to 1855 he and his family lived in the Seminary building; in later years he seems to have been involved in

disciplinary matters, but his primary function was raising money.

23. ML to ZPG, place unspecified, December 1834; Hitchcock, *Mary Lyon*, p. 132. Also Hitchcock, *Mary Lyon*, p. 204, and T. Packard to ——, Shelburne, December 25, 1834, ABCFM Collection, Houghton Library. Mary Lyon had not hesitated to contribute to the proprietary scholarship arrangement at Oberlin in behalf of a nephew. She had given $150 to this new and struggling institution in January 1834—when Zilpah and the Ipswich students together gave $200—though she already knew how much money her own undertaking would require. Six months later she wrote to Father Shipherd, bespeaking a place as soon as possible for Aaron Ezra Lyon, age 21. Robert Samuel Fletcher, *A History of Oberlin College From Its Foundation through the Civil War* (Oberlin, Ohio, Oberlin College, 1943), 1:135. ML to Rev. John J. Shipherd, Ipswich, July 28, August 11, 1834, letters owned by Oberlin College.

24. ML to J. Felt, Amherst, December 23, 30, 1834, January 26, 1835, Joseph B. Felt Papers, Vol. 1, Essex Institute collection. Joseph B. Felt, scribe, Minutes of the Committee, December 3-5, 1834, January 8, 1835.

25. John Todd to J. Felt, Northampton, March 29, 1835, Joseph B. Felt Papers, Vol. 1, Essex Institute collection. Felt, Minutes, April 15, 1835. Hitchcock, *Mary Lyon*, p. 245.

26. ML to ZPG, South Hadley Canal, October 1, 1835; Hitchcock, *Mary Lyon*, p. 217. ML to EC, Amherst, November 13-16, 1835.

27. Stow, *History*, p. 49.

28. ML to EC, n. p., January 11, 1836; ML to ——, Boston, April 25, 1836; Hitchcock, *Mary Lyon*, pp. 222, 223. Hannah Porter to ML, Monson, May 6, 1836. Stow, *History*, p. 63.

29. Fisk, *Recollections*, pp. 94-95: "She would say: 'I want everyone of my pupils to know the names of Dana, Felt, Choate, Heard, and Packard. We owe them much. They were our friends when our cause had hardly taken a place among the good objects of our day. . . .' One of the early pupils says: "I had hardly been a week in South Hadley before I had heard of all these early friends of the seminary from Miss Lyon's lips. She had so told us of Dr. Humphrey and Dr. Hitchcock, that the very mention of their names filled us with reverence. We had heard of the faithfulness of Mr. Tyler and Mr. Bowdoin, and were assured that Deacon Safford, Deacon Porter, and Deacon Avery would soon come to see us.'" As a member of the original committee but not one of the five incorporators, Professor Hitchcock was formally elected a trustee on October 3, 1836, along with Heman Humphrey, President of Amherst. ML's letter to Mrs. Edward Hitchcock, Ipswich, July 7, 1834, is in the Amherst College Archives. Mrs. H's answer, though surely cordial, was slow to come; on August 1, Mary Lyon in a letter to Hannah White, who was then teaching at Amherst Academy, asked her to find out if the July 7 letter had been received.

30. Tyler, *History*, p. 168. ML to ZPG, Boston, October 25, 1836; Hitchcock, *Mary Lyon*, p. 232.
31. "Pangynaskean Seminary," *Boston Recorder*, 30, nos. 9, 10, 11 , for February 27, March 6, 13, 1835. "A Pangynaskean," "Location of Female Seminaries," *The Religious Magazine*, 2, no. 7 (1835), 326–328. "Paterfamilias" to Editor of *Boston Recorder*, June 10, 1837; unpublished. [Edward Hitchcock] to [Roswell Hawks] , Amherst, October 20, 1851, Amherst College Archives.
32. David Choate to Mary W. Chapin, Essex, July 19, 1862.
33. ML to J. Felt, Amherst, December 30, 1834; Joseph B. Felt Papers, Vol. 1, Essex Institute collection.
34. J. Todd to J. Felt, Northampton, March 29, 1835; Joseph B. Felt Papers, Essex Institute collection. ML to the Reverend Mr. Tyler, Amherst, April 12, 1835. Some of ML's questions, which follow in full, apparently were considered: although ground was not broken until the following summer, an executive committee was named at the meeting and empowered to proceed with specific plans.

Queries relating to the new seminary at South Hadley

Will there not be considerable hazard with regard to the impression on the Christian community to defer the commencement of building till another year? May it not be better to put up, or at least to commence a small part of the buildings the present season? In such a case, would it not be best to lay out the whole plan, according to the design of the Committee for the whole establishment, with the estimated expense, & then take a definite portion to be built the present year, deferring the cost till another year or longer?

If anything of this kind should be judged expedient by the Committee, will there not be some very important business to be accomplished at the next meeting, which ought not to be deferred till the last of May? Would it not be necessary to have a small executive Committee appointed, who can take the time immediately to do all the business, which would suffer by delay? If any contracts are to be made, could not some part of this business be done to much better advantage early in the season than later? Ought not measures for deciding on the building spot, & for obtaining a plan for buildings to be immediately adopted?

If there are not now on the General Committee a sufficient number of business men, who can take the time to fulfil the duties of an executive Committee on every branch of business, ought not some measures to be adopted at the next meeting to add to the General Committee such men as are needed? And is it not important that great care should be taken about adding more to the Committee, lest the number should be filled up without accomplishing the object?

There are two important objections to making preparations immediately for commencing buildings the present summer. 1. The smallness of the sum already raised. 2. The longtime before some part of it will become due. In carrying out the undertaking, it will undoubtedly be the path of wisdom, to avoid presuming on means which have not been literally secured, & to avoid spending money faster than it has been obtained. But in the small undertaking of erecting a small part of the buildings the present year, will it not be safe to venture a little farther than can be done hereafter? Would it not do to calculate on the raising of a few thousand dollars more during the course of the summer considering the reception which the enterprize has hitherto met, & the extent of ground which is yet to be gone over? And in this small beginning, would it not do to endeavor at a suitable discount, to turn some that will be due in future years into ready money? If the gentlemen of the Committee should judge it expedient, considering the urgency of the case, to venture something, & go forward, possibly they would be disappointed in their expectations. But on such a result, could not the builders cease from their work, & the waiting walls be delayed till funds could be raised, & till the money to be paid in future years, should become due?

35. ML to ZPG, fragment, endorsed "Rec'd Nov. 26. '35"; Letters and Documents, 1:68–70.
36. ML to ———, July 7, 31, 1836; Hitchcock, *Mary Lyon*, p. 230. ML to ZPG, Norton, July 18, 1836; Letters and Documents, 1:71–74; Hitchcock, *Mary Lyon*, p. 231.
37. Hitchcock, *Mary Lyon*, pp. 404–405. Deacon Porter, who estimated Mary Lyon's contributions, was auditor and worked closely with her on accounts. For one investment, see Aaron Ezra Lyon to ML, Shelburne Falls, December 9, 1836; her nephew, temporarily in the East, reported that Uncle Cyrus Alden, who had just bought some expensive machinery, found Squire White's request for payment on his notes to Mary Lyon "inconvenient," but her money seemed to be safe and everything could probably be straightened out when she came. See also ML to H. White, fragment, n.d. [1836?], and South Hadley, January 9, 11, 1837, Boston, May 26, 1837. Also ML to Thomas White, South Hadley, October 26, 1837.
38. ML to ZPG, Granby, November 16, 1836; Letters and Documents, 1: 87–90. The following autumn she arranged to borrow $500 from Zilpah, secured by notes signed by Mr. White. "My name connected with anything of the kind can be handled in a very unpleasant manner," she wrote.
39. Hannah Porter to ML, Monson, May 11, 18, 1837. Mrs. Porter told Mary in strict confidence that her husband was expecting to collect $5,000 owed him and he planned to lend it to the seminary.
40. Journal and reminiscences in *The Echo*, no. 9, published in July 1898 by Monticello Seminary.
41. Hitchcock, *Mary Lyon*, pp. 245–246.
42. "Pangynaskean Seminary," *Boston Recorder*, 30, no. 9, February 27, 1836. J. Todd to J. Felt, Northampton, March 29, 1835; Joseph B. Felt Papers, Vol. 1, Essex Institute collection. ML to ZPG, n.p., June 29, 1835; Hitchcock, *Mary Lyon*, pp. 213–214.
43. ML to mother and sister, Northampton, July 23, 1835, ML to ZPG, Northampton, July 24, 1835; Hitchcock, *Mary Lyon*, pp. 214–215.

Harriet Martineau, *Retrospect of Western Travel* (London, Saunders and Otley, 1838), 2:84–86.

44. Hitchcock, *Mary Lyon*, p. 218. ML to ZPG, South Hadley Canal, October 1, 1835; Hitchcock, *Mary Lyon*, pp. 216–217; ML to Rev. Mr. Tyler, Amherst, October 17, 1835.

45. Manuscript in Archives. The version in Hitchcock, *Mary Lyon*, pp. 218–219, has cuts at the beginning and end.

46. ML to ZPG, fragment, endorsed, "Rec'd Nov. 26. '35"; Letters and Documents, 1:68–70.

47. J. Felt to E. Hitchcock, Boston, December 23, 1851.

48. Hitchcock, *Mary Lyon*, pp. 201–202.

49. ML to ZPG, n.p., September 6, 1836; Hitchcock, *Mary Lyon*, pp. 229–230.

50. ML to ZPG, Boston, March 13, 17, 1837; Letters and Documents, 1:95–98, 99–102. ZPG to Rev. Rufus Anderson, Ipswich, February 23, 1837; see also Hitchcock, *Mary Lyon*, pp. 239–240. Mrs. Ann E. Safford, *A Memoir of Daniel Safford By His Wife* (Boston, American Tract Society, 1861), pp. 382–383.

51. Betsy Chickering to ML, Phillipston, February 6, 1837.

52. Harriet Johnson to Nancy Johnson, Ipswich, November 10, 1836, April 5, 1837. In a letter to her father, February 28, 1837, she mentioned having written an appeal for funds for Mount Holyoke to her vacation hostess and future mother-in-law. In the April 5 letter she urged Nancy to consider attending Mount Holyoke.

53. Bethiah Miller to Priscilla Maxwell (at Ipswich Seminary), Heath, January 16, 1837, Both she and her sister Hannah did attend Mount Holyoke the first year, though Hannah did not stay long enough to get her name in the catalogue.

54. ML to Abigail Moore, Enfield, Conn., June 26, 1837; Letters and Documents, 1:107–110. Hannah Porter to EC or ML, Monson, July 29, 1837. ML to D. Choate, South Hadley, September 21, 1837.

55. Hitchcock, *Mary Lyon*, p. 203. ML to ZPG, [Ipswich], October 7, 1834; Hitchcock, *Mary Lyon*, p. 203. One retreat at the home of the Rev. Mr. Tyler in South Hadley Canal was recorded in a letter to Eunice Caldwell March 9, 1836. Mary Lyon found the Tylers "a very kind hospitable family" who gave her "toasted bread made of wheat meal" and provided her with everything she needed.

56. Hitchcock, *Mary Lyon*, pp. 230–231, 246. *Hampshire Gazette*, 51, no. 34, April 19, 1837.

57. ML to EC, Framingham, June 1835; Hitchcock, *Mary Lyon*, p. 211. Miss A. was probably Martha Abbott, a student at Ipswich 1835–36 who did attend Mount Holyoke the first year but did not complete the work for a diploma. The other three "ladies of distinguished ability" who made up the first senior class, also recruited by Miss Lyon's "private efforts," all received diplomas and all became members of the Mount Holyoke

faculty the following year. One was Abigail Moore, who did not get the supervising job but was made an assistant pupil, along with Persis Woods, who had followed Miss Caldwell from Wheaton. The third was Sarah Brigham, who, in order to come the first year, turned down Miss Grant's offer to return to Ipswich as assistant pupil, with a salary of $60 for a twenty-four week term plus free board and the opportunity to take one course without charge.

58. ML to her mother and sister, Northampton, July 23, 1835; Hitchcock, *Mary Lyon*, pp. 214-215. ML to ZPG, Norton, July 18, 1836; Letters and Documents, 1:71-74. The trustee meeting three days later settled the site permanently, and her spirits must have risen then.

59. ML to ZPG, South Hadley, October 9, 1836; Letters and Documents, 1: 79-82. ML to ZPG, Boston, October 25, 1836. Happily they decided to wait in order to try Boston, and Deacon Safford took over the following March.

60. ML to Rev. Mr. Tyler, Boston, April 30, 1836. Mrs. Cowles pointed out (Hitchcock, *Mary Lyon*, pp. 247-248) that with lightning speed she made decisions about the color of the floors and other matters of taste and convenience in the building but was capable of reversing herself, "for reasons not at first seen, to the annoyance of the workmen."

61. ML to ZPG, Norton, July 18, 1836, South Hadley, October 9, 1836; Letters and Documents, 1:71-74, 79-82.

62. C. E. Beecher to ML, Boston, Friday evening (June 26?, 1836); ML to C. E. Beecher, July 1, 1836; Hitchcock, *Mary Lyon*, pp. 225-229.

63. Hitchcock, *Mary Lyon*, pp. 243, 244.

64. Ibid., pp. 244-245. Her scriptural allusions were often pointed, as in the last sentence quoted. Nehemiah, in the midst of his heroic struggles to rebuild the walls of Jerusalem, was rejecting specious proposals that would have thwarted his efforts. See Nehemiah 6:3.

65. *The Religious Magazine and Family Miscellany*, 1(1837), 184-189.

66. Ibid., pp. 239, 320-324. The May issue of the *American Annals of Education*, 7 (1837), 219-222, quoted two paragraphs by Professor Andrews as a point of departure for editor William Alcott's own objections to boarding schools. He gently rebuked the aspersions on Ipswich graduates, represented as going West supposedly to teach but really to hunt husbands, but said nothing about the personal attacks on Miss Grant and Miss Lyon. In the ensuing two years before its demise in 1839, the *Annals* carried no reference to Mount Holyoke, although it devoted considerable space to ideas about female education and to individual schools for young women.

67. "Paterfamilias" to Editor, *Boston Recorder*, n.d., covering note to Deacon Safford, June 10, 1837, unpublished. Edward Hitchcock, "A Chapter in the Book of Providence," *Twelfth Anniversary Address before Mount Holyoke Female Seminary*, August 1, 1849, Amherst, Mass., p. 35. Mr. Hitchcock was probably well advised in selecting his outlet. The *Boston*

Recorder had carried serially long articles by him and by Mary Lyon and a number of shorter announcements. Mrs. Stow, *History*, p. 41, reported that when Miss Lyon asked the *Recorder* to carry news items about her enterprise, she was told she would have to pay for them as advertisements. This might have happened even with a reasonably sympathetic editor. Over the protracted three-year struggle, some of the "news" offered must have seemed repetitious.

68. ML to H. White, Ipswich, February 26, 1834. ML to Susan Brigham, Ipswich, August 25, 1834.

69. ML to Mary Hitchcock, Ipswich, February 8, 1836. For children's letters to ML, see Marion Lansing, ed., *Mary Lyon Through Her Letters* (Boston, Books, Inc., 1937), pp. 181–183.

70. ML to Laban M. Wheaton, Ipswich, July 8, 1834. ML to Trustees of the Female School in Norton, n.p., September 25, 1834; typed copies in Letters and Documents, 1:39–42, 53–56, originals in Wheaton College Archives.

71. ML to Mr. and Mrs. Laban M. Wheaton, Ipswich, March 4, 1835, Letters and Documents, 1:63–64, original in Wheaton College Archives. Apparently some of these provisos were at times disregarded. Persis Woods, one of the 1837–38 seniors at Mount Holyoke, had roomed with Miss Caldwell at Wheaton.

72. Agnes Wardrop to ———; extracts copied from her letters when she was a student at Wheaton Seminary 1836–37, from Wheaton College Archives.

73. ML to ZPG, Norton, May 19, 1835; Hitchcock, *Mary Lyon*, pp. 210–211.

74. William S. Tyler, *Autobiography of William Seymour Tyler* (privately printed, 1912), pp. 65–66. Tyler, *History*, pp. 166, 168. The mention of Mary Lyon by name was made by the Rev. Elias Riggs, D.D., who became a missionary of some note.

75. ML to her mother, South Hadley, September 6, 1837; Hitchcock, *Mary Lyon*, p. 242. ML to ZPG, South Hadley, September 14, 1837; Letters and Documents, 1:121–124; see also Hitchcock, *Mary Lyon*, p. 248.

76. ML to D. Choate, South Hadley, September 21, 1837.

77. Ibid. ML to Harriet Wheeler, South Hadley, October 16, 1837. *Hampshire Gazette*, 52, no. 13, November 22, 1837. The statistics in this issue, 80 students and 200 applicants, were accompanied by a brief correction of the preceding week's report of the opening and presumably came from Mount Holyoke officially.

78. Stow, *History*, pp. 86–87. Harriet Wheeler to her mother, South Hadley, December 28, 1837.

5. The Hazards of the Start

1. Donald G. Tewksbury, *The Founding of American Colleges and Universities Before the Civil War* (New York, Teachers' College Press, Columbia University, 1932), pp. 15–17, 28.

2. For ML's references to the first building see the so-called "Circular to Ladies," a three-page printed letter asking for furniture (n.d. but probably November 1836). One student in 1837-38 who encountered hostility was a junior who returned home to Deerfield early because of health. She "heard much said against her [Mary Lyon] and her school. I wish people would learn to wait until they are acquainted with a person before they make remarks abouts them . . ." Theresa Arms to Nancy Everett, Deerfield, July 30, 1838; typed copy in Everett correspondence.

3. ML to ———, South Hadley, December 1, 1837, November 27, 1837; Letters and Documents, 1:127-128, 125-126; both apparently to ZPG. The student was Persis Woods Curtis, recorded in Memorabilia, p. 149. Mrs. Cowles's report is in Hitchcock, *Mary Lyon*, p. 379.

4. Elizabeth Bull to her sister in Danbury, Conn., South Hadley, November 10, 1837. Nancy Everett to her uncle, South Hadley, November 26, 1837. For her romance, see Elizabeth Hawks to Nancy Everett, South Hadley, October 8, 1838; typed copy. Nancy first met her future husband, John Dwight, one of the volunteer helpers from South Hadley, when he was cording her bedstead. Their married life was long and happy, he prospered and in 1900 made a substantial gift toward an art building on the site of his and Nancy's house, which was moved across campus and for many years served as the college infirmary.

5. Hitchcock, *Mary Lyon*, pp. 271-272. Hannah Bailey to her brother, South Hadley, January 22-30, 1838; typed copy. It is not surprising that she became one of the "general leaders," assuming part of the supervision originally expected of Miss Peters. Miss Lyon's account book for 1837-38, detailed but incomplete, shows that for one eleven-week period, Hannah had averaged nearly 25 hours a week of supervision and that she was paid $14.34 in June and $13.32 in August. The account book indicated that there were three other general leaders during the year: Mary Whitman of East Bridgewater, paired with Miss Bailey, and Bethiah Miller of Heath and Wealthy Shepard of Buckland, probably the first pair so to function.

6. Lucy Goodale to various members of her family, South Hadley, April 10, July 13, August 6, August 8, 1838; typed copies, originals owned by Mrs. H. Rush Spedden, Salt Lake City, Utah.

7. ML to Rev. Theron Baldwin, South Hadley, July 12, 1838, postmarked July 30; Letters and Documents, 1:133-160.

8. ML, Report of the Teachers, fragment, n.d. [August 1839?]; Letters and Documents, 2:376. ECC, Hitchcock, *Mary Lyon*, ed. 1858, p. 200.

9. Julia Hyde Clarke in Memorabilia, p. 191. Mary Burr to her family, South Hadley, July 20, 1838; uncatalogued. The students who recorded Professor Cowles's frequent visits to the Seminary that spring were unenthusiastic about him and suspected that Mary Lyon felt the same way.

10. Hitchcock, *Mary Lyon*, ed. 1858, p. 203. ML to Rev. Theron Baldwin,

July 12, 1838; Letters and Documents, 1:135. Harriet Wheeler to her mother, South Hadley, December 28, 1837. Harriet Hollister to her sister Ann Marie, South Hadley, December 24, 1837. Nancy Everett to her uncle, South Hadley, November 26, 1837.

11. Hitchcock, *Mary Lyon*, ed. 1858, p. 205. Lucy Goodale to her family, July 2–13, 1838.

12. Mary C. Whitman to Eunice Caldwell, East Bridgewater, April 26, 1837. Alice Stone Blackwell, *Lucy Stone: Pioneer of Women's Rights* (Boston, 1930), p. 40. In evaluating the hostility to William Lloyd Garrison among the devout, it is worth remembering that "Throughout 1838 Garrison waged as furious a campaign against the church and ministry as against the slave traffic." Timothy L. Smith, *Revivalism and Social Reform in Mid-Nineteenth-Century America* (New York, Abingdon Press, 1957), p. 183.

13. Lucy Goodale to her family, South Hadley, March 17, 1838; typed copy, original owned by Mrs. H. Rush Spedden. Harriet Hollister to her sister, South Hadley, December 24, 1837.

14. Harriet Hollister, ibid.

15. Harriet Wheeler to her mother, South Hadley, December 28, 1837. Julia Hyde Clarke, Memorabilia, p. 189. Hitchcock, *Reminiscences*, pp. 151–158, 300. Professor Hitchcock was a prime mover in 1830 in founding the Antivenenean Society of Amherst College; its name came from the Latin for "against poison." All the faculty and more than half the students enrolled that year joined by taking the pledge against "spirit, wine, opium, and tobacco." For the next thirty years more than half of each entering class joined.

16. Fletcher, *History of Oberlin College*, 1:326, 432–434. Other reasons for his summary dismissal in October 1839 were his public attacks on the president and the trustees for what he felt were curricular and theological heresies. He started a boys' school in Elyria, Ohio; after a few years he and Eunice came back East and together revived Ipswich Seminary, which Miss Grant had given up in 1839.

17. Hannah Bailey to her brother, South Hadley, January 22–30, 1838; typed copy. Other visiting speakers in 1837–38 included President Humphrey of Amherst, the Spauldings, enfeebled but dedicated missionaries from the Sandwich Islands, and Professor Cowles, who, on his courting visits, preached sermons "pretty much tinctured with the spirit of Abolition," according to Mary Burr, (July 20, 1838), and lectured on literature.

18. Julia Hyde to her father, South Hadley, March 2, 1838; postmarked March 6. Lucy Goodale to her family, March 17, 1838, and to Warren, [1838]; typed copies, original owned by Mrs. H. Rush Spedden. Mary Burr to her family, South Hadley, July 20, 1838; uncatalogued.

19. ML to Mr. and Mrs. Heard, South Hadley, August 7, 1838; Letters and Documents, 1:161–162. Julia Hyde to her mother, South Hadley,

August 4, 1838. ML to ZPG, South Hadley, April 23, 1838; Hitchcock, *Mary Lyon*, pp. 390-391.

20. ML to ZPG, South Hadley, August 27, 1838; Letters and Documents, 1: 167-170. See also Hitchcock, *Mary Lyon*, pp. 309-311.

21. Fisk, *Recollections*, pp. 102-103. Julia Hyde to her father, South Hadley, March 2, 1838; postmarked March 6. Lucy Goodale to her family, South Hadley, August 8, 1838; typed copy, original owned by Mrs. H. Rush Spedden.

22. Sarah Miner to ML, Northfield, September 7, 1839. *Female Education: Tendencies of the Principles Embraced, and the System Adopted in the Mount Holyoke Female Seminary*, South Hadley, Mass., June 1839, passim.

23. Elizabeth Hawks to Nancy Everett, South Hadley, December 18, 1840; typed copy. For four weeks in the fall of 1840 Elizabeth, advised to travel for her health, had kept her father company; her mother had gone with him for six weeks the preceding winter. When he was in South Hadley, Mr. Hawks apparently helped with Seminary transactions and enterprises; in her 1837-38 account book Mary Lyon noted that $100 of Mr. Hawks's salary should be paid by the boarding department to the trustees. Records of the Board of Trustees, August 12, 1840. ML to Hannah White, South Hadley, December 18, 1840; Letters and Documents, 2:199-200.

24. Hitchcock, *Mary Lyon*, p. 321. Lucy Goodale to her mother, South Hadley, March 17, 1838; typed copy, original owned by Mrs. H. Rush Spedden.

25. Hitchcock, *Mary Lyon*, pp. 321-322.

26. Perry Miller, *The Life of the Mind in America from the Revolution to the Civil War*, Books One through Three (New York, Harcourt, Brace and World, 1965), pp. 3, 5. Fletcher, *History of Oberlin College*, 2:889. Smith, *Revivalism*, p. 60. Hitchcock, *Reminiscences*, pp. 159, 162.

27. Frederick Rudolph, *The American College and University* (New York, Alfred A. Knopf, 1962), pp. 160, 170. ML to Mrs. Hannah Porter, South Hadley, October 27, 1848; Hitchcock, *Mary Lyon*, pp. 329-330, 324.

28. Elizabeth Hawks to Nancy Everett, South Hadley, March 20, 1839; typed copy. Caroline LeConte to her sister, South Hadley, March 16, 1839. Lucy Goodale to her mother, South Hadley, April 18, 1840; typed copy, original owned by Mrs. H. Rush Spedden.

29. Sarah Brigham to Nancy Everett, South Hadley, October 29, 1838; typed copy.

30. Elizabeth Hawks to Nancy Everett, South Hadley, March 20, 1839; typed copy. Lucy Goodale to her brother, South Hadley, November 4, 1839; typed copy, original owned by Mrs. H. Rush Spedden.

31. *Mount Holyoke Female Seminary, Preparation for Admission*, South Hadley, September 1840.

32. ML to Rev. William A. Hallock, South Hadley, March 2, 1841; Letters

and Documents, 2:207–210. Her objections seem to have had effect; there is no Mary Anne Hallock in either catalogue or directory.

33. Mary Burr to her family, South Hadley, November 2, 1839. Taking extra time for Latin would complicate the tandem arrangement by which Mary and her sister Caroline alternated at home and at the Seminary. What happened about the Latin is nowhere recorded, but Caroline did complete the three-year course in 1841 and Mary in 1842. Lucy Goodale to her brothers, South Hadley, November 4, 1839; typed copy, original owned by Mrs. H. Rush Spedden. *Third Annual Catalogue of the Officers and Members of the Mount Holyoke Female Seminary* (South Hadley, Mass., 1839–40), p. 8.

34. Lucy Goodale to her parents, South Hadley, December 28, 1839 – January 6, 1840, February 7, 1840; typed copies, originals owned by Mrs. H. Rush Spedden.

35. Mellicent Warren Goodale, account of Lucy Goodale's last illness and death, May 1841.

36. Caroline LeConte to her brother, Granby, September 14, 1840. Fisk, *Recollections*, p. 139. ML to ZPG, South Hadley, March 8, 1841; Hitchcock, *Mary Lyon*, p. 393.

37. ML to Dr. [Rufus] Anderson, South Hadley, November 5, 1840, ABCFM collection, Houghton Library, Harvard. Extracts from the journal of Eliza Antoinette Hubbell, October 14, 1840.

38. Sarah Brackett to ML, Washington, Ga., February 16, 1841. Elizabeth B. Haven to ML, New London, Conn., March 2, 1841. Faith in Mary Lyon and the operation of the Seminary remained unshaken even in some of the families whose daughters had died. The two younger sisters of Lucy Goodale came to Mount Holyoke; Mary was a member of the middle class in 1849–50, and Harriet graduated in 1855. Harriet Hollister of Manchester, Vt., would have been a senior in 1840–41; she was the oldest of four sisters to attend the Seminary. She was accompanied by Julia in 1839–40 and followed by Ann Marie, who graduated in 1845 and taught there for two years, and by Sarah, who attended in 1846–47.

39. Fisk, *Recollections*, pp. 119–123. Remedies dispensed by the teachers were mainly plasters, poultices, sage tea, wormwood tea, and the like. An anonymous student notebook contained directions for dosing a "Cold with a cough"; the compound to be administered contained 1 tablespoon molasses, 2 teaspoons castor oil, 1 teaspoon paregoric, 1 teaspoon spirits of camphor. Sketch Book, M.H. Fem. Sem., September 1839.

40. ML to ZPG, South Hadley, March 8, 1841; Hitchcock, *Mary Lyon*, pp. 393–394.

41. Ibid., pp. 381–382.

42. Julia Hyde to Mrs. David Goodale, July 20, 1841, December 15, 1840; uncatalogued. Antoinette Hubbell to Caroline E. Coles, South Hadley, March 8, 1841.

43. Caroline LeConte to her mother, Granby, August 25, 1840. Because the

round-trip fare home would have cost more than twice what she was paying for board, she spent the long vacation with a friendly family, originally found for her by Mary Lyon, less than two miles from the Seminary.

44. Milo P. Jewett to ML, Perry C.H., Ala., December 3, 1838. L. H. Sigourney to ML, Hartford, Conn., July 13, 1839.
45. Fisk, *Recollections*, p. 235.

6. In High Gear

1. ML did not take credit for the large number of applicants, which she termed "a favor of Divine Providence" that might at any time be withdrawn. See printed letters to applicants of July 27, 1847, and February 9, 1848.
2. Fletcher, *History of Oberlin College*, 2:694.
3. ML, 14 work sheets, undated and unidentified except for class headings.
4. The texts on which Mount Holyoke differed from Amherst were Wood's *Botany* (not Gray's), Alexander's *Evidences of Christianity* (not Paley's), Upham's *Mental Philosophy* (not Stewart's or Brown's), Paley's *Natural Theology* (not the *Bridgwater Treatises*, which were, however, in the Seminary library). Thomas Woody, *A History of Women's Education in the United States* (2 vols., New York, Science Press, 1929), 1:418, 562, 2:161 ff. Martineau, *Retrospect*, 2:24.
5. Elizabeth Gordon to Eliza Hayden, South Hadley, October 16, 1845. *Candidates for Mount Holyoke Female Seminary*; see ML's letters to Osborn Mysick, South Hadley, July 27, 1847, and to Helen M. Graves, South Hadley, February 9, 1848, for first and revised versions.
6. Louisa Torrey to her mother, South Hadley, April 1844; typed copy. Her sister Delia, who had entered with her, went home early but Louisa stayed through the summer term. Neither returned for the senior year; instead, they spent the winter and spring in New Haven and attended chemistry lectures by Professor Silliman and Professor Olmsted at Yale, along with 25 other ladies. Both sisters taught at Monson Academy in 1847; some years later Louisa married Alphonso Taft. Their oldest son was William Howard Taft, the 27th president.
7. Emily Dickinson to Abiah Root, South Hadley, November 6, 1847. Maria Savage to Rhoda Roys, South Hadley, March 19, 1842.
8. Emily Dickinson to Abiah Root, South Hadley, November 6, 1847. Ariel Parish to ML, Westfield, January 13, 1843. Of the eight young women, Sarah Crane and Emmeline Alling seem to have attended Mount Holyoke in 1843 for part of the year; neither stayed long enough to get her name in a catalogue. There is no identifiable Seminary record of the others. Mr. Parish was well known and highly respected in western Massachusetts; he was to be principal of the Public High School in Springfield for twenty years and in 1864 to be elected a Mount Holyoke trustee.

9. Rhoda Roys (the friend whom Maria Savage had persuaded to enter in 1842), her mother, and her husband all helped Lydia Shattuck reach out for a better education. For Miss Shattuck's standing in the scientific world, see "A Scientific Heritage" by Charlotte Haywood, in the *Mount Holyoke Alumnae Quarterly* (Fall 1959), pp. 122-125.

10. Rudolph, *American College*, p. 130.

11. Abigail Moore to ML, Boxford, September 10, 1845.

12. ML, "Items for personal and private use," covering parts of 1842-43, 1843-44, 1844-45. ECC, Hitchcock, *Mary Lyon*, ed. 1858, p. 221.

13. Duties at Mount Holyoke Seminary, n.d., p. 51. Julia Hyde to her mother, South Hadley, November 15, 1841.

14. Maria Savage to Rhoda Roys, South Hadley, April 28, 1842. Lucinda Guilford to Frances Greene, South Hadley, March 13, 1846, November 17, 1846; typed copies. Among ML's private papers is a list of 20 names, all members of the class of 1845, headed "Candidates for teacher 1845." Beside each is a notation as to knowledge of French, Latin, music. Out of the 20, only one, Ann Marie Hollister, appeared on the faculty roster in the 1845-46 catalogue, which did, however, include three other members of the class: Susan Tolman, Persis Thurston (who taught drawing), and Martha Scott (who took on much of the domestic work supervision). Had these three been appointed before ML considered as possibilities two fifths of the rest of the class? Mrs. Cowles spelled out what she saw as the motives of those who returned to teach: "A desire to do good, the pleasure of unfolding minds of a high order, delight in communing with congenial spirits, the identification of the seminary with themselves, and the luxury of living in what seemed to them a miniature paradise, and of anticipating the millennial glory . . ." Hitchcock, *Mary Lyon*, ed. 1858, pp. 221-222.

15. William G. Hammond, *Remembrance of Amherst: An Undergraduate's Diary 1846-1848*, ed. George F. Whicher (New York, Columbia University Press, 1946), p. 109. Julia Hyde to Lucy Goodale, Wayland, March 1, 1840; the plays were *King John, Merchant of Venice, Macbeth, Richard III*, and *King Lear*. Emily Dickinson to Abiah Root, South Hadley, May 16, 1848; Thomas H. Johnson and Theodora Ward, eds., *The Letters of Emily Dickinson* (Cambridge, Harvard University Press, 1958), 1:65-67. For ML on reading see Harriette Wells, journal, November 17, 1845. For the teachers' reading group, see Martha Chapin to her cousin, South Hadley, December 18-25, 1844.

16. Louisa Torrey to her mother, South Hadley, January 24, April –, 1844. Lucinda Guilford to Frances Greene, South Hadley, March 13, 1846. Professor Hitchcock received modest remuneration; in ML's surviving account books there are two entries under his name—$70 for 1843-44 and $40 for 1844-45. In 1837-38 he had given his geology lectures without charge to stimulate individual contributions to the Seminary library. Mary Burr to her family, South Hadley, July 20, 1838.

17. For the cost of the manikin, which came from Paris, see Hitchcock, *Reminiscences*, p. 293. References to the series are found in Diantha Lee, Memorabilia, p. 194; Lucy Lyon, journal letter, January 31, February 9, 1844; Marietta Sherwood to her sister and brother, January 30, 31, 1844; Mrs. Elijah Grant to her husband, South Hadley, February 2, 1844. Of Professor Snell's lecture on architecture, Caroline LeConte wrote her mother on May 30, 1840, that she wished for a half dozen more on the same subject.

18. Some students recalled that ML's method of making time for such extras in the daily schedule was simply to set the Seminary clock back. Lyman Beecher, in the words of Barbara Cross, "stood at the center of the transformation of American Protestantism between 1790 and 1845"; *Autobiography*, 1:xxxvi. Catharine Beecher's visit is recorded in Harriette Wells's journal, May 1, 1846; Lucy Lyon, journal letter, May 5, 1846.

19. Abigail Cowles to Martha Grant, South Hadley, July 22, 1845.

20. Lucy Lyon, journal letter, March 10, 1844, May 7, 1846. Susan Tolman, journal letter, April 8, 1847. Elizabeth Bell, journal, May 5, 1846; typed copy.

21. Between 1837-38 and 1840-41, enrollment averaged just over 110; between 1841-42 and 1848-49 it averaged just under 210. Hitchcock, *Reminiscences*, pp. 161-163; *Mary Lyon*, pp. 344-345.

22. ML to ZPGB, South Hadley, March 8, April 13, 1843; Hitchcock, *Mary Lyon*, pp. 339, 343. ML to Mrs. Safford, South Hadley, March 9, 1843; Hitchcock, *Mary Lyon*, pp. 331-332. Dr. Kirk continued to be much interested in Mount Holyoke as long as he lived. He delivered the anniversary address in 1844. In 1856 he was elected a trustee and two years later succeeded Roswell Hawks as president of the board, serving until his death in 1874.

23. ML to Mrs. Safford, South Hadley, March 21, 1843; Hitchcock, *Mary Lyon*, pp. 335-337. Lydia Pomeroy to her mother, South Hadley, March 30, 1843.

24. Rhoda Perkins to her parents, South Hadley, April 5, 8, 1843.

25. Susan Tolman, journal letter, December 10-31, 1846, January 1-8, 1847.

26. Mary Whitman to Fidelia Fiske, South Hadley, March 9, 1848. ML to ZPGB, South Hadley, April 27, 1848; Hitchcock, *Mary Lyon*, p. 400. Martha Benedict to her family, South Hadley, January 1-9, 1845.

27. Susan Tolman, journal letter, December 10, 1847 – January 20, 1848, passim. Emily Dickinson to Abiah Root, South Hadley, January 17, May 16, 1848; Johnson, *Letters*, 1:60, 67. For full and discriminating treatment of Emily Dickinson's year at Mount Holyoke, see Sydney R. McLean, "Emily Dickinson at Mount Holyoke," *New England Quarterly*, 7 (1934), 25-42, and Richard Sewall, *The Life of Emily Dickinson* (New York, Farrar, Straus and Giroux, 1974), 2:357-367.

28. Lydia Pomeroy to her mother, South Hadley, March 30, 1843. Henry Francis to ML, Hartford, March 11, 1843.

29. Hitchcock, *Mary Lyon*, p. 417. *Memorial: Twenty-fifth Anniversary of the Mt. Holyoke Female Seminary* (South Hadley, Mass., 1862), p. 51. ML's approach to salvation was strictly non-denominational. Some of the students who found Christ joined the village church, which was Congregational, but as a rule a new convert waited to return home and join the church attended by her family. No records seem to have been kept in ML's lifetime of the denomination of any student or teacher. The only recognized categories were those to which the students assigned themselves on entrance: (1) professing Christian, (2) indulging hope, (3) without hope. This indifference to sects did not, of course, extend to the Roman Catholic church. Susan Tolman was distressed to get a letter from a classmate, "a person of fine talents, & a good scholar," saying that she had become a Catholic. ML also "felt it much" but predicted that the young woman would return to the Protestant fold. For once she turned out to be wrong. Susan Tolman, journal letter, June 28, 1847.

30. Fisk, *Recollections*, p. 170. Antoinette Hubbell, journal, February 20–26, 1844.

31. Mary C. Weaver to her family, South Hadley, February 29, 1844; typed copy. A member of the middle class, Mary was glad to be spending a year at the Seminary but thought one was quite enough for ordinary "minds and constitutions." ML discussed freely with the young ladies her methods of winning support. She once told them, "We ought to appear benevolent, as well as to be really so. This is the reason I think it best to have our missionary contributions in the form of subscriptions." Fisk, *Recollections*, p. 325.

32. ML to Fidelia Fiske, South Hadley, March 4, 1844; Hitchcock, *Mary Lyon*, pp. 351–352.

33. *Missionary Offering*, pp. 17, 39.

34. Ibid., pp. 44–45, 45–46, 49–50.

35. Ibid., pp. 57–61, 74.

36. Ibid., pp. 53, 65, 84.

37. Jefferson Church to ML, Springfield, November 17, 1845; Frances Gillette to ML, Bloomfield, Conn., May 29, 1846; Fisk, *Recollections*, p. 245. Church had evidently corresponded earlier and waited on Miss Lyon in person. His twelve-page letter refers to a note written by her on October 22, reporting that the trustees had refused his request. Of this vote there is no record; it must have been an action of the executive committee, as Cole points out. Arthur C. Cole, *A Hundred Years of Mount Holyoke College: The Evolution of an Educational Ideal* (New Haven, Yale University Press, 1940), p. 352. Miss Gillette's letter was also long (seven pp.) and, like Church's, earnest and very respectful.

38. *Missionary Offering*, pp. 99–101. The story of Achan is told in Joshua 7, the story of Phinehas in Numbers 25:6–18.

NOTES TO PAGES 260-264

39. *A Missionary Offering* was advertised by the printers, Crocker and Brewster, along with other new books, in the *Boston Recorder* on July 13 and 20, 1843. A brief unsigned review on July 20 was favorable: "The author has admirably personified Covetousness."

40. The successor of the first Mrs. Walker was also a student in the Seminary in 1837–38 and a graduate in the class of 1840. Zeviah Shumway married Mr. Walker in 1845 and went back with him to West Africa, where she died two years later at the age of 30.

41. For ML on foreign missions see Antoinette Hubbell, journal, January 11, 1843.

42. Fisk, *Recollections*, pp. 138, 172–173. Antoinette Hubbell, journal, January 16 – February 24, 1843. Justin Perkins to ML, Oroomiah, July 7, 1843, February 13, 1845. He wrote Miss Lyon of Fidelia's "rare merits" as well as her fine health and spirits and her effectiveness as a teacher: "She contributes a great deal, as you presumed she would, to the comfort, cheerfulness and happiness of our whole mission."

43. One graduate called the Seminary a "missionary wive's depot" in reporting the engagement of Ebenezer Burgess, missionary to India long known to ML, and Abigail Moore, the most indispensable of all the teachers who left for foreign shores. Amelia Dickinson Bangs to Tirzah Williams, Springfield, February 14, 1846. ML traced the teacher exodus to a meeting of the ABCFM in Norwich, Conn., in September 1842 when she gathered all the former Mount Holyoke students present for group prayer, reconsecrating the Seminary once again to God and the missionary cause. Although in later years ML used to say, "I little knew how much that prayer-meeting would cost me," it was only one of many occasions on which she extolled the saving of heathen souls. See Fisk, *Recollections*, pp. 170–171.

44. The Webb visit is mentioned in Lucy Lyon's journal letter, June 4, July 11, 1845. For Lucy's romance see *Memoir of Mrs. Lucy T. Lord of the Chinese Baptist Mission* (Philadelphia, American Baptist Publication Society, 1854), pp. 122–123. For Susan Tolman's marriage see Elias Olan James, *The Story of Cyrus and Susan Mills* (Stanford, Stanford University Press, 1953), pp. 88–95. The Foote-Webb marriage endured; they had five children who grew to maturity; they survived 19 years in India and lived together in amity for 53 years. Susan and Cyrus Mills, who had no children, collaborated on mission work and school teaching and administration for their 36 years together; Cyrus died in 1884, and Susan was president of Mills College for the next 23 years. Lucy's lot was far less fortunate; the two children born in Ningpo, China, died in infancy, and she suffered nearly four years of incapacitating illness before dying of tetanus in 1853.

45. Stow, *History*, pp. 204, 319–322. Sarah Locke Stow, ed., *Semi-centennial Celebration of Mount Holyoke Seminary, 1837–1887* (South Hadley, Mass., 1887), p. 38. The earliest figures include service to the Cherokees and the Choctaws in the United States, which was counted by the

ABCFM as foreign until the middle of the century. It is illuminating to compare the number of young women recruited during the first 12 years of the Seminary, 35, with the total at Amherst at the same time. Between the opening of Amherst in September 1821 and early 1849, the number of alumni who went into foreign missions was 41; between 1837 and 1849, the total was only 14. Hitchcock, *Reminiscences,* pp. 193-204.

46. For alumnae statistics see successive Catalogues of the Memorandum Society, *Semi-centennial Celebration,* pp. 38-43.

47. Kathryn Kish Sklar, *Catharine Beecher: A Study in American Domesticity* (New Haven, Yale University Press, 1973), p. 122. C. E. Beecher, *Educational Reminiscences and Suggestions* (New York, J. B. Ford, 1874), pp. 97-99. This letter from ML is undated but was probably written in the spring of 1847; see Susan Tolman, journal letter, March 30, 1847. ML to Reverend Henry Brown, South Hadley, November 8, 1847; typed copy.

48. ML to Rev. Charles Beatty, August 27, September 16, 1846; originals belong to Historical Society of Pennsylvania. In both notes she said explicitly she was writing in confidence. Understandably, she made no reference to one striking evidence of Cornelia Martin's tact and authority. The preceding June she had been detailed to escort from South Hadley to home in central New York state a student expelled for slipping out of the Seminary and presumably spending the night with a man. In spite of threats to run off to New York City, the culprit was safely delivered to her parents' charge. See Harriette Wells, journal, June 8-16, 1846.

49. Susan Tolman, journal letter, August 3, 4, 1847. ML to Lydia Bailey, South Hadley, August 20, 1846. ML to Sarah Bonney, South Hadley, March 4, 1846; Letters and Documents, 2:251-254.

50. ML to Susannah Fitch, South Hadley, September 17, 1848; Letters and Documents, 2:305-307. There is no indication that any of the five did join Susannah Fitch, but all of them were soon teaching somewhere. ML's response follows:

I have been absent a few days, have just returned & find your letter. I do not know of one of experience who could be obtained, who could teach music. Do you remember a Miss Harriet C. Haile of Hinsdale, who was a member of the Junior Class the year you were a member of the Middle Class. She completed her course last year. She can teach music. Perhaps you can obtain her. I am going to write & ascertain. Do you recollect Miss Norcross one year behind you. She had devoted considerable time to music. I am not quite certain that she considers herself qualified to teach. I shall write to her in case Miss Haile fails. In the mean time I wish you would write to me stating further particulars which I can give to any one, compensation etc. If I cannot find any one who can teach music, do you wish to have me procure any one? If I fail of finding a teacher, I will let you know as early as I can.

Affectionately yours,
Mary Lyon

*If you do interest one who can teach music, how would you like to have
Miss Graham go & take the place equally with you. She has had many years
experience in teaching, & is I understand an excellent teacher.*

*Miss Jane A. Cook [was] a member of the Senior Class the same year which
you were of the Junior Class. Perhaps she might be obtained as an associate.
Miss Sarah G. Fenn of the last Senior Class, of Southington, Ohio, would be
a good teacher. Perhaps she has another engagement. Miss Cook is now with a
sister in Galena Ill.*

51. *Semi-centennial Celebration*, pp. 38-43. ML, "Circular to Ladies,"
    [probably November 1836].
52. Hitchcock, *Mary Lyon*, p. 318.
53. ML to R. C. Galbraith, two drafts, both undated and unsigned; Letters
    and Documents, 2:223-230. Each draft is written on the back of a
    letter from Galbraith, the first dated June 2 and the second June 27,
    1842. There is no evidence as to what extent the first draft was altered
    or whether the second draft was sent in any form.
54. For strong dissent see the contribution of Caroline Fanning, class of 1847
    in Memorabilia, pp. 55-56: "I believe there was not one pupil who
    chose to do domestic work even one hour a day." She resented being
    "chambermaid for two teachers" but thought the experience in domes-
    tic hall had proved valuable to many students in later life. The quoted
    letters were written on October 13, 1843, by Louisa Torrey, on Octo-
    ber 18 by Lydia Baldwin, on October 19 by Elizabeth Wolcott.
55. For enthusiasm about wash day and other domestic work, see Harriet
    Crane to her cousin, South Hadley, February 1845, and H. —— to
    a friend, South Hadley, January 4, 1849; uncatalogued. Lucinda Guil-
    ford, Memorabilia, p. 75, and letter to Frances Greene, South Hadley,
    November 4, 1845.
56. Sarah Fenn to Jerusha Moore, South Hadley, February 2, 1847; uncata-
    logued. Susan Tolman, journal letter of June 7, 1847, reported that ML
    had filled "many important places" in domestic work for the next year,
    including leaders for washing, ironing, dinner, baking. For teacher
    supervision of domestic work, see lists in ML's hand, "1846, Nov.
    Description of Miss Curtis's duties, House Department"; "Sick Depart-
    ment, Miss Curtis"; and "Duties of Room Visitors."
57. For the Beecher comment, see Louisa Torrey to her mother, South
    Hadley, October 13, 1843. She had entered the Seminary only two
    weeks earlier and could not have heard the August speech. For Susan
    Tolman's report, see journal letter, May 14, 1847.
58. Joseph Avery to ML, Conway, September 25, 1842. Daniel Safford to
    ML, Boston, July 1, 1843, July 16, 1844. ML, various household hints,
    n.d.
59. Sarah Wingate to her parents, South Hadley, September 30, 1848. Jerusha
    Babcock in a letter by Mary Weaver to her parents, South Hadley,
    February 29, 1844. Emily Dickinson to Abiah Root, South Hadley,
    November 6, 1847; Emily Dickinson to Austin, South Hadley, Novem-
    ber 2, 1847; Johnson, *Letters*, 1:50-52. Mount Holyoke students had

far fewer grievances than the patrons of the commons in the institutions for men. In the 1840's college-administered student dining rooms were in a sad decline. Yale closed its commons about 1845, Harvard in 1849. For the changes that had altered the residential structure of established colleges, see David Allmendinger, Jr., *Paupers and Scholars* (New York, St. Martin's Press, 1975).

60. Miss Whitman's scarlet fever is recorded in Lucy Lyon, journal letter, March 16, 26, 1845. For the 1846 influenza see Lucinda Guilford to Frances Greene, South Hadley, May 6, 1846; for smallpox, Harriette Wells, journal, March 7, 1846, and Fayette Moody to Abner DeWitt, Granby, April 12, 1848.

61. Helen M. Graves, "Journal at Mount Holyoke Seminary 1848," p. 1; typed copy. Three days later, after many details about washing day and domestic work, she was writing, "Miss Lyon is certainly a wonder of the age. She is such a planner. And she is so affectionate and kind too." Mary Ware to Ann Batchelder, South Hadley, December 1, 1848. Mary closed her letter by urging Ann to try to come to Mount Holyoke because she "would value the privileges so much."

62. The exact number of Seminary rules at any given moment is difficult to determine. An undated printed sheet in the archives, beginning with "Recorded Items," has only 63 entries, but there is only one entry for "Fire Laws," which seem never to have been fewer than seven. Mary Lyon did make new rules whenever she saw the need, but most of the added regulations seem to have been assimilated with the old when the entire list was issued at the beginning of the next year. In any case the number was not excessive by collegiate standards. The colleges for men also prescribed bells and rules. At Amherst for many years beginning in 1833 the bell for morning prayers sounded at 5:45 a.m. in the winter and 4:45 a.m. in the summer. At Harvard, least puritanical of all the New England colleges, *The Statutes and Laws of the University* had 153 rules in 13 chapters when it was published in 1825; the last edition in 1866 had 204 rules filling 16 chapters. Students at Amherst could not bathe or exercise during study hours, shoot off a gun near college buildings, play a musical instrument (prohibitions traditional on most campuses); young men at Harvard could not smoke in public, walk on Sunday, or attend the theater. The reason Mount Holyoke rules seemed more forbidding was, no doubt, as Professor Cole suggests, that they were enforced, while the rules at the men's colleges were often ignored or evaded. See Tyler, *History of Amherst*, pp. 187–188; Morison, *Three Centuries of Harvard*, pp. 232, 357–358; Cole, *Hundred Years*, p. 76.

63. On student cheating see Anna Hodges, Memorabilia, p. 184.

64. Persis Thurston to her sister Mary, South Hadley, December 20, 1841. Ann Webster, Memorabilia, pp. 34–35.

65. Estimates of the number of offenders must be very rough; references to

discipline cases in early letters and diaries are very sparse. Most students must have heeded Miss Lyon's injunction not to talk about these cases afterward. On theft see Mary Ellis, Memorabilia, pp. 43–44, and H. Cleveland Bush to her uncle, South Hadley, December 23, 1844. The midnight escapade was recorded by Harriette Wells in her diary, June 8, 9, 10, 1846.

66. Stow, *History*, pp. 112, 122. Lydia Pomeroy to her sister, South Hadley, December 7, 1842. Elizabeth Gordon to Eliza Hayden, South Hadley, November 11, 1845. Louisa Torrey to her mother, South Hadley, April 1844; typed copy. Marietta Sherwood to her father, South Hadley, July 30, 1847.

67. Emily Dickinson to Abiah Root, South Hadley, November 6, 1847.

68. For the Hutchinson family and menagerie visits see Amelia Jones, Memorabilia, pp. 86 ff. For the daguerreotype ban see Susan Tolman, journal letter, January 1, 1848. Attendance at the Hitchcock inaugural is mentioned by Lucy Lyon, journal letter, April 19, 1845. The Jerusalem trip is recorded by Sophia Hazen and Mary Chapin, journal letter, November 16, 1848. The coming of the railroads in the 1840's—the line from Springfield to Northampton was opened in December 1845—was taken by ML in stride. "The cars" replaced stages and private carriages for Seminary outings and for the student trips home as the changing travel instructions in successive catalogues tell.

69. Lucinda Guilford to Frances Greene, South Hadley, December 17, 1845; typed copy.

70. Emily Dickinson to her brother, South Hadley, October 21, 1847; Johnson, *Letters*, 1:48. For the rules about wild flowers, see Rebecca Fiske, journal letter, June 3, 1848. In the spring of 1847 the care of the grounds in front of the building became another of Mary Whitman's extra responsibilities, assisted by Susan Tolman, a young man to do all the heavy work and four students who put in an hour a day as required domestic work. Susan Tolman, journal letter, May 24, 1847.

71. Rebecca Fiske, journal letter, June 22, 1848.

72. Hitchcock, *Reminiscences*, pp. 220–226, 227–234. The speeches given both years are quoted at some length. Lucinda Guilford to Frances Greene, South Hadley, July 7, 1846; typed copy.

73. On Amherst kinship, David Allmendinger has found that of nearly 350 young women who completed the course at Mount Holyoke between 1838 and 1850, 10 percent had brothers at Amherst. Hammond, *Remembrance of Amherst*, pp. 108–109, May 19, 1847. On his fifth visit a few months later when he arrived on Thursday instead of Wednesday, Miss Lyon invited him to stay to supper. For early morning socializing, see Louisa Ware, journal, November 1, 2, 1848.

74. For the detailed account of one lively village vacation, see Harriette Wells, journal, January 16–29, 1846.

75. Helen M. Graves, journal, ——, 1848; typed copy.

76. Sophia Hazen and Mary Chapin, journal letter, December 1, 1848.
77. Lydia Baldwin to her father, South Hadley, July 2, 1845. In 1843, when
    Lyman Beecher was the speaker, the church was so jammed that a
    representative of the *Springfield Republican* had trouble getting a seat
    where he could hear. *Springfield Republican*, 19, no. 188, August 5,
    1843.
78. Ibid. Hammond, *Remembrance*, p. 162.
79. Hitchcock, *Mary Lyon*, p. 453. Amanda Robinson, Memorabilia,
    p. 109. *Springfield Republican*, 22, no. 1145, August 8, 1846.

7. From Generation to Generation

1. ML to ZPG, South Hadley, December 1842; Hitchcock, *Mary Lyon*,
   pp. 395-396. ML's announcement at morning devotions of the coming
   marriage and departure was reported in detail by Lucy Lyon, journal
   letter, November 22, 1845. An Amherst graduate and tutor, Burgess
   was an old acquaintance of ML; they had both boarded at the Hitchcocks, and his first wife, a niece of Zilpah Grant, had been Miss Lyon's
   pupil in Buckland as well as Ipswich. ML's doubts, at the time he was
   wooing Mary Grant, about his immediate appeal as a prospective husband were suggested in two letters to Eunice Caldwell, postmarked
   April 3 and April 11 [1836]; ten years later he was still ungainly, but
   most student and faculty comments during his protracted visits to the
   Seminary concerned his lectures and sermons, which they admired.
2. ML to Fidelia Fiske, South Hadley, January 15, 1846; Hitchcock, *Mary
   Lyon*, p. 352. ML announced the engagement to the school November 21, 1845, according to Susan Tolman in the journal letter. In the
   1840's when student enrollment averaged 200, the number of young
   teachers fluctuated from 8 to 18; the average was 12 or 13 a year. In
   1845-46 Abigail was one of the 15 young teachers listed in the catalogue, 5 of whom had just graduated and joined the staff. In 1846-47
   there were only 12, 2 of whom were 1846 graduates, new to the
   cumulative pressures of teaching in the Seminary. In 1847-48 there
   were 11 teachers, 3 of them new; in 1848-49 there were 12 teachers, 5
   new.
3. Susan Tolman, journal letter, July 12, 1847. Mary Whitman to Mrs.
   Hannah Porter, South Hadley, December 10, 1847.
4. Rebecca Fiske, journal letter, July 14, 1848.
5. Hitchcock, *Mary Lyon*, p. 247.
6. ML to Hannah White, South Hadley, January 8, 1848; Letters and Documents, 2:283-284. Joseph Avery to ML, Conway, September 27, 1847.
   Mary Whitman to Mrs. Hannah Porter, Monday afternoon, [South
   Hadley, January 18, 1848]. The new minister, Mr. Thomas Laurie, a
   returned missionary, was cordially welcomed by ML and promptly
   installed by the congregation but left within three years because of
   difficulties over collecting his salary.

7. The word tuberculosis was not yet in the medical vocabulary, but some of the pulmonary forms of the disease were widely known as consumption. This term nowhere appears in accounts by teachers and students of Miss Lyon's illnesses, but there are repeated references to her lungs as weak or sensitive. Dr. Carol Craig and Dr. William Putnam independently found in the medical descriptions in letters and diaries convincing evidence that she had tuberculosis.

8. Susan Tolman described the progress of ML's illness and recovery in great detail in the journal letter for 1846–47.

9. Eliza Noble to her sister, South Hadley, November 19, 1845; original in library of St. Lawrence University. Susan Allen to a friend, South Hadley, January 19, 1847. Mary Whitman to Mrs. Hannah Porter, South Hadley, December 10, 1847.

10. Her will was witnessed November 27, 1846. ML to Susan Howland, Monson, April 19, 1847. Account of Springfield visit in September 1848 by Louisa Russell in Hitchcock, *Mary Lyon*, pp. 409–414. ML to Thomas Laurie, South Hadley, May 5, 1848. ML to ZPGB, South Hadley, June 5, 1848; Hitchcock, *Mary Lyon*, p. 401; the book was McCheyne's *Life, Letters and Lectures*. ML to Ann Marie Hollister, South Hadley, July 21 – August 10, 1848; the extra care included four students too ill to leave at commencement. Shortly thereafter they did recover, and ML recouped sufficiently to attend the ABCFM meeting in Boston in mid-September. ML to Abigail Moore Burgess, Monson, January 20, 1849. ML's last letter to Mary Whitman on February 15, 1849, proposed that they take a vacation trip together the next autumn.

11. Of a half-dozen detailed accounts of the last illness, the most comprehensive are the ones by Sophia Hazen and Mary Chapin in the journal letter dated March 9, 1849, and the letter from Rebecca Fiske to Fidelia, March 5, 1849.

12. Sophia Hazen and Mary Chapin, journal letter, March 9, 1849. Mary Q. Brown to her mother, South Hadley, March 14, 1849.

13. Sophia Hazen and Mary Chapin, journal letter, March 9, March 30, April 12, May 4, 1849. Laura Corbin to her parents, South Hadley, March 7, 1849.

14. The missionary subscription, finally taken in July, reached $856.75. It may have been more of a tribute to the strong memory of Miss Lyon's zeal than to Mr. Hawks's eloquence, but in any case it was an impressive total, considering that the teachers were few and no one could make up the $90 Mary Lyon had been giving each year. Sophia Hazen and Mary Chapin, journal letter, March 30, May 16, 21, July 16, 1849.

15. Ibid., March 30, 1849. Mary Q. Brown to her mother, South Hadley, March 14, 1849.

16. Sophia Hazen and Mary Chapin, journal letter, May 16, 21, 1849.

17. Ibid., March 30, 1849. Mary Whitman to Mrs. Hannah Porter, South Hadley, June 1, 1849. Julia Hyde Clarke to Mary Goodale, Middlefield, July 16, 1849.

18. Mary Reed to her sister, South Hadley, February 26, 1850. Harriet Johnson to Mrs. Hannah Porter, South Hadley, July 12, 1850. Mary Whitman to Mrs. Hannah Porter, Saturday morning, n.d. [probably December 22, 1849].

19. Mary C. Whitman, "To the Trustees of the Mt. H. Fem. Sem.," n.d. [April 1850]. This document was accompanied by a physician's statement which has not survived.

20. No copy has been found of the journal letter covering the period from August 1849 through September 1850; the main source for events in the last half of 1849–50 is a single letter written by a teacher, Harriet Johnson, to Mrs. Hannah Porter, South Hadley, July 12, 1850.

21. Harriet Johnson, ibid.

22. Sarah Damon to M. A. Cary, Amherst [N.H.?], August 28, 1850; uncatalogued.

23. Helen Peabody, journal letter, October 11, November 8, 27, 1850.

24. Mary Whitman, "To the Trustees of the Mt. H. Fem. Sem.," n.d. [April 1850].

25. Helen Norton, *Memorials of Mary W. (Chapin) Pease and Lydia W. Shattuck* (Boston, Beacon Press, 1890), pp. 9, 31.

26. Mary Chapin was principal of Mount Holyoke from 1852 to 1865. Sophia Spofford was associate principal from 1852 to 1855, when her health gave out, and she was followed by Emily Jessup. Martha Scott taught at the Seminary for eleven years. Harriet Johnson headed the Cherokee Female Seminary in Oklahoma Indian Territory and then married a missionary to the Creeks. Helen Peabody became the first principal of Western Seminary, a daughter institution over which she presided for more than thirty years.

27. Apparently the whole Thanksgiving operation in 1850—dinner, wedding, reception and all—went more easily than the celebration had gone in 1848, when Miss Hazen and Miss Chapin were impressed to find that they actually had managed without either Miss Moore or Miss Whitman at the helm. The source for teacher activity from 1850 to 1852 is the journal letter, kept most of the time by Helen Peabody.

28. Abbie Nims of Greenfield, who died March 26, was "the jewel of Miss Gilbert's section." Gertrude de Bruyn Kops, who died April 25, a remarkable young woman whose family had emigrated from Holland two years earlier, was teaching French and racing through the Seminary curriculum as she improved her English. Sarah North to her sister, South Hadley, April 2, 1852; journal letter, May 26, 1852, author unknown.

29. It seems likely that when Mr. Hawks was leading morning devotions or other regular services, he did not go out on fund-raising trips. In the absence of any records at all, it is impossible to guess how much soliciting for Mount Holyoke he undertook after Mary Lyon's death. Some of the teachers, including Helen Peabody, were strong partisans of Mr.

Hawks in all the conflicts; she deplored "the injuries that have been heaped upon him" and praised his "most lovely and exalted Christian character," in the journal letter of November 5, 1851. For Humphrey's stay at the Seminary, see Helen Peabody, journal letter, June 2, 6, 9, 19, July 10, 16, 1851; she copied the *Springfield Republican* item in her July 10 entry.

30. Hitchcock et al. to the president of the board of trustees of the Mount Holyoke Female Seminary, October 10, 1851. [Hitchcock] to [Roswell Hawks], Amherst, October 20, 1851; superscription and signature are missing; Amherst College Archives.

31. *South Hadley First Congregational Church Records, 1848-1878*, pp. 177-179. Records of the Board of Trustees, August 5, 1852. Helen Peabody, journal letter, February 16, 1852; anon., journal letter, May 26, 1852. Albert Hopkins to Rev. Mr. Swift, Stockbridge, September 20, 1852.

32. [Edward Hitchcock], "Objections to Holyoke Sem.," n.d. [October 1852?], no signature. Records of the Board of Trustees, August 7, 1851, August 5, November 18, 1852. There was probably some residual trustee friction. One senior writing to her sister in the spring of 1854 believed that Mr. Hawks and Mr. Swift were "inveterate enemies"; Sarah North to her sister Harriet, South Hadley, March 21, 1854. Mr. Hawks's influence in disciplinary matters seemed to continue, though perhaps moderated, until 1855, when he was replaced as steward by John Chapin, Mary's brother. Within another two years he had left South Hadley for Painesville, Ohio, to raise money for Lake Erie, one of the daughter colleges; in 1858 he resigned as president of the Mount Holyoke board, though he remained a member as long as he lived.

33. Norton, *Memorials*, p. 11. Mary Nutting to William Nutting, South Hadley, November 12, 1850; *Vermont History*, 31, no. 3 (July 1963), 183; letter owned by Wesley Herwig, Randolph Center, Vermont.

34. For examination crowds, see Helen Peabody, journal letter, November 5, 1851. For the Chinese child, see Sarah North to her sister, South Hadley, July 21, 1852. For the Beecher visit, see the journal letter of May 26, 1852, author unknown.

35. For Mr. Rankin from Texas see Mary Phinney to her mother, South Hadley, December 24, 1850. Miss Chapin had already corresponded about faculty appointments and curriculum for the Cherokee Seminary. See David Vann and William P. Ross to Miss Chapin, Washington, D.C., June 19, 1850; also Ellen Whitmore to Miss Chapin, Park Hill, Cherokee Nation, March 16, 1852. Within a year Harriet Johnson was wooed and won by a missionary to the Creek Indians; she was succeeded by Paulina Avery, an 1850 graduate who had taught two years in Alabama and one at Mount Holyoke.

36. For the spotless senior record, see Helen Peabody, journal letter, January 26, 1852.

37. Mary Nutting to William Nutting, South Hadley, November 12, 1850;

Vermont History, 31, no. 3 (July 1963), 183-184; letter owned by Wesley Herwig.

38. Susan Lennan to Emily Whitten, South Hadley, January 8, 1852; paragraphing supplied.

39. Julia Newell to Mary Ann ———, South Hadley, October 17, 1852. Susan Hammond to her sister, South Hadley, October 19, 1852. Melissa Usher to Mollie ———, South Hadley, October 23, 1852. Julia Tolman, journal letter, November 10, 1852.

40. Julia Tolman, journal letter, October 27, 1852.

41. ML's morning and afternoon talks, which made such a lasting impression on Seminary students, are nowhere recorded in full, but series of excerpts and summaries appear in notebooks carefully preserved by their owners. One such collection is the three-part journal of Sophia Spofford, dated 1844-45, 1845-46, and 1846, upon which Miss Spofford must have drawn heavily when, as associate principal, she herself conducted morning devotions. Sophia Spofford, journal for 1846, pp. 15, 13. Fisk, *Recollections*, p. 242.

42. Sophia Spofford, journal for 1846, p. 30; journal for 1845-46, pp. 7, 14.

43. Antoinette Hubbell, journal, January 29, 1843.

44. Sophia Spofford, journal for 1845-46, p. 11; journal for 1846, p. 8; journal for 1844-45, p. 3.

45. R. Emerson, *Joseph Emerson*, p. 421.

46. Susan Tolman, journal letter, January 29, 1847. Sophia Spofford, journal for 1846, p. 6.

47. Elizabeth Eaton, entry of April 16, 1845, diary for 1844-45; typed copy. Lucinda Guilford to Frances Greene, South Hadley, November 4, 1845; typed copy. Excerpts copied from letter of Mrs. Dean Walker to Arabella and Isabella, November 9, 1848; location of original letter unknown.

48. Mrs. Blackwell, Memorabilia, p. 202. ML to Mary Susan Rice, South Hadley, June 17, 1847; Hitchcock, *Mary Lyon*, p. 355.

49. Hitchcock, *Reminiscences*, p. 306. Thomas Whittemore to his sister Eliza, Fitzwilliam, N. H., June 14, 1847. Hitchcock, *Mary Lyon*, pp. 404-405. In 1854 the yearly student charge had to be raised to $68.

50. Rebecca Fiske, journal letter 1847-48, July 5, 1848.

51. For the Beloit inquiry, see A. L. Chapin to Joel Hawes, Milwaukee, Wisc., January 20, 1846. Reverend Chapin served as president of Beloit for thirty-six years. For the Boston salon, see Mrs. S. A. S. Lawrence to ML, Amherst, N. H., September 23, 1847. The publisher of Hitchcock, *Mary Lyon*, was Hopkins, Bridgman and Company (later Bridgman and Childs) of Northampton. The successive editions were unaltered except for the one issued in 1858, which was considerably revised by Mrs. Cowles and published by the American Tract Society.

52. Stow, *History*, pp. 327-347. The 50th anniversary in 1887 provides a useful dividing line for categorizing Seminary students; the official shift

by state charter to the name of college began in 1888 and was completed in 1893. The *One Hundred Year Biographical Directory of Mount Holyoke College 1837–1937*, edited by Mary C. J. Higley and published by the Alumnae Association, contains data about the great majority of the students enrolled in the first fifty years.

53. Most of the tributes were initialed or unsigned. The *Observer* obituary was initialed A and may have been the work of Dr. Rufus Anderson, secretary of the ABCFM, who also may have written a sonnet on her death which was initialed A and published in both Boston and New York. The *New York Observer*, 17, no. 10 (March 10, 1849), and 17, no. 11 (March 17, 1849). The *Boston Recorder*, 34, no. 11 (March 16, 1849). Hitchcock, *Mary Lyon*, pp. 484, 485.

Index

ML is the abbreviation of Mary Lyon.
Sem is the abbreviation of Mount Holyoke Female Seminary.

Library of Congress Cataloging in Publication Data

Green, Elizabeth Alden, 1908–
Mary Lyon and Mount Holyoke.

Includes bibliographical references and index.
1. Mount Holyoke College—History. 2. Lyon,
Mary, 1797–1849. 3. Education of women—United States—
History. 4. College administrators—United States—
Biography. I. Title.
LD7092.65.L9G73   378.744'23   78-68857
ISBN 0-87451-172-0